THE TIMETABLE OF TECHNOLOGY

THE TIMETABLE OF TECHNOLOGY

HEARST BOOKS
224 West 57th Street, New York, N.Y. 10019

Editor	**Patrick Harpur**
Assistant editors	**Pip Morgan**
	Ruth Binney
	Rosanne Hooper
	Caroline Gilfillan
	Barbara Westmore
	Paulette Pratt
	Gwen Rigby
Art director	**Barry Moscrop**
Art editor	**Simon Blacker**
Design assistant	**Graeme Little**
Picture editor	**Zilda Tandy**
Picture researcher	**Mary Corcoran**
Production	**Barry Baker**
	Janice Storr

The Timetable of Technology was conceived,
edited and designed by
Marshall Editions Limited,
71 Eccleston Square,
London Sw1V 1PJ

First published in the USA by
Hearst Books
224 West 57th Street,
New York, NY 10019

Copyright © 1982 by Marshall Editions Limited

**Library of Congress Cataloging in Publication
Data**
Main entry under title:

Timetable of Technology

   Summary: Chronological listings, from 1900
through 1981, of significant discoveries and
developments in medicine, communications,
transport, energy, food technology, and other fields.
   1. Technology – History – 20th century.
2. Technology – Chronology. [1. Technology –
Chronology. 2. Science – Chronology. 3. Twentieth
century – Chronology]
T20.T55 1982   609′.04   82-11899
ISBN 0-87851-209-8

10 9 8 7 6 5 4 3 2 1

Printed and bound in The Netherlands by
Royal Smeets Offset BV, Weert

Consultant editors

Dr Edward S. Ayensu (The Smithsonian Institution, Washington D.C.)

Michael Marshall, MP (Former Parliamentary Under-Secretary of State in the Department of Industry with special responsibility for Space)

Dr Philip Whitfield (Lecturer at the Department of Zoology, King's College, University of London; co-author of *The Rhythms of Life*)

Consultants and contributors

G.W.A. Dummer, MBE, C.Eng, FIEE, FIEEE, FIERE (Author of *Modern Electronic Components* and *Electronic Inventions and Discoveries*)

Dr Ghislaine Skinner, MB, BS, MRCS, LRCP (Wellcome Museum of the History of Medicine at the Science Museum, London)

From the Science Museum, London
A. Hall-Patch (Rail transport)
M. Andrewartha (Aeronautics)
A. Patterson (Agriculture)
R.S. Taylor (Electrical power)
M.T. Wright (Stationary motive power)

Basil W. Bathe, ISO (Formerly in charge of water transport, the Science Museum, London; author of *Seven Centuries of Sea Travel*)
Brian Coe, FSA, FBKS (Curator, the Kodak Museum, Middlesex)
Peter Payne, FIOP, FIRT (Head of Graphic Reproduction, the London College of Printing)
John Roberts, BA, RIBA, MCIT (Director, Transport and Environment Studies, London)
M.J. Willis (Imperial War Museum, London)

Contents

The year 1900 launched a technological revolution whose effects on communication, energy, medicine and transportation have been multiplying geometrically ever since. We look over our shoulders and see the development from wireless to radio to television to cable networks; we glance ahead and see homes equipped with satellite receiver 'dishes', electronic mail equipment and instant access to databanks. The generation that dubiously witnessed the début of the 'horseless carriage' has watched the automobile develop into an economic and lifestyle institution. Energy supplied by coal in many instances gave way to oil; the crunch of oil prices has the pendulum swinging back again, while controversy rages over directing our resources towards nuclear and solar energy.

We can now travel faster than the speed of sound; telephone literally anywhere on earth; successfully operate a manned space station; employ robots to undertake mundane and disagreeable tasks; vaccinate against previously fatal or debilitating diseases; transplant organs and reattach limbs. And, though these many advancements affect every aspect of our lives, we tend to lose perspective on the vastness of the transformations that have taken place during the past eighty-odd years of this century. For many of us, the consideration of predicted technological transformations for the remaining part of this century, and beyond, conjures a feeling of apprehension and bewilderment.

The Timetable of Technology is a work that allows us to comprehend our technological history and contemplate our technological future. In a manner that is both fascinating and accessible, it charts the progress to date and documents the remarkable achievements of the twentieth century's men and women of science and technology. Its theme of taking stock transcends its contents — we must consider where we have been so that we can make wise choices about where we are heading. We can shoot for the stars figuratively as well as literally: the developing technological innovations have the potential to be shared and applied by all nations to meet the universal needs of humankind. Furthermore, I see the impending technological innovations as instruments that will offer very positive new approaches to redress the scientific and technological imbalance that has existed between the industrialized and the less affluent nations. The possibility also exists for a new cultural renaissance to emerge, with the time and means available for greater personal fulfillment. It is my hope, therefore, that in the best of all possible circumstances technology will enable us to reach ever-increasing heights of both equality and individuality on a worldwide scale.

Professor Edward S. Ayensu
Smithsonian Institution, Washington D.C.

COMMUNICATION AND INFORMATION

Radio takes a leap forward as Canadian Professor R.A. Fessenden uses a telephone link to transmit human speech on radio waves for the first time.

Printing undergoes a radical transformation. Tolbert Lanston's Monotype typecasting machine, invented some four years before, makes it possible to set type mechanically in single characters. Corrections can thus be made with ease; and, since the processes of composing and casting are now separate, the type can be melted down and recast.

Cinema-in-the-round is a novelty at the Paris Exhibition. In R. Grimoin Samson's Cinéorama show, 10 cinecameras record a 360° view of the horizon and the films are projected on a cylindrical screen. The first—and only—film seen is of Paris shot from an ascending balloon. After a few screenings the Cinéorama is closed down because the public, who stand on the roof of the projection box containing highly inflammable film, are deemed to be at risk.

TRANSPORT AND WARFARE

The first international motor car race is run from Paris to Lyon. Five cars from France, Belgium and America compete for a trophy put up by Gordon Bennett, a wealthy American publisher living in Paris. The competitors have to contend with serious breakdowns and the problem of dogs hurling themselves under the wheels of the noisy machines. The winning car, a French Panhard-Levassor, averages 38.5 mph (62 km/h).

Two separate sets of cylinders on France's 'Atlantic' steam engine, largely built by Gaston du Bousquet, make it more economical to run than any other train—but also more difficult to drive. The French custom of assigning each engine to the care of one driver, who sees to its overhaul as well, ensures the locomotive's long-lived success.

Orville and Wilbur Wright fly their first glider, mainly as an unpiloted kite, over the dunes at Kitty Hawk, North Carolina. The brothers have been experimenting with biplane kites for a year and have been building gliders since 1896.

ENERGY AND INDUSTRY

The electric arc steel-making furnace is used for the first time. Paul Heroult employs an electric arc—formed between an electrode and the metal being heated—to generate the heat to melt the metal. The lack of solid, liquid or gaseous fuel in the furnace prevents any contamination of the steel by impurities. The process will be developed during World War I, particularly in Sheffield, England, the principal centre of the alloy steel trade.

Charles Palmer of the USA makes a breakthrough in gasoline technology when he finds he can obtain good quality gasoline by using high temperatures and pressures to decompose crude petroleum. In 1916 he will sell the rights of this thermal process to the Standard Oil Co.

The machine tool trade sees the introduction of the magnetic chuck. This gives a very smooth finish to steel components, such as cylinder heads for automobile engines, because it holds the component magnetically, avoiding the use of clamps. It also allows surface grinders to give a quick, all-round finish, so increasing production.

Two similar storage batteries are developed: the nickel-iron cell by Edison and the nickel-cadmium cell by Junger. The Edison cell will develop faults in service and a successful version will not be developed until 1908.

MEDICINE AND FOOD PRODUCTION

Kiyoshi Shiga prepares an antiserum against bacillary dysentery—later called Shigella in his honour—which will be one of the scourges of World War I.

Karl Landsteiner, working at the Institute of Hygiene in Vienna, postulates three incompatible blood groups (later designated A, B, and O). A fourth group (AB) will be identified by other investigators two years later. This work leads to safer blood transfusions and opens the way for more adventurous surgery.

In Vienna, Sigmund Freud sees publication of what many consider to be his most original and important work, *The Interpretation of Dreams*.

FRINGE BENEFITS

'Ever Ready' electric torches give instant illumination.

An eaterie in New Haven, Connecticut, pioneers the hamburger.

Valdemar Poulsen unveils his Telegraphone at the Paris Exhibition. He has discovered that sound can be recorded on steel piano wire by passing it across an electromagnet connected to a microphone. Two decades will pass, however, before its full potential is realized—in Germany.

"HORSE AND PONY" MOWER.

Shown with arrangement worked from the Handles for delivering the Grass without stopping the horse.

STOP — HANDLE — SPRING — BEARING — FRAME

ENLARGED VIEW OF PATENT SPRING

The cheap Kodak Brownie camera brings photography to the masses. The simple box camera, which uses roll film, is especially popular with children. The Brownie is the first of hundreds of models bearing the famous Kodak name.

The 'Portrait Parlant', a talking movie, using a gramophone coupled to a film projector, is shown at the Paris Exhibition by Leon Gaumont. But the gramophone speed varies and quality is poor.

The first fully automatic telephone exchange, accommodating 10,000 lines, is installed at New Bedford, Ma., and successfully demonstrated over a distance of 1 ml (1.6 km). To connect a caller, an idle line is selected by a motor-driven rotary interrupter. The ringing tone, initiated by the press of a button at the caller's end, can be heard by both caller and called. When the receiver at one end is replaced, the connection is broken because both lines become earthed.

New potential for sound transmission arrives with the 'singing arc', a high-frequency generator which can produce musical sounds from a direct current. When the frequency is increased the sound can be sent a long way.

As the new century begins there are around 470,000 mls of railway in the world.

After long scientific research and extensive study of US locomotives—as well as the purchase of three French 'Atlantic' steam engines—G.J. Churchward produces an engine that will dictate the basic design of virtually all subsequent British steam railway trains. After spending his entire working life on British railways, Churchward will be killed by a train one misty morning in 1933 while inspecting a piece of rail.

The Browning 7.65 mm (.32 in) Model 1900 is the first commercially successful pocket automatic gun. By 1912 the Belgian manufacturers, Fabrique Nationale, will have produced one million Brownings, one of which begins World War I—it is used by Gavrilo Princip to assassinate Archduke Franz Ferdinand at Sarajevo in 1914.

The Packard is the first US car to feature a three-speed and reverse gearbox. The 12 hp car is otherwise much like a horse-drawn carriage with buggy styling, wire wheels and a central chain drive to the rear wheels.

Escalators and moving pavements will both be improved as a result of H. Ward Leonard's first demonstration, at the Paris Exhibition, of his automatic motor speed control system. The control system maintains a steady speed no matter how many pedestrians stand on the escalator.

British inventor Charles Topham gives the budding man-made fibre industry a boost by devising a rotating box which winds viscose rayon yarn off the spinning machines. Only 7 in (18 cm) wide, the Topham box revolves 10,000 times a second, processing the fibre into a form acceptable to the weaving machines.

The first offshore oil wells, fixed to piers, are drilled along the shore of the Caspian Sea and the west coast of the USA.

Metal parts such as screws and the teeth on gears are made quicker and more precisely as John Parker installs the constant-speed geared drive in the milling machine. With an independent electric motor, it replaces the dangerous overhead belting drives.

The excellent cutting performance of tools made from so-called high-speed steel is displayed at the Paris Exhibition by F.W. Taylor. High-speed steel contains tungsten and carbon and is so hard that it remains rigid even when red hot. These new tools show a three-fold increase in cutting speed over existing machine tools, which become obsolete.

Major Walter Reed heads the US Yellow Fever Commission, sent to Cuba to investigate recurrent epidemics of this deadly disease, which has held up completion of the Panama Canal for two decades. With the help of human volunteers, Reed establishes that yellow fever is transmitted by the *Aedes aegypti* mosquito.

Gregor Mendel's laws of inheritance, neglected and misunderstood when published in Germany in 1866, are rediscovered and reappraised by scientists wishing to improve livestock and crops by selective breeding.

Sir Patrick Manson publishes his classic paper identifying the *Anopheles* mosquito as the carrier of malaria. The disease is transmitted when, after sucking the blood of an infected person, the mosquito bites someone else. Eradication of malaria (which afflicts up to 10% of the world's population) will now begin by waging war on the insect.

Artificial flints for cigarette lighters are introduced.

The paper clip—indispensable office aid—is patented.

The US Post Office issues books of stamps.

The 'Horse and Pony' mower is introduced by Ransomes, Sims and Jefferies, a Suffolk-based manufacturer of high-quality agricultural machinery. Seen illustrated in a contemporary catalogue, this 48-in (120-cm) machine dwarfs its domestic cousins, whose sales have soared as a result of the rising popularity of tennis.

His earlier plans for an 'aerial express train' turned down by the German government, Count von Zeppelin turns his energies to the promotion of airship flight. In a floating shed on Lake Constance, at the Swiss-German border, he builds the Luftschiff Zeppelin 1, the world's first rigid airship. Its 420 ft (126 m) long cotton-covered aluminium frame contains 400,000 cu ft (11,200 cu m) of hydrogen in 17 separate gas bags. Unfortunately, tiny rudders at both bow and stern, and a shifting weight, prove totally ineffective aerodynamic controls for such a behemoth, and its two Daimler engines are capable of producing a mere 16 mph (25.6 km/h). After three test flights, the underpowered giant is scrapped.

COMMUNICATION AND INFORMATION

The gramophone record destined to dominate the market in the years ahead is introduced in Britain by the Gramophone and Typewriter Co Ltd. Black, and made of the hard, resinous plastic shellac, the first disc is 10 in (25 cm) across. Two years later, the same company launches a 12 in (30 cm) disc and by 1904 double-sided discs can be bought in Europe.

The 'Disc Gramophone', to play shellac discs, goes into production in the latter months of 1901; but sound quality is still poor.

TRANSPORT AND WARFARE

Acetylene gas lamps replace candles and oil lamps on motor cars for night driving. The first acetylene lamps generate gas by dripping water on lumps of carbide; but in later models, steel cylinders provide a steady, rechargeable source of gas. The new lamps produce a light so bright that thin wooden slats are sometimes placed over the glass to prevent dazzle.

The Scottish Clyde River steamer *King Edward* is the first merchant vessel to be driven by steam turbines—a form of propulsion which attracted world-wide attention four years before when Sir Charles Parsons' *Turbinia* became the world's fastest vessel.

A 100,000-franc prize is won by Brazilian aviator Alberto Santos-Dumont when he flies his No.6 airship over a 7-ml (11-km) course in under 30 mins, circling the Eiffel Tower *en route*.

ENERGY AND INDUSTRY

The first coin-in-the-slot meters for regulating the domestic supply of direct current electricity are approved for use in Britain. The first pre-payment meter for alternating current electricity will be introduced in 1908.

G. Eneas builds a solar-powered water pump to transport water for irrigation on an ostrich farm in Pasadena, California. The solar reflector, made up of 1,788 little mirrors, focuses the sun's rays on a boiler, where the steam produced sets in motion a nearby pump that drives the water.

More than half the world's oil output is produced from the Baku oil fields around the Caspian Sea in Russia. The fields have been developed by Ludwig Nobel—brother of Alfred, founder in 1896 of the Peace Prize—who has already devised the world's first oil tankers and vehicles for carrying oil by rail, and has installed Europe's first oil pipeline.

MEDICINE AND FOOD PRODUCTION

Wooden tower silos are introduced to Britain from the USA, so boosting the production of silage, a nutritious livestock feed made by compressing and storing grass or green crops in airtight conditions for about a month while they ferment. Over the next 50 years they will be used worldwide.

At Cambridge, England, J.N. Langley discovers the properties of adrenaline—the so-called fight-or-flight hormone—in speeding the heart rate and raising blood pressure.

German bacteriologist Emil von Behring receives the first Nobel Prize for Physiology and Medicine for his pioneering work on the conquest of diphtheria. One of the founders of serum therapy, he infects animals with disease microbes, extracts defensive substances from the blood serum, calls them antitoxins and uses them to confer immunity on human beings.

FRINGE BENEFITS

Strings of carbon-filament lights decorate Christmas trees.

Fingerprints go on file at Scotland Yard, London's Police HQ.

Guglielmo Marconi and his assistants, Kemp and Paget, pose by the equipment they used to arrange the first-ever transatlantic wireless communication. By attaching an aerial to a kite flown over St John's, Newfoundland, they were able to give it sufficient height to receive the Morse letter 'S' tapped out in Poldhu, on England's Cornish peninsula—a record-breaking transmission distance of over 1,800 mls (3,500 km). The Marconi Wireless, Telegraph and Signal Co is already producing transmitters and receivers for the military to use in conjunction with telegraph decoding apparatus, and within six years Marconi will have established a commercial radio telegraph service across the Atlantic.

Typewriters go electric as the world's first successful model, the 'Blickensderfer Electric' is designed. Manufacture of this sophisticated typewheel machine will begin a year later, although lack of mains supply to most offices will restrict its popularity.

Alternative audio is the aim of Professor Rühmer's Photographone. Sound waves are recorded as variations on photographic film. A beam of light is then passed through the film on to a light-sensitive cell which converts the variations into a varying electric current. A telephone receiver is used to hear the sound.

For the first time, recorded sound can be played back with no loss of clarity. The breakthrough is achieved by Professor Nernst, a German physicist, who adapts Poulsen's phonograph by using a revolving copper disc instead of wire. The result: an early form of 'tape' recorder.

US scientist Samuel Pierpoint Langley takes a step towards powered flight by fitting a gasoline engine to—and flying—a quarter-sized model of his plane *Aerodrome*. The real thing will attempt flight in 1903.

Wilbur Wright's first lecture, modestly entitled 'Some Aeronautical Experiments', is delivered to the Western Society of Engineers in Chicago. He describes the No 1 and No 2 gliders of 1900 and 1901, showing how cables that 'warp' or twist the wings allow aircraft to imitate the action of a gliding bird and so give a greater measure of flight control.

The Curved Dash Runabout Oldsmobile is the world's first car built at a rate of more than 10 a week. Well suited to town driving, the car has a two-speed gearbox and a single-cylinder engine that produces a top speed of 22 mph (35 km/h). The numbers sold annually will rise from 425 in 1901 to over 5,000 in 1904.

The first vacuum cleaner is invented by Hubert Booth and becomes the first real alternative to the Bissell carpet sweeper. Built on to a horse-drawn cart, it consists of a petrol-driven pump and a long hose.

The first synthetic vat dye, Indanthrene Blue, is successfully made. Like the natural vat dyes, it is fast—it neither washes out nor fades, even when exposed to light for long periods.

The Spindletop oil field, near Beaumont in Texas, starts to produce 80,000 barrels of oil a day, considerably boosting world oil production, and making the USA the world's major supplier of petroleum. The Spindletop, a field which contains more oil than the rest of the USA put together, gives Rockefeller's Standard Oil Co its first real competitor.

A forerunner of the fluorescent lamp tube is demonstrated in the USA by Peter Cooper-Hewitt. Four feet long and 1 in in diameter (1.2 m by 2.54 cm), this is the first successful light-discharging lamp to be made since the carbon arc lamps of the last century. It contains liquid mercury that vaporizes to produce a blue-green light when an electric current is passed through it. Its disadvantage—having to tilt it by hand before the mercury connects with the current—will be overcome by 1910.

Neurosurgeon Harvey Cushing makes an important contribution to US surgery by introducing the Italian Riva-Rocci sphygmomanometer—the first practical apparatus for measuring blood pressure.

The Nobel Prize for Physics is awarded to German doctor-turned-physicist Wilhelm Roentgen for his discovery of X-rays, which are already revolutionizing the practice of medicine.

Injected into the lower end of the spinal canal, the 'sacral epidural' anaesthetic successfully blocks pain in the pubes without ill-effects. Developed at the Salpetrière in France by Athanase Sicard, it is locally more effective than a general anaesthetic, and will be used in surgery.

Four years before the word 'hormone' enters medical terminology, Japanese biochemist Jokiche Takamine turns over to Parke, Davis and Co purified adrenaline, extracted from the adrenal glands of animals. This is the first hormone to be marketed (under the name of epinephrine in the USA) in pure form.

Sew-on press-studs are invented in Paris.

Meccano—the model engineering kit—is patented.

An early multi-storey car park in London eases city parking problems.

The low chassis, long bonnet and revolutionary vertically mounted honeycomb radiator of the first Mercedes, establish the shape of the modern motor car. It is named after the daughter of Count Emil Jellinek, Austro-Hungarian consul at Nice, who has requested the new model from Daimler.

13

COMMUNICATION AND INFORMATION

Invented by German craftsman Carl Zeiss, the four-element Tessar camera lens is destined to prove one of the most successful of all time. The same basic design will still be in use in the eighties.

Using Professor Rowland's octoplex typographic telegraph, 20 operators can send out messages at 18,000 words an hour. Letters are fed in via a keyboard, and arrive at the receiving station as a print-out.

Books can now have more illustrations. Instead of using hand-cut wood blocks, the latest method of production etches illustrations into zinc with acid. But to get good results, more sophisticated printing machinery and better quality paper and ink prove essential.

TRANSPORT AND WARFARE

Frenchman Capt. Ferdinand Ferber, one of the few Europeans still making gliding experiments, reads the 1901 Wright lecture and immediately abandons his hang-glider in favour of a Wright-type. Although only a primitive copy, lacking rudder and wing-warping, Ferber's craft sparks off the revival of European aviation.

The Belgian firm of Déchamps offers the first car with an electric starter system fitted as standard.

The flamboyant Selwyn Francis Edge wins the Gordon Bennett Trophy—Britain's first success in an international car race. His winning Napier, like most cars of the time, has engine inlet valves which are opened and shut by atmospheric pressure—a 'hit-and-miss' system soon replaced by the mechanically operated valves already operative in Mercedes and Lanchester cars.

The first practical airship is built by the Lebaudy brothers in France. *La Jaune's* 40 hp Daimler engine gives it sufficient power to be fully controllable, unlike earlier dirigibles which were under-powered for their size.

ENERGY AND INDUSTRY

The first electric lamp to employ a metal filament—the osmium lamp—is made in Europe. Although more efficient than the previous carbon filament lamps, the cost and rarity of osmium inhibits the lamp's adoption.

The first patent in the USA for the manufacture of a man-made textile yarn—acetate rayon—is taken out by W.H. Walker (and others). Acetate rayon is one of four types of rayon discovered around the turn of the century. It will be used in World War I, in a different form, in the production of aircraft varnish and, as the fabric Celanese, will be spun commercially after the war and used mainly for women's underwear.

German inventor Carl von Linde discovers a way of 'liquefying' air to produce, in liquid form, the pure oxygen and nitrogen that will become essential to many industrial processes. The production of high-quality oxygen in Buffalo, NY, for instance, will shortly help to perfect the oxyacetylene torch.

Any part for a particular machine will be interchangeable throughout the world as C.E. Johansson patents his gauge blocks in Britain.

MEDICINE AND FOOD PRODUCTION

Philadelphia chemists Albert Barnes and Herman Hille produce a non-caustic antiseptic to combat eye infections. Within a few years their 'silver vitellin', marketed as Argyrol, will be in widespread use to protect infants against eye infections (such as gonorrhoeal infection of the newborn) which could lead to blindness.

Swedish ophthalmologist Allvar Gullstrand invents one of the most useful tools of the eye doctor's trade: the slit-lamp. A brilliant beam of light illuminates the area to be examined, while the rest of the eye is left in darkness.

Paris physiologist Charles Richet describes anaphylaxis—an allergic reaction so acute as to cause collapse, disablement or even death.

FRINGE BENEFITS

The Pepsi-Cola Co is founded.

An early automat offers food for a 'nickel in the slot'.

Experimental runs of the Thorneycroft steam motor bus in London earn it the description 'the sensation and distress of Bayswater Road and Oxford Street'. The bus, which travels at about 8 mph (12.8 km/h) is not a financial success and confirms that other sources of power must be found to replace metropolitan horse-drawn services.

The secret of Marconi's success is explained as Oliver Heaviside in Britain and A.E. Kennedy in the USA discover that the upper, ionized layer of the atmosphere reflects radio waves. Later to be dubbed the Heaviside layer, its existence and reflective behaviour show how Marconi can make radio contact round the curved surface of the Earth. It also explains why signals are clearer at night: during the day the sun's heat expands air and pushes the layer upward, making signals weaker.

A pair of US naval vessels, the *Virginia* and the *Connecticut*, are the first ships to install radio telephones. After successful tests, with speech received from 21 mls (33.6 km) away, an entire US naval fleet, which is about to embark on a round-the-world voyage, accepts radio telephone equipment from the de Forest company.

Bringing down the cost of keeping in touch, the first trans-Pacific telephone cable, laid between Canada and Australia and New Zealand, halves the cost of a cablegram between the two continents. London-Brussels telephone calls become feasible with the help of a cross-Channel cable between St Margaret's Bay, Kent, and La Panne on the Belgian coast.

A marine internal combustion engine, combined in one unit with gearbox, drive shaft and propeller, can be clamped to the stern of a boat: the 'outboard' motor is introduced in France and Sweden.

Steam superheaters dramatically improve the performance of railway engines. Devised by German engineer Wilhelm Schmidt, the system of tubes raises the temperature of the steam so that it can expand and produce more power in the engine's cylinders, while cutting down fuel and water consumption. Within 10 years superheaters will be adopted in most of the world's steam engines.

Louis Renault produces a simple but efficient drum brake which will soon be developed for the majority of the world's vehicles. When the brake is applied, two shoes in the hub are pushed outwards and forced against a rotating drum fixed to the inside of the wheel. This type of internally expanding drum brake will still be used on the rear wheels of most passenger cars in the eighties.

German chemist Wilhelm Ostwald patents a process for the conversion of ammonia to nitric acid. This important step in the history of explosives' manufacture—nitric acid is the basis of TNT—will be exploited industrially after 1906.

The internal shaping of a keyhole in a metal doorlock is just one of the précise operations that Lapointe's new machine tool, called a pull-broacher, can accurately and speedily perform.

The Aswan Dam on the Nile is completed and is considered one of the finest dam-building achievements of all time. Made of locally quarried granite, the dam reaches an unprecedented length of 6,400 ft (1,950 m) and has 180 low-level sluices which control the flow of the river and feed water to the irrigation system. The dam wall will be raised in 1912 from 65.5 ft (20 m) to 88.5 ft (27 m), and again in 1933, to 118 ft (36 m).

The first motorized lawn mower is designed by James Ransome and manufactured by Ransome, Sims and Jeffries Ltd of Ipswich, England. The model incorporates a passenger seat and is run by a 6 hp engine.

Electric kettles are introduced into Britain, where they become popular for tea-making. Originally appearing in Chicago in 1894, the kettle takes 12 mins to boil a pint of water. This model, with a few improvements, will remain basically unchanged for the next 80 years. In 1981, over 75% of British households will have an electric kettle, the fastest of them boiling a pint of water in 96 secs.

Two British physiologists, William Bayliss and Ernest Starling, initiate the science of endrocrinology when they discover a substance they call secretin. Released from the walls of the intestine, it stimulates the secretion of pancreatic juice as an aid to digestion. They will introduce the word hormone—from the Greek 'to rouse to activity'—to describe its effect.

British Army pathologist Sir Almroth Wright immunizes soldiers in the Boer War with the 'killed' vaccine he has developed against typhoid. He is unable to persuade the War Office to make immunization compulsory, but the 14,000 enlisted men who receive the vaccine fare much better than their companions when the disease strikes.

In New York, Miller Hutchinson, inventor of the klaxon, patents the first electrical hearing aid—the Acousticon. It goes into production with large batteries, and a telephone receiver to be held to the ear. Among early users is Princess Alexandra, who has suffered partial deafness since early childhood.

The British public get their first taste of a dried breakfast cereal when Force Wheat Flakes are introduced.

Frank Clarke, a Birmingham gunsmith, patents the first automatic tea-making machine. Springs and levers connect an alarm clock to a match, spirit burner and pivoted kettle. When the water boils, the flame is extinguished and the kettle's contents tilted into the teapot.

The Wright No 3 glider is man-launched on the Kill Devil Hills in North Carolina, with Orville Wright piloting—one of nearly 1,000 flights. Control problems highlighted by its two predecessors have resulted in intensive research, with model wings undergoing tests in a Wright-designed wind tunnel—the brothers having decided 'to rely entirely upon our own investigations'. The modified No 3's movable rudder is connected to the warp cradle on which Wright is lying, and the simultaneous use of wing warping and the rear rudder at last give him proper control of the glider.

COMMUNICATION AND INFORMATION

19 January: from the transmitting station he has built at Wellfleet, Ma., Marconi transmits a greeting from President Roosevelt to Britain's King Edward VII. The station has four 250-ft (75-m) towers and a 3-ft (39-cm) spark gap rotor for generating electrical waves. The message, tapped out in Morse code at 17 words a minute, creates a signal so powerful that the station in Cornwall picks it up direct, rendering Marconi's Newfoundland relay station unnecessary.

In Bonn, 100 companies acquire more communication power as the German Post Office opens the first commercial telegraph service. The companies are connected to a manually controlled exchange which switches tapped telegraph messages to their destination, where they are printed out automatically.

Gramophones are improved with the invention of the 'tone arm', which reduces the pressure on the needle point created by the back of the horn and leaves the horn free to point in any direction.

TRANSPORT AND WARFARE

Flyer 1 takes to the air on 17 December. The Wright Brothers combine a gasoline engine with an airframe that allows them control of their craft—and the first powered, sustained and controlled aeroplane flights are achieved at Kitty Hawk, North Carolina. The best flight of the day lasts 59 secs, a time unequalled by European pilots until 1907.

Henry Ford founds the company which will bring motoring to the average American citizen, and encourages the mass production of cars around the world. The Model A, the Ford Motor Company's first car, is built from bought-in parts, and sells for $850.

William Harley and Arthur Davidson build the first Harley-Davidson motorcycle in a small shed in the Davidson family's Milwaukee backyard.

ENERGY AND INDUSTRY

The first skyscraper in the world to have a reinforced concrete framework—the 16-storey Ingall's building in Cincinatti, Ohio—forces the construction industry to redefine its concepts for design of buildings.

The first notions of manpower planning are the subject of the ideas F.W. Taylor introduces to industry. He initiates the important trend towards the scientific management of men and machines: economic success can be achieved only by minimizing the amount of human effort and making the most efficient use of raw materials, equipment and buildings. Henry Ford will be first to put Taylor's ideas into practice when he opens production-line automobile plants.

Welding metals will become easier and safer in the future with Edmond Fouce's invention of the oxyacetylene burner, which, by burning a combination of oxygen and acetylene, produces a flame of very high temperature.

MEDICINE AND FOOD PRODUCTION

To prevent patients choking on their tongues during surgery, Atkin Thompson devises forceps to secure the tongue with a tiny pin, leaving only a minute puncture at the tip, and causing the patient no pain on waking.

As New York faces an outbreak of typhoid fever (with around 1,300 cases reported), the infamous 'typhoid Mary' is named. Mary Mallon is traced as a carrier of the disease, but not a victim. She acquires notoriety when she continues to take jobs—sometimes under assumed names—which involve the handling of food. Finally she will be placed in detention in 1915, remaining in confinement until her death in 1938.

Dutch physician Willem Einthoven revolutionizes the diagnosis of heart disease when he invents the string galvanometer to record the electrical behaviour of the heart. Subsequently, this apparatus—the forerunner of the electrocardiogram (ECG)—will be used to reveal patterns of electrical activity, which can usefully be correlated with various kinds of heart disorder.

FRINGE BENEFITS

A mould for ice cream cones is patented by an Italian immigrant living in New Jersey.

The Williamsburg Bridge, the second to span New York's East River, opens to traffic. Designed by Lefferts L. Buck, a specialist in arches, it is the first major suspension bridge to use steel, rather than masonry, towers. It is also the ultimate in truss stiffening—its 1,600-ft (488-m) roadway deck is kept rigid by deep trusses.

The 'talkies' begin to improve as Gaumont manages to cut down sound distortion. He does this by using an electrical synchronizer to allow the gramophone's constant speed of rotation to control the film projector. The 'Photo-scenes' are still limited, however, by the lack of amplified sound from the acoustic gramophone.

Using the newly laid Pacific telephone cable, US President Theodore Roosevelt sends a message from San Francisco to Manila via Honolulu.

Radio transmission, dogged by interference, is given a fillip by Oliver Lodge's self-restoring coherer. By employing the interaction between mercury and oil the coherer maintains sensitive reception of electromagnetic waves.

British newspapers claim a double 'first'. In February the *Globe* announces that, for the first time, it is printed entirely by electricity. November sees the birth of the *Daily Mirror*, the founder of the pictorial press and the world's first daily to illustrate its news stories and features with halftone blocks throughout, rather than a mixture of halftones and line drawings.

The newly founded Cadillac car company is the first US firm to sell cars with fully interchangeable parts. The success of its policy is demonstrated five years later when one of three Cadillacs, taken apart and then reassembled from random piles of parts, wins the prestigious US Dewar Trophy.

Although powered by an advanced radial engine, Langley's *Aerodrome* is a complete failure when launched by catapult from a houseboat on the Potomac river. It plunges into the water on both test flights owing to its disastrous method of take-off and lack of flight controls.

Frenchman Clément Ader puts eight cylinders in his racing car for more power, but finds that the extra cylinders need to be arranged in two banks, set at an angle to each other, to keep the car compact. V–8 engines will soon become commercially available.

The Newcastle-upon-Tyne Electric Supply Co install the world's first alternator to have a rotating field magnet, at their new Neptune Bank power station. Designed by Charles Parsons, this type of high-speed alternator—a generator that produces alternating current—will subsequently be installed in power stations all over the world.

Harry Decker, a well-known figure in the early days of Gulf Coast oil development, patents the first blow-out preventer for oil rigs. Fitted between the drill stem and the casing, the blow-out preventer is first used a year later at the Humble field, Texas.

A bottle-making machine—the first to be fully automatic—begins production. Invented by the American M.J. Owens, it leads to greater output and decreases both production costs and hand-blowers' wages. By 1920 almost all bottles in the USA will be made on machines like this one.

R.W. Paul invents the Unipivot Movement for the portable measuring instruments used by electricians. The delicate needle and spring are resistant to shock and highly accurate.

James Sequira, a dermatologist at the London Hospital, devises a radiation therapy to destroy the malignant tumour of the face, known as rodent ulcer. Healing begins with the formation of scar tissue, and plastic surgery completes the treatment.

German surgeon Georg Perthes initiates radiation therapy for cancer when he finds that X-rays inhibit the growth of malignant tumours.

The Nobel Prize for Physiology and Medicine goes to Danish physicin Niels Ryberg Finsen for his success in killing the bacterium involved in the skin disease, *lupus vulgaris*, brought on by the TB bacillus, by using ultraviolet light.

The flavour and texture of margarine is improved by hardening vegetable oils. Replacing skimmed milk and animal suet, these oils will quadruple the world's annual margarine production to 2.1 million tons by 1950.

In Boston, J.H. Cunningham and Frank Lahey revive a technique of rectal anaesthesia pioneered in Russia more than 50 years earlier. They operate on patients using air to conduct ether vapour into the rectum.

Wolseley build a track to test-drive their cars.

'Pagliacci' becomes the first complete opera on disc.

Marie Curie, *left*, Polish-born physicist, publishes her Ph.D thesis outlining the discovery of the elements radium and polonium, and shares the Nobel Prize for Physics with her husband, Pierre, and Henri Becquerel, the discoverer of radioactivity. Later acclaimed the greatest-ever female scientist, her findings concerning the nature of radioactivity will form the basis of most subsequent nuclear research. She will die of leukaemia in 1934, a victim of the forces she has studied for most of her life, but her name will live on in the curie—the unit of measurement of radioactivity used by scientists all over the world.

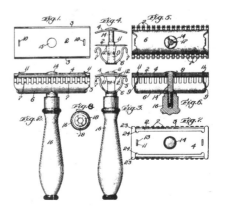

Advised to 'invent something that will be used once and thrown away', King Camp Gillette dreams up the safety razor. The manufacture of thin, sharp blade steel eludes him until he joins forces with mechanic William Nickerson. They file the patent shown in 1901. The 51 razors sold so far will blossom to 90,000 in the next year.

COMMUNICATION AND INFORMATION

The answerphone makes its début. Now, using a form of Poulsen's telegraphone, the telephone can be answered—and a message taken—quite automatically.

Members of Britain's Royal Society witness a demonstration of the 'Auxetophone', a gramophone incorporating a sophisticated new means of audio amplification. Within two years the Gramophone Company begin a successful marketing campaign, with machines priced at £100. Soon the Auxetophone is used to give concerts in venues such as London's Albert Hall, and an elegant drawing-room model in a Chippendale-style cabinet becomes available.

TRANSPORT AND WARFARE

The 'Victorian', built in Belfast, and the *Virginian*, in Glasgow, are the first transatlantic liners to be driven by steam turbines and the first with triple screws. The *Virginian's* 1,200 hp turbines, directly coupled to each of its three propeller shafts, raise its speed to 19.8 knots.

Five submarines join the British navy for training and experimental use. Built in Barrow to an American design, the cigar-shaped *Hollands* are each armed with one torpedo and powered by an Otto gasoline engine.

Dr. Rudolf Diesel's heavy oil engine of 1893 is adopted for use in small vessels. The first motor-ship is the oil tanker *Wandel*, built at St. Petersburg (now Leningrad), for use on the Caspian Sea.

The 'City of Truro' steam locomotive is the first train to break the 100 mph barrier—officially (other steam trains have probably travelled as fast). Its actual record speed is disputed, but 102.3 mph (164.6 km/h) is most likely.

ENERGY AND INDUSTRY

Gas is used for the first time to power central heating and to provide a large-scale supply of hot water. Gas-fired equipment is installed in London both at a high school in Clapham and at the Sandow Institute of Physical Culture.

A. Fasenmeyer builds the first plant that can extract gasoline from natural gas by the compression and cooling method. It is located near the Drake well, Pennsylvania—the first well to be drilled for the purpose of finding oil.

Initial efforts to generate power by harnessing the steam from volcanic regions are made at Lardarello, in Tuscany, Italy.

MEDICINE AND FOOD PRODUCTION

In London, Alexander Glenny, seeking to improve on Emil Behring's diphtheria antitoxin, accidentally discovers a safer and longer-lasting serum. By diluting diphtheria toxin with formalin, he prepares a harmless mixture which gives complete protection. But it will be 20 years before it is adopted as the basis of immunization against diphtheria.

Emil Fischer and J. von Mering, synthesize barbitone (Veronal), first in a long line of barbiturates which will be used for intravenous anaesthesia.

Former shoe salesman and Illinois medical school graduate William Scholl patents the Dr Scholl arch-support. Scholl, who will advertise himself as 'foot doctor to the world', later promotes his famous corn, callous and bunion pads, used to relieve sore feet.

FRINGE BENEFITS

The vacuum flask, designed for lab work, is first used in the home.

George Parker patents his lever-fill pen.

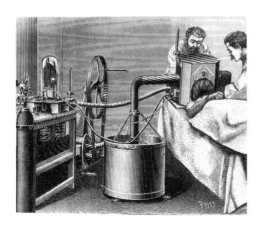

Ludolf Brauer of Marburg, Germany, facilitates thoracic surgery with his pneumatic cabinet. Linked with Roth-Draeger's chloroform apparatus for anaesthesia, it maintains normal pressure within the chest cavity during surgery, so preventing the lungs from collapsing.

John Ambrose Fleming patents the diode as a radio wave detector. Edison had discovered that an electrode introduced into one of his light bulbs would permit a flow of current between it and the filament in one direction only. Fleming's inspiration makes possible the development of sophisticated radio communication.

Advertising is an exploding source of revenue for US newspapers. The total spent in this year is a staggering $40 million.

German physicist Christian Helsmeyer takes the first halting steps towards the invention of radar when he hits on a way of using radio echoes to prevent collisions at sea.

As double-sided 10-in (25-cm) needle-cut shellac gramophone discs gain in popularity, their British price falls to 5 shillings—still expensive, but by 1912 they will cost only a twelfth of this price.

Offset lithography for printing on paper becomes commercially viable by working faster and using cheaper paper. Architect of the advance is Ira W. Rubel of New York, who designs a printing press capable of transferring the image to be printed from the litho stone to the rubber roller which comes into contact with the paper.

Michelin popularize a pneumatic car tyre whose raised, flat tread is stronger and provides a better grip on the road than the smooth, round tread common for the time.

Even stalling on tight turns does not prevent the Wright Brothers from making over 100 flights in the second of their Flyers. An improved design and larger engine allow them to remain airborne for over 5 mins, and to turn and fly a circuit.

A famous motoring partnership is formed when car enthusiast the Hon. Charles Stewart Rolls decides to boost flagging trade at his London motor agency by selling cars built by Henry Royce, a Manchester electrical engineer. The two men will found the Rolls-Royce car company in 1906.

Frenchman Robert Esnault-Pelterie builds and tests a glider—without success; but his is the first glider to use ailerons, the hinged surfaces on a wing edge that control the plane's rolling movement.

Frederick Simms invents the first motor car fender, or bumper, basing his design on the buffers used for railway engines.

The first metal alloy to be virtually unaffected by changes in temperature is discovered by Charles-Edouard Guillaume. Called Invar, this new alloy contains 66% steel and will be used for clock pendulums, watch escapements and all other precision instruments which would otherwise be affected by temperature fluctuations.

Experiments in house central heating, using gas as a fuel, are begun in St Louis, Missouri, by the Laclede Gas Light Co.

Stainless steels are first made by French scientist, Leon Guillet. However, interested only in the metallic and mechanical properties of the new alloys, which contain the crucial stainless ingredient chromium, he fails to notice their remarkable resistance to corrosion and will not receive full credit for his work.

Russian physiologist Ivan Pavlov receives the Nobel Prize for Physiology and Medicine for his work on digestion. Famous for his work on dogs, Pavlov will be remembered for his discovery of the conditioned reflex and his subsequent contribution to behavioural psychology.

Alfred Einhorn discovers the anaesthetic procaine—as effective as its relative cocaine, but without the worrying side-effects. Simpler and more stable than cocaine, it will be first used intravenously in 1909, and will become known under its trade-name Novocain.

Russell Chittenden, founder of the first US laboratory of physiological chemistry at Yale, is the first to isolate glycogen, the form in which the body stores carbohydrates.

The folding metal push chair proves a boon to parents and servants.

Coin-operated ticket machines save time on the London tube.

The trans-Siberian Railway, the longest continuous stretch of track in the world, is completed. It runs for 5,778 mls (9,297 km) between Moscow and Vladivostok. Early trains are often hauled by wood-burning locomotives such as the one pictured at a provincial station. By the eighties, the railway will contain the longest stretch of electrified track in the world—3,240 mls (5,213 km) from Moscow to Irkutsk—and a through journey will take about $7\frac{1}{2}$ days.

COMMUNICATION AND INFORMATION

Picture postcards are the craze of the year. Most are printed in a single colour (usually sepia), but the most expensive are also hand-coloured.

Always aiming to improve radio reception, Marconi discovers that an antenna wire laid on the ground gives better reception when its free end points away from, not toward the transmitting station. This directional or 'bent' antenna (aerial) is incorporated into his Glace Bay Station in Canada and broadens the range of reception. Marconi's discovery marks the first step toward radio direction finding which will prove so vital during World War I.

The New Zealand Post Office introduces the franking machine—for official use only—as an alternative to the postage stamp. It takes another 17 years for such machines to reach Britain and the USA.

A flood of tabulating machines for processing statistics is generated by the mass of information gathered by the US Census Bureau—by 1910, 300 different types will have been produced.

TRANSPORT AND WARFARE

The first illuminated track diagram in the world is installed in a London railway station signal box. For the first time, a signalman no longer has to rely on his actual view of the track to operate points and signals; instead he can monitor train movements as their positions are pin-pointed in small electric lights on the diagram—a system which will change little in 75 years.

Dr Anschutz-Kaempfe patents the gyrocompass, an electro-mechanical device which has the advantage over the magnetic compass of being entirely independent of the Earth's magnetic field.

The Wrights' Flyer III solves its older sister's stalling problems and becomes the world's first practical aircraft. It even has fewer test runs than its forbears, but is soon making sustained flights of over 30 mins with ease—as well as turning, circling and flying in figures of eight.

ENERGY AND INDUSTRY

Non-shatter safety glass is patented for the first time, the basis being a simple sheet of celluloid, glued between two sheets of glass. By 1910, it will be made under the name Triplex and become widely used for windshields and even for gas mask lenses.

Artificial silk is commercially produced for the first time by Courtaulds of England, who have spent 13 years developing the viscose process. Samuel Courtauld will buy the US rights to this viscose rayon, and by 1911 will begin commercial production there. By 1913, over 3 million lb (1.4 million kg) of the new fabric will be manufactured each year.

Cars move nearer to becoming mass-produced with the introduction of two new grinding machines. Charles Norton's specialized grinder enables crankshafts to be made with greater precision and a smoother finish. James Heald's planetary spindle cylinder grinder allows engine cylinders to be manufactured economically and with a greater degree of accuracy. Both machines also make large savings in time and labour—Norton's grinder, for instance, does in 15 mins what a skilled worker has previously taken 5 hrs to do.

MEDICINE AND FOOD PRODUCTION

The Nobel Prize for Physiology and Medicine goes to German physician Robert Koch, for his discoveries concerning tuberculosis.

US physician David Marine, concerned at the high incidence of goitre in the Cleveland area, begins a ten-year series of experiments with iodine-containing compounds. But 20 years will go by before his discovered remedy for goitre is widely accepted: that iodine supplements should be added to table-salt and water in areas where the soil is poor in iodine.

FRINGE BENEFITS

Strip lighting twisted into words is used for advertising.

The first pre-selective jukebox, the 7 ft high Multiphone, uses cylinder recordings.

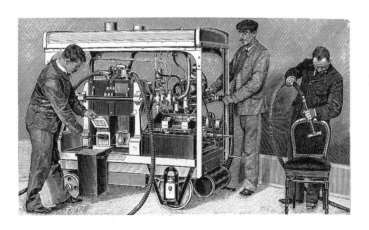

Sweeping changes in home maintenance are heralded by the first domestic vacuum cleaning equipment. Originally invented by Hubert Booth in 1901, this French version is typical of the unwieldy contraptions that will soon be replaced by the smaller electrically powered Trolley Vac and Hoover.

The Pathé Company of France automates the colouring of movie films—previously they were laboriously hand-coloured, frame by frame, at the rate of 1,000 frames for each minute of screen time. The secret is Pathé's stencil system by which colour can be transferred to the black and white film at high speed. The system will remain in use for 25 years and, well used, will prove remarkably effective.

Recorded music arrives in British homes as several German companies market Puck cylinder-playing phonographs at bargain prices. But success is short-lived as discs begin to replace cylinders.

Dr J.A. Fleming's portable wavemeter—for checking signal wavelengths simply and quickly, and for tuning—is now an indispensable item of equipment for all radio operators.

All ships on the North Atlantic route equipped with Marconi radios send out weather bulletins. For the first time *Daily Telegraph* readers in Britain can read printed versions of these weather bulletins.

British mainline trains follow the lead taken by London's Underground when the first regular service to run on electricity is opened in Newcastle.

The Long Island Railroad becomes the first US railway to abandon steam completely in favour of electrification. Although an electrified railway system is more expensive to install than one run on steam, the swift acceleration of electric trains makes them especially attractive for the many commuter rail routes under construction.

London's underground railway system says farewell to steam forever: the programme of electrification begun in 1900 is completed.

The submarine U1 is launched, the first of a long succession of German submarines which will take such an important part in the two World Wars.

Strong, wire-reinforced glass becomes more of a reality when Chance Brothers of the USA patent the first machine to manufacture it. The process embeds iron wire mesh—and, later, an iron-nickel alloy—into glass.

A remarkably futuristic bridge opens over the Rhine in Switzerland. The Tavanasa Bridge, in Canton Grisons, incorporates the prototype of the three-hinged arch and is built from concrete slabs, reinforced by steel rods embedded in them. The architect, Robert Maillart, will become the most famous designer of reinforced concrete bridges, but his work at Tavanasa will be destroyed by a landslide in 1927.

A new world of comfort for women is discovered when elastic rubber replaces traditional whalebone and lacing in foundation garments.

Richard Sutcliffe, an Englishman, installs the first endless-belt conveyor at a Yorkshire colliery.

Electric light bulbs with filaments made from the metal tantalum are placed on the market by Siemens and Halske Co, Berlin, and are immediately successful. So strong and malleable is tantalum that very long-lasting and thin filaments can be made; but, although they will be used for many years in lamps on vehicles, tantalum light bulbs do not produce enough light to ward off competition from later tungsten lamps.

J.B. Murphy of Chicago pioneers arthroplasty—the creation of artificial joints—when he operates on a patient with an arthritic hip.

The first successful corneal graft is performed by Eduard Konrad Zirm in the little Moravian town of Olmutz. But the operation does not become widespread until the end of World War II.

French-American surgeon Alexis Carrel experiments with the transplantation of living organs and blood vessels, and perfects a technique of surgical anastomosis: reconnecting severed blood vessels to restore normal circulation. His work with animals at the Rockefeller Institute helps pave the way for organ transplants in human beings.

Vick's Magic Croup Salve—later re-named VapoRub—is introduced by the Vick Chemical Co, N. Carolina, to relieve chest congestion.

A new dimension is given to man's understanding of the universe by a young examiner at the Swiss Patents Office: Albert Einstein, *left*, propounds his Special Theory of Relativity. He hypothesizes that the concept of absolute motion is valueless and that the measured speed of light is constant for all observers, irrespective of relative motion. His deductions from this basis reverse many fundamental assumptions. Notably, he claims that mass and energy are interchangable; their relationship is expressed in the equation $E = MC^2$, where C is the speed of light. Later experimentation will confirm most of his disturbing assertions; most spectacularly, the first atomic bomb demonstrates that a tiny amount of matter can be turned into enormous energy.

Early electric kettles kept water and watts well away from each other: a metal plate bolted to the base is heated by bare-wire filaments sealed in a separate compartment. This inefficient system will remain in use until the 'Swan' kettle, with an immersed element is introduced in 1921.

Oil's troubled waters

For millions of years, the bodies of a multitude of primitive organisms have been waiting, poised in the pores of the world's rocks to burst into the 20th century as oil. The role of this vital liquid has been to sate the ever-increasing appetite of man's energy-consuming machines, and to provide the raw material for the paints, plastics, cosmetics and countless other products that elevate living standards, and keep them high.

Since 1859, when Edwin Drake drilled the first oil well in Titusville, Pennsylvania, oil engineers employed by entrepreneurs and corporate giants have been puncturing the Earth's surface to extract crude oil. Chemists cracked the crude to make kerosene and gasoline, and, from the early years of the century, began to make the first of the products the average western family now finds indispensable. Huge fortunes were made and even whole nations have been held hostage for vast ransoms—the price payable in black gold.

By 1979, 70 per cent of all the world's total of 4,800 million tonnes of annual energy production came from oil. And man has become so dependent on oil that over half the energy of the industrialized world is now supplied by oil, with a further 16 per cent provided by natural gas, a close relation of oil and always found in association with it. Yet the continuing discovery of new sources suggests that it may be premature to predict the exhaustion of the world's oil, as some have, by the year 2030, even though man has never before scoured the Earth so thoroughly for a mineral resource.

In the early days of oil exploration, engineers looked first for surface seepages of oil, but then devised more and more sophisticated techniques for charting and locating the sandstone and limestone rocks where petroleum—oil and natural gas—is known to accumulate. Offshore and onshore drilling rigs were sent to explore the most likely sites and huge oilfields were discovered and exploited. Year by year, as oil production increased, more efficient transport techniques were devised so that now oil pipelines stretch like arteries and veins across the land and along the sea bed, pumping oil into vast storage tanks.

Even after it has been expensively unearthed, the oil is still crude and unusable. In sprawling refineries, strategically located around the world's coastlines, and each a monument to technology, crude oil is refined by heat, pressure and a whole variety of catalysts, and can be used for the many domestic products we take for granted.

When the Middle East War of 1973 triggered the Arabs into using their oil as a political weapon against western nations, it was clearly time to subject the oil situation to close scrutiny. Just as oil had so rapidly become a

symbol of technological advance, so it could equally become a symbol of decline—unless the ongoing development of oil went hand in hand with that of new resources.

In a world that daily consumes all the fossil fuel laid down in 1,000 years of prehistory, including coal as well as oil and gas, it would be foolish indeed to ignore the warning bells of dwindling and wasted resources. For nations such as the USA, where six per cent of the

Like a vast chemistry laboratory, the 1,000-acre (404-hectare) Fawley refinery on Southampton Water, England, owned and run by the oil giant Esso, distils crude oil and separates it into many pure products. These include gasoline, paraffin, lubricating oils, heavy fuel oils, naphtha, gas oils and bitumen. From the refinery, each product is transported for later use as fuel or as feedstock for a wide range of manufacturing industries. Naphtha, for example, is used to make Perspex and nylon, while gas oil is employed in the manufacture of plastics.

The massive concrete production platform of the Shell/Esso Brent B field in the North Sea, *left*, handles up to 150,000 barrels of oil a day. Perfectly suited to the North Sea, where water depths do not exceed 656 ft (200 m), the platform rests on the sea bed secure under its own weight. It pumps oil down a pipeline to the Shetland Isles off the Scottish coast, and transfers gas to a separate pipeline to the Scottish mainland.

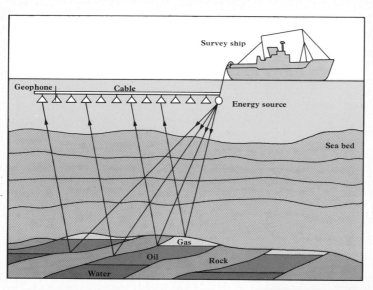

Survey ship

Geophone   Cable   Energy source

Sea bed

Gas

Oil   Rock

Water

Underwater surveys of oil-bearing rocks are carried out by prospectors on a computer-equipped ship behind which is towed a 'sleeve exploder'. This device emits regular, controlled pulses of energy which are reflected from the rocks below and picked up again on a series of geophone detectors spaced along a cable. The computer then processes the reflected signals and displays a picture of a cross section of the ocean bed on a monitor. Such surveys greatly improve the chances of finding oil.

Early oil wells were drilled by the age old percussion method used to sink wells for water: a hole was punched by repeatedly pounding soft rock with a heavy cutting tool hanging from a cable. This was superseded by the rotary drill bit, *below right*, which the Hughes Tool Co introduced in 1908 for drilling deep wells through hard rock. The rotary bit on the Brent B platform used in the North Sea, *below left*, shows that it has remained virtually unchanged.

world's population consumes 35 per cent of its energy, conservation of that energy is no longer merely desirable but a necessity, along with the development of new resources such as hydrogen and shale oil fuels. This said, the USA is expected to consume more energy in the next 30 years than in its entire history. No cause for alarm, but caution is advisable: the watchwords must be conservation and development.

COMMUNICATION AND INFORMATION

Colour printing arrives for general-interest books and cards. Novel, comparatively cheap techniques allow colour printing using only three hues—cyan, magenta and yellow—instead of the wide range of colours previously needed.

Large display type, ideal for headlines and handbills, and invaluable to the daily press, is now available thanks to Washington I. Ludlow's invention of the typecasting machine in the USA.

On Christmas Eve, Fessenden makes the first successful radio broadcast from the National Electrical Signalling Co's radio station at Bryant Rock, Ma. Opening with a violin rendition of Gounod's *O Holy Night*, he goes on to recite verses from St Luke's Gospel and ends with a Christmas greeting. The broadcast is heard by ship's wireless operators over a radius of more than 100 mls (161 km).

H.C. Dunwoody patents the carborundum crystal radio detector which is to be the heart of the new wireless industry. Despite the investigation of many other crystals, carborundum is to prove the most reliable.

TRANSPORT AND WARFARE

Swiss railways adopt electric locomotives which immediately prove much better than steam engines for hauling trains up steep mountain slopes. Abundant hydroelectric power helps to put Switzerland among the world's leaders in railway electrification; and by 1975 all but 12 mls (20 km) of its rail network will be electrified.

The longest railway tunnel in the world is completed. The Simplon Tunnel, linking France and Italy, runs for 12.3 mls (19.8 km) and reaches a depth of 6,890 ft (2,100 m). A slightly longer tunnel, driven parallel to the first, will open in 1921; and this will remain the world's longest until Japan's Seikan tunnel of the eighties.

Herbert Austin founds Britain's most successful pre-World War I car company after he resigns from the rival firm of Wolseley.

ENERGY AND INDUSTRY

A major breakthrough in the development of electric fires is made by A.L. Marsh when he patents a coiled wire, made from a nickel-chrome alloy, that will subsequently be used in heating elements. Previous iron wires tended to break but Marsh's alloy stays intact for long periods of intense heat.

The term 'air-conditioning' is coined by American Stuart Crawer when he combines his dust filter with W.H. Carrier's 1902 device for cooling air in buildings. The machine is first used in a textile mill to condition cotton by using air, but 'air-conditioner' soon comes to mean a machine that conditions the air itself.

MEDICINE AND FOOD PRODUCTION

The first change in amputation procedure this century comes when Italian surgeon Giuliano Vanghetti introduces cineplastic treatment of the stump. This is shaped so as to ensure maximum movement of any artificial limb after it is fitted.

Victims of African sleeping sickness will benefit from the first synthetic drug, discovered in Germany by Paul Ehrlich. Working on the bactericidal properties of organic arsenical compounds, he finds one—Atoxyl—that kills the trypanosome of sleeping sickness.

Columbia University zoologist Thomas Hunt Morgan launches the science of genetics with the novel idea of using the fruit-fly *Drosophila* to study heredity in action. Results will be achieved even more readily when, in 1926, one of Morgan's former colleagues, Herman Muller, discovers a way to speed up the rate of mutation in the fruit-fly, so that inheritance of genetic changes can be observed more quickly. This work is vital to the understanding of hereditary disease.

FRINGE BENEFITS

Cornflakes lose their 'health food' image and appear on the general market.

The Trolley Vac—the first portable domestic vacuum cleaner to be powered by an electric motor—is introduced by Hubert Booth.

American Lee de Forest invents the three-electrode vacuum tube—the triode valve—by adding a third valve to Fleming's diode. Using an electric power source, this 'Audion' amplifies feeble electric currents and translates them into sound. As a sensitive detector and an efficient amplifier of radio waves, the triode revolutionizes radio communications. The human voice can now be broadcast loud and clear over long distances.

The first pre-selective juke box to hold 24 10-in (25-cm) discs is named the John Gabel Automatic Entertainer, and is manufactured by the Automatic Machine and Tool Co of Chicago.

Marketing the first fully panchromatic plates, Britons Wratton and Wainwright put photography firmly into the 20th century. Their 'London' plates are the first to be equally sensitive to all colours of the spectrum.

American undertaker Almon Brown Strowger, frustrated by losing business through wrongly connected telephone calls, devises a switching system controlled automatically by a dial instead of a fallible human operator. The Bell Telephone Laboratories are quick to latch on to the idea and install Strowger-type telephone exchanges across the USA. Such exchanges will still be widely used in the eighties.

The first aircraft factory is set up by Charles and Gabriel Voisin in Billancourt, France. Their biplane becomes a favourite among European pilots despite having no system of lateral control.

Leon Levasseur builds the water-cooled Antoinette engine. Named after a friend's daughter for good luck, the eight-cylinder V-type is designed first as a 24 hp, then as a 50 hp model. Although its direct fuel injection system gives an irregular performance, it will remain the main European engine for aircraft until the development of the Gnome rotary in 1909.

A tailfirst 14-bis biplane piloted by Alberto Santos-Dumont makes Europe's first officially recognized powered flights or 'hops'—the longest lasts only 21½ secs. Its nickname *canard*, or duck, is soon applied to all similar machines built with fuselage and tail unit in front of the engine.

In France Romanian-born Trajan Vuia builds a primitive monoplane. By combining a propeller, mounted forward of the engine, with a monoplane wing and rear tail, Vuia anticipates virtually all modern aircraft.

Light bulbs using tungsten as the metal filament are introduced commercially. Made by Just and Hannaman's squirted filament process, they will remain delicate and inefficient until Coolidge devises a new method of preparing tungsten in 1908.

US engineers Harvey Williams and Reynolds Janney develop the first true variable speed hydraulic transmission system. Used to raise and lower the guns on the US warship *Virginia*, this prototype of later hydraulic systems is also the first to be powered by its own electric motor.

The cutting edge of high-speed steels—used in lathes for the machining of metals—attains such high quality that their usefulness cannot be fully exploited. The steels are now so hard, as a result of electric furnace melting, that existing lathes are neither powerful nor fast enough to capitalize on their strength.

Austrian paediatrician Clemens von Pirquet coins the word 'allergy' to describe hypersensitivity to any one of a number of environmental substances. Allergic reactions may vary in intensity from a mild rash to outright collapse.

Italian physiologist Camillo Golgi and Spanish neurologist Santiago Ramón y Cajal share the Nobel Prize for Physiology and Medicine for their research on the connections of the cells in the brain and spinal cord.

Six years after two Belgian bacteriologists, Jules Bordet and Octave Gengou, tracked down the whooping cough bacillus, they succeed in cultivating it in the laboratory. This is an essential step towards the development of the whooping cough vaccine.

Freeze-drying is invented, by A. d'Arsonval and F. Bordas in Paris, as a means of storing biological material for long periods. It will be used on a large scale in 1940 when blood plasma is freeze-dried in the USA.

German bacteriologist August von Wasserman introduces a serum reaction test for the detection of syphilis. The Wasserman test becomes the best-known example of a diagnostic procedure of this kind.

The permanent wave promises 'naturally' curling hair.

The 'hot dog' gets its name from an American cartoonist's drawing of a dachshund in a bun.

Built in a year and a day at an estimated cost of £1¾ million, the HMS *Dreadnought*, launched in October, carries 2½ times as many heavy guns at greater speed than any existing battleship. Its smooth-running turbine drive reduces maintenance costs and enables it to spend more time at sea. Its unique design and efficiency render all other battleships afloat obsolete. Rapid naval expansion follows its début, and its success is such that future craft of all naval powers will be designed along the same lines.

The first commercial cinematograph projector made in England appeared in 1896—used by its designer Robert Paul at the Alhambra Theatre. His new 'Animatograph' projectors are larger—the 11-in (27.5-cm) spools of this 'Reliance' model can take 1,500 ft (450 m) of film—and they produce steady images with much less flicker.

25

COMMUNICATION AND INFORMATION

London's 'Daily Mirror' publishes the first front-page newspaper photograph transmitted by wire—a shot of King Edward VII taken in Paris. The radio telegraph system flashes the photograph between the two cities in only 12 min.

The direction of aircraft on long-distance routes can be plotted more accurately then ever before, thanks to the invention of the radio-goniometer by Italian Alessandro Artom. Now navigation by radio waves is possible, making the old, cumbersome slide-rule calculations obsolete.

TRANSPORT AND WARFARE

British Daimler cars are fitted with the new sliding sleeve valve engine invented by US publisher Charles Knight. It has fewer mechanical parts and so is quieter than other contemporary car engines, but its high oil consumption and limited performance will eventually lead Daimler and other companies to drop it.

Over 100,000 route miles of railway, added since 1900, bring the world's total to around 600,000.

A French bicycle-dealer, Paul Cornu, designs the first man-carrying helicopter to rise vertically. His fragile twin-rotor machine, powered by a 24 hp Antoinette engine, remains airborne for just 20 secs at a height of 6 ft (1.8 m) and breaks up on landing.

ENERGY AND INDUSTRY

The electric light industry will be among the main beneficiaries of the first commercial production of the five inert gases found in the air. Neon, argon, xenon (to be used in the manufacture of light bulbs), helium (to be used for airships) and krypton (ultimately to be used in laser technology) are all made available when Georges Claude and Carl von Linde independently perfect the method of liquefying air and separating its component gases.

A tin can, a broomstick, a flour sack and an electric motor are the components of Murray Spangler's lightweight vacuum cleaner. He sells the rights to W. Hoover, a leather manufacturer, who will introduce the first commercial model in 1908. Selling for $75, it becomes so popular that 'hoovering' will become a household term and even find its way into the dictionary.

MEDICINE AND FOOD PRODUCTION

In the USA a calorimeter is devised to assist work on nutrition and metabolism (the conversion of food into usable energy). It measures both the consumption of oxygen and the elimination of carbon dioxide, as well as the production of heat in the body. This provides a way of measuring the effects of disease on metabolic efficiency.

The Nobel Prize for Physiology and Medicine goes to French parasitologist Alphonse Laveran, for his work on the role of protozoans in causing diseases such as malaria, leishmaniasis and sleeping sickness.

Francis Benedict, director of the Nutrition Laboratory in Washington D.C., discovers how, in starvation, the human body begins to consume itself. Normal sources of life-sustaining energy are fats and carbohydrates in the diet. In starvation, these sources are used up, and the body begins to metabolize protein—devouring its own tissues.

FRINGE BENEFITS

The self-threading sewing-machine needle is introduced.

The Lumière brothers, Louis and Auguste—12 years after their invention of cinematography—introduce the first commercially successful single-plate colour process. Their 'Autochrome' glass plates are coated with minute starch grains each dyed red, green or blue to act as filters, and overlaid with a photographic emulsion. Exposing the plate to good light for one or two seconds, and then reversing the image into a positive picture during the development process, eventually produces a full colour transparency. Such plates will remain on the market for nearly 30 years.

The range of radio transmission is broadened hugely when Ernst Alexander of GEC in the USA builds a high-frequency radio alternator which can generate an alternating frequency of up to 100 kHz. He later invents a magnetic, and an electronic, amplifier and a multiple-tuned antenna.

Regular radio broadcasts begin. Made from a studio on New York's 4th Avenue by the de Forest Radio Telephone Co, they consist solely of gramophone music.

Russian physicist Boris Rosing realizes that the cathode-ray tube can be used for receiving images. His idea—later taken up by Baird—is that electrical signals can be transformed into visible patterns, using a mechanical transmitter and a cathode-ray tube as a receiver.

Encouraged by the response to their first, homemade motorbike, William Harley and Arthur Davidson found the famous motorcycle company which will produce over 18,000 bikes a year by 1917.

Influenced by Trajan Vuia's pioneering work on monoplanes the previous year, French airman Louis Blériot abandons his biplane in favour of the VI and VII—the first full-sized cantilever monoplanes (their wings are free of external bracing) which set the style of aircraft to come.

The basis of modern aerofoil theory is set out in F.W. Lanchester's two books *Aerodynamics* and *Aerodonetics*, arguably the most important written works on aviation since Sir George Cayley's *On Aerial Navigation* of 1809-10.

HMS 'Invincible', the first battle-cruiser, is commissioned by the British First Sea Lord, Sir John Fisher, whose radical reforms of the navy create a fighting force to rival the rising power of Germany. The weight of the battle-cruiser's heavy guns is redressed by a reduction in armour to maintain a high surface speed of over 25 knots—a slight edge over the German cruisers which carry guns to menace British commercial shipping.

Changes in the character of road traffic in Britain demand that the dust of the old tracks be covered by road-surfacing, and crude coal-tar is now used for this purpose. Later, when it will be employed for binding Tarmacadam, road-surfacing will become coal-tar's primary use.

The Atlantic Refining Co introduces the tower still refinery, which incorporates a new method of improving the efficiency of producing gasoline and other oil-based products, from solvents to waxes and greases. The process permits the petroleum to be separated in a continuous process rather than in batches, thus increasing productivity, and will be used in many refineries from 1910.

The paint spray gun is introduced, giving paint technology its greatest advance to date; it will rapidly be adopted by the car and furniture industries in particular. Not only does the spray gun speed up the application of paint, but it will also accelerate the introduction of those lacquers that are unsuited to brush application. Spraying lacquer on car bodies will give them a finer finish, with no brush marks, and will reduce their price by about $100.

Amino acids are joined together to form part of a protein, the basis of all living matter. German chemist Emil Fischer gives the name peptide to the synthesized chain of glycine molecules—the simplest amino acid.

Ross G. Harrison and colleagues at Johns Hopkins University usher in a new era in the study and prevention of disease, with the introduction of tissue culture: keeping alive in the laboratory cells removed from animal tissues.

Surgeons, fearing for their handiwork, have been insisting on several weeks' bed-rest for their patients after surgery. Now, US gynaecologists H.J. Bolt and Emil Ries show that patients recover more quickly, and suffer fewer post-operative complications—from thrombosis and pneumonia, for example—if they quickly become mobile after surgery.

In America, new techniques for growing cells outside the body enable scientists to see activity within individual cells. Montrose Burrows becomes the first person to observe cells dividing, in the process called mitosis. He also isolates a single cell from the heart muscle which contracts spontaneously, thus proving that the heart-beat originates within the heart itself.

Persil, produced by a German firm, will be marketed in Britain as 'The amazing oxygen cleaner'.

Many companies vie to improve the filaments of electric lamps. Osram-GEC introduce their tungsten-osmium filament lamp and, in 1908, will be the first in Britain to use drawn-tungsten. A publicity campaign begins to win consumers over to electric light—this advertisement will be seen in the early twenties.

The 'Mauretania', pictured here before her maiden voyage, will hold the Blue Riband for the fastest Atlantic crossing for more than 20 years. Her reputation is built on luxury as much as speed and reliability. Christened 'the monstrous nine-decked city' by Rudyard Kipling, her sumptuous interior includes staterooms furnished in the style of Adam and Chippendale.

COMMUNICATION AND INFORMATION

Standard stationery for home and office is becoming popular. Seizing a marketing opportunity, the famous British stationers W.H. Smith invest in their first printing plant—the Arden Press.

Using the world's first transatlantic radio-telegraph stations at Glace Bay, Canada and Clifden in Ireland, messages can be sent across the Atlantic by members of the public. The cost: 15 cents a word.

British scientist Campbell Swinton outlines a method of electronic scanning which, 15 years later, becomes the basis of the TV tube in the form of the iconoscope. Swinton proposes the use of a cathode-ray tube at both camera and receiver ends of the system. The image is focused on a mosaic screen of photoelectric elements in the camera, and the TV signal is created by the discharging effect of a scanning cathode-ray beam. The scan is traced out, line by line, in the receiver to form a TV picture.

TRANSPORT AND WARFARE

Gaston du Bousquet, co-builder of France's 'Atlantic' steam engine, branches out to build an engine of his own. To achieve a tighter grip on the track without sacrificing any power, he uses six (instead of the 'Atlantic's' four) driving wheels, and reduces their diameter by 1 ft (0.305 m) to 5 ft 9 in (1.7 m).

In May Charles Furnass becomes aviation's first passenger when he accompanies Wilbur Wright on a 28.6-sec flight at a height of nearly 2,000 ft (610 m). In August, Wright takes the Flyer to France, where his practical demonstration of flight control spellbinds spectators and stimulates the development of European aviation.

LZ4 is flown on a 20-hr journey down the Rhine to show the German army the practicality of rigid airships. Although LZ4 is wrecked during this trial, public donations pay for LZ5 which is later bought by the Air Ministry.

ENERGY AND INDUSTRY

A purer white for paper, rubber, leather, textiles and ceramics becomes possible when two US chemists extract the whitest known pigment—titanium dioxide—from its natural sources, rutile and ilmenite.

The Howard Hughes Tool Co designs, builds and successfully uses the first steel-toothed rock-drilling bit, to sink an oil well at Goose Creek, Texas. The bit revolutionizes oil drilling because it can drill easily through hard rock to oil deposits beneath. Previously, only the oil under softer rock could be reached—by pounding a way through.

The prototype of all future filament electric light bulbs is made by Coolidge, a US scientist. He successfully produces a filament made from tungsten by compressing tungsten powder into rods and then, after extreme heating and hammering, drawing the metal into very fine, strong filaments. Tungsten's high melting-point enables the filament to be run at greater temperatures, giving more light for a given wattage than previous filaments.

MEDICINE AND FOOD PRODUCTION

Russian biologist Ilya Metchnikoff is joint winner (with German bacteriologist Paul Ehrlich) of the Nobel Prize for Physiology and Medicine for his discovery of important agents in the body's immune system—the white blood cells, known as phagocytes, which devour bacteria.

In Britain Sir Archibald Garrod gives a series of lectures relating the rare disorder, known as alkaptonuria, to an 'inborn error of metabolism'. He extends his studies to other metabolic disorders, suggesting that each arises from a single inherited defect.

The first international meeting of psychiatrists, held in Salzburg, Austria, attracts such notable delegates as Freud, Jung and Adler.

FRINGE BENEFITS

'Use once and throw away' paper cups are introduced.

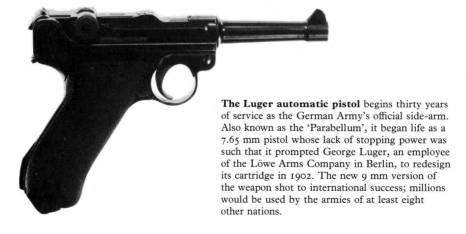

The Luger automatic pistol begins thirty years of service as the German Army's official side-arm. Also known as the 'Parabellum', it began life as a 7.65 mm pistol whose lack of stopping power was such that it prompted George Luger, an employee of the Löwe Arms Company in Berlin, to redesign its cartridge in 1902. The new 9 mm version of the weapon shot to international success; millions would be used by the armies of at least eight other nations.

German Hans Geiger and Briton Ernest Rutherford develop the Geiger counter, a device for detecting radioactive radiation. It contains a high-voltage wire carrying an electric current running through a gas. The gas becomes ionized into charged particles, and a pulse corresponding to each alpha particle can be observed on a dial. The Geiger counter reflects the growing interest in nuclear research.

Thomas Edison's Amberol cylinders double the playing time of a single recording from 2 to 4 mins. The secret is simply the addition of more grooves to the inch.

The Telharmonium, an electric organ the size of a small power station, is demonstrated by American Thomas Cahill. An impressive if cumbersome device, it uses alternator generators for all the frequencies needed. Musical signals, controlled by switches, are transmitted over telephone lines.

'The Times' of London needs more pages per issue. To speed up production enough to achieve its aim, the paper installs Monotype composing machines.

Henri Farman, an Englishman living in France, makes the first cross-country flight, covering 16.78 mls (27 km) from Bouy to Reims. His Voisin biplane is fitted with four ailerons, which allow him lateral control of his craft.

Sir J.W. Isherwood patents his longitudinal system of framing for ships: widely spaced vertical frames between numerous tank bulkheads combine with narrowly spaced girders to give great longitudinal strength.

Further experiments to find the best method of electrifying trains include the first use of high voltage alternating current (a.c.) to power British locomotives. The unwieldy wiring of low voltage direct current (d.c.) systems is avoided; but difficulty in controlling speeds prohibits the widespread adoption of a.c. for several years.

Powered aviation suffers its first fatality when Orville Wright's Flyer crashes during US army trails and his passenger, Lt Thomas Selfridge of the Signal Corps, dies.

A.V. Roe tests a biplane at Brooklands, England. Graduating from model aircraft, Roe constructs a shaky Wright-derived machine that, despite being air-towed behind a car, fails to achieve true flight.

Waste heat from the exhaust system is used to heat a car's interior for the first time. But until the twenties, portable, solid-fuel foot warmers will be the usual source of heating for car travellers.

To heat water by utilizing the sun's rays, E.G. Abbot uses a series of highly polished, bowl-shaped troughs to concentrate the rays on to glass-enclosed, water-filled metal pipes that run along the troughs.

Willsie and Boyle build a solar-powered water pump to drive an engine similar to a simple steam engine. A conical reflector heats water, which in turn heats sulphur dioxide. The sulphur dioxide vaporizes and is used to drive the engine. This device, though uneconomic, demonstrates for the first time the use of two fluids for generating power.

Cheap, mass-produced good-quality gears for cars will be the result of Ward and Taylor's new gear-cutting machine. Tiny diamond cutting edges continually and automatically correct the form of the gear-cutting wheel, ensuring that each set of gears is identical to the next, without the need to change worn-down cutters. The machine saves time and labour and allows the uninterrupted production of gears which are now precise, strong and also quiet.

Agriculture is improved by the first gasoline-engined tractor with crawler (caterpillar) tracks, produced by Holt of California. The tracks provide a good grip on wet sticky soil and, although the tractors are slower than wheeled machines, they can pull the wider implements that large US farms require.

When only hard tissues, such as bone, can be seen on X-rays, the German Hammeter shows up a gastric ulcer for the first time. He uses the barium meal technique: the patient swallows barium sulphate, which, being opaque to X-rays, clearly outlines the stomach and the ulcer.

Already there is a notion that micro-organisms may be involved in cancer, and now two Danes, Wilhelm Ellerman and Olaf Bang, show that leukaemia in poultry is associated with a virus. But leukaemia is not recognized as a cancer at this time, and so the significance of this discovery is not appreciated.

The new oscillating electric fan is the first to offer controllable ventilation.

Henry Ford's Model T brings the automobile to the masses by introducing the assembly line to the motor industry. The first low-priced car to combine speeds of up to 45 mph (72 km/h) with mechanical reliability, the 'Tin Lizzie' offers such good value for money that it will remain in production for 19 years—during which time a total of 15 million will be sold. By leaving it mechanically unchanged for so long and by gaining control of sources of raw materials and means of distribution, Ford is able to reduce the original price of $850 to $260 by 1923. It will remain available in a selection of colours until 1914, when the production line is moving so rapidly that only black paint dries with the requisite speed.

G.A. Smith presents the first true colour movies. His Kinemacolor process uses two-colour analysis: the film is both taken and projected through red and green segments on a rotating wheel. Paradoxically, due to severe colour fringing on fast-moving objects, it will be best used on static subjects.

COMMUNICATION AND INFORMATION

US inventors Elmer Sperry and Hannibal Ford install their gyroscope—already proved a success in stabilizing ships—in an aircraft. It detects and corrects any deviation from level flight immediately.

Europe's first automatic telephone exchange is installed in Munich, Germany. It operates by Strowger's step-by-step dialling system. The dialled digits 'route' the call through a series of switches, first to the local exchange and then to the called line, where either the ringing or engaged tone is triggered.

Rural Chelmsford, in Essex, England, is the testing ground for the 200-ft (61-m) steel radio transmitter masts which will soon traverse both the Amazon rainforest and Europe's concrete jungle.

TRANSPORT AND WARFARE

Fresh from a number of lesser conquests but nursing a badly burned foot, Blériot makes the first cross-Channel flight on 25 July, pipping his rival, Hubert Latham, to a £1,000 prize. Blériot makes the 37-min crossing without a compass, navigating by following ships bound for Dover. His achievement attracts huge publicity—and alarm, as governments realize the potential of a machine that can overcome hitherto impregnable geographical barriers.

Photographs of the military installations at Mourmelon, France, are the first taken from a plane. They demonstrate the potential of aerial reconnaissance.

In the USA an entirely non-magnetic survey ship, the *Carnegie*, is built to investigate the problems of the Earth's magnetic field at sea.

In France, Houdaille devises a suspension system better suited to cars than the arched spring damping inherited from horse-drawn carriages. His telescopic shock absorbers will become standard equipment on most cars by the twenties.

ENERGY AND INDUSTRY

General Electric Co make the first electric toaster, which goes on sale in the USA. The heating element, composed of wires wound around strips of mica, glows red hot and toasts the bread—one side at a time.

Welding metal to metal is considerably improved as the welding machine's electrode—from which an electric arc is generated—is covered for the first time. The asbestos yarn shield around the electrode gives much better control of the heat from the arc, and a stronger, more reliable weld is achieved.

The age of plastics dawns when Leo Baekland, a Belgian chemist working in New York, patents his process for making Bakelite. This is the first plastic to solidify on heating, and it will be used to make telephones, gramophone records, billiard balls, pipestems and as a substitute for hard rubber, amber and celluloid.

MEDICINE AND FOOD PRODUCTION

Following belated recognition of the work of Gregor Mendel (the Austrian monk who did valuable experiments on heredity in the 1860s), the Danish biologist Wilhelm Johannsen gives the name 'genes'—from the Greek word meaning 'to give birth to'—to the factors governing heredity.

French physician, Charles Nicolle, shows that typhus is spread by the body louse. It is subsequently shown that Rocky Mountain spotted fever is also transmitted by lice, and that both are caused by organisms distinct from bacteria and viruses. They are later named rickettsiae after the US pathologist, Howard Ricketts, who will die of typhus in Mexico City in 1910.

The United States Congress bans the import of opium for anything but medical use.

FRINGE BENEFITS

Castrol introduce their first motor oil, specially designed for car engines.

The Silver Ghost, the first car produced by Rolls-Royce, survives a 14,671-ml (23,473.6-km) Royal Automobile Club test unscathed, to become a legend in reliability. The thirteenth chassis was given silver-plated fittings and the nameplate, *The Silver Ghost*—an appellation that will be used for all their 40/50 models until 1925.

'Women's Suffrage' is the subject of the first broadcast 'talk'. It is no coincidence that the speaker is Harriet Stanton Black, mother-in-law of Lee de Forest, one of America's leading radio experts.

The 35 mm film format, introduced in 1893 by Thomas Edison, is agreed as standard for the movie industry by an international conference of film producers. This concordance finally disposes of the problems of incompatibility between films and equipment made to different standards, and paves the way for development of still cameras using perforated ciné film.

Architectural wonder of the contemporary world, the Eiffel Tower in Paris, France, is saved from demolition: a radio antenna atop its 1,000-ft (305-m) superstructure ensures its future.

Radio saves 1,700 lives when the US liner *Republic* collides with an Italian vessel, the *Florida*. The radio distress signal brings help in time to rescue all but five passengers.

The first military aircraft is a Wright Model 'A', adopted by the US Army. The biplane remains airborne for 1 hr 12 min and averages 42.5 mph (68.4 km/h) in a speed test, earning its designer a $5,000 bonus. Wilbur Wright then trains two flyers; but almost at once they crash the Model 'A', destroying the embryo air force.

Despite the advent of the monoplane, biplanes continue to dominate aviation. This year's Goupy II, with a new open fuselage and staggered wings, vies for attention with the more powerful Breguet I, which boasts a three-blade propeller plus rear rudders and wing-warping for flight control.

The cargo ship *Vespasian* is the first turbine-powered vessel to have a gearbox between its engines and the driving propellers, giving the master the flexibility and delicacy of control that car-drivers have.

The American six-masted schooner *Wyoming* is built. At 329.5 ft (100 m), it is the longest wooden sailing vessel in the 5,000-year evolution of the sailing ship.

The first successful hydrofoil is designed by Enrico Forlanini. The foils act like aeroplane wings to generate lift as the speed of the vessel increases, and so raise the hull out of the water.

Working for Standard Oil Co, W. Burton begins his pioneering work on turning the oil not used for producing gasoline into marketable by-products. A process not to be used at an oil refinery until 1913, the fruits of his work will spread to many other refineries by 1916.

A fire extinguisher is patented which smothers flames with the heavy, non-flammable gas carbon tetrachloride, expelled from the container by pressurized carbon dioxide. Devised by Edward Davidson in New York, this extinguisher provides an alternative to the foam mechanism invented in 1905 by the Russian Alexander Laurent.

An accidental discovery leads to the production of lightweight, high-strength aluminium alloys. Working at the Durenner Metalwerke in Germany, Alfred Wilm prepares an alloy, containing small amounts of copper and magnesium, which is found to be strong but light. Duralumin will be used first to make girders and rivets for Zeppelin airships, and will later radically influence the evolution of the aircraft industry.

William MacCallum at Johns Hopkins University shows that it is fatal to remove the parathyroids—four tiny glands clinging to the thyroid—because they control calcium metabolism. From now on, partial removal only of an over-active thyroid will be the treatment for hyperthyroidism, whose symptoms include bulging eyes, weight loss, and increased activity.

Samuel Meltzer and John Auer devise a tube to assist breathing during operations on the mouth, throat or chest. The Meltzer-Auer tube, developed at the Rockefeller Institute, is inserted into the windpipe to allow a constant flow of air to reach the lungs.

US neurosurgeon Harvey Cushing realizes that acromegaly—the enlargement of the jaws, extremities and some organs—is due to overgrowth of the pea-sized pituitary gland at the base of the brain. He removes a part of the gland in an acromegalic patient, whose symptoms then abate and who will survive in good health for 21 years.

Gasoline cigarette lighters appear on the market.

The expanded-rubber industry begins as the three Pfleumer brothers perfect a technique for making the first puncture-proof bicycle tyres.

38 aircraft are entered for the first aviation meeting, a sparkling event held at Reims in France. Organized by the local champagne industry, which also donates considerable prize money, it attracts the world's top pilots. 120 take-offs are watched by thousands of spectators who include many heads of state and military chiefs—Britain's David Lloyd George comments that 'flying machines are no longer toys and dreams'. Henri Farman, *right*, wins the Grand Prix for the longest non-stop distance—112.5ml (180 m) covered in just over three hours—after fitting a Gnome rotary engine, *left*, to his standard biplane. The Seguin brothers, by designing an engine that spins with the propeller, have obviated the need for a bulky cooling system.

The wide world of radio

In 1900, the existence of electromagnetic radio waves had been common knowledge for at least forty years. But the only way of exploiting them for communication was through the 'wireless telegraph' transmitter, which filled the air with millions of Morse code 'dots and dashes'. The transmission of human speech remained elusive until 1904, when John Ambrose Fleming elegantly adapted Edison's light bulb to produce his thermionic valve, which could both detect and amplify radio waves.

Thanks largely to the ingenuity of Guglielmo Marconi in promoting the potential of radio, regular broadcasts were firmly established in the twenties. In 1921, for instance, an avid American public listened to the Presidential election results, either on cheap crystal sets—known as 'cats' whiskers'—fitted with headphones, or on more expensive valve sets with loudspeakers. Transmitting aerials mushroomed on both sides of the Atlantic—by 1925 there were 600 broadcasting stations— and serious experimentation with the airways began. In Britain, the use of long waves (1000–2000 metres) brought eighty per cent of the population within range of a transmitter; and, while Europe followed suit, the Americans were trying out the long-distance capacity of the short wavelengths (10–100 metres). Once again it was Marconi who capitalized on the opportunity offered by the higher frequency, shorter wavelengths: in 1926, he broadcast across the globe to Australia.

All this activity caused serious congestion of the airwaves, which had to be divided into internationally agreed portions. The first result was fewer, more powerful, twinwave transmitters; the second was the demise of the crystal set, which relied on single-wavelength signals from nearby transmitters, and the rise of the thirties 'cabinet' radio set, which was more selective in response to wavelength— and, above all, able to be tuned.

By the mid-fifties, radio was faltering as the focus of home entertainment under the growing popularity of television. Fortunately, the dawn of miniaturized electronic gadgetry was breaking: the transistor had been invented to replace the unwieldy valves. The first pocket-sized, portable transistor radios were an immediate success—not least because they were cheap—and, this time, the Japanese were quickest to capitalize. The 4,000 'trannies' they exported to the USA in 1959, along with innovatory car radios, were merely the trickle before the flood.

At the same time, over thirty years after Marconi's pioneering work with higher frequencies, transistor radios were modified to pick up very high frequencies or VHF (1–10 metres), as well as the usual medium and long wave transmissions. A new clarity of sound, free of radio interference, transformed radio programmes; and the wide spacing between channels on VHF also suggested that two separate sound signals could be accommodated. In 1961, stereophonic musical broadcasts began, giving rise to the modern trend towards sophisticated hi-fi radios and, incidentally, to the return of headphones.

While radio has proved its worth over long distances—astronauts can talk comfortably to their mission controls, for example—the future of radio may lie just as much in local communication, where it began. Community needs have never been served so well as by local commercial radio, and individual communication has taken on a new look—and a new language—with the spread of CB (Citizens' Band) radio.

In the early days of the 'wireless', the excitement caused by the tapping out of Morse code messages on a telegraph machine, *left*, would not be equalled until the spoken word was successfully captured on the airwaves by Fleming's 1904 invention of the thermionic valve.

Travelling was no obstacle to keeping in touch, as radios were installed in trains and aircraft. News bulletins, concerts, weather forecasts or even the running commentary on the 1923 Grand National, *right*, were received loud and clear through horn loudspeakers installed in first class railway carriages.

Early valve radios were often used with headphones instead of loudspeakers. Although more expensive and complicated to operate, valve sets proved more selective than crystal receivers.

The highest radio technology that 1951 had to offer was incorporated into Britain's Daventry broadcasting station, the home of the first long wave broadcast some 25 years earlier. Inaugurating the largely musical 'Third Programme', the BBC installed hi-fi disc recorders to begin with, but soon changed to magnetic tape.

From fantasy to fact . . . The idea that radio sets could ever become portable was subject to ridicule in the early 1900s, as this contemporary cartoon shows. But with the advent of the transistor in the fifties, aerials were brought down from the rooftops, loudspeakers were built into the radio sets and power was supplied by batteries. The first portable transistor radio was the US Regency, introduced in 1954; but Sony of Japan were soon to become the experts at translating the new technology into commercial success, and they lead the market to this day. Their latest model, *below*, can receive medium and FM (frequency modulation) bands, as well as seven short wavebands which allow clear reception from as far afield as Moscow and Peking.

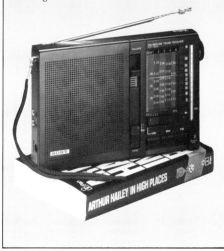

The thirties were, in a sense, the great age of radio—'furniture' sets, encased in mahogany or walnut, were as much a home's focal point as the TV is today. They superseded the old crystal sets, and were not only reliable and tunable, but also able to receive short, medium and long wavelengths from considerable distances.

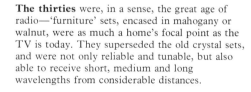

When the BBC became a public corporation in 1927, restrictions placed on it by the newspapers were lifted, to allow outside broadcasts of sporting events. England's Derby at Epsom, *left*, was one of the first (it was also the first TV outside broadcast), offering the chance to test the new, smaller yet more sensitive carbon microphones.

COMMUNICATION AND INFORMATION

Investing a fortune of $500,000, the USA aims to speed the production of a 'noiseless' typewriter. First attempts to make such a machine are a disaster. Some manufacturers even try—unsuccessfully—to encase their typewriters in padded wooden boxes.

The first criminal capture by radio takes place in Canada, after the captain of a transatlantic liner sailing from England is alerted to the presence on board of the notorious wife-killer, Dr Hawley Harvey Crippen, and his mistress Ethel LeNeve.

TRANSPORT AND WARFARE

Over the next four years the German DELAG company will establish an enviable aviation standard: its Zeppelins, on routes between five German cities, will safely carry 33,722 passengers and crew on 1,588 flights.

Henri Fabre's *Hydravion* is the first powered seaplane to fly. The success of his tailfirst craft is largely due to its Gnome rotary engine, making the plane exceptionally light yet powerful.

Henry Ford steps up mass production of the Model T. He cuts costs by making more components in his own factory, by buying shrewdly from outside suppliers, and by constantly improving the efficiency of the assembly line. The annual production of Model Ts will rocket from 18,000 in 1909, to half a million in 1916, to an astonishing two million in 1923—the peak of production. In all 15 million will be made.

ENERGY AND INDUSTRY

Air pollution from factory chimneys is reduced by the electrostatic precipitator, invented by F. Cottrell. The precipitator removes solid or liquid particles from gases by attracting them to an electrically charged capacitor, and in doing so can clean ventilating air or reduce the emission of smoke from factory flues.

The first colliery to have all its machines driven by electricity is opened at Monmouth, Wales. The advance epitomizes the trend away from manual, and towards mechanical, methods in coal-mining.

Swedish engineers build the world's first underground hydroelectric power station at Mockfärd. Power is generated by turbines driven by water which is forced by gravity along sharply inclined tunnels.

MEDICINE AND FOOD PRODUCTION

Paul Ehrlich, the German bacteriologist leads the search for what he calls 'magic bullets'—drugs which can 'home in' on, and kill, syphilis. Doggedly working through more than 600 arsenical compounds, he produces Salvarsan, which is effective in treating the disease. Salvarsan is hailed by some as a miracle drug, by others as an encouragement to sin.

An hereditary blood disorder, in which the red blood cells are sickle-shaped, is recognized for the first time in a young West Indian by Chicago physician James Herrick. Common in negroes, this serious disease kills most of its victims before the age of 21; few live beyond 40. It will not be named sickle-cell anaemia until 1922.

Holt, a US company, develop the first self-propelled, gasoline-powered combine harvester. It replaces previous combines towed by horse or tractor, and rapidly improves crop production.

FRINGE BENEFITS

The Manhattan Bridge is the third of New York City's bridges over the East River and carries traffic between Brooklyn and downtown Manhattan. Completed in 1909, its pioneering design by O.F. Nichols is the first to make allowance for the horizontal displacement of the cables of a suspension bridge under load. Its central span of 1,470 ft (447 m) and side spans totalling another 722 ft (220 m) are carried by four parallel cables held aloft by flexible steel towers, a system that will be adopted by all the world's great suspension bridges.

The fabulous voice of Italian tenor Enrico Caruso escapes from the confines of New York's Metropolitan Opera House with the first ever outside radio broadcast. But his audience is restricted to those with radio receivers. Among the lucky ones are people in ships in New York Harbour, in large hotels in Times Square and workers at the de Forest Radio Laboratory.

The sale of radio apparatus to the public begins at the demonstration room in the Metropolitan Life Building, New York. Lee de Forest's Radio Telephone Co have produced, and are now selling, radio receiver kits to amateur radio enthusiasts.

The birth of aircraft-carriers is presaged when Eugene Ely becomes the first person to take off from a ship: he flies a Curtiss biplane from a temporary flight deck on the US light cruiser *Birmingham* moored in Hampton Roads, Va.

A fruitful year for aeronautical 'firsts', 1910 sees J.B. Moisant fly across the English Channel—with a passenger; air-to-ground communications open up when John McCurdy, a pilot working for seaplane pioneer Glen Curtiss in America, transmits radio messages from his plane; and a practical airspeed indicator is invented to become an indispensable aid in the cockpit.

The conquest of the oceans by motor-ships begins with the launch of the small Dutch tanker *Vulcanus*. Opting for six-cylinder diesel engines, instead of steam or turbine power, the *Vulcanus* is the first ocean-going motor-ship.

An anti-rolling device invented by Dr H. Frahm is pioneered on the steamer *Ypiranga*: the weight of water in a horseshoe arrangement of tanks is used to steady the ship as it rolls.

Without the reassuring red glow offered by ordinary electric fires, the new convector heaters—which contain concealed elements to warm the air passing over them—seem doomed to failure. However, because they are safe and easy to install, in 1914 the British War Office will order thousands of them to heat the wooden barracks where troops will be billeted.

The first artificial silk stockings, made from the synthetic fibre viscose rayon, are produced at the Bamberg rayon factory, Germany.

The red light of a neon tube is demonstrated at the Grand Palais, Paris, by Georges Claude. Within a few years a big industry will develop around neon tubing, which is ideally suited to advertising displays because of the intensity of the light. New and improved neon tubes will make a major contribution to street lighting, as well as becoming a familiar feature of city life from Piccadilly Circus to Times Square.

Commercial mass production of synthetic nitrogen fertilizers will soon follow German chemist Fritz Haber's novel way of making ammonia: he extracts nitrogen from the Earth's atmosphere and 'fixes' it with hydrogen. Fertilizers made from this cheap and inexhaustible raw material will dramatically improve crop yields the world over.

Aided by Mendel's laws of genetic heredity, British scientist Rowland Biffen breeds Little Jos, a wheat suitable for the British climate and resistant to the yellow rust fungus disease, which regularly reduces wheat yields.

Major Frank Woodbury of the US Army Medical Corps finds tincture of iodine to be an ideal surgical disinfectant and antiseptic. It is cheap, readily obtainable and safe.

Botulism takes its name from the Latin word for a sausage because German physicians, who first studied the condition, found it sometimes in connection with contaminated sausages. In fact, this deadly toxin can occur in contaminated meat, fish or canned foods. Now it is L. Leuchs who prepares the first antitoxic sera for botulism.

The appliance of electricity in the home reaches the kitchen, typified by the 'Carron' range—complete with its daunting wall-mounted switching panel and fuse-board. The oven, equipped with glass viewing door, is heated above and below by two circular elements of coiled wire mounted on firebrick. Like those in the smaller warming oven, and on three of the hotplates on the hob, the heat from each element in the oven is controlled by a switch with only three settings: low, medium and high. Accurate temperature control will not be available on electric ovens until thermostats are introduced in the thirties.

COMMUNICATION AND INFORMATION

The first wireless company, attached to the Cavalry Brigade, is formed to cater for the British Army's communication needs. Its equipment, consisting of engine, generator and 50-ft (15-m) telescopic steel mast, however, weighs two tons, needs two horses to draw it and takes 20 mins to erect. Nevertheless it has a range of 50 mls (80 km) and represents the Army's growing acceptance of the value of radio.

The portable pack radio set, originally designed for the British Army by the Marconi Co, sees action in the hands of the Italian Army fighting in Libya.

TRANSPORT AND WARFARE

The Colt .45 automatic pistol goes into service with the US Army, after winning a government competition to find a heavy calibre weapon simple enough to be taken apart without tools, yet reliable under adverse conditions.

The first aerial bombing is carried out by an Italian in a German aircraft. Lt. Gavotti's attack on the Turkish camp at Ain Zara from his Etrich plane is too inaccurate to cause much damage, but it inspires debate on the ethics of air bombing.

Racing driver Louis Chevrolet founds the Chevrolet Motor Co with Billy Durant—and builds a bargain-priced car to challenge Ford's ascendancy over the market.But, infuriated by his high-handed partner, Chevrolet will quit within a few years leaving Durant to outsell Ford by 1931 and make a fortune under the banner of his name.

The Great Powers begin to take a military interest in aircraft: an exhibition of planes with potential for war is held at Reims; meanwhile, the Italians fighting in Libya are using a Blériot monoplane for reconnaissance.

Flamethrowers are issued to three German battalions. Each man carries a steel cylinder of fuel; a rubber pipe gives him flexibility of aim. At the hand-held nozzle, the pressurized liquid is ignited to unleash a 20-yd (18.3-m) jet of flame.

ENERGY AND INDUSTRY

The anti-corrosive quality of stainless steels is discovered for the first time by a German scientist, P. Monnartz. Though stainless steels were made by Guillet in 1904, Monnartz is the first to explain their resistance to corrosion and the first to patent one of many types of stainless steels.

Steel production throughout the world, in millions of tons, is: USA 23.6, Germany 14.7, Britain 6.4, France 3.8, Russia 3.8, Austria/Hungary 2.3, Belgium 1.9.

MEDICINE AND FOOD PRODUCTION

US military authorities introduce compulsory vaccination against typhoid fever for soldiers. In 1916, a mixed vaccine against typhoid, paratyphoid A and paratyphoid B is made available to Allied troops.

Amateur microscopist Joseph Barnard publishes *Practical Photomicrography*, the book which will become a standard work of reference in medical laboratories. A London businessman, in 1925 he will develop an apparatus using ultraviolet light to obtain clear photomicrographs of some germs, including some of the larger viruses, too small to be seen by light microscopy.

Short of opening up the patient, a gastroenterologist has no way of investigating abdominal troubles. Now, however, William Hill, a London doctor, reduces the need for exploratory surgery with his gastroscope. A tube leading to the stomach gives a clear view of the stomach lining, and a little periscope increases the field of vision to include the entry to the small intestine.

FRINGE BENEFITS

Actors are filmed miming to recordings as a number of systems for synchronized sound are developed using electrical or mechanical coupling of projector and gramophone. Hepworth's 'Vivaphone' and Walturdaw's 'Singing Pictures' both use existing commercial records.

Photogravure, the method of reproducing pictures by relief printing in reverse, goes rotary. The system of producing gravure cylinders is now commercially viable and is tipped to replace the halftone block for the reproduction of pictures in newspapers. But although photogravure is ideal for magazine printing, which does not have to be totally topical, it is not so good for dailies because the production of the cylinder is very slow.

Kamerlingh Onnes, a Dutch physicist, discovers superconductivity. By passing an electric current through mercury, cooled to a temperature approaching absolute zero ($-273\,^\circ$C), he finds that the current meets no resistance—it does not heat up the mercury and so loses no power.

The building of the *Selandia* in Copenhagen starts the era of the marine heavy oil engine. The vessel's main propulsion—two eight-cylinder engines—is augmented by two oil engines: one supplies electricity for lighting and steering gear, the other supplies compressed air for reversing the main engines. Exhaust gases are carried off through the ship's tubular mizen-mast; but later motor ships will be fitted with funnels for appearance's sake.

Gas engines are tested on *Holzapfel I*, an experimental sea-going cargo vessel launched at South Shields, England. The 120-ft (36.5-m) vessel is equipped with a gas plant to provide fuel for its six-cylinder, vertical gas engines.

Air meetings proliferate, catching the public imagination. Country-to-country events prove especially popular: 700,000 flock to Vincennes, France, to watch the start of the Circuit of Europe race on 13 June.

Smarting from injuries sustained while crank-starting his car, Henry Leland, founder of the Cadillac Co, adopts Charles Kettering's electrical system for car ignition, starting and lighting. By 1912, electric starter systems will be a standard feature of Cadillacs, encouraging an increase in the number of drivers among crank-shy women.

Charles Parsons' improved turbo-alternator for generating electricity in power stations can resist the huge bursting forces caused by rapid rotation of its magnet. Cast in solid steel and balanced by winding its conducting cables around deep slots, the magnet can rotate at 4,000 rpm without dangerous vibration.

Moving staircases, invented nearly 20 years before, are introduced to a wary British public at Earl's Court underground station in London. A man with a wooden leg is employed to ride up and down the twin 40-ft (12-m) escalators to demonstrate their safety.

Males who have inherited haemophilia from their mothers are prone to continuous bleeding because their blood lacks a vital clotting substance. T. Addis now offers haemophiliacs their first ray of hope: by giving transfusions of normal plasma, he can dramatically shorten clotting time and halt bleeding when it occurs.

The British medical journal, *The Lancet*, pleads for a return to real bread. Bakers should provide nutritious loaves containing wheatgerm rather than 'dazzling white tasteless rolls and slices'.

By examining the reactions of white blood cells to infections and the abnormal conditions of blood-forming organs, Paul Ehrlich helps pathologists create a complete 'blood picture' of many human diseases.

New York orthopaedic surgeon Russell Hibbs devises a spinal fusion operation which revolutionizes the treatment of scoliosis, or curvature of the spine, and spinal TB.

A white road marking, called the 'center line safety strip', first appears on US roads.

An electric fire, *left*, based on H.J. Dowsing's patent for using incandescent lamps as sources of heat, is put on the market by Britain's GEC. The use of curved copper reflectors behind the tubes increases their efficiency, but it is still low compared to later coiled-element fires.

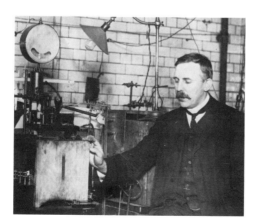

Ernest Rutherford, a British physicist born in New Zealand, puts forward his theory of the structure of atoms to account for recent discoveries about energy and radioactivity. He replaces the concept of the atom as a featureless indivisible sphere, originally conceived by Democritus 23 centuries before, with a model consisting of a tiny nucleus—composed of a number of heavy, positively charged protons—surrounded by a cloud of light, negatively charged electrons. By the end of the decade, Rutherford will have realized one of the alchemists' dreams by becoming the first man to transmute one element into another.

COMMUNICATION AND INFORMATION

London's first automatic telephone exchange is installed. Equipped with 480 lines and using a variety of electro-mechanical devices, the system proves successful in eliminating the frustrations and delays previously a hazard of making telephone calls.

Gaumont presents his improved sound film system. The 'Chronophone' uses discs whose mechanically amplified sound can fill a large auditorium, and Chronophone shows prove highly popular. In the same year Gaumont demonstrates his Chronochrome colour system, a full three-colour process and the first to be commercially exploited. Soon Gaumont will present both together in his public showings of the first colour talkies.

The heterodyne radio system, invented by Canadian professor R.A. Fessenden, will play a large part in the evolution of modern radio. The receiver picks up the transmitted signal, and also generates its own local signal to beat in synchrony with it. Reception of the resulting intermediate, or modulated, signal is improved still further by the use of amplifying circuits insensitive to other frequencies. Within six years the superheterodyne system becomes—and remains—the standard for all radio.

TRANSPORT AND WARFARE

Strong, lightweight and streamlined aircraft are the result of the revolutionary monocoque structure: a cylindrical fuselage made of plywood is given a 'skin' of cloth wound spirally over the tapering frame. The skin carries the primary stresses, freeing the plane from bulky internal bracing.

Louis Paulham constructs a metal aircraft, the Tubavion, for French military trials.

The Bowden brake cable, passing through a flexible tube, enables drivers to steer their cars while braking. The cable will be in almost universal use until the fifties, when hydraulically operated brakes will relegate it to the handbrake alone.

ENERGY AND INDUSTRY

Cellophane, perfected as a thin flexible wrapping material in 1910 by Swiss inventor Edwin Brandenberger, is manufactured for the first time by a French rayon company, La Cellophane.

'This fire is warmed by electricity so do not use a poker' is the warning that comes with the new electric fire introduced by Belling from Middlesex, England. The first electric fire to use the nickel-chrome wire developed by Marsh in 1906, it has a series of coiled elements set in front of fire-clay and supplies far more heat than any previous electric fire.

Schlumberger develops the technique of measuring the properties of subsurface rocks from electric impulses discharged from the surface to holes bored deep into the earth. This important advance in geophysical exploration will be used to locate the rocks most likely to have trapped oil—in 1927 in Alsace, 1929-30 in Venezuela, Baku and the Dutch East Indies, and 1932 in the USA.

MEDICINE AND FOOD PRODUCTION

Polish-born biochemist Casimir Funk uses the name 'vitamine' for several substances he has earlier discovered to be essential trace factors in food. The final 'e'—later dropped to avoid confusion—is added because Funk mistakenly believes that these substances are amines. But he leads the field in showing that vitamins are essential to life, at a time when deficiency diseases such as beri-beri, rickets and pellagra are legion.

The human body can produce many of the amino acids essential to life, but there are eight of these nitrogen-containing compounds which must be acquired from the diet. Scientists at Harvard University and the Rockefeller Institute demonstrate that a meat meal provides humans with these crucial amino acids. Absorbed by the intestine, they appear in the blood before being used by the body to synthesize proteins.

Sir William Macewen of Glasgow delivers his famous monograph, *The Growth of Bone*. He elaborates on the notion of bone grafts to reinforce or to replace diseased or damaged bone.

FRINGE BENEFITS

The first neon advertising sign lights up in Paris—for the famous aperitif Cinzano.

A 5-litre Bugatti racing car competes in the Le Mans road race meeting. The car's Italian designer, Ettore Bugatti built his first car in 1900 at the age of 19. Now in the throes of establishing a company to market his sporty Type 13—the first car bearing his name to go into mass production—Bugatti has maintained his interest in racing by building his small series of heavier chain-driven competition cars. A natural showman and noted eccentric—throughout his life he will always insist on being photographed in riding clothes and a bowler hat—Bugatti is also an inventive engineer who, during World War 1, develops aero-engines and patents many new manufacturing processes.

A process of colour photography using three light-sensitive layers on a single plate is patented as a principle by R. Fischer in the USA. Fischer's idea will not prove practicable until the thirties, but will then become universally adopted and remain in use.

An SOS in Morse code (. . . – – – . . .) is adopted as the universal distress signal. Used for the first time in 1909, when two steamers received it from the shipwrecked liner *Slavonia*, the signal is to prove valuable in saving lives in World War I.

Accidents in Britain and France cause a hiccup in the evolution of the monoplane whose limitations, outlined by Blériot, deter designers until a better grasp of materials and structure is obtained.

'The Illustrated London News' installs rotary photogravure, the first such production in Britain. The same year sees the 40,000th issue of *The Times*. To mark the occasion, the paper publishes a supplement on the history of printing and newspaper presses.

The first US flying-boat takes off, thanks to Glen Curtiss and his invention of a hull that is 'stepped' to break the suction of water—a design feature that is still used.

Seven companies produce 50% of all US cars and more than 22% are Fords.

The first monoplane with an enclosed cabin is built by A.V. Roe in England.

The regenerative or 'feedback' radio receiver arrives—within the decade it will replace the ubiquitous crystal set. Its heart is a sensitive feedback circuit which amplifies weak signals and tones down strong ones, to achieve balanced reception; it is vastly more effective over long distances than the crystal set. After years of legal dispute, the invention of the regenerative radio is eventually credited to US scientists de Forest, Armstrong and Langmuir, in preference to German scientist Meissner.

The BSI is the first single-seat scout plane. The combination of monocoque fuselage and 100 hp Gnome engine enables it to reach a top speed of 92 mph (148 km/h) in tests at Farnborough, England.

In an effort to end the 'free for all' chaos on the air waves, the US Congress legislates that all radio transmitters and receivers must be licensed. In Britain, meanwhile, the Post Office nationalizes the private telephone companies.

To ensure that holes are drilled in exactly the right places, a machine that accurately positions the precise centres of the holes is introduced to the machine tool shop. Made by the Société Génèvoise d'Instrument de Physique (SIP), it is the forerunner of their later machine, the jig borer, and it will increase the accuracy of mass-production techniques.

The forerunner of the electric blanket is invented by American doctor Sidney Russell, who discovers the warming effect of passing an electric current through insulated metal tape covered on both sides by blanket. Designed as a small heating pad for patients suffering from chest complaints, his idea will not be commercially introduced as an electric underblanket until 1930.

Key West is linked by road to mainland Florida for the first time with the opening of the 37-ml (59.5-km) highway. Designed by Henry Flager, this remarkable feat of engineering contains 20 mls (32 km) of embankments, 38 bridges of both steel and concrete, 29 concrete viaducts and 3 drawbridges. The Long Key Viaduct, at 2.15 mls (3.5 km), will be for many years the longest open-water crossing in the world.

US physician Bertram W. Sippy, recognizing that ulcers in the gullet, stomach or duodenum cannot occur if there is no acid present, introduces both his special diet and the aphorism 'No acid, no ulcer'.

The first specific treatment for pneumonia is serum therapy, developed in the USA by Rufus Cole and Alphonse Duchez. Infecting a horse with mild pneumonia, they separate from its blood the serum carrying the antibodies.

Chicago physician James Herrick documents the first heart attack to be diagnosed in a living patient. He points out that what appears to be an acute attack of indigestion or food poisoning may in fact be a coronary—something which, up to now, doctors have encountered only by way of evidence in the post-mortem room. Herrick's patient, a middle-aged banker, survives only 52 hours; but the episode shows that a heart attack need not be fatal.

Hugh Young, a surgeon at Johns Hopkins, engineers relief for men with urinary retention due to an enlarged prostate gland. He devises the famous 'punch operation' to remove prostate tissue blocking the urinary tract: two metal tubes, one inside the other, are inserted into the urethra, and the inner cutting tube is used to 'punch' out the tissue, which can then be withdrawn.

The era of the hand-driven movie-camera winds to an end as motorized models are developed in reponse to the rapid growth and output of the motion picture industry. In the USA some directors are turning out two films each week.

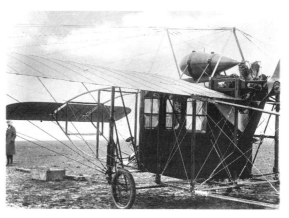

Louis Blériot, best known for his pioneering flight across the English Channel in 1909, also designed and built aeroplanes: this Blériot-Limousine—a large monoplane with an egg-shaped petrol tank perched dangerously above the passenger cabin—was made for M. Deutsch de la Meurthe.

COMMUNICATION AND INFORMATION

Already a confirmed success at sea, with over 3,000 ship stations, radio is gradually making an impact on land. A total of 1,650 land and coastal transmitting stations are now operating all over the world.

Some of the latest cameras, including the American Tourist Multiple and the French Homéos stereoscopic model, use the 35 mm perforated film common in movie cameras. Oscar Barnack, working for Leitz in Germany, designs (for his own use) a small, compact camera for 35 mm film which will become the prototype for the Leica camera to be introduced in 1925.

The first regular time signals are broadcast from the Eiffel Tower and can be picked up in any Paris home with just a telephone and cheap antenna attachment.

TRANSPORT AND WARFARE

Ford opens his mass production Highland Park car manufacturing plant. Conveyor belts carry parts along the assembly line at the correct speed for the workers, cutting the time taken to assemble a car from $12\frac{1}{2}$ to $1\frac{1}{2}$ hrs. Minimum daily wages are raised from $2 to $5, an incentive that boosts profits to $60 million in 1916.

The first 'loop' (flying a plane in a vertical circle) is achieved by Lt Peter Nesterov of the Imperial Russian Air Service. Immediately arrested for endangering government property, Nesterov is later awarded a medal by the Russian Royal Aero Club for accomplishing this daring manoeuvre.

Electric transmission is installed in the collier *Jupiter* and tested for the US Navy. The system uses turbo-generators to supply current to electric motors driving the propellers.

ENERGY AND INDUSTRY

F. Bergius converts coal into oil by using a catalyst to combine hydrogen with the carbon in coal. The resulting hydrocarbons can be used as a fuel. BASF of Germany will develop the process, which will be of great importance during World War II.

A steam turbine and a generator are installed at Lardarello, in Tuscany, Italy, where they will be driven by underground volcanic steam to produce electricity. Lardarello will become the only large and successful geothermal power station for many years.

Victor Kaplan, a German engineer, patents his turbine and thus enables hydroelectric power stations to be more consistently efficient. The turbine has adjustable blades which can be set to suit the load of water on the turbine, so maintaining a level output of power.

World petroleum production reaches 407.5 million barrels, compared to 5.7 million in 1870.

The first domestic electric refrigerator, called the Domelre, goes on sale in Chicago. An electric motor, instead of a small steam engine, drives the compressor that produces the compressed air to reduce the temperature of the insulated cabinet.

MEDICINE AND FOOD PRODUCTION

John J. Abel and colleagues at Johns Hopkins are the first to isolate amino acids—the building-blocks of protein—from blood.

German surgeon A. Salomen develops the technique of mammography: diagnosing breast tumours by X-ray.

US physician Victor Heiser virtually clears the Philippines of leprosy by organizing the segregation of lepers in the Cullion Island Colony. He claims that 11.1% of patients here are 'apparently cured' by treatment with injections of chalmoogra, camphor oils and resorcin.

FRINGE BENEFITS

The first automatic totalizer is installed at a New Zealand race track.

In Russia, Igor Sikorsky develops the first large multi-engined aircraft. The 'Bolshoi' ('Big One') has four engines mounted in a row along the bottom wing. This will be developed into the Ilya Mouromeťz, forerunner of World War II heavy bombers, which will carry 920-lb (414-kg) bombs in 1914 Russian Army trials.

Telegraph communications become more reliable. Previously, quality has been poor owing to the break in transmission at the point where cables meet land lines; but British scientist John Gott devises a method of using current reversals for transmission which solves the problem.

The Decca Portable, a gramophone manufactured by Barnett Samuel & Co, London, comes on the market. Now discs can be played in the garden or countryside. Soon the gramophone will be used by troops in World War I.

Typefaces change their looks as type composition enters the mechanical age. The British Monotype Corporation brings out two new typefaces, named Plantin and Imprint, designed specifically for composing machines. The first factory-made Intertype composing machine, developed by W.S. Scudder, produces type slugs—lines of type all in one piece. Scudder also breaks with the practice of producing individual machines, making instead a basic model which can be adapted to specific use.

French industrialist Jacques Schneider offers a trophy for the first of several seaplane races held at Monaco. Intense international interest in the race aids the rapid development of seaplanes, which become the fastest aircraft in the world.

The first—and, for 60 years, the only—South American underground railway system opens in the bustling city of Buenos Aires.

Designed to a British military brief by Geoffrey de Havilland, the BE2 aircraft is inherently so stable that pilots can fly 'hands-off' during reconnaissance missions.

The synthesis of ammonia by the Haber process frees German munitions manufacturers from dependence on Chilean nitrates as their only source of nitric acid—the key ingredient of most explosives.

A stainless steel is accidentally invented by Harry Brearley in Sheffield, England. He discovers that a new steel alloy he has developed for rifle barrels does not corrode. Then, persuading a local cutler to make knives from the alloy—which contains 12.7% chromium and 0.25% carbon—he finds that neither water nor the mild acids in foods will stain the alloy. Though not the first to invent a stainless steel, Brearley will be given most of the credit for its general acceptance.

All the light bulbs and incandescent lamps made so far have contained a filament in a vacuum, and, after a time, have collected a metallic deposit on the inside of the glass case which dims the light. Irving Langmuir of GEC in the USA now fills a bulb with nitrogen—and later with the gas argon—which reduces the rate of evaporation of the tungsten filament. This keeps the glass case clearer and also allows the filament to be heated to a higher temperature, so radiating more light.

Sheet glass of high quality is produced as the Fourcault machine starts commercial operations. Using a continuous process, which makes many skilled manual workers redundant, Fourcault machines will be responsible for 72% of the world's sheet glass by 1950.

At New York's Mount Sinai Hospital, Hungarian-born physician Bela Schick perfects the Schick test for determining susceptibility to diphtheria. An inflammatory response occurs if the patient is not immune.

John J. Abel and colleagues develop a prototype artificial kidney—an apparatus for cleansing the blood by passing it through a network of collodion tubing. But human kidney patients must wait for the introduction of vividiffusion, later known as haemodialysis, before they can reap the benefits.

The slide-fastener—later nicknamed the zip—is perfected.

Brillo pads give a shine to kitchen pots and pans.

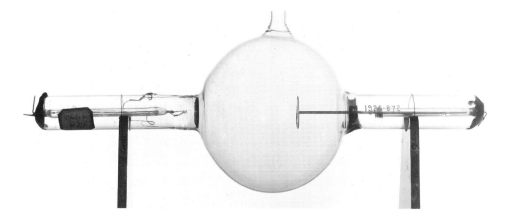

William David Coolidge, an American physicist, constructs a tube for the generation of X-rays that replaces earlier short-life gas discharge versions. A stream of electrons is accelerated towards a water-cooled tungsten anode where 1% of the beam's energy is converted into X-rays and the rest becomes heat. The Coolidge tube is the prototype for all later such sources and will be responsible for liberating the X-ray from the laboratory and facilitating its use in industry and medicine.

41

COMMUNICATION AND INFORMATION

Using a vacuum tube, US physicist R.A. Heising shows that the modulation of high-frequency radio waves is important in the transmission of speech and music. Heising shows that a modulated wave consists of a carrier wave, plus two sidebands which can be separated off by filters. With this discovery, the possibility of squeezing more information into the airwaves becomes feasible.

In the USA, Langmuir perfects de Forest's triode valve by inventing a pump to create a vacuum up to 1,000 times more efficient than any used before. The triode is now set to take radio into a new era.

In the USA, Eastman Kodak introduce a range of Autographic cameras which, using special roll film, enable the user to 'write' information on the film at the time of exposure, which is revealed when the film is developed. This feature remains standard on most Kodak cameras until the thirties, when further improvements in the sensitivity of photographic films will make it impractical.

TRANSPORT AND WARFARE

The Atlantic and Pacific oceans are connected by the opening of the Panama Canal. The 42½-ml (68-km) channel, cut through the Isthmus of Panama, shortens previous sea routes round the tip of South America by many thousands of miles.

The first electric traffic lights to control the flow of different streams of traffic are set up at a crossroads in Cleveland, USA. The red and green lights are reinforced by a warning buzzer.

Following the 'Titanic' disaster in 1912, the British and American governments send ships to patrol the ice regions in the North Atlantic. Two years later the International Ice Patrol will be formed to observe and report the position and course of drifting ice.

'Big Bertha', a massive howitzer, is used in the German advance on Belgium. Designed to destroy concrete fortifications, the 75-ton monster levels the forts of Liège and Mauberge with 2,052-lb (931.6-kg) projectiles.

ENERGY AND INDUSTRY

The world's first major sewage works to use bacteria in the decomposition of waste open at Manchester, England. This biological treatment of sewage, which replaces chemical methods, will be used all over the world, and is so safe that, by 1980, over a million tons of treated sewage will be fed into the River Thames each day.

Ammonia starts to be produced on a large scale, by the Haber process, at Oppau, Germany. Fritz Haber has earlier developed a method of heating a mixture of nitrogen and hydrogen until these gases, combined and form ammonia. Now, increased demand for ammonia to make explosives and fertilizers pushes production at the Oppau plant up to 6,000 tons by the end of its first year.

MEDICINE AND FOOD PRODUCTION

Zinc, like iron and manganese, is discovered to be a vital trace element, essential for healthy growth in crops and plants. Copper (1931), molybdenum (1939), and chlorine (1954) will later be added to the list.

In the USA, Henry Dakin and Alexis Carrel advocate the use of an antiseptic chlorine compound, known as Dakin's solution. It proves to be useful in preventing wound infection and will be widely applied.

A British company develops a process for making potent synthetic phosphate fertilizers, containing high concentrations of phosphates, by the interaction of phosphate rock with phosphoric acid.

FRINGE BENEFITS

Aluminium-foil tops for milk bottles are produced in Sweden.

The brassière, whose prototype comprised two handkerchiefs, pink ribbon and thread, is patented.

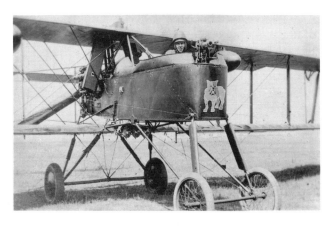

This Voisin Type 10 fighter-scout is a direct descendant of the Voisin biplane which claims the first air-to-air victory on 5 October. Shortly after the reorganization of the French Air Force into specialized units, Sergeant Franz and Caporal Quénault of *Escadrille* V24—the initial letter for each unit identifying the type of plane used: V for Voisin, D for Deperdussin, and so on—shoot down a German reconnaissance aircraft using a Hotchkiss rifle-calibre machine-gun mounted in a steel-tube pyramid.

The Telescribe, a new device for recording telephone conversations, can now provide useful proof in business transactions or disputes. During a call, the telephone receiver is placed against a transmitter which passes the sound waves to the recording element of a phonograph. The subscriber then uses a second receiver for conducting his conversation.

A tide predictor, dubbed 'the great brass brain', arrives after 15 years' work by scientists E.G. Fischer and R.A. Harris for the US Coast and Geodetic Survey. It gives advance information on tidal movements which enables Allied ships to manoeuvre in shallow water and outwit German U-boats during World War I.

The 'loaded' telephone line between New York and Denver, Colorado, the largest in use, transmits so clearly that callers cannot believe they are conversing over 2,000 mls (3,200 km). John Ambrose Fleming predicts that, by further loading or modulation of power to the lines, clear conversations between London and California could soon be possible.

With the incentive of the start of a world war, the development of the aviation industry is taken over from the private sector by governments eager to improve their military strength. By 1918, the idea of an air force will be an inseparable part of any nation's defence strategy.

A single-engined flying-boat operates the world's first scheduled airline service between St Petersburg and Tampa in Florida. A second flying-boat is soon needed to cope with demand—over 1,000 passengers are carried in the first three months.

Tear gas shells are developed in Germany by Dr von Tappen, who uses howitzer shells packed with TNT and a small canister of xylyl bromide—a tear-producing compound released when the shell's explosion breaks the canister.

The first purpose-built anti-aircraft gun is issued to British troops. While other nations are still experimenting with weapons light enough to be mounted on trucks and armoured cars, the UK-designed 3-in (7.62-cm) gun weighs in at one ton; it will remain in service for the next 30 years.

The Italian aircraft designer Allesandro Guidoni drops a torpedo of 750 lb (340.5 kg) from a specially built seaplane. Experiments with a Farman biplane, carrying lighter weights, have indicated the potential of torpedo-carrying planes.

The production of cast iron pipes is mechanized by S. de Lavaud's centrifugal casting process, which means the pipe moulds can now be used repeatedly and the casts are of better quality. The first foundry for using the process will be built in 1922 and many other uses for cast iron—such as making cylinder liners and piston rings—will be found.

Engineers in Britain build an 8-in (20.3-cm) pipeline to carry coal from barges on the Thames to a power station. Patented in 1891, it is the world's first commercial system designed to pump slurries—mixtures of liquid and solid coal. Not until 1957 will the system be used for the long-distance transport of coal in Ohio and of asphalt in Utah.

The treatment of thyroid disease takes an important step forward when Edward Kendall, biochemist at the Mayo Clinic, isolates the thyroid hormone, thyroxin. Thyroxin will be used to treat various kinds of thyroid insufficiency (hypothyroidism), which cause goitre, mental dullness and sometimes retardation.

In London, Allen and Hanburys announce a small, portable sterilizer-tank for surgical instruments. Cylindrical in shape, it is useful for operations performed outside hospitals.

A solution of sodium citrate, added to freshly donated blood, prevents clotting. This makes it easier to store and transport blood in large quantities for transfusion. But, although this technique is widespread by 1917, it is not until 1937 that the first blood bank opens in the USA, replacing the hospital donor-registers which are a legacy of World War I.

The protein plastic, casein, made from skim-milk, is used to make knitting needles and crochet hooks—used in their turn to make sweaters for the troops.

Fixed driving-mirrors on cars are in general use.

Marconi's type 16 balanced-crystal receiver has two crystals connected in such a way that one picks up the normal Morse pulses, while the other screens out any more powerful signals. Vital wartime ship-to-shore messages can thus now be clearly received without interference from the 'atmospherics' of thunderstorms.

Since German Puck Phonographs now sell for the price of a Sunday lunch, the gramophone has become the centre of family entertainment. To boost the sale of cylinders, some manufacturers have even taken to giving away players with a boxful of cylinders.

The conquest of infection

For centuries mankind has been powerless in the face of an enemy more terrible than war: infectious disease. The shadow of such plagues as the Black Death, which killed a quarter of Europe's population in the 14th century, lingered over the face of the Earth until the final decades of the last century. Then, thanks to the genius of a handful of men, the physical cause of diseases began to be identified and steps taken to wipe them out. Louis Pasteur discovered that bacteria caused infection; Joseph Lister banished germs from operating theatres with his carbolic acid spray; Robert Koch showed how specific bacteria could be cultured in the laboratory; Sir Almroth Wright initiated immunization against typhoid by using killed typhoid organisms.

In England and Wales, 100,000 people died of infectious diseases in 1899—60,000 from tuberculosis (TB) alone, and over 14,000 from measles. By the end of the seventies, the number of deaths (still largely from TB) was down to under 10,000. The reason for the reduction mostly lies with the range of available vaccinations which, from the BCG vaccine against TB in 1922 to the Salk polio vaccine in 1954, have all but obliterated such diseases—along with smallpox, typhoid,

cholera, whooping cough and diphtheria—from the developed world. There have been setbacks: for instance, no vaccine against influenza existed during the worldwide epidemic of 1918–1919, and 20 million people died—more than were killed in World War I. But help was at hand; if diseases could not be prevented, they could be cured.

The science of microscopy made a particular contribution. Early in the 20th century, Paul Ehrlich noticed that the same dyes which were used to stain tiny organisms under the microscope to render them visible, might also be used to destroy them. He treated malaria with methylene blue and developed Salvarsan for curing syphilis. Following in his footsteps, Gerhard Domagk saw in 1935 how prontosil red destroyed a variety of streptococcal bacteria; and he was soon initiating the range of sulphonamide drugs which have proved so vital in the fight against infection. The wounded of World War II were treated with new kinds of drugs derived from soil micro-organisms: the antibiotics. Penicillin, discovered in 1928, was still virtually unobtainable in 1939; by 1944, it was active in virtually every theatre of war in the world. Other antibiotics arrived rapidly throughout the forties—

streptomycin, for example, was found to be effective against 70 types of bacteria that penicillin could not kill.

But drugs have shortcomings; bacteria and viruses can build up a resistance to them so that the disease recurs in a new, more virulent form. One highly effective method of combatting diseases lies in the destruction of their carriers and the eradication of the conditions that foster them. The mosquitoes which, in 1900, were found to carry yellow fever and malaria, the body lice which spread typhus and Rocky Mountain spotted fever, and the tsetse flies which propagate sleeping sickness—all have been systematically attacked.

Meanwhile, the fundamental enemies of health continue to flourish: malnutrition, squalor and inadequate medical facilities. Such conditions prevail for about eighty per cent of the world's population, whether in neglected rural areas of overcrowded urban slums. The World Health Organization has made some inroads into these areas with mass immunization programmes. New tools will be placed in its hands—vaccines against malaria, cholera and even leprosy are in their early stages, promising total eradication of these major diseases within the next decade.

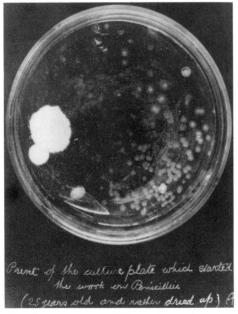

Print of the culture plate which started the work on Penicillin (25 years old and rather dried up) A.F.

A momentous piece of history is preserved on this culture plate. After its lid had come off by mistake, it was found to be contaminated: a mould clearly visible as the large white colonies on the left, was destroying the much smaller staphylococcus colonies on the right. Alexander Fleming's genius lay in his ability to turn this accident into discovery. Instead of throwing the plate away, he investigated the powerful mould, called *Penicillium notatum*, and so, in 1928, discovered the 20th century's most famous antibiotic: penicillin.

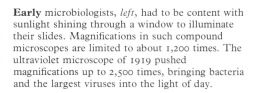

Early microbiologists, *left*, had to be content with sunlight shining through a window to illuminate their slides. Magnifications in such compound microscopes are limited to about 1,200 times. The ultraviolet microscope of 1919 pushed magnifications up to 2,500 times, bringing bacteria and the largest viruses into the light of day.

Like a window on to the invisible, the electron microscope opened up the universe of viruses and bacteria. A wealth of detail about bacteria suddenly became available, as well as the exposure of a number of the much smaller viruses. Not all such organisms cause diseases: the *Escherischia coli*, *below*, are benign bacteria, inhabiting human intestines. They are magnified 21,000 times. The electron microscope began to be developed in 1932 and, two years later, it had the same magnifying power as the most powerful light microscope. By 1937, it could magnify 7,000 times and, by 1944, the pattern of future microscopes was established, magnifying over 200,000 times.

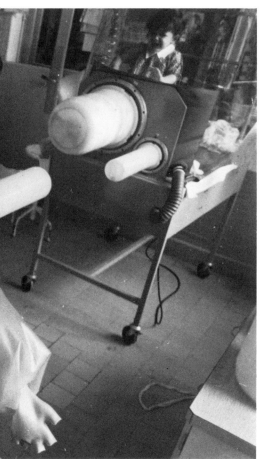

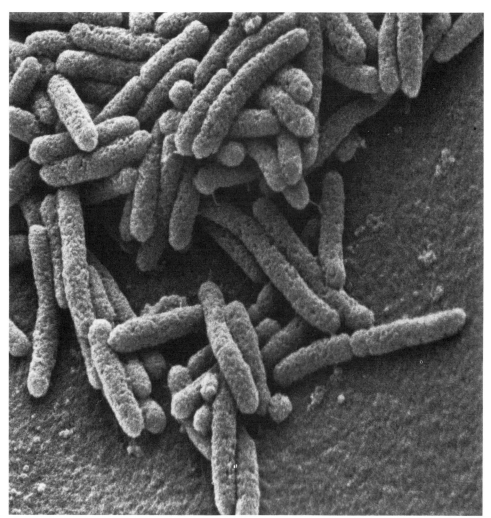

'Bubble' chambers such as this sterile unit at the Edouard Herriot Hospital in Lyon, France, protect the lives of patients who are particularly at risk from infection because of some defect in their immune system. The 'bubble' baby is Akim, the world's first recipient of a bone marrow graft, and even his clothes, food and drugs have to be kept in a sterile closet. Doctors who deal with cases like Akim's are becoming known as clinical ecologists: the patient's environment can make a difference between life and death.

COMMUNICATION AND INFORMATION

By discovering that the germanium crystal can be used to convert a.c. to d.c., US physicist Manson Benedicks lays the basis for the integrated circuit. The same crystal will later be used in the 'chip'.

In the first direct transatlantic radio-telephone transmission, speech is relayed from Canada to the Eiffel Tower in Paris. The callers are B. Webb of A T & T in Arlington, Va., and Lt Col Ferries, representing the French Government.

Japan and the USA—the technological giants of the future—are put in touch via wireless for the first time.

TRANSPORT AND WARFARE

Early fighter-scout planes have flown with the pilot or observer using a hand-held rifle or a pistol; but it is now evident that a forward-firing gun, fixed to the upper fuselage, is far more effective. Engineers at the German Fokker factory devise an interrupter gear which allows the firing of a gun mounted in this way to be synchronized with the propeller's movement, so as not to damage the blades.

Explosive paravanes—torpedo-shaped devices—are towed behind British destroyers to combat U-boats and mines. They either explode on contact or are detonated from the ship, but find little favour with captains who dislike trailing TNT-packed devices.

The tractor trailer is invented in Detroit by local blacksmith and wagonmaker August Fruehauf. The trailer, hauled by a Model T Ford, is for a local lumber dealer who wants to transport his boat to a Michigan lake. Out of this quick improvization, the Fruehauf Trailer Company will be born in 1918, eventually to become the world's largest trailer manufacturer.

Ford produces his millionth motor car.

ENERGY AND INDUSTRY

Pyrex glass emerges from the Corning Glass Works laboratories in the USA. Resistant to the effects of both heat and chemicals, this glass will be much used in domestic cooking ware and in laboratories everywhere, and will facilitate the construction of large-scale chemical plants.

Hard and soft metal parts, crucial to a wide range of equipment, can now easily be produced in large quantities, quickly and at low cost, as L.R. Heim introduces his centreless grinding machine to production engineering. It will be developed by the Cincinnati Milling Machine Co and made ready for industrial use in 1922.

MEDICINE AND FOOD PRODUCTION

The first of a long line of carcinogens (cancer-producing agents) is identified by two Japanese scientists, K. Yamagiwa and K. Ichikawa. They succeed in producing cancer in rabbits by exposing them for long periods to coal tar. This is the first known example of a cancer being experimentally produced by a continuous stimulus.

Dr Ulrich, head of a centre for epilepsy in Zurich, reports on a new compound called Sedobrol. This bromide treatment is used effectively, in conjunction with a low-salt diet, for the control of epilepsy.

George Crile of the Cleveland Clinic in Ohio recognizes that there is more to anaesthesia than rendering the patient unconscious, and introduces pre-operative medication—scopolamine to relieve anxiety and morphine to deaden pain. He also suggests injecting a local anaesthetic (procaine) in conjunction with a general anaesthetic—a technique called 'anoci-association'.

FRINGE BENEFITS

The Bayer Co begins retailing aspirin (first introduced in Germany in 1888) in handy, over-the-counter packs of 20.

William Lawrence Bragg, at 25, becomes the youngest recipient of a Nobel Prize. He and his father, William Henry Bragg, share the Physics award for their studies of X-ray diffraction and its use in elucidating crystal structure. X-ray crystallography will determine the make-up of many molecules, the most famous being the double-helix of DNA.

In the USA, Arnold and Carson of AT&T (American Telephone and Telegraph) demonstrate single sideband radio. They prove that each sideband of a modulated wave can carry a separate channel. This helps make multi-channel transmission possible and increases telecommunications potential.

Following the sinking of the *Titanic* three years before, French professor P. Langevin is inspired to invent the first ship's detector of icebergs and submarines. His sound navigation and ranging (SONAR) system uses quartz crystals to send out very short—ultrasonic—sound waves which are reflected back to the sender. Although destined to be largely replaced by radar, sonar plays a significant part in medical and industrial ultrasound technology for another half-century.

The world's first motor scooter, the Auto-Ped, comes on to the US market. It looks like a child's scooter—the rider stands on a platform (there is no seat)—but has a single cylinder engine fixed to the front wheel.

Cadillac market the first mass-produced US car with a V-8 engine (the eight cylinders are arranged in a V-shape). But after initial success, the V-8 will be eclipsed in the twenties by the 'straight-eight' engine (the cylinders are arranged in a line)—only to make a comeback in 1932 with the launch of Ford's low-priced Model 18.

An AB-2 flying-boat is catapulted into the air from the USS *North Carolina*, lying in Pensacola Bay, Florida. This novel form of launch from a ship at sea is one of many US Navy experiments to find a way of using aircraft in naval warfare.

Hungarian engineer Kalman Kando builds the first electric locomotive to be powered by high-frequency current (50Hz instead of 15-25Hz), so that power can be drawn from the public electricity supply, instead of from an independent generating station.

The acoustic mine is invented by Dr A.B. Wood: he fits a mine with a reed which is set vibrating at a certain frequency by the sound of approaching ships—and so triggers an explosion. Later mines have counters, and are set to explode only after a number of ships has passed.

The quality of a car's gears is improved with the introduction of the successful gear-hobbing machine—it cuts faster and with no distortion—produced by the Brown and Sharpe Manufacturing Co of Rhode Island, USA.

The structure of rocks beneath the earth's surface is revealed by the torsion balance, an instrument that can detect minute differences in the gravity of rocks. Used for the first time in Czechoslovakia, it will later become a key tool in the detection of oil and gas fields.

Stellite, a new hard, corrosion-resistant copper-based alloy, is developed. It will soon be used to make high-speed cutting tools because the alloy retains its strength even when it reaches very high temperatures, as encountered, for example, in the manufacture of gas turbine engines.

English bacteriologist Frederick W. Twort discovers germs that prey on germs—viruses which enter and destroy bacteria. He calls this kind of virus a bacteriophage—'bacteria-eater'. Later, the bacteriophages will become important in revealing how viruses in general affect cells.

Morgan Parker, a 23-year-old US inventor, patents one of the simplest and most convenient of surgical tools: the disposable scalpel.

Processed cheese, first made in Switzerland, is launched in the USA by Kraft. Although it costs more than fresh cheese, the new product is popular because it keeps indefinitely in its sealed packet.

Margaret and Warren Lewis watch the activities of a living cell using time-lapse cinephotography. Film of the stages of cell growth and function is speeded up so that the minute changes become visible.

Lipstick first appears in a metal cartridge.

The wind-on mechanical pencil never needs a sharpener.

'Little Willie', *left* is an early example of tank design. The British Admiralty and War Office began experiments a year earlier with 'landships' intended to protect infantry advances from machine-gun fire and thus break the stalemate of trench warfare. The successor to 'Little Willie', 'Mother', is the first to be designed in the lozenge shape that will become standard, and is able to cross trenches and climb vertical parapets. The 100 production models which follow are built in two versions: the Male, fortified and equipped with naval and attack guns, and the Female, armed with machine-guns to give covering fire.

Box 'respirators', with a tight-fitting facepiece connected to a charcoal-filter canister, are an early defence against the chemical warfare that will kill an estimated 91,000 in the trenches. The first masks—cotton pads impregnated with chemicals—are devised after the Germans use chlorine gas at Ypres in April.

47

COMMUNICATION AND INFORMATION

A human voice fills the vast arena of Madison Square Gardens, New York, for the first of countless times: loudspeakers linked to an open-air public address system are successfully tested at a conference of the National Educational Association.

Cameras with coupled rangefinders make their début. Several special models in Eastman Kodak's Autographic range have optical rangefinders connected to the focusing mechanism for accurate judgement.

TRANSPORT AND WARFARE

The German submarine *Deutschland* transports much-needed nickel, tin and rubber from the USA, breaking the British blockade. But the idea of cargo-carrying subs is dropped by the Germans when the USA enters the war.

The Nissen hut provides temporary shelter for newly conscripted troops. First erected at Hesdin, France, the bow-shaped hut of corrugated iron is the best of many such designs, and wins its Canadian-born inventor, Peter Nissen, the DSO (Distinguished Service Order).

The US Dodge company mass produces the first motor car with bodywork made entirely of steel. Advanced pressing and welding techniques produce a tough car used as an ambulance in World War I.

ENERGY AND INDUSTRY

Pipes made from asbestos cement are produced commercially in Italy. They are light, free from corrosion and provide a smooth bore—ideal for carrying water from reservoirs and waste from disposal systems.

World War I and US domestic demands create such shortages of oil and gasoline that engineers predict the exhaustion of petroleum reserves within 30 years.

Acetone, a colourless, flammable liquid that will be used in the manufacture of explosives and later as a solvent, is prepared in significant quantities by the British Admiralty Powder Department. The secret of their high production rate, crucial to the war effort, lies with a bacterium (*Clostridium acetobutylicum*) which makes the acetone by fermenting grain; this may well be the first example of what will be called biotechnology.

MEDICINE AND FOOD PRODUCTION

In the USA, General Electric's William Coolidge (who has already introduced the tungsten filament for X-ray tubes three years earlier) again revolutionizes X-ray technology when he patents the hot-cathode tube.

In an era of intense preoccupation with deficiency diseases, Elmer McCollum and Marguerite Davis declare vitamins A and B—which they identified in cow's milk in 1913—as essential for growth. Later work will show that vitamin B is a mixture of compounds with different properties, which will become known eventually as the 'B-vitamin complex'.

US public health physician Joseph Goldberger shows that pellagra, a disease widely prevalent in the Mediterranean area and southern United States, is due to dietary deficiency, not to infection, as has previously been thought. He cures jail inmates of the disease by adding milk to their diet.

In New Orleans, Rudolph Matas teaches that no operation should be performed on a wounded patient until the effects of shock have been reduced with adrenaline, intravenous saline and glucose.

FRINGE BENEFITS

Vulcanite is used for moulding teeth fillings.

A US grocery store installs a turnstile and checkout in a move towards the 'super' market.

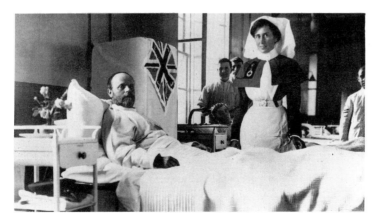

The first hospital ward in the world to be entirely devoted to the practice of plastic surgery opens at Cambridge Military Hospital in Aldershot, England. About 11,000 British soldiers and airmen will undergo successful restorative treatment in this, and other hospitals, thanks to the dexterity of such men as Harold Gillies and T.P. Kilner. Their wartime experience will later be turned to good effect in repairing inherited deformities, such as harelips and cleft palates, and in grafting skin in severe burns cases.

In front of Lord Kitchener, British Secretary of State for War, Major C.E. Prince gives an impressive demonstration of ground-to-air communications. Over his wireless telephone Mark I, the major talks to a pilot in flight. Airborne communication is speeded up from this moment.

Marine navigation goes electronic with US scientist Frederick A. Kolster's radio direction finder. Soon radio beacons are erected around the world's coastlines so that ships can take bearings in all weathers, and many vessels install large rotating loop receivers.

Invented by Italian Abiel Betel Revelli, the first sub-machine-gun—the Villar Perosa 9 mm —is issued to Italian troops. Originally designed for aircraft, the double-barrelled gun is light enough to be mounted on a motorbike side-car.

Driving in the rain is now safer with the first mechanically operated windshield wipers, introduced to US cars. 1921 will bring the first automatic wipers, and 1932 the first electric windshield wipers for cars in Britain and America.

Britain's Great Northern Railway pioneers the use of railway coaches articulated in pairs. A specially modified bogie links each pair, so that three instead of four bogies are needed. The coaches are lighter and cheaper than conventional ones, but problems with maintenance—two carriages instead of one are affected by a fault in a bogie—will discourage other railways from pursuing this innovation.

Spanning 1,000 ft (305 m) between Wards Island and Queens, New York, the Hell Gate Bridge is opened, an outstanding example of the use of steel in bridge building. Its designer, Gustav Lindenthal, has used a great 'through arch', the first of its kind, with the deck that carries the railway track cutting through the line of the arch. The central part of the deck is suspended from the arch above.

British electrical engineers Duddell and Mather develop the first industrial wattmeter for measuring directly and accurately the electric power in high voltage cables.

US engineer John Fisher develops the prototype of agitator washing machines. Having used an electric motor to drive a rotating dolly in 1908, Fisher now puts the motor beneath the tub, with successful results: the motion of the dolly pushes the clothes, not the water, around the tub to give an efficient wash. The agitator machine, marketed by the Hurley Machine Co of Chicago in 1927, will be the forerunner of all single- and twin-tub machines.

The body louse is already known to spread typhus. Now Henrique da Rocha-Lima, a Brazilian working in Germany, discovers the cause—one of the rickettsial group of micro-organisms—and names it *Rickettsia prowazeki* after two researchers who died of it.

Jean Comus, director of physical treatment at the Grand Palais de Paris, introduces whirlpool baths to relieve pain and stiffness in wounded joints and limbs. Jets of warm water are used to mobilize the affected part, ready for massage or manipulation.

British physiologist Edward Sharpey Schafer suggest that the Islets of Langerhans in the pancreas—already known to be abnormal in diabetics—must secrete some kind of substance controlling carbohydrate metabolism. He calls this hypothetical substance 'insulin'.

An early exponent of antiseptic measures, Sir Almroth Wright suggests washing open wounds with a saline solution to prevent infection. His recommendation helps to safeguard the wounded at the Battle of Jutland.

Two years after coining the phrase 'birth-control', US feminist Margaret Sanger, author of *The Woman Rebel*, pioneers the first birth-control clinic in the USA. Located in Brooklyn, the clinic is raided by police a month after it opens.

Long-life stainless steel, designed specifically for cutlery, is patented.

Enamelled baths begin to replace cast iron tubs.

An early road-safety campaign is launched in London.

The Direction-Finding (D/F) Loop Aerial, the first navigational aid fitted to aircraft, is capable of receiving signals from ground stations. Rotating it until a given signal is at its strongest gives the bearing of the source; by doing this for two separate transmitters, in quick succession, the navigator can determine his position.

How the word travels

The way in which we communicate by word is typified by today's super-secretary. She types and corrects documents on a word processor with a display monitor. The processor stores its input on disc and, while it automatically types out the required number of copies, the secretary can pick up a push-button telephone and be connected direct to the other side of the world. If the number is busy, the press of a button will ensure that it is 'nagged' until free. Orders can be placed by telex and facsimile pictures sent direct to clients by phototelegraphy. While the secretary is out at lunch, telephone calls will be answered by machine and the telex will print out any messages.

When the century began, the picture was different indeed. Most day-to-day communication was by letter, and the telegram was the best way of sending a message at speed. Typewriters were still in their infancy, as were telephones. The telephones that did exist mostly required the intervention of the operator who could connect the caller with a recipient at most 300 miles (480 km) away. Messages could be sent by telegraph across the Atlantic, but only via the operator at the appropriate telegraph company, who tapped out each letter for translation into a code.

Although telegraph services were soon introduced in which subscribers could transmit and receive messages, these still had to be controlled by an operator. The secret of the telephone's success was the automatic exchange which was invented in the 1890s by Kansas City undertaker Almon Strowger, fired by annoyance at the inefficiency of his local operator. The Strowger system incorporated a push-button device on the handset for generating pulses which then triggered a selector at the exchange, but this device was quickly replaced by the dial still widely used today.

As communicators became more ambitious in their aims, the telegraph system was boosted in 1920 by a transatlantic radio link. But it was the rapid proliferation of automatic exchanges, and the opening of the first transatlantic telephone service in 1927 that gave the telephone the fillip it has never lost. Like their telegraphic counterparts, the telephone links were made across the Atlantic by means of radio.

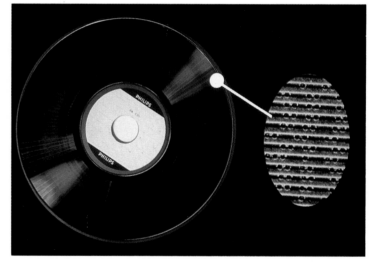

The office clerk, *above left*, laboriously keeping records and writing letters in duplicate with a quill pen in copperplate handwriting, typifies the way in which the written word was communicated at the start of the twentieth century. By the eighties, the situation had changed out of all recognition, *left*. At the offices of London's *Observer* newspaper, even the conventional typewriter has become obsolete. Journalists enter their stories directly into the Ferranti computerized composing system. The words are displayed on the monitor and corrected 'on screen'. They are then stored until required for checking by the editor. To see a display of any article, the editor dials up its code. He can then use his own keyboard to make any corrections. When all the copy for an issue has been approved, the computer is activated and transfers it to the typesetting machines for printing.

As the volume of printed material increases, storage space is an ever-growing problem. One possible solution is the optical disc recorder, with which the entire *Encyclopedia Britannica* can be housed on a disc no larger than a long playing record. The information is stored in the form of microscopic holes, burnt into a disc by a laser beam and 'read' by another laser beam.

The next step up the communications ladder came in the thirties with the launch of the telex or teleprinter. It consisted of a keyboard on which messages were typed, a dial to key in the correct number of the person who was to receive a message, and a print-out for receiving incoming information. This operator-free system was made possible by the introduction of an electrical code which incorporated stop and start signals before and after each letter.

The international telephone network began its most dramatic advance in the fifties and sixties. The first undersea transatlantic cable was laid in 1956 and, four years later, trials with all-electronic, computer-operated telephone exchanges were begun in the USA by the Bell Telephone Company. In 1962, the communications gap across the Atlantic was bridged by the satellite Telstar, which was able to carry a dozen telephone calls simultaneously and bounce them down to a receiving station. Also in the sixties, experiments in fibre optics were begun: their aim was to increase the carrying capacity of the telephone system.

Since the sixties, both satellites and computers have played an ever more important part in communications. Geostationary satellites, so named because they are launched into orbit over the Equator in synchrony with the spin of the Earth, and so appear to be stationary, are ideal for this task because they are high enough above the Earth's surface to circumvent the problems of transmitting over the Earth's curved surface. Communications satellites currently in orbit number nearly 100.

Like the satellite, the computer—particularly in the form of the chip—promises to extend the scope of communications. The computer is, for example, the heart of the word processor, a machine that has a memory, disc storage system and printer. The next step in sophistication promises to be a link up between the word processor and a high-speed telex system. Using this, it will be possible to type out material and, by punching in one or more numbers, ensure that it is displayed simultaneously on the processor's own monitor and the monitor of chosen recipients. Add to this a video telephone and the day of the globe-trotting business commuter could be over.

To celebrate the laying of the first undersea transatlantic cable, London's satirical magazine *Punch* of 11 August 1866 depicts Neptune holding out both hands in blessing on the marriage of Britannia with 'Uncle Sam'.

Optical fibres, *below*, made out of transparent glass, are gradually replacing copper coaxial cables in many forms of communications. Data is converted from electrical to optical wave forms before being transmitted. The great advantage of the new cables, which are in use in both telephone and television systems, is that they can transmit more data faster than ever before.

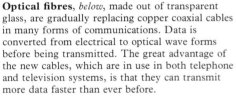

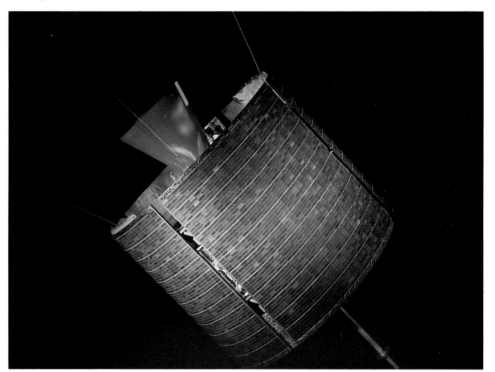

Long-distance communication by satellite began in earnest in 1965 with the launch of Early Bird 1 by NASA for the international group, Intelsat. Orbiting the Earth once every 24 hours, it could carry 240 voice channels, one television channel or a high-speed data service. The active life of the first Early Bird, predicted at 1½ years, was in fact three years. It has been succeeded by Early Bird 2, launched in 1967, and three more Early Birds, the latest launched in 1980.

COMMUNICATION AND INFORMATION

Photocomposing—printing by photography—is christened with the advent of the Bowtree Automatic Pantograph. The machine consists of a projector unit carrying a negative disc on which there are 78 characters. The disc is rotated until the required character is opposite a pointer, then a photographic exposure is made. More than 300 characters can be photographed in an hour.

Canny interruption of radio signals from German aircraft enable Allied troops to pinpoint enemy artillery and to launch air attacks before it can open fire.

With the vast expansion in Government printing induced by the war, HMSO (His Majesty's Stationery Office) acquires its first printing works.

TRANSPORT AND WARFARE

A sea-going vessel built of concrete, the *Namsenfjord*, is launched. Concrete barges and pontoons are already in use and a number of concrete vessels will be constructed during both the World Wars.

A prototype 'aerial torpedo', built by the Curtiss Company for the US Navy, is delivered to the Sperry Flying Field at Long Island, New York. It is a biplane without a pilot, pointed in the required direction and launched; gyroscopes control its flight. A pre-set timing device causes it to stop over its target where the wings automatically drop off so that the fuselage containing 300 lb (136.2 kg) of explosives plummets down to earth.

The US Baldwin Locomotive Works build the largest railway engine in the world. Designed primarily to haul coal trains up steep gradients, the massive Triplex steam engine weighs 384 tons and has a boiler 50 ft (15.2 m) long.

ENERGY AND INDUSTRY

The old wives' tale that cloth dyed green is never eaten by moths is found to contain a grain of truth. E. Meckbach demonstrates at the German Dye Trust that Manchester Yellow—a common ingredient in green dye mixtures—does in fact mothproof wool. Few later dyestuffs will prove as effective in this area.

Black and Decker improve their electric hand drill by adding an on/off switch and a 'universal' motor. The drill, originally invented by German Wilhelm Fein in 1895, is now more controllable, since the switch is trigger-operated, and more versatile, as the motor can be powered by both alternating and direct current.

The Howard Hughes Tool Co introduce the reaming cone bit into oil-drilling technology. The reamer, a metal sheath around the drilling cones on the bit, guarantees that deep bore holes maintain a uniform gauge.

MEDICINE AND FOOD PRODUCTION

French doctors describe the condition known as 'trench foot', defining three forms from slight (painful, swollen feet) to severe (gangrenous). It is due to standing for long periods in water and using footwear which restricts the blood supply.

In the USA Graham Lusk and R.J. Anderson bring further understanding of nutrition, by showing that the body's energy production is related to the number of calories it consumes, regardless of their source.

Walter Dandy, a student of Harvey Cushing at Johns Hopkins, pioneers new techniques of contrast radiography—ways of improving X-ray images—in neurosurgery. He injects air into the cerebral ventricles, causing the outline of the brain to show up on the X-ray, so making it easier to locate brain tumours.

FRINGE BENEFITS

Wartime shortages of paper and paper-making materials encourage experiments with grasses.

M. Hammers and C. Lewis of the USA produce a fully automatic, electrically ignited oil burner—the first automatic home heater.

At the height of his powers, Sigmund Freud completes his *Introductory Lectures in Psychoanalysis* at Vienna University. They confirm his reputation, established worldwide in 1900 by the publication of his *Interpretation of Dreams*, as one of the century's most influential thinkers. Despite the onset of cancer and public burnings of his books by the Nazis in Berlin, he will continue to work in Vienna until he is driven into exile in London in 1938—to die a year later.

Microphones become more efficient. The condenser microphone, introduced into the USA by E.C. Wente, produces a clearer, more uniform sound. Improved versions of the microphone will soon be employed to make high-quality recordings and broadcasts.

The USA enters the war and all US commercial radio stations come under naval control, including Marconi's coastal stations and 540 ship radios.

A new electronic circuit vastly increases the sensitivity and selectivity of radio receivers over a wide band of frequencies. This superheterodyne circuit, which makes it unnecessary to vary the amplifier tuning, is designed by Armstrong. It rapidly becomes part of the basic design of all AM radios.

US car manufacturers produce 1,745,792 vehicles, of which 42% are Model T Fords.

Scouting aircraft need to be highly manoeuvrable. Britain introduces the Sopwith Camel, capable of a maximum speed of 122 mph (196 km/h) and soon to become famous for its lightning right turn. Its destruction of nearly 1,300 enemy aircraft forces Germany to reply with the Fokker D VII, built with a welded steel fuselage that makes it highly resistant to battle damage.

Nearly 300 mls (483 km) of rail, laid in the heat of the barren Nullarbor Plain, complete the trans-Australian railway. This final section of the east-west link is the longest dead-straight stretch of track in the world.

Only five years old, the Japanese company Kwaishinsa enjoys success with its small car, the DAT, whose name derives from the initials of the firm's partners. In 1932, the Japanese national emblem—a rising sun—is added to name a much better known car, the Datsun.

Soap for washing clothes is in short supply during the war and this stimulates the Germans into making Nekal, the world's first commercial detergent. The superior cleaning power of synthetic chemical detergents, discovered in 1913 by a Belgian, A. Rechler, will soon put them into washing machines all over the world; and in 1967, Proctor and Gamble will introduce a powerful detergent which contains enzymes which digest dirt.

Ninety skilled glass hand-blowers are made redundant for each automatic glass-tubing machine installed at glass works. The machine, which uses a continuous process of blowing compressed air to make the tubes, is introduced by Edward Danner of the Libbey Glass Co, USA, the first company to make real cuts in the cost of glass tubing.

The Catskill aqueduct is completed, 372 yds (340 m) below the Hudson, to bring fresh water to the still-exploding population of New York City. Ninety three miles (150 km) long, its tunnel is 15 ft (4.5 m) wide and, in many places, driven through solid rock. The aqueduct makes use of an unusual engineering device, the pressure tunnel, which in the forties will also convey water to New York from the Delaware catchment area.

In Britain, J.D. Speid Sinclair perfects an appendicectomy clamp to snip out the diseased organ and trap it in a container for removal. This cuts the risk of infection of surrounding tissues.

British and US obstetricians report how 'twilight sleep' eases pain in childbirth and prevents unpleasant memories for the mother. Introduced originally by von Steinbüchel of Graz in 1902, a light state of scopolamine-morphine narcosis is induced, notably in first-time mothers. Unwanted side-effects can include prolonged labour, depression of breathing in the infant and complete amnesia of the birth.

Clarence Birdseye makes the connection between freezing and freshness. Having eaten fish in Labrador which was still palatable weeks after being frozen, he experiments with ways of freezing perishable foods to preserve them.

Ford begins production of the cheap, hard-wearing Fordson frameless tractor which, within 10 years, will be responsible for a vast increase in farm mechanization in Britain and the USA.

The roll-towel cabinet provides cleaner, more hygenic linen.

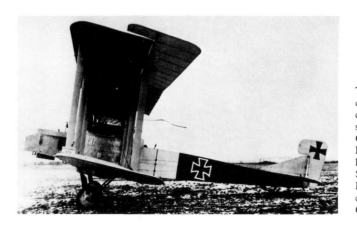

The German Gotha is the first aircraft to be designed as a bomber, replacing the bomb-carrying Zeppelins shot down by Allied fighter-scouts. In May four squadrons of twin-engined Gothas begin a series of daylight raids on England, flying with 1,000-lb (450-kg) bomb loads at high altitudes from bases in Belgium. Switching to night raids when higher-flying British fighters are developed, the Gothas will carry out 52 raids before the German High Command ends operations in May 1918.

The fastest cars

Grand Prix racing made its début in France in 1906. Far from being the bumbling buggies of the previous decade, the monstrous machines that competed in that inaugural event were propelled at speeds of up to 100 mph (161 km/h) by 12 or 13 litre engines. The fact that they had inadequate tyres, brakes and steering did not deter their daredevil drivers.

This was the first year in which a special formula—later named Formula 1 and subject to continual change—was laid down for high-powered racing cars. By 1914, following several fatalities, engine size was limited to 4.5 litres and an era of recklessness was over.

Only in 1923 was Grand Prix racing radically changed with the introduction of the supercharger, which blew pressurized air into the engine to increase its motive power. Although engine size was now restricted to 2 litres, these 'blowers' greatly improved speeds and acceleration. By 1925, blowers had become standard, and bred a new, nimble generation of racing cars that was to flourish until the advent of World War II.

In 1934, rising speeds and a dangerous surge in power prompted the introduction of a formula limiting the weight of cars to 1,666 lb (750 kg). Some firms promptly responded by constructing cars of expensive, light-weight alloys which ran on costly, technically advanced fuel mixtures. Engine power reached an all-time peak in the 1937 W125 Mercedes: its 5.66-litre supercharged engine had a top speed of 195 mph (312 km/h).

With the financial restrictions of war, this phase was abruptly ended, and even in the fifties, modest 'unblown' engines were the rule. But change in car design continued. In 1958 the Cooper Car Company began an irrevocable trend when they turned their cars back to front and put the engine behind the driver. This practice, which reduces wind drag, has been used in Formula 1 ever since.

When, in the sixties, manufacturers could at last buy adequate engines 'off the shelf', experiments in aerodynamics could begin in earnest. In 1968 Grand Prix cars first sprouted fins and huge, movable aerofoils. Although now restricted for safety reasons, they have remained a feature of Formula 1 cars.

The first 'ground effects' car, the Lotus 78, fitted with a skirt (side panels reaching to the ground) to harness the airflow beneath the car, appeared in the late seventies. The skirt provided added downforce and so increased cornering speed. Even more significant were the innovatory Renaults unveiled in 1977, whose turbochargers—superchargers driven by hot exhaust gases—began to win them races two years later. Other manufacturers turned their attention to such engines, and, by the start of the eighties, turbos promised to herald a new age in which the supercharger will again rule.

'One ton' monsters, such as this 14-litre Clement-Bayard, contested early Grand Prix. Although hard to handle, they achieved extraordinary speeds—in the 1908 French Grand Prix, 20 of the 48 starters managed to maintain 100 mph (161 km/h) over a flying kilometre. Riding with each driver was a mechanic whose duties were to warn of overtaking and monitor the dashboard instruments. After many accidents, such mechanics were banned in 1925.

Voiturette races for cars less powerful than the Formula 1 types were run alongside Grand Prix races in the twenties and thirties. The supercharged 1½ litre ERA (English Racing Automobile), *right*, scored many successes with an engine developed from that of the Riley Six production car. Its chassis was designed by Reid Railton, who later built land speed record-breaking cars.

Germany's Nürburgring, once notoriously dangerous and now the home of vintage car rallies, witnessed many of the developments in Formula 1. In the fifties, for example, Grand Prix regulations encouraged the design of engines that were not supercharged. The reasoning was that 'unblown' engines would benefit production car builders. The new-style cars had typically rounded bodies as this poster well illustrates.

The Grand Prix winner of the seventies, *below*, was a fantastic, wedge-shaped machine which scorched around fast circuits at speeds above 200 mph (362 km/h). In 1980 the skirts which created the 'ground effects' car were banned by a new ruling that bodywork should clear the ground by a minimum of 2.4 in (6 cm) when stationary. But teams bypassed the ban by building cars with skirts lowered by hydraulic suspension or by the flick of a switch, once the race had started.

The Lotus 49, *above*, dominated the 1967 Grand Prix season, although its lack of reliability cost British driver, Jim Clark, the Drivers' Championship. Powered by the high-performance Cosworth-Ford DFV V8 engine—destined to be the mainstay of Grand Prix cars for another decade—the car had a body and chassis cast in one piece in light, rigid, metal. This monocoque method of construction was pioneered by Lotus chief Colin Chapman six years before. The wide tyres typified the mid-sixties trend towards the huge 'slicks' universal in the seventies.

Supercharging came back to Grand Prix racing in 1977 with the turbocharged Renault, *below*, whose supercharger was driven by hot exhaust gases. From the off, these French cars showed tremendous power, but overheating and unreliability plagued them in the first two seasons. A split-second delay between the application of the throttle and the car's response made manoeuvring difficult. But in 1979, after a design with smaller, twin turbos was adopted, the car scored its first triumph—the French Grand Prix. Since then the success enjoyed by turbos racing for Grand Prix giants, Ferrari and Brabham, has confirmed the turbo car's potential.

COMMUNICATION AND INFORMATION

In Germany, the cause of crackle on the line—it has drowned many wartime radio messages—is identified by W. Shottky. Defining the interference as random fluctuations in the power of a current, Shottky inspires many scientists to devise ways of counteracting this unwanted spasmodic noise.

Wireless inadvertently saves German airships in the last Zeppelin raid of the war, on the night of 5/6 August. Misled by their wireless information, the airships drop their bombs into the sea, well short of the British coast, and turn for home. They thus avoid a large force of British fighters.

TRANSPORT AND WARFARE

ASDIC (Anti-Submarine Detection Investigation Committee) detectors replace passive microphones for detecting enemy submarines and mines. The ASDIC apparatus employs sound-ranging (SONAR) principles, developed by Langevin in 1915; and in its first test at the Admiralty Experimental Station at Harwich, British and French scientists witness its detection of a submarine at the range of a few hundred yards. Further development will lead to the 1922 echo sounder.

The Americans take delivery of their first SPAD XIII scouts. The famous French aircraft will be used to equip many US squadrons, including the 94th Aero Sqn, which on 1 March becomes the first US unit to patrol over enemy territory.

Red, green and amber electric traffic lights are installed for the first time in New York, nine years before they reach British streets (in Wolverhampton)—although London does experiment with a set of manually operated three-colour lights in 1921.

ENERGY AND INDUSTRY

Van der Gracht of Shell introduces to the oil company the first drill to have diamond cutting edges.

Paint technology enters the modern age as alkyd resins, which will become essential components of paint, are developed and manufactured on a large scale from petroleum. Widely used in the USA by 1928 and later in the rest of the world, alkyd-based oil paints will improve the craft of painting and decorating because of their good drying performance, colour characteristics and durability.

MEDICINE AND FOOD PRODUCTION

In France, following the recent discovery of gas gangrene antidotes, the British Army starts using mixed antitoxin against two of World War I's deadliest killers: tetanus and the most important of the gas gangrene bacilli.

In Britain, Dr S.A. Kapadra improves upon an existing method of preserving perishable food in a sealed chamber filled with a special gas medium. He replaces carbon monoxide with a less volatile mixture of carbon dioxide, nitrogen and a trace of oxygen. Raspberries preserved in the new gas medium remain fresh after two weeks of storage.

A wood cellulose substitute for cotton, known as Celucotton, is developed to answer the urgent need for bandages and other dressing materials at war casualty stations in Europe.

FRINGE BENEFITS

The USA announces a method of distilling alcohols, used in munition manufacture, from a cactus plant.

Jubilant Allied troops, standing in a captured German gun emplacement near recently fallen Grevillers in France, proudly display one of their trophies—a 13 mm Mauser rifle. The first purpose-built anti-tank weapon, its steel-core bullets fired at high velocities can penetrate the thin armour-plate of a tank with ease. The Mauser is the forerunner of several generations of shoulder-fired anti-tank weapons which will be made by many countries and used in active service until the end of World War II.

The electronic swing, or multivibrator circuit, is invented by H. Abraham and E. Block and clears the way for the use of vacuum tubes in computers. The circuit, which instead of producing wave-like vibrations induces the bouncing of waves between two unstable points, will prove invaluable in computer technology.

The US public is quick to appreciate the improved stability of radio reception produced by the neutrodyne circuit of Professor L.A. Hezeltine. By feeding the current back into the circuit at the right strength, he succeeds in neutralizing the imbalance in high-frequency reception.

The optimistically titled Liberty engine is fitted to thousands of American and British planes. Eager to put a rapid end to the war, the US government has charged a team of designers to produce a standard aircraft engine; the water-cooled V-12 Liberty is the result, going into mass production just five months after it was commissioned.

On 14 October a Handley Page aircraft of the British Independent Air Force—first formed to bomb Berlin in reply to the Gotha raids on London—lets fly with a 1,650-lb (747-kg) 'Block Buster', the largest bomb to be dropped during World War I.

HMS 'Argus', known in the British navy as the 'flat iron', is the first aircraft carrier to have a purpose-built flight-deck allowing its squadron of Sopwith Cuckoo torpedo-bombers to take off from, and land on, the same area. Earlier cruisers were fitted with separate platforms for taking-off and landing.

The quality of white paint is improved with the introduction of the whitest pigment of all, titanium dioxide, which, by 1945, will oust white lead paint from 80% of the white paint market. Although expensive, its success will result from its remarkable covering power and its lack of toxicity.

The first food mixer to be powered by an electric motor—the universal food mixer and beater—is introduced in the USA. Essentially similar to the manual mixer, the beaters extend downwards from the motor and into the bowl. Not until 1952 will this design be changed, with the invention of a model that has the motor in the base and the blades actually fitted into the bowl.

Curtains, upholstery, stairs and car interiors can all now be cleaned by the new vacuum cleaner produced by the Swedish firm Lux, which will become part of Electrolux. A metal cylinder encloses the motor and the fan, and a variety of fixtures is provided, to be attached to the end of the hose. It will be superseded in 1930 when Hoover introduce the first small hand-held vacuum cleaner.

In Britain, doctors succeed in coaxing ex-servicemen out of their hysterical paralysis. Not expecting to be cured, men with 'paralysed' limbs are encouraged to talk with helpers at the treatment centre who have themselves recovered from the same hysterical manifestations. When a man's expectations are correct, the affected limb is massaged in warm water to improve circulation and total recovery usually follows within minutes.

The death rate in the trenches from open wounds of the chest is running at an alarming 47.7%. Improvement comes when army surgeons revive the old practice of closing chest wounds.

British research establishes that epidemic encephalitis, though similar to polio in its early stages, is a separate disease. Fatalities mostly occur within the first three weeks; otherwise, recovery is slow, often leaving patients with facial palsy.

Airmail labels, inscribed *Par Avion*, are used by the French civil airmail service.

The DI, a low-wing Junkers monoplane, is clad in corrugated metal panels. In fighter trials held in June it proves both fast and manoeuvrable. However, its unconventional structure slows down production, and only 41 reach the Front before the Armistice in November.

Life on film

Taking colour photographs can be anything from an absorbing hobby to a steady source of professional income. For family snapshots, good colour reproduction is available at the touch of a Polaroid button or via the low-cost, foolproof, cartridge-loaded camera which is the modern colour equivalent of the black and white box Brownie so popular for the first 50 years of the century. The more serious photographer can choose from a wide range of ever more efficient and ingenious cameras.

The earliest surviving photograph of any kind was taken in 1827 on an asphalt-coated pewter plate and needed eight hours' exposure. In 1888, George Eastman offered the public the first Kodak hand camera. Its now familiar roll film took 100 pictures, each with an exposure time of a fraction of a second. The popularity of this camera encouraged the search for a workable form of true colour photography, not just the hand tinting of black and white prints.

In the 1850s, Niépce and Daguerre managed to produce colour images but were unable to fix them, except by manual means such as varnishing. It was not until Louis and Auguste Lumière launched their Autochrome process in 1907 that the public were afforded the first practical means of taking colour photographs.

Since that time, cameras and film have evolved and diversified in such a way that the photographer can now choose anything from a low-error automatic system to a sophisticated camera with ample scope for artistic and technological expertise and experiment.

The first practical technique for producing a colour image, now known as the additive method and derived from a system invented by James Clerk Maxwell in 1861, involved taking three separate pictures: in 1893, John Joly made a combination filter screen composed of minute bands of red, green and blue which was placed against the glass plate inside the camera. On exposure, the screen allowed varying degrees of light to pass through, and recorded the resulting tonal values on the glass plate in black and white. By projecting the transparency on the plate in register with the original screen, a multi-coloured image was produced. The Lumière brothers improved this technique, substituting dots for lines and coating them directly on to the glass plate. They thus achieved the first practical three-colour process. A number of screen-plate processes followed, including the Paget plate which was renowned for the subtlety of its colouring. *Girl with Flowers, below*, was taken on a Paget plate in about 1913.

Screen plates remained popular for colour photography for more than 30 years, but because the filter used in the additive process absorbed a lot of light and produced rather dark pictures, photographers continued their search for a new method of colour reproduction. The subtractive method approached the problem by beginning with white light—which is a mixture of all colours—and removing certain hues to create a copy of the original image. Research in Germany had shown that colour-forming substances, or dye couplers, worked by absorbing primary colour components of light. Much later, two professional musicians, Leopold Godowsky and Leopold Mannes, used dye couplers in experiments which led to the advent of Kodachrome film in 1936. The film had three light-sensitive layers and a single exposure produced three negatives which analyzed the image in red, green and blue. By 1942, negatives could be developed by Kodak's special process to give Kotavachrome prints, such as this wedding group, in clear, natural colours.

Screen filters, shown as microphotographs, *left*, made stable colour photographs possible. The 1907 Autochrome process used a filter of starch particles dyed in three primary colours.

The 1916 Agfa Colour process had its origins in Germany. The film was composed of three gum solutions which had been dyed and emulsified, then poured on a sticky plate and held in a mosaic.

The 1935 Dufayacolor process was the last additive method ever to appear. Printed on film, it reflected the permanent trend away from glass plates, but was soon to be ousted by subtractive methods.

By the forties, the colour print had gained great popularity, and this was when the American Polaroid Corporation introduced the world to the miracle of instant photography. The film of Polaroid inventor Edwin Land's black and white camera promised 'finished pictures in a minute'. In 1963, the instant print process was extended to colour. The film used was based on the same three-colour subtractive process still used today for conventional film, but was coated with developer as it was drawn from the camera. Whilst this developer penetrated and developed the three negative layers, the subtractively coloured dye molecules were released in inverse proportion to exposure to form a colour image. The Polaroid SX–70, introduced in 1972, improved on this process by combining the negative and positive materials in a single unit containing 14 coatings. With automatic ultrasonic focusing, the system has captured the imagination of an impatient generation. The snapshot can be in the family album in a matter of minutes.

Colour photography has come of age with the single lens reflex (SLR) camera: it uses 35 mm film and is popular with amateurs and professionals alike. Among the many advantages of the SLR is its versatility—a wide range of lenses, filters and other accessories can be fitted quickly and easily—and the fact that no matter what lens or other attachment is fitted to the camera, the viewfinder always shows exactly what is 'seen' by the lens. With built-in electronic flash, to which the shutter is synchronized, the SLR can be used both indoors and out to equal effect. The most advanced models are totally automatic with exposure meter, shutter and film advance all electronically controlled. Much of the improvement in the quality of colour photography has also been due to refinements in the quality of emulsion used on the films. The skill of the photographer in setting up a shot such as the one below, and in selecting the most appropriate filters, is enhanced by the subtle skin tones and clear primary colours which the film produces.

COMMUNICATION AND INFORMATION

The superheterodyne radio receiver goes into mass production and a new era in radio begins. Uniform reception over a wide range of station frequencies is now possible because the superheterodyne changes the frequency of an incoming signal by offsetting it against a second one, and only amplifies that precise frequency. Since it is more sensitive to weak signals, and can tune into stations more selectively, the 'superhet' monopolizes the US luxury market throughout the twenties.

America's first dial telephones are introduced by AT&T in Norfolk, Va. Ironically, the company has earlier rejected the possibility of using the system.

President of America's GEC, Owen Young, founds RCA (Radio Corporation of America). An anti-trust court action soon splits GEC and RCA apart, leaving RCA to grow into a giant of the radio industry.

TRANSPORT AND WARFARE

Stationary radial engines make a comeback in aircraft after being largely superseded some 10 years before by the lighter, spinning rotary engine, which is fixed directly to the propeller and rotates with it. The improved stationary radial engine saves the power which would be required to spin it, driving the propeller via a crankshaft instead.

A single foot pedal operates the first coupled four-wheel brakes, featured on the French luxury car, the Hispano-Suiza H6B. Drivers no longer have to apply a hand and foot brake simultaneously. The H6B's brakes will be copied by all major car manufacturers within the next decade.

A Vickers Vimy is the chosen plane of Ross and Keith Smith on their historic flight from Britain to Australia. The 11,294-ml (18,172-km) journey is completed in just under a month and wins them a £10,000 prize, offered by the Australians.

Motor scooters enjoy a brief vogue in Europe. Unlike their American forbear, the 1915 Auto-Ped, most of them have seats, and a few—the 1920 British Unibus, for instance—have streamlined, enclosed bodies which anticipate later scooter design.

ENERGY AND INDUSTRY

Shock waves created by man-made explosions are the key to a new technique for probing the structure of the rocks beneath the earth's surface. This seismic survey notes the time taken for the waves to be reflected back to a device at the surface, and then builds up a profile of the rocks.

Machines continue to replace manpower at an accelerating rate in US industry. In the 60 years since 1859, the output of goods has increased 33 times but with only a seven-fold increase in manpower, from 1.3 million workers to 9.1 million.

MEDICINE AND FOOD PRODUCTION

Danish zoologist and physiologist August Krogh shows that blood supply is diminished to parts of the body which are temporarily idle—such as an empty stomach or resting muscles—while capillaries remain 'open' in those parts, like the liver, brain and skin, which are always active. His observations are important for the understanding of vascular disease.

In Britain, W.B. Cannon and W.M. Bayliss report that the drop in blood pressure which occurs in shock is triggered by the release of some chemical substance from the injured muscle.

The prevention of botulism comes nearer when US bacteriologist Georgiana Burke brackets the causative organisms into two strains, types A and B, each of which requires a separate antitoxin.

FRINGE BENEFITS

The first airline companies offer pre-packed lunchboxes at mealtimes.

16½ hours after struggling to take off from Newfoundland under the weight of extra fuel tanks on their Vickers Vimy, John Alcock and Arthur Whitten Brown are forced by low cloud to land in a peat bog in Clifden, Ireland—an early end to the first non-stop transatlantic flight. In the air, the engines iced up so badly that Brown was forced to crawl out on the wings to clear them. To make up for their unceremonious landing, the two airmen will go on to a heroes' welcome in London, where they will receive a £10,000 prize and will be knighted by King George V.

Three US Navy flying-boats attempt the first flight across the Atlantic. Only one—the NC-4—finishes the 3,925-ml (6,315-km) journey to England, completed in stages via the Azores in about 57 hrs. 68 US Navy destroyers, stationed at 50-ml (80-km) intervals, monitor the aircraft's progress and safety.

Hanso Henricus a Idzerda begins transmitting his 'Dutch Concerts' from The Hague. British radio enthusiasts are inspired to press for similar broadcasts in Britain, following the relaxation of wartime restrictions.

The flip-flop electronic switching circuit, so called because it 'flips' and 'flops' from one stable state to another, is the heart of the high-speed electronic counting system which will become the key function of the digital computers of the future. Inventors are US physicists Eccles and Jordan.

The crystal microphone, destined to be widely used in home tape recorders and public address systems, is made in the USA by Nicholson. The mike works on the piezo-electric principle, by which small voltages are produced on the surface of a solid such as a crystal. Sound quality is good, and costs low, but the mike reacts adversely to heat, humidity and rough handling.

Transatlantic flights become all the rage...the first, made in stages, is eclipsed by Alcock and Brown's non-stop crossing. A month later, the British R34 becomes the first airship to cross the Atlantic, carrying the first aerial stowaway. The R34 attracts large crowds at the end of its 4½-day journey to the USA, and makes a dramatic midnight circuit of the Empire State Building as it leaves for home.

Trams approach the peak of their popularity in Britain. The number of fare-paying journeys on trams has doubled since 1905 to nearly 5,000 million a year. In 1923 the number of US tram passengers will rise to 14,000 million—the highest ever, and nearly three times as many as in 1902.

The Italian Isotta-Fraschini Tipo 8 introduces the straight-eight engine to production cars. Improved engineering solves the problem of vibration caused by setting the engine's eight cylinders in a line. The engine will soon become fashionable for higher-priced cars.

Commercial air travel expands as a result of the post-war surplus of pilots and planes: small, fast aircraft are adapted to carry mail or fare-paying passengers, while larger, multi-engined bombers become peaceful transporters of commercial cargo.

Belling introduce the first popular electric domestic cooker, which has been developed during the war for cooking in submarines. Called the Modernette, this small cooker is cheap, lightweight and reliable; but its success is limited, since only a fifth of British homes have a mains supply of electricity.

The large turbo-alternators generating electricity at Blaydon Burn power station in Britain are cooled for the first time by forcing air into them. Air cooling will soon be widely employed to prevent alternators from overheating.

Light bulbs without 'pips' appear. When a bulb was sealed after air had been evacuated, a little glass spike was left on its crown; now, by extracting air through the base instead of the crown, one of the bulb's points of weakness—the 'pip'—is eliminated.

While treating victims of mustard gas poisoning, E.B. Khrumbaar notices that the poison has a marked cell-destroying action on lymph tissue. This stimulates research into cancer of the lymph, which establishes that, given in controlled doses, the deadly gas brings about temporary remission.

British scientist R.A. Fisher statistically analyses data, gathered since 1843, concerning 13 plots in one field which have been given the same fertilizer treatment every year. His analysis paves the way for a more methodical approach to agricultural field trials. For example, the minimum size and number of test plots can be calculated more accurately, and the results more reliably assessed.

Belgian Jules Bordet, a pioneer of immunology, discovers that a second substance in the blood serum, apart from the specific antibody, is involved in the destruction of invading bacteria.

Lines of the Citroën Type A assemble in Europe's first mass-production motor car factory. A maker of car gears during World War I, André Citroën astutely adapts Henry Ford's revolutionary methods to produce a large output of low-priced cars.

Rethinking trains

The trains of the world are hauled by three sorts of motive power—steam, electric and diesel. Of the three, it is steam that fires train lovers with emotion, and although many might think that the age of steam is long gone, steam engines still play a significant role on the world's railways. In much of Asia, Africa and South America, for example, steam engines are needed to fill gaps in diesel services caused by breakdowns. And of the 9,000 locomotives in China, some 80 per cent are powered by steam.

In 1829, when George Stevenson's 'Rocket' reached 26 mph (47 km/h) it proved once and

An American steam locomotive hauls a fast passenger train out of Chicago in 1952. For countries such as the USA and Britain, the old age of steam was, after a century and a half, drawing to a close. But steam is still in use in China and India, and in Eastern European and African countries with plentiful coal supplies. As oil prices soar, plans are now afoot for a new steam era: South African railways, for example, have already put their computer-designed 'Red Devil' steam locomotive into service.

Diesel locomotives, *below,* brought faster, smoother services to the many railways that adopted them in the fifties and sixties. They were most popular in the USA, where long sidings permitted them to be worked in twos, threes, fours and even fives, giving enormous power from a unit whose weight was well distributed and therefore did not cause excess track wear. By the mid-seventies, the prohibitive cost of oil had made them inordinately expensive to run. In the eighties, only oil-rich nations such as Saudi Arabia and Iraq—who has recently ordered 72 new, high-powered diesel units from France—were investing in large diesel fleets.

for all that steam traction was swift enough to oust the horse. Steam locomotives were set to haul nearly all the world's locomotives for well over a century. The electric train—either hauled by a locomotive or propelled by motors driving some of the train's axles—was developed in the late nineteenth century. Initially, it met the need for cleaner locomotives to haul trains in cities and through tunnels. However, railway bosses soon found that although an electrified railway system is expensive to install, it is the most economical to operate—provided that it is intensively used.

And because an electric train can draw on extra reserves of power (from the generating station) for special tasks, acceleration and hill climbing are excellent, and high speeds can be reached and maintained with ease.

Diesel locomotives, first used to haul trains in the USA and Tunisia in 1924, also proved superior to steam: acceleration was better, and they required smaller crews. Like most contemporary diesel locomotives, these early prototypes were diesel-electric units. A diesel engine was used to power an electric motor which, in turn, drove the wheels.

If the running costs of the three types of locomotives are compared, *below,* results reveal that a diesel locomotive is three times as costly as an electric one. If the three were hitched to trains of equal weight, and the same amount spent on fuel for each, the electric locomotive would haul the train three times as far as the diesel and the steam locomotive twice as far. According to one estimate, by 2010 diesel prices will have risen 175%, electricity prices only 50%.

Diesel

Steam

Electricity

In the fifties large diesel fleets were established in countries unwilling to meet the high capital costs of electrification. But by the seventies, most of the 56 countries who depended upon diesel-powered trains found themselves in an unenviable position when oil prices rocketed following the world energy crisis of 1973.

The price of coal has, in contrast, increased at roughly the general rate of inflation. As a result, many railway administrators are being forced to rethink the future of their fleets. Denmark, for instance, after replacing all her steam locomotives with diesels, has now begun to implement electrification plans so that by 2005, some 90 per cent of all her rail traffic will be hauled by electric power.

With world oil supplies uncertain, and coal expected to be plentiful for another 200 years, electrified trains, most of which draw their power from coal-fired power stations, appear to be the best candidates for a railway system of the future. Although by the early eighties only 103,120 miles (165,000 km) of track was electrified—13 per cent of the total—by 2050, the figure is expected to have tripled.

The next few decades may see the redesign of diesel locomotives so that they can use low-cost heavy oil fuels, alcohol fuel or even burn the hydrogen released as a by-product from nuclear power stations. As railways rethink their attitudes, the re-emergence of steam is an even more likely proposition. In the USA, a steam locomotive for the future, the ACE 3000, is already being planned. It would burn low-smoke coal and would be controlled by computer for maximum efficiency of fuel use. So the new age of steam may be just around the next corner.

An electric train draws its power from a generating station. The electricity is conveyed to the train by two main systems. Overhead wires, *left*, carrying high-voltage current, are preferred on long-distance routes because they require fewer costly substations. Trains run on this system use electricity more efficiently than those in which current is picked up from a third rail laid on the track. This system, used by Britain's 'Brighton Belle', *below*, is suited to short commuter routes and underground services in which trains are compelled to make frequent stops.

The amount of heat energy a locomotive can extract from its fuel and convert into hauling power is termed its 'thermal efficiency', and is expressed in percentage form, *right*. Although steam locomotives seldom topped a thermal efficiency of 7%, those built by the French engineer André Chapelon attained an impressive 12%. Diesel and electric locomotives are considerably more efficient than steam.

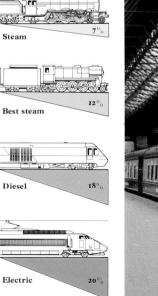

Steam 7%

Best steam 12%

Diesel 18%

Electric 20%

COMMUNICATION AND INFORMATION

Printed labels are in ever-increasing demand. Their production is aided by the advent of a step and repeat machine which can take a negative image and make multiple copies of it, accurately positioned on an offset printing plate. Thus the printer can produce a single sheet of printed paper, with many copies of the same information on it, which is then cut up to make individual labels.

Radio interference generated by engine noise in aircraft is effectively removed by an ignition system developed by H.C. Van de Velde in the USA. The Marconi Co successfully test the device in an experimental DH6 aircraft.

Flying in fog, the pilot of a Handley Page Hannibal demonstrates the first practical radio-telephone service to aircraft. By 1922, radio is fitted to all passenger aircraft flying more than 100 mls (161 km) at a stretch.

An immediate message service with France, Germany and Argentina is established by RCA. With the lifting of wartime restrictions, experimental radio stations flourish: by the end of 1922 there will be 500.

TRANSPORT AND WARFARE

Electric arc welding is introduced into shipyards and immediately proves its superiority over rivetting. With the launch of the first all-welded ship, the *Fullagar*, welded construction is shown to cut building time, save weight and reduce a vessel's resistance when moving through the water.

Advances are made in aircraft design. The US Dayton-Wright RB Racer is the first plane with an efficient retractable undercarriage to reduce drag; while the addition of split flaps and Handley Page slots on the wings makes the aircraft easier and safer to handle at low speeds.

ENERGY AND INDUSTRY

As electricity supplies spread throughout the industrialized countries and demand for electricity increases, power stations produce a higher voltage output to minimize power loss and to meet commercial needs. In so doing, electric cables break down mysteriously until Martin Hochstadter introduces, in the USA, a three-core power cable that does not deform or become burned by the high-voltage electricity.

The first reasonably priced electric hand iron goes on sale in London. As this coincides with the spread of an electricity supply to an increasing number of homes, the iron is soon popular. However, burning of clothes will remain a hazard until the thermostatically controlled iron is introduced in 16 years' time.

The first synthetic, colour-fast green dye is Caledon Jade Green, announced by James Morton in Scotland.

The first practical water-immersion heater has a thermostat to control the temperature of the water automatically—unlike Belling's 1912 electric geyser that boiled 12 pints of water a minute, but used so much power that lights dimmed while the heater was on.

MEDICINE AND FOOD PRODUCTION

German surgeon Ludwig Rehn pioneers surgical intervention in constrictive pericarditis, a condition where the membranous sac around the heart becomes inflamed and thickened, constricting the heart muscle. Rehn cuts a portion of the diseased pericardium to allow the heart room to work.

A London firm markets energen rolls—a bread substitute for diabetics and others anxious to avoid starch in the diet. Energen, made from fresh wheat gluten, is high in nutritional value.

In the USA, A.C. Broders of the Mayo Clinic says that cancer of the lip is much more common in men than in women. Some kind of sore or ulcer often precedes the malignant growth, and pipe smoking is associated with more than three-quarters of all cases seen.

FRINGE BENEFITS

A Detroit newspaper carries radio programme announcements.

At 20.00 hours on 2 November, the first US commercial broadcasting station, Pittsburgh KDKA, goes on the air in time to carry the results of the Harding-Cox presidential election to 300,000 listeners. Operated by the Westinghouse Co, its daily service is financed by advertisements and by sales of the company's 'Music Box' receivers—the first manufactured sets to appear on the US market. The new station immediately establishes message services with France, Germany and Argentina, opening up international as well as domestic communications.

Magnetic tape recording becomes possible outside the laboratory. The reason is the introduction, by Austrian researcher Dr Pfleumer, of plastic tapes in place of steel wires or tapes. The magnetophones marketed by the Germans in the thirties will incorporate these plastic tapes.

In June, Marconi opens the first British public broadcasting station near Chelmsford, Essex. By wireless telephony he transmits a concert by Dame Nellie Melba over 1,000 mls (1,610 km).

The first radio compass is successfully tested when a Curtiss F-5-L naval seaplane flies from Norfolk, Va., to the battleship *Ohio*, 95 mls (153 km) out to sea, and returns, guided by radio signals.

The X-ray fingerprint method of forensic investigation is devised by Dr Pilou in Paris and warmly welcomed in Britain by Scotland Yard. The ball of the finger is powdered with salt, which is opaque to X-rays, then photographed with X-rays and enlarged to reveal the unique pattern of the fingerprint and the shape of the nail.

Former champion cyclist William Morris learns a lesson from Henry Ford and introduces assembly-line production of his Morris Cowley and Oxford cars to Britain. It soon pays off—by 1923 his company, founded 10 years before, will be Britain's biggest car manufacturer.

The US Duesenberg Model A car attracts attention less for its straight-eight engine (it is the first US production car to have one) than for its hydraulically operated brakes. The first system to use brake fluid as a link between pedal and mechanism, it will be employed in most of the world's cars within 30 years.

The Queensland and Northern Territory Aerial Service is formed in formed in Australia, opening scheduled services in 1922. QANTAS will soon partner Britain in experimental mail flights between the two countries, finally joining Imperial Airways in 1934 to start a regular service.

A new type of cable to carry high-voltage electricity from power station to consumer is introduced by Luigi Emanueli of the Italian Pirelli Co. The cable is filled with oil, which is fed from elevated reservoirs and permeates the entire system, so that any distortions caused by the expansion or contraction of the cable core immediately fill with oil, thus overcoming the damage and breakdowns that occurred with previous high-voltage cables.

An imitation coal fire, the 'Magicoal', is invented by H.H. Berry and becomes fashionable among those who want to be modern and electric, while retaining the charm of a real fire. The fuel-effect flicker is made by a red electric bulb shining through perforations in an aluminium wheel, which rotates from the heat rising from the bulb.

US oil wells produce nearly two-thirds of the world's oil supply.

Henry Ford accelerates the production rates of car engine components—particularly cylinder heads and engine blocks—when he introduces the continuous casting of cast iron: instead of one component being moulded at a time, a production line is created on which large numbers of the same component are moulded simultaneously. The technique will spread rapidly and will mechanize many forms of iron foundry moulding.

Karl Spiro and Arthur Stoll extract the alkaloid drug ergotamine from the ergot fungus, *Claviceps purpurea*, which is parasitic on grasses, especially rye. In small doses it will prove effective for treating migraine and, in some cases, for causing abortions.

As France makes abortion illegal, Russia becomes the first country to legalize it. Russian doctors will discourage women from seeking abortion, especially after 10 weeks; France, wanting to build up its war-torn population, threatens severe penalties for anyone performing or undergoing abortion.

William Mayo of Rochester, Minn., advocates a conservative attitude to the removal of female organs, the ovary and uterus, because of the important, though unidentified, hormones they secrete.

Feminine characteristics (such as lack of facial hair or enlargement of the breasts), which result in a man with damaged gonads, are claimed to disappear after R. Lichtenstern transplants a new testis.

Coco Chanel introduces her No 5 perfume.

Dial telephones appear in Britain following the installation of an automatic exchange in Leeds. Local calls can now be made without an operator: the dial triggers electrical pulses which can identify the correct line.

The Dutch embark on the greatest ever land-reclamation scheme. 1,289 million cu ft (36.5 million cu m) of boulder clay and sand will be dredged from the Zuiderzee to build embankments which, by 1932, will join North Holland to the island of Wieringen and that to Friesland.

Plastics come of age

Plastics have changed the face of domestic and industrial life in the twentieth century. All plastics are giant molecules or polymers which, under heat and pressure will soften so that they can become moulded and extruded. Perhaps surprisingly, plants provided the raw material for celluloid, the first man-made plastic and the one plastic widely available as the new century dawned.

Brushes, boxes, spectacle frames and many other domestic items were moulded from celluloid, largely with three visual effects—tortoiseshell, ivory and pearl—and celluloid was soon to become the material base for the newly flowering movie business. Two other plastics with natural connections had anticipated celluloid in the market-place. The first was casein, made from skimmed milk and fashioned in several colours as a substitute for bone and horn in the manufacture of buttons, buckles and hair slides; the second, shellac, was made from the secretion of an Asian beetle, and formed the first phonograph discs.

Bakelite, a brittle resin originally produced in 1910 as a coating material to protect precious metals, was moulded in the twenties into useful items such as electrical components, door handles and knobs for crystal sets. In 1924 the first amino plastic (a polymer derived from ammonia) entered the market and, as Beetle-ware, was made into cream-coloured or pale green picnic sets, cream telephones and white electrical fittings. For more than a decade it was the only pale-coloured plastic that could be bought.

Scientifically speaking, the thirties was the golden age of plastics. In this decade, new moulding and extrusion techniques, combined with the fruits of chemists' curiosity, led to the invention and development of such now familiar plastics as polyvinyl chloride (PVC), polystyrene, polyethylene (polythene), melamine, nylon and acrylics such as Perspex. Although the intervention of World War II delayed the commercial exploitation of these plastics, the

Plastics have shaped everyday domestic items since the start of the century. Celluloid, the first truly domestic plastic, was the material used for the 'mother of pearl' box and tortoiseshell hairbrush, *below*, and the clock casing, *centre*. Both the Sonorette radio, *right*, and Michelin Man ashtray, *below*, are made from Bakelite, a brittle plastic that can be pigmented only in black, dark brown, maroon, green and blue. A good insulator, Bakelite has also been widely used for plugs, sockets, lampstands and telephones.

The pink plastic ashtray, *below left*, was moulded from urea formaldehyde, a resin first marketed in 1924; but, when used for utensils such as picnic cups, the plastic often became badly marked with a 'crazed' pattern. The dark red lidded box, *below*, was made from melamine formaldehyde. Introduced in 1939, it was so resistant to water and scratching that it quickly ousted urea formaldehyde ware.

Beetleware, the trade name for the plastic thiourea, made an immediate impact when first marketed in the twenties. For the first time, colourful plastics such as the pale green cruet, cup and saucer and vacuum flask, *above*, flooded into the home. In the USA Mickey Mouse Beetleware teasets were bought in their thousands.

The perfume bottle, mirror and napkin ring, *left*, are all composed of Catalin, a plastic with a chemical composition similar to Bakelite. As a transparent liquid it was used to coat wood, producing a *bois glacé* effect for jewellery and desk coverings in the thirties.

changeover from plastics made from natural, organic materials, to those synthesized in the laboratory from organic chemicals, was nearly complete. Coal had become the essential raw material for making plastics, and would remain so until petroleum took over in the early fifties.

The post-war explosion of new plastics was powered by techniques such as rotational moulding which made PVC into dolls, toys, beach balls and artificial flowers. Blow moulding was employed in the early fifties to make polythene bottles for cosmetics and pharmaceuticals, while extrusion techniques made polythene and PVC into improved electrical cable insulators, and made PVC into sheets, pipes and gutterings.

Huge stocks of war surplus styrene were seized on by the plastics industry and either used to make high impact polystyrene, or compounded with rubber to form enormously strong, chemically resistant plastics. With the advent of vacuum techniques, these plastics could be moulded into boats, sinks, surfboards and interior panels for cars. By the same method, polystyrene could be shaped into refrigerator linings, egg boxes and plant holders; acrylics into baths, light fittings, advertising signs and aircraft windows; high-density polythene into water tanks and deep freezers; PVC into food containers, packaging materials and machine covers and cases.

The image of plastics has somehow suffered from a 'bad press': they have been branded since their birth with the notion that they are substitutes for something better. In reality, they have revolutionized industry worldwide. And, although there have been few startling innovations since the fifties, steady advances in plastic manufacture over the last 20 years have produced a total of 60 different types. It has been estimated that one third of the world's chemists and chemical engineers are currently engaged in plastics research and development; in 1983, the total volume of plastics made will equal the volume of metals produced.

Polythene was used to make the plastic flowers, and the bottles for the orange juice and face cream, *below*. The dustpan and brush and clothes pegs, *below left*, and the pen tops, *below right*, are polypropylene.

A 'double plastic' or copolymer, based on styrene, was the material of which the pepper grinder and red container filled with felt tips, *below*, the mug and toothbrushes, *left*, the barrel of the blue fountain pen, *below left*, and the construction toy, *below*, were made. The knife and fork, *below left*, are of toughened polystyrene, while the green plate is a mixture of plastics filled with wood. The spectacle lenses are polycarbonate.

The versatile plastic PVC (polyvinyl chloride) was used to make the credit cards, hamburger, sandals and the bristles on the green brush, *above*, plus the barrels of the felt tip pens, *above right*. The coloured discs, *right*, were pressed from a copolymer, combining PVC and polyvinyl acetate.

COMMUNICATION AND INFORMATION

The blind can now read by sound, thanks to the optophone invented in Paris by Dr Fournier d'Albe. Using selenium, an electric battery and a telephone receiver, the optophone 'sings' a series of musical notes corresponding to letters on the printed page.

Regular broadcasts of music begin in Britain. Until, after a few months, a monopoly of the airwaves is assumed by the BBC, the transmissions are made from Marconi's research station near Chelmsford in Essex.

More space is found on the air waves. While the first medium-wave radio broadcast is transmitted in the USA, amateurs are discovering the potential of short-wave radio bands which, until now, have been thought useful only for short-distance transmission. Trial broadcasts from the USA to Britain prove that broadcasts on short-wave can be heard thousands of miles away. When Franklin introduces directional antennae to 'beam' short-wave signals, the problems of interference are also significantly reduced.

TRANSPORT AND WARFARE

Jack Knight covers 672 mls (1,081 km) through ice and snow in only 10 hrs on the first stage of an experimental flight across the USA to demonstrate the feasibility of a transcontinental airmail service. Two more pilots take his aircraft on to New York, setting a total west-to-east flight time of 33 hrs 20 min.

ENERGY AND INDUSTRY

The incredibly accurate free-pendulum clock— it loses only one hundredth of a second each year—is perfected by W.H. Shortt, a British civil engineer who works for the railways. Powered electromagnetically, the clock is so accurate that it indicates the irregularities in the earth's rotation, and its precision means that it will be installed as the main timekeeper in the principal observatories of the world.

The first electric kettle to have its heating element totally immersed in water is introduced by Bulpitt & Sons, Birmingham, England. This 'Swan' kettle has more than double the heating power of previous kettles.

The first steel pipes with electrically welded seams go into production for use in the gas pipeline industry.

MEDICINE AND FOOD PRODUCTION

Harvard biologist Edward Murray East, and Princeton botanist George Harrison Shull, perfect a hybrid corn (maize) variety that will greatly improve crop yields.

The chance of a reprieve for millions of diabetics comes when Canadians Frederick Banting and Charles Best succeed in isolating insulin from the pancreas. Insulin reduces blood-sugar which, in diabetes mellitus, builds up to dangerous levels, leading eventually to coma and death. The first diabetic to benefit from this discovery—a 14-year-old boy—will begin life-saving insulin therapy in January 1922.

Contrast radiography takes an important step forward with the use of a new radio-opaque substance to yield clearer X-ray images of some internal organs. At the Mayo Clinic at Rochester, Minn., sodium iodide is injected into the subject's vein; rapidly excreted by the kidneys, it produces a clearer outline of these organs on the X-ray. This is quickly followed by the use of similar contrast media for viewing the blood vessels (1923) and the gall-bladder (1924).

FRINGE BENEFITS

The new automatic fire extinguisher fights fires quicker.

Californian medical student John Larson invents the lie detector.

US Director of Arsenals, General John Thompson, sees the Colt Co put his 'tommy-gun' into production. Small enough to fit into a violin case, the gun will become a favourite with gangsters. In 1928 it will be modified to become the first sub-machine-gun to be adopted by the US armed forces, and thousands will later be issued to British forces waiting to repel the expected German invasion during the Battle of Britain in 1940. British Prime Minister, Winston Churchill, is seen examining one during a tour of north-eastern coastal fortifications.

Fog signals—the first radio beacons in the USA—go into operation in three lighthouses at the entrance to New York harbour. By beaming radio waves around the horizon, they enable ships and aircraft to establish their positions.

The quartz crystal brings a new stability to the fluctuating radio signal, thanks to US scientist Walter G. Cady's discovery of the remarkable stabilizing quality of the crystal. The quartz crystal oscillator, similar to that used in a quartz clock, maintains a steady carrier frequency and prevents any overlap of frequencies at the receiver.

Playwright Karel Câpek coins the word 'robot' in his play *RUR* (Rossum's Universal Robots): the word (from the Russian for 'work') becomes a synonym for the remote-controlled mechanical 'men' built in the twenties and thirties.

The first telephone call from a private number to an aircraft is made. With the cooperation of the British Post Office and the Croydon Ground Station, near London, Sir Samuel Instone speaks to the pilot of a Vickers G-EASI.

Automatic steering for ships is introduced. The gyrocompass is the primary component of an automatic pilot which keeps a ship on a set course without the intervention of a helmsman.

US scientist Thomas Midgley synthesizes tetraethyl lead which, when added to gasoline, eliminates engine 'knocking' and improves a car's performance. Its universal addition to gasoline by the late twenties will be questioned later in the century: pumped out by car exhausts, it will be seen as a hazard to health and environment.

The first modern escalator, the Otis L, is adopted by US department stores and railroad stations. The new model has a safer comb-plate landing device in place of the side exit door of its precursor, invented by Elisha Otis.

Acetate rayon fibre starts commercial life in Britain under the trade-name Celanese. In the same year Arthur Eichengrün designs a prototype of the modern injection moulding machine for the shaping of rubber and plastic materials. This machine will improve the production of acetate rayon, which will become the chief thermoplastic moulding material until after World War II, when it will be replaced by polystyrene and polythene.

Rifles and revolvers are the first products of the jigs and fixtures made on a new jig-boring machine produced by the Société Génèvoise d'Instrument de Physique (SIP). Commissioned by the Royal Small Arms Factory at Enfield, England, the jig-boring machine will find wide application in the machine tool world for boring precision holes in exactly the right place. A delicate instrument, it has to be kept in an air-conditioned room and insulated from floor-transmitted vibrations.

Heart disease takes over from tuberculosis as the leading cause of death in the USA. Currently, heart disease accounts for 14% of deaths each year, but this figure will increase to 39% in the next half-century.

US farmers produce a massive surplus of corn and other farm products: the price paid for corn drops from a high of $2 in 1919, to 42 cents per bushel; for wheat, the fall is from $3.50 to $1.

Microsurgery is pioneered by ear specialists who operate using a powerful magnifying instrument to see the delicate structures of the middle and inner ear. In Scandinavia, C.O. Nylen leads the way, performing surgery with a monocular microscope. A year later, G. Holmgren develops the first binocular instrument, which gives a much clearer view of the operating site.

Swiss psychiatrist Hermann Rorschach perfects his 'ink-blot' test as an indicator to personality. Subjects are assessed on their reactions to a series of cards, each bearing a different ink-blot shape.

Johnson & Johnson introduce Band-aid, the first stick-on bandage.

Artificial or 'cultured' pearls are produced.

Van Heusen's stiff but starchless collar appears in the shops.

The virtues of the Austin 7 put thousands of British families on the road for the first time. Soon to be acclaimed as the best small European car of the twenties and thirties, the 7 salvages the fortunes of the company founded by its designer, Herbert Austin. A mere 8 ft 8 in (2.6 m) long, the four-seater has four-wheel brakes and is powered by a four-cylinder engine that can produce speeds of up to 38 mph (61 km/h). Versions of the 7 will be made by companies all over the world: in Japan it is the car on which the Datsun empire is built, and in the USA it will be used to launch the Bantam company—which will go on to create the Jeep during World War II.

The 'box in the corner'

All over the world, more than 300 million people can turn on their television sets and watch the same football game. At the touch of a button, the producer can give viewers the chance to see the vital goal again in slow motion. Hours, days, or even weeks later, the video owner who missed the game can see it on tape. This typifies the scope of television, arguably the most potent communications medium ever invented, which has revolutionized home life and now promises to spearhead the arrival of a new era as the display centre of the home computer.

Despite its modern sophistication, including infrared remote control, slimline transistorized sets and plug-in video, all television works by translating images into signals which are transmitted in the ionosphere, then picked up by a receiver which converts the signals back into visual form. The resulting series of separate images is seen in such quick succession that they appear to move.

With this aim of image transmission in mind, scientists of the 1880s and 1890s had in fact laid many of the practical and theoretical foundations of television at a time when even radio was in its infancy. Much of this early work was done in Germany where inventor Paul Nipkow had patented a system of rotating discs which used a photoelectric cell to generate the signal for transmission. Also in Germany, Ferdinand Braun had invented the cathode-ray tube which, since it translates variations in light intensity into electrical impulses, and can be made to glow when bombarded with electrons, was to become the heart of the television receiver.

Further intensive research into television was carried out in Europe and the USA in the early years of the century, but it was not until John Logie Baird's historic first television transmission in 1926 that the possibilities of television really caught the public imagination. But Baird's achievement was, in a sense, a step backward. The reason: his system was mechanical, that is, it created signals using rotating Nipkow discs, rather than employing the all-electrical system for signal generation, transmission and translation which had been proposed as early as 1906.

Within a decade of its inception, Baird's system had become obsolete. By the end of the thirties it had been ousted by the high-definition Marconi-EMI system in Britain and the RCA system in the USA, both of them based on the cathode-ray tube and both fully electronic. The signals and the final monochrome picture were produced by the horizontal scanning of an electron beam along lines of light-sensitive dots, which were activated when struck by the electrons.

Now the scene was set for the development of colour television, but, ironically, it was again

a mechanical system that was first in service—this time the whirling disc equipped with colour filters (made by American inventor Peter Goldmark) which rotated in front of the camera tube. But it did not last long. In 1953, two years after the first transmission, RCA had perfected an electronic version to a standard still used in the USA. Uniformity still, however, eludes the medium, so that worldwide there are no less than three different colour systems.

The 'box in the corner' has been a permanent piece of domestic furniture for nearly half a century, but new discoveries and technologies promise television a bright new future. Soon television will be readily available in a large-screen format big enough to fill a whole wall, or small enough to slip into a coat pocket or even wear on the wrist.

The scope of television is increasing too. With the launch of new communications satellites it may soon be possible for viewers in Europe to see American broadcasts direct as they are beamed to dish-shaped antennae on the roof or in the garden. On a more parochial level, cable television, fed direct from television companies to subscribers via underground cables, promises to serve more and more minority interests through the creation of speciality 'narrowcasts'.

In the Sony Trinitron, introduced by the Japanese company in 1968, the shadow mask is replaced by an arrangement of several hundred vertical slits, while the luminous areas on the screen are phosphor stripes of red, green and blue. This design, which uses a single electron gun to produce three electron beams side by side, made it possible to make much slimmer sets and give brighter, better registered pictures. The set's main problem is that, on large screens, the stripes are visible.

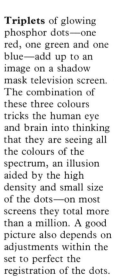

Triplets of glowing phosphor dots—one red, one green and one blue—add up to an image on a shadow mask television screen. The combination of these three colours tricks the human eye and brain into thinking that they are seeing all the colours of the spectrum, an illusion aided by the high density and small size of the dots—on most screens they total more than a million. A good picture also depends on adjustments within the set to perfect the registration of the dots.

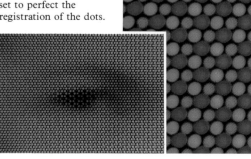

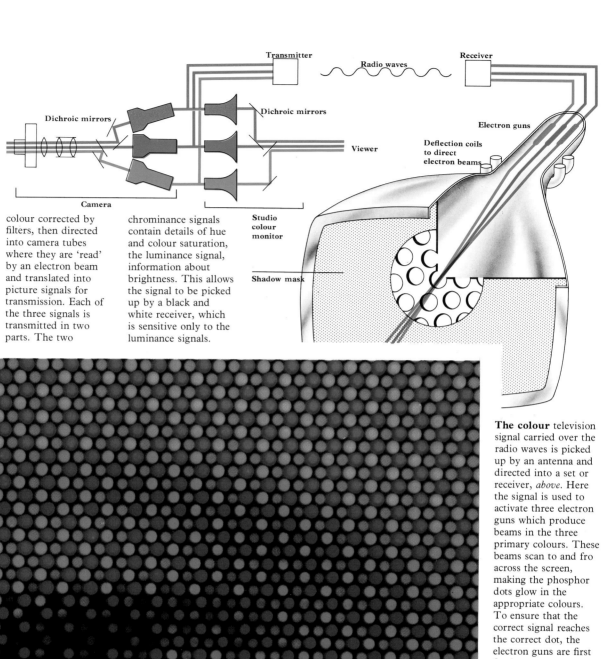

Transmitter

Radio waves

Receiver

Dichroic mirrors

Dichroic mirrors

Electron guns

Viewer

Deflection coils
to direct
electron beams

Camera

Studio
colour
monitor

Shadow mask

The story of a colour television picture begins in the television camera. The beam of light entering the camera is split by dichroic mirrors into its three primary components: red, blue and green. The images from these mirrors are colour corrected by filters, then directed into camera tubes where they are 'read' by an electron beam and translated into picture signals for transmission. Each of the three signals is transmitted in two parts. The two chrominance signals contain details of hue and colour saturation, the luminance signal, information about brightness. This allows the signal to be picked up by a black and white receiver, which is sensitive only to the luminance signals.

The colour television signal carried over the radio waves is picked up by an antenna and directed into a set or receiver, *above*. Here the signal is used to activate three electron guns which produce beams in the three primary colours. These beams scan to and fro across the screen, making the phosphor dots glow in the appropriate colours. To ensure that the correct signal reaches the correct dot, the electron guns are first fired at a screen or shadow mask studded with nearly 400,000 holes. These holes, precisely aligned with the dots on the screen, mask all dots except those of the appropriate colour, so producing a precise image.

COMMUNICATION AND INFORMATION

With the movie *Toll of the Sea*, the Technicolor company, in business in the USA since 1915, has its first commerical success with an improved two-colour process. The double prints, made by cementing two thin films back to back, cause problems for projectionists, but the public are impressed. The process will be used in several movies throughout the twenties, notably in Douglas Fairbanks's *The Black Pirate* (1926).

In Berlin, Tri-Ergon give one of the first commercial demonstrations of sound-on-film. An optical sound track, producing sound said to be of good quality, is carried on the edge of a film strip bearing the pictures.

The phonograph record graver improves sound recording dramatically. Now, instead of singing or playing directly into phonograph horns, artists can record in acoustically correct studios. Electrical impulses from the sound waves vibrate the graver which chisels an impression into wax at the rate of 30 to 5,500 wiggles a second.

In Britain the world's first regular radio broadcasts intended purely for entertainment are transmitted by the BBC. The British Post Office responds by instituting radio licenses. In the USA, 99 new stations open in a single month.

TRANSPORT AND WARFARE

A turning point in railway history is reached when main line electric traction is established as the rail power of the future. Although far more expensive than steam to set up, electric traction is much cheaper to run.

ENERGY AND INDUSTRY

The St Pierre de Vouvray Bridge is opened in France, its span of 430 ft (131 m) over the River Seine setting a record for a bridge made from concrete. The bridge is built from pre-stressed concrete, a technique the designer, Eugène Freyssinet, first proposed nearly 20 years ago.

The light from lighthouses can now stretch farther into the night since high-power incandescent electric lights are available for the first time.

Oil is discovered on the shores of Lake Maracaibo, Venezuela, by US surveyors, and in the future, oil will become the country's most important export.

MEDICINE AND FOOD PRODUCTION

Danish neurologist V. Christiansen is ahead of his time in recognizing that injury to the central nervous system, including the brain, can have repercussions in later life. At his clinic in Copenhagen he has seen cases where symptoms may develop as long as 30 years after the event. He deplores the fact that the Danish Working Men's Compensation Act specifies that all claims must be settled within three years.

An apparatus for measuring minute quantities of liquid is demonstrated in London. The micropipette is initially designed to deliver 0.02 cc of liquid for the Schick tests for diphtheria.

Harriette Chick, in Vienna, shows how rickets can be cured either by cod liver oil or by sunlight. Cod liver oil, used widely in the 19th century, contains Vitamin D; the healing properties of sunlight, first shown by Palm in 1890, are due to the formation of Vitamin D in the skin when exposed to ultraviolet radiation. Vitamin D is established as the essential factor in the building of strong bones in children.

FRINGE BENEFITS

Mah Jongg, the western version of a Chinese game played with tiles, enjoys a vogue among Americans.

Roll your own with a cigarette-making machine.

Stimulated by Marconi's first broadcasts in 1920, the British wireless industry gears up to prepare for the demand generated by the first BBC broadcasts. Burndept (Burnham from Deptford) produce their Mark IV 4-valve receiver, the Rolls-Royce of radio. Well beyond the means of the average worker, it is worth saving up for: the Burndept IV can receive broadcast concerts anywhere in Britain and, if used within 50 mls of a high-powered transmitter, can be heard from more than 500 yds away. For the more modest, crystal sets are available at chemists' and stationers' shops, for the price of a radio licence (10 shillings—less than $3).

Printing technology and education advance as the St Bride's Foundation Printing School moves to larger, more modern and better equipped premises in London's Stamford Street and is renamed the London School of Printing and Kindred Trades. The school is gaining—and will retain—international renown for educational excellence and technological innovation.

Using an echo sounder, the depth of the oceans can be accurately measured. The sounder, which makes full use of the fact that water is an excellent medium for transmitting sound, bounces sound waves off the ocean floor and measures the distance by timing the return echo. Born out of the research of Professor R.A. Fessenden, it is to become crucial for submarine detection in World War II.

Anticipating a radio boom, the Marconi Co market their Marconiphone Crystal Junior V1 and V2 models, the first ready-made home radio sets to appear in British shops. But many enthusiasts continue to build their own sets.

A home cinema system, using 9.5 mm safety films printed by reduction from standard professional movies, is launched in France by Pathé. Next year, Pathé make home-made movies possible by introducing a camera using the same format.

The first underground railway train with automatic doors goes into service on London's Piccadilly Line.

A German sailplane makes an hour-long unpowered soaring flight. Because of restrictions placed on their aviation by the peace settlement of 1918, the Germans do not join the 'Flying Club' but concentrate on the development of heavier-than-air sailplanes. By the thirties they will lead the world in this field.

The largest hydro-electric power station in the world is completed at Queenston, Ontario. Using the cascade on the Canadian side of the Niagara Falls to drive its turbines, it will generate enough electricity to supply the needs of over half a million people.

The future of acetate rayon fibre for silky-looking clothes is assured when A. Clevel discovers an entirely new class of dyes—the disperse dyes—which are unique in their ability to colour the rayon fibres.

Named after two researchers at the Pasteur Institute—Albert Calmette and Camille Guérin—the BCG tuberculosis vaccine is first introduced in France. This vaccine, developed from a strain of bovine TB, is used initially on infants.

Roumanian hospital director Louis Hartmann uses hypnosis in obstetrics for safe, painless deliveries without the use of drugs. The duration of labour is shortened as the mother has contractions at the doctor's suggestion, and little blood is lost.

Colostrum is the first milk produced by mammalian females after giving birth. Theobald Smith and Ralph Little carry out experiments with calves to test the importance of colostrum to the newborn. They discover that, while it does not seem to provide any special nutritional benefits, colostrum has the effect of conferring immunity to infection on the young until its own defences begin to function.

The first US soybean processing plant opens in Illinois. It extracts 96% of the oil from the beans; the remaining cake is sold as a protein supplement for animal feed.

Paper manufacture from hardwood is pioneered in Australia.

In the last days of its broadcasting monopoly, Marconi House, in London's Strand, transmits a duet. The two singers cannot share a microphone, as the 'telephone' models are only suitable for close use. The BBC will adopt the Marconi-Sykes 'magnetophone' which, although unwieldy, does permit performers to stand at a distance. The chimes seen behind the pianist are used to give the time signal—a service shortly to be taken over by the BBC. Fearing the same surge of activity that overloaded the US airwaves, the Post Office gives the BBC exclusive broadcasting rights and limits the number of transmitters. Most rural districts will have to wait at least three years for a radio service.

COMMUNICATION AND INFORMATION

Speaking from his office at the American Telephone and Telegraph office in New York on 14 January, H.B. Thayer makes the first telephone call from Britain to the USA. The recipient of the call is Frank Gill, AT & T's British chief engineer. The call lasts two hours. Another part of the experiment is the use of a loudspeaker using 20 valves. The result is a massive improvement in sound strength and clarity.

The spectroheliograph is invented in the USA by astronomer G. Hale, who uses it to photograph the surface of the sun in a single wavelength of light, corresponding to a solar element such as hydrogen or helium. By slowly moving the instrument's aperture over the image of the sun, the entire solar disc can be photographically recorded.

Ship-to-ship communication begins: a spoken message transmitted from the White Star liner *Olympic* in the Atlantic is received loud and clear by the *Celtic* in New York Harbour.

A microphone, with a ribbon of aluminium foil suspended between the poles of a magnet, becomes standard in many recording studios. Replacing the clumsy, immovable carbon-granule mike, it gives unimpaired sound and allows performers freedom of movement.

TRANSPORT AND WARFARE

Although World War I ships of all kinds were converted into aircraft-carriers, HMS *Hermes*, launched in 1919 and now completed, is the first ship to be specifically designed as an aircraft-carrier.

The larger US car manufacturers decide to introduce new models of their cars every year, in order to squeeze out of the market those small companies which cannot afford an annual change of style. Success is not long in coming: by 1935 the number of US car companies will have dropped from 43 to 10, confirming that the future of the motor car industry lies in mass production.

A diesel engine is used to drive the Benz Sendling agricultural tractor—a rare power source for a motor vehicle because, although its economy is ideal for industry, ships and trains, the diesel engine is heavier and slower to accelerate than a gasoline engine. But Benz will persevere with it, building the first diesel truck in 1924 and, in the thirties, his diesel-powered Mercedes-Benz cars.

ENERGY AND INDUSTRY

The world's first wide strip mill for producing sheet steel goes into operation in the USA. The process involves rolling at high speed a very long strip of steel, up to several feet wide, and then cutting the strip into sheets of the required length. Cars and domestic items, such as refrigerators, will be immediately affected.

The search for cheaper materials to build houses for the lower-income groups leads to the introduction of 'cellular concrete', which has a mere one in nine ratio of cement to clinker. The concrete is used to build a group of two-storey houses at Scheveningen, Holland, and later at Edinburgh, Scotland.

MEDICINE AND FOOD PRODUCTION

In Britain, Sir Henry Souttar pioneers cardiac surgery by attempting to widen a constricted mitral valve. Other surgeons tentatively follow his lead, but surgery on the heart itself will not be common for 30 years.

A new tetanus toxoid vaccine is developed by French bacteriologist Gaston Ramon. It will be widely used for immunization against tetanus— also known as 'lockjaw'—which is caused by infection through open wounds.

FRINGE BENEFITS

The music typewriter types scores as well as words on the same machine.

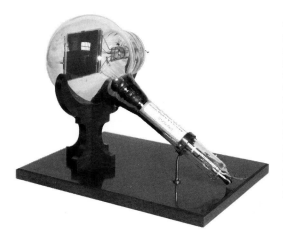

Vladimir Zworykin's invention of the iconoscope marks the first step towards the development of electronic television. The image is focused, by an external lens, on a screen inside the glass vacuum tube, while a high-velocity electron beam scans this screen from the other side in a sequence of horizontal lines. As they are struck by the beam, the mosaic of photoelectric elements which constitute the screen emit impulses varying in strength according to the amount of light falling upon them. This information is built up into a picture signal which can then modulate the intensity of an electron beam in a receiver tube, as it scans a fluorescent screen in the same line pattern.

WARNER BROS. SUPREME TRIUMPH
AL JOLSON in *The* **JAZZ SINGER**

A portrait is successfully broadcast by wireless telephony at the first attempt..For the experiment French scientist Fournier d'Albe chooses a picture of King George V. The image is coded by dividing it into 30 lines, each split into 20 squares. Each square is assigned a letter indicating its shading, and each letter is then dictated into the microphone. Within 22 mins the King's face is reproduced as a series of dots.

Britain's first truly portable radio receiver comes on the market. The Burndept Ethophone V Portable is the size of—and designed to look like—a suitcase.

Eastman Kodak introduce 16 mm film, with a camera and projector for home movies. The system is inexpensive because the film is small and reversal processing almost halves the cost of development. Unlike professional film, the home version is non-flammable.

The largest cable ever manufactured for deep-sea operations is laid between Britain and the USA establishing the sixth transatlantic cable circuit. Containing 80,000 mls (128,000 km) of iron and steel wires—more than enough to encircle the Earth three times—and with 4,000,000 lb (1,800,000 kg) of copper and 1,800,000 lb (815,000 kg) of gutta-percha, it has twice the capacity of any other existing cable and can transmit 1,200 letters a minute: 600 in each direction simultaneously.

Pan American World Airways starts life as a New York air taxi service, using nine US Navy flying-boats that are about to be scrapped.

Spanish aeronaut Juan de la Cierva cracks the most complex aerodynamic problems of rotorcraft. His autogyro looks like a propeller-driven monoplane topped by a large rotor. The rotor is set in motion by the engine, but continues to turn by the action of the slipstream through the blades—a principle Cierva called autorotation.

ZR-1, known as the *Shenandoah*, is the first rigid airship to be inflated with safe, incombustible helium gas instead of hydrogen. Authorized by the US government in 1919, but not completed until this year, the Navy airship will make 37 flights before its destrucion in a storm in 1925, when it breaks up in flight with the loss of 14 lives.

Aboard his yacht *Elettra*, Guglielmo Marconi conducts experiments in the development of shortwave wireless communications, which will prove crucial for ship-to-ship and ship-to-shore communications.

Chicago's electricity supply is greatly increased when the Crawford Avenue Power Station installs steam turbines which use excess steam to regenerate heat. The turbines so successfully raise the thermal output that many power stations around the world will adopt the system.

The photoelectric cell is developed and, acting as an 'electric eye', opens the way to future devices such as automatic doors, intrusion alarms and the light-activated counters used to assess the numbers of people passing a certain spot.

The 'Regulo', the first commercially successful thermostat in domestic ovens, is fitted to the New World H16 Radiation Gas Cooker made by the Davis Gas Stove Co, giving the user total control over the cooking process. The thermostat expands to control the flame according to one of 15 temperature settings on the control knob.

A new inhalation anaesthetic, ethylene, is introduced into US surgery by Isabella Herb, A.B. Luckhardt and J.B. Carter. It works more quickly than ether, but is just as explosive.

Thorvald Madsen of Copenhagen produces a 'killed' vaccine to combat whooping cough (pertussis), which is very common in children. Trials in the Faroe Islands, and elsewhere, prove its effectiveness in preventing the disease. It is many years before it is overtaken by the 'triple-antigen' injections: a three-fold package of immunizations against whooping cough, diphtheria and tetanus.

Lee de Forest demonstrates his 'Phonofilm' sound-on-film system, and by 1925 over 30 cinemas in the eastern USA will be equipped for 'talkies'. However, silent films will remain popular until 1927, when the irresistible appeal of Al Jolson in *The Jazz Singer* leads to the general adoption of sound.

The first successful in-flight refuelling of an aircraft is made during a record-breaking endurance flight by two US Army aviators. They keep their DM 4B airborne for 37 hrs 15 mins, replenishing their fuel supply 15 times from a sister aircraft.

COMMUNICATION AND INFORMATION

The New Year is ushered in by the first broadcast of the chimes of London's Big Ben. The chimes are then instituted as a daily radio time signal.

In Britain, S.G. Brown Ltd bring out their supersensitive Crystavox loudspeaker in time for the opening of the wireless station at Daventry, Warwickshire, next year. Attached to a home crystal set in place of earphones, it can fill a whole room with high-quality sound. Needing no valves, batteries or accumulators, it cuts down the radio's running costs considerably.

Photographs are transmitted from Britain to the USA for the first time. Devised by R. Ranger of RCA, the method involves mounting a print on a rotating cylinder, which is then scanned by a light beam.

The Ernemann 'Ermanox' camera, with an ultrafast f/2 Ernostar lens, promotes the rise of 'candid' photography at night and indoors.

TRANSPORT AND WARFARE

Nigel Gresley's famous 'Flying Scotsman' steams over the tracks between London and Edinburgh in the record-breaking time of 8¼ hrs. But its claim to the title of Britain's most powerful express train is immediately challenged by the smaller 'Caerphilly Castle'. Gresley reluctantly accedes the title and, swallowing his pride, borrows the 'Castle' to improve the 'Flying Scotsman's' design.

The German Junkers G-23 ushers in the age of the trimotor airliner. One-engined aircraft cannot carry heavy enough payloads; two-engined aircraft can— but run the risk of engine failure; a third engine on the nose gives both power and reliability.

The constant-speed propeller brings new efficiency and safety to aircraft. The propeller is geared to the engine so that it automatically adapts the pitch of its blades to the engine's revs, maintaining a constant speed and hence the most efficient use of the available power. Widely adopted in the thirties, it will enable twin-engined aircraft to fly safely with one engine dead.

ENERGY AND INDUSTRY

The Aga cooker, which provides perfectly controlled and clean cooking from solid fuel, is invented by a blind Swedish physicist, Dr Gustav Galen. Later models will be equipped with a built-in water tank, connected to the mains supply, to provide domestic hot water; others will be designed to be run by gas or oil.

Rubber products, such as car tyres, are given a greater life-span when the first commercial antioxidant, whose application prevents oxygen corroding natural rubber, becomes available.

German engineers construct the world's first concrete shell roof at Jena, so creating a new structural technique for building. The thin shell's inside surface will be laid out as a 'sky' for the planetarium designed by Zeiss.

MEDICINE AND FOOD PRODUCTION

Soybeans are gathered for the first time by combine harvester, in the USA. The soybean will be planted in increasing quantities by Mid-west farmers as demand grows for its oil and protein. By the eighties, the USA will produce about two-thirds of the world's soybeans.

In Melbourne, Australian surgeon R. Hamilton Russell publishes his classic paper on the balanced traction treatment of fractures of the thigh bone's shaft. The knee is elevated to allow the traction to work in a direct line on the fragments.

In the USA George and Gladys Dick isolate the scarlet fever streptococcus and devise a way to test human susceptibility to it.

FRINGE BENEFITS

Celluwipes, the first disposable handkerchiefs—later known as Kleenex—are introduced by Kimberley Clark.

The self-winding watch is patented.

In Czechoslovakia, Vaclac Holek develops the 7.22 mm (0.284 in) light machine-gun which, after modification, is known as the ZB26—the forerunner of the Bren gun. This will become the standard light machine-gun of the Czech army, and will soon equip soldiers all over the world.

Spiral binding, named Spirex and invented by Staale, revolutionizes the notebook. A loose coil of wire binds the leaves, which can be carried over to the back of the book, or torn out without the book falling to pieces.

British explorer Sir Napier Shaw discovers, when half way across the Atlantic, that a weather map of the whole northern hemisphere can be made using information from both sides of the Atlantic and from passing ships.

In the USA, Rice and Kellogg of GEC patent their moving coil loudspeaker which cuts down audio distortion drastically. On the market the following year, the loudspeaker can fill a hall with high-quality sound.

'We speak across space and some day we shall see as we speak': so ran the message conveyed in the first direct wireless link-up between Cornwall, England and Cape Town, South Africa. The message, foretelling the advent of television, was transmitted by the short wave 'beam' system.

Eleven new radio transmitters are set up in Britain to serve large towns not covered by the main stations; 70% of the British population are now within 'crystal range' of a transmitter.

The new US Wills Sainte Claire car features the first electric fuel pump fitted to a production-line model. During this period, most car manufacturers are moving gas tanks from the front of the car to a safer position at the rear; and the new pump is one of several developed to feed the fuel over the greater distance to the carburettor.

The Italian Milano-Varese *autostrada*, with a carriageway designed solely for high-speed, inter-city traffic (two-wheeled vehicles are forbidden) is the first modern motorway opened to traffic. By 1932—the year in which Germany opens her first *autobahn*—Italy will have 330 miles of motorway paid for by income from tolls and roadside advertising-billboards.

Chrysler's first car, the '70', is a closed sedan, costing $1,645, which starts a trend away from the only slightly more expensive open touring cars.

Imperial Airways is founded in Britain and is soon operating a fleet of Handley Page HP Hannibal and Heracles four-engined biplane airliners. Although slow, these planes gain such a reputation for safety and comfort that they will carry more passengers between London and Europe in the thirties than the planes of all the other airlines combined.

Morris Motors of Coventry, England, start to use the engine block machine in automobile production. A large—181 ft (55 m)—special-purpose machine, it combines the operation of 53 machine tools which in sequence, produce an engine block in a cycle time of 4 mins. Other companies will follow and introduce similar machines to suit their own particular mass-production needs.

The spin dryer is used for the first time in washing clothes by the Savage Arms Corp, Utica, NY. Incorporated into a washing machine, a high-speed electric motor spins the drum, extracting water by centrifugal forces.

Industrial equipment needing direct current electricity can now be run on alternating current, if it is fitted with the new selenium rectifier. Able to convert a.c. into d.c., this component is cheap and efficient, but will be superseded by later germanium and silicon rectifiers.

Amputation of the breasts has been carried out from earliest times, but mammoplasty—cosmetic surgery of the breasts—is still in its infancy. Now the Lexer-Kraske operation is introduced for the reduction of pendulous breasts, which also often relieves infertility.

German scientists synthesize plasmochin, the first of two quinine substitutes for treating malaria (the other is atebrin, synthesized in 1930, and later known as mepacrine). Ironically, it will prove invaluable to Allied troops in jungle areas during World War II.

A.L. Tatum, A.S. Atkinson and K.H. Collins at the University of Chicago are concerned at incidents of acute poisoning during treatments conducted under local anaesthesia. Their experiments with animals are rendered much safer by the preliminary use of a barbiturate and paraldehyde.

The dead-bolt lock promises greater home security.

Quick-drying enamel paint speeds up car production.

Using the effect whereby wind incident upon a rapidly rotating body drives it at right angles to its own direction, Anton Flettner attempts to design a more economic ship. He adapts the small motor-ship *Buckau* by mounting two light tubular towers, each 9 ft (2.7 m) in diameter and 50 ft (15 m) high, above the deck. The towers are rotated by a small electric motor to take advantage of the auxiliary power supplied by the wind effect. It is claimed that by fitting three similar rotors to a larger vessel, the *Barbara*, an extra 2 or 3 knots has been achieved. However, as good performance is only possible in perfect wind and weather conditions, the project will be discontinued.

London's first automatic switchboard, nearing completion, will soon handle the increasing volume of business calls—with fewer crossed lines and less delay. The success of the first such exchange in Leeds has stimulated mass production of telephones to cater for a national conversion to automatic systems.

COMMUNICATION AND INFORMATION

At Cambridge University, British physicist Edward Appleton lays the foundations for the development of radar: he measures the height of the ionosphere and finds that radio waves are reflected from the upper atmosphere to a height of 310 mls (500 km) above ground level.

The loudspeaker horn, hallmark of the gramophone, disappears. Instead, the gramophone becomes all-electric, with a built-in cabinet loudspeaker.

The demise of the crystal set is hastened as the BBC sets up twin-wave radio stations. The new stations transmit two programmes at the same time but on different wavelengths, at moderate strength, and over a wide area. Crystal sets are designed to pick up strong signals on a single wavelength close to an urban transmitter and cannot separate the two wavelengths.

TRANSPORT AND WARFARE

Headlights that can be dipped are introduced to cars. They depend on a new type of bulb which has two separate filaments: one provides a long, straight beam, while the other gives a wide, unfocussed pool of light with less range. A foot-operated dipping switch allows the driver to shine either beam of light on the road.

Perfectionist Henry Royce coaxes an impressive performance from the new Rolls-Royce, the Phantom, by the use of an improved 7.7-litre engine. But, sadly, the car will never quite cut the dash of its predecessor, the Silver Ghost.

ENERGY AND INDUSTRY

Picnics need never be the same again as the first plastic-covered vacuum flasks go on sale. Cheap and pint-sized, they are far more popular than Reinhold Burger's 1902 model, which was large, fragile and covered in nickel.

Lateral thinking from aviation and mass-production engineering is brought to bear on Holland's windmills. Fred Dekker introduces aerofoil-section sails and roller bearings for the working shafts, tripling the windmills' power output. His improvements will be used in Holland's windmills for several decades.

The modern age of glass manufacture dawns when the Corning Glass Co of the USA makes a new type of refractory for glass-making. Before this, the pots and furnace parts used in glass works were made from natural rocks and clays. Corning's refractories—the first of their kind to be used—are made from materials which, when fused together, are highly resistant to molten glass: they therefore last longer, operate at higher melting temperatures and generally increase output.

MEDICINE AND FOOD PRODUCTION

An elderly doctor begins a revolution in the treatment of mental illness at a farmhouse in Topeka, Kansas. With his sons, Karl and William, Charles Menninger pioneers a group practice for disturbed people, providing a family atmosphere and what he calls a 'total environment' approach. 'No patient is untreatable', says Menninger.

In Italy, L. Lazzarini experiments with transplants of living bone. Using laboratory rabbits, he finds that bone, taken from the same animal and regrafted at once, heals in place, producing new growth. When grafts from another rabbit are used, there are signs of rejection at first and the biological process is much more sluggish, but the final result is practically the same.

Thomas Cooley describes thalassaemia, an hereditary blood disorder common in Mediterranean areas. Sometimes called Cooley's anaemia, it appears in childhood and usually proves fatal by the age of 20.

FRINGE BENEFITS

Air-conditioning makes New York theatre-going more comfortable.

Dodgem-cars, new in Britain, increase the fun of the fair.

Pneumatic tyres replace ones made of solid rubber on a London bus. Until the twenties, heavy vehicles have not made use of pneumatics, as they are prone to punctures and unable to support their weight. However, the corded carcass and short side walls of the new 'balloon' tyres are safer, sturdier and more hard-wearing.

Nearly two decades after its invention, the photoelectric cell gets its first public demonstration at the Grand Central Palace in New York. The Westinghouse Electric and Manufacturing Co reveals how the device can open doors automatically and count objects each time a light beam is interrupted by the approach of a person or object.

The daily demands of the press for up-to-the-minute photographs are met by the development of methods of transmitting pictures by wireless or cable. Scotland, once 9 hrs from London pictorially, is now less than 9 mins away.

Britain's Daventry wireless station, the largest and most efficient in the world, is opened. With a radius of 100 mls (160 km), and the first to use the new long wavelength of 1,500 m, it consists of twin triangular steel masts, 500 ft (150 m) tall, which support the antenna, the power house and a zinc earthing system.

The de Havilland Moth makes its first flight. The lightweight biplane, powered by a 4-cylinder engine, will become a favourite with flying clubs the world over after it is chosen offically to start the British Flying Club—an organization in which many of its famous cousins, the military Tiger Moths, will end up after World War II.

Three companies— Chrysler, Ford and General Motors— produce 80% of US cars and are steadily increasing their share of the market: for example, Ford now has 10,000 US dealers.

A 'never-stop' railway is installed at a British industrial exhibition in London. This ingenious railway system, first demonstrated in 1923, features a set of railway cars which travel non-stop, slowing to a crawl at stations for passengers to board or alight, then speeding up to 16 mph (26 km/h) between stations.

Glass bottles start to be produced on a new type of machine which, in 50 years, will make over 90% of all bottles. Known as the individual section machine, it continuously feeds into bottle-shaped moulds individual lumps of glass of the correct size and weight, and then blows the glass to form bottles. It is more productive and efficient than the turntable machine introduced by Owens in 1903.

After-images from the filament in clear glass light bulbs—long thought to damage the eyes— are prevented as British manufacturers introduce internal frosting to the glass. Giving a diffuse source of light, to hide the bright filament, and superseding earlier 'obscured' lamps where the outside of the glass was sand-blasted, internal frosting will become standard manufacturing procedure.

A new kind of pump—the balanced-vane hydraulic pump— is developed by US engineer Harry Vickers. It will be used for pumping oil from the bottom of oil wells to the surface.

At the University of Alberta in Canada, James Collip isolates the parathyroid hormone involved in the absorption of calcium from the blood, and calls it parathormone.

The first quarter of the century has brought steady advances in eye surgery. Now Jules Gonin of Lausanne pioneers an operation for the repair of a detached retina.

Californian agriculturists conduct some of the earliest successful experiments in hydroponics, the soil-less cultivation of plants fed only by nutrient-rich water. Their experiments will later prove valuable to people living or working on isolated islands where there is no soil to grow fresh vegetables.

US physiologists L.S. Fridericia and E. Holm show that vitamin A deficiency causes night-blindness.

Battery cages for laying-hens are introduced in the USA. Poultry farmers find that hens kept indoors, in carefully controlled conditions, lay more eggs than those kept in a chicken-run or farmyard. Within fifty years most laying hens will be kept in battery cages.

Production of potato crisps increases as automatic peeling machines are introduced.

Twelve years after Oscar Barnack developed a compact camera for his own use, the German company Leitz base their Leica on his design. Despite reservations—Leitz has previously made only scientific optics—the 35 mm camera is a great success.

Radio manufacturers are quick to respond to the discovery that shortwaves bounce repeatedly between the ionosphere and the earth's surface, facilitating long-distance communication. Before long, most such transmissions will be carried on the 3-25 MHz wavelengths previously consigned to amateur use.

COMMUNICATION AND INFORMATION

Using audio discs synchronized with the projected film, Warner Brothers launch their Vitaphone sound system in the USA. The first feature film to use the system is *Don Juan*, in which only the musical score is carried on the 16-in (24-cm), $33\frac{1}{3}$ rpm discs. But it is Al Jolson's ad-libbed dialogue in their next movie, *The Jazz Singer*, which catches the public imagination and leads to the success of the talkies.

The days of the triode as a radio wave amplifier are numbered when H.J. Round of the Marconi Co replaces it with the screened grid valve or tetrode. The new valve, marketed by Marconi in Britain and GEC in the USA next year, solves the problem of static interference and vastly improves the stability of high-frequency reception.

The first radio fitted with automatic volume control, the Philco Model 95, arrives on the US market. The circuitry, invented by H.A. Wheeler, makes it unnecessary to touch the volume control once it has been properly adjusted.

TRANSPORT AND WARFARE

The German car firms of Mercedes and Benz amalgamate. The Mercedes star, symbol of elegant cars since the company's creation in 1901, is set inside the Benz laurel wreath to form the new badge.

Four aspect railway signals, (one red, one green, and two amber electric lamps) are introduced to stretches of Britain's Southern Railway in the wake of track electrification. Combinations of colours tell the driver what the next two sets of signals may say, enabling him to gauge the maximum possible speed for the track ahead.

Forcing steam out of a locomotive's cylinders more smoothly than ever before, the Kylchap exhaust system both extracts more power per portion of coal, and allows coal of lower quality to be burnt. First fitted to French steam engines by André Chapelon and his Finnish partner, the exhaust system will soon be widely fitted to European steam engines.

ENERGY AND INDUSTRY

A popular alternative to the electric fires that used the coiled nickel-chrome alloy is introduced in the USA, one of the best known being the 'Globar', made by the Carborundum Co. The element is a rod of a new silicon-carbide material.

The rapid growth of the plastics industry is ensured when German engineers Eckert and Zeigler build the first injection moulding machine. The injection ram on the machine is operated by compressed air, but within five years it will be controlled more accurately by hydraulic compression.

The first pop-up toaster, invented in the USA, is soon popularly regarded as a device that hurls slices of flaming toast several feet into the air. A 1937 version will become popular in Britain after World War II, and later models will be used in a third of Britain's homes by 1980.

The cutting speed of lathes is increased six times with the introduction in German industry of tungsten-carbide cutting tools.

A transit mixer—a huge concrete mixer mounted on the back of a truck—is first used in the USA and becomes an indispensable piece of equipment in civil engineering.

MEDICINE AND FOOD PRODUCTION

The newly founded British Company, Imperial Chemical Industries (ICI), starts production of compound fertilizers. Containing nitrogen, phosphorous and potassium—the three major chemicals needed for plant growth—they will save the farmer time and labour, while improving crops.

British neurologist W.J. Adie describes idiopathic narcolepsy, where a patient either falls asleep irresistibly or, triggered by amusement or anger, collapses fully conscious because his muscles give way.

The first factory ships to freeze and process fish—and to remain almost permanently at sea—go into service for France and Britain.

FRINGE BENEFITS

Zips replace buttons on blue jeans.

The first artificial ski slope is installed in London.

Scottish inventor John Logie Baird demonstrates television to 50 scientists in his Soho laboratory, London. Facial features, albeit dim and flickering, are seen on the screen for the first time. The system transmits images of an object, such as a doll's head, by mechanical scanning: light from the object passes through the spiral of holes in a rotating disc, and falls on a photoelectric cell which converts it into electrical signals. These are translated back into variations in the intensity of a beam of light which, projected through a second rotating disc, reconstructs the image on a screen.

Inks coloured by aniline dyes extend the range of colour printing. Used with flexible rubber plates, they allow printing on a variety of surfaces, including plastics, fabrics, rough paper or card. This aniline, or flexographic, printing starts a revolution in the packaging industry, but particularly in food packaging because the dyes are less toxic than their predecessors.

The background hum on radio is eliminated at last with the advent of the Metrovick AC/R valve. The valve, which facilitates the arrival of the all-mains radio receiver, becomes standard in radios until it is replaced by the transistor.

The BBC becomes a public corporation. Restrictions on the live broadcasting of sports events—imposed on the private company by the newspapers—are lifted.

The newly laid Permalloy transatlantic telegraph cable increases carrying capacity four times. Thanks to the iron-nickel alloy coating of the copper conducting cable, which increases the cable's magnetic permeability—and thus its sensitivity—2,500 letters a minute can now be transmitted between Cornwall and Newfoundland.

Steel railway cars developed in the USA between 1902 and 1910—trams used them first—at last reach Britain. Other European railways will soon follow suit, replacing their wooden rail cars with steel ones to reduce risk of fire.

A power steering system is installed in a Pierce-Arrow Runabout car. Francis Wright Davis, formerly an engineer with the US prestige car company, will demonstrate his innovation to Detroit car manufacturers in 1927, but power-assisted steering will not be fully developed and introduced to passenger cars until the fifties.

US pilot Floyd Bennett makes the first flight over the North Pole, narrowly beating the Norwegian explorer Amundsen who is preparing his airship for the same journey.

British government scientist A.A. Griffith proposes a turbine-driven propeller for aircraft; but further experiments on the aerodynamics of his turbine-blades—they will influence later turbojet design—are curtailed when he is transferred to a new post.

Driverless trains carry London's mail through an underground railway unique for its time. The remote-controlled trains reach speeds of 35 mph (56 km/h) over their $6\frac{1}{2}$-ml (10-km) track.

Good quality steel is made quicker than ever before at the world's first continuous hot-strip steel mill in Butler, Pennsylvania. The mill produces hot strips of steel up to 48 in (122 cm) wide without human intervention, and the process will allow the steel industry to keep abreast of the car industry's demand for all-steel car bodies.

British electrical engineers W.A. Whitney and E.B. Wedmore invent the first air-blast circuit breaker to be used at power stations for preventing overloads, or simply for routine switching off. The air-blast 'blows out' the arc of electric current formed across the contacts, and disconnects the high-power circuit.

The Central Electricity Board is created in Britain, and the national 'grid'—the network of power lines resembles a grid on a map—is proposed. The public supply of electricity will have a standard frequency of 50 Hz (50 cycles per sec). The first section will open in 1929, and most of the network will be in operation by 1935.

Abraham and Edgecumbe commercially produce an 8 ft high (2.4 m) electrostatic voltmeter, designed to measure the voltage—up to 500,000 V—of electricity supply circuits.

Recognizing pernicious anaemia as a deficiency disease, George Richards Minot and William Parry Murphy announce that they have been treating this previously fatal condition successfully for two years by giving patients raw liver to eat. Later, Vitamin B12 is pinpointed as the therapeutic substance contained in liver.

In Britain, H. Gardiner-Hill and J. Forest Smith report a new treatment for abnormalities including lack of growth, amenorrhea (absence of menstruation) and sudden weight gain with decreased carbohydrate tolerance. When the affected children are treated with pituitary extract, their condition improves dramatically, but the doctors admit they do not know why.

US bacteriologist Thomas M. Rivers, with an influential paper which distinguished between viruses and bacteria, establishes virology as a separate discipline. His textbook, *Filterable Viruses*, published two years later, will be the first in America devoted to virus disease.

Anti-freeze for car radiators allows year-round motoring.

Safety glass windshields become standard car fitments.

A thin layer of varnish makes cellophane seven times more resistant to moisture than normal. Developed by Du Pont chemists Charch and Prindle, the waterproof film will package Carreras' Craven 'A' cigarettes in Britain by 1931.

The most sought-after sports car in Europe, the new Mercedes boasts Ferdinand Porsche's supercharger. It is the first to be fitted to a non-racer and the first to be engaged only when the driver chooses—by pressing the accelerator flat on the floor.

COMMUNICATION AND INFORMATION

Utah engineer Philo Farnsworth devises a complete electronic TV system. The system uses the inventor's image dissector tube which transmits moving pictures by electricity.

In France, Professor Henri Chrétien demonstrates his 'Hypergonar' lens which compresses a wide field of view on to a standard movie film. The distortion is corrected by a similar lens on the projector, to give a wide-screen image. Although little used at the time, this anamorphic lens comes into its own with the advent of the wide-screen processes of the fifties.

'Movietone News', the first sound newsreel, begins regular showings, thanks to the Fox Film Corporation's sound-on-film system. The process is used for the first all-location talkie, *In Old Arizona*, in 1928.

TRANSPORT AND WARFARE

Japan's first underground railway system is opened. The Chikatetsu line is just $1\frac{1}{4}$ mls (2 km) long, but by the sixties, Japan's dense population will benefit from some of the most efficient urban rapid transit systems in the world.

The first Volvo car comes out of the factory built by two Swedish industrialists to halt the flood of imported cars into their country. The P4 is the first of a series of solid family cars which sell consistently in Scandinavia. After World War II, Volvo will gain a wider reputation for the safety of their cars.

ENERGY AND INDUSTRY

In Britain, the newly created Central Electricity Board begins the construction of the national electricity grid with the erection throughout the country of steel transmission towers. The towers—commonly called pylons—carry steel-cored aluminium conductors 0.79 in (20 mm) in diameter. Eventually, a 2,860-ml (4,600-km) network of overhead high-voltage transmission lines will be in operation, linking power stations and local electricity distribution systems.

To carry yet more electrical power from power station to consumer, single core paper-insulated cables—designed to handle 132,000 V—are laid in the USA for the first time.

Silent electric refrigerators are first manufactured in Britain by Electrolux. Earlier compressed air machines had noisy compressors, but these new machines use electric heating elements to evaporate liquid refrigerants. To encourage the refrigerant to condense, however, a constant supply of cold water is required—a weakness that Electrolux will remedy in their 1932 model.

MEDICINE AND FOOD PRODUCTION

A.J. Hosier, a British farmer, invents the milking bail, or portable milking shed. An economical, hygienic system of milking cows in open pasture, it is an early step towards the labour-saving mechanization of milking.

Frank Meleney reports the death from gas gangrene of a patient, following surgery. Tracing the infection to the catgut stitches, his report ensures all suture material will be sterilized before use.

Austrian-born Karl Landsteiner, working at the Rockefeller Institute in New York, identifies two minor blood groups—M and N. Not as significant for blood transfusions as the ABO system he discovered earlier, they will be sometimes useful in determining paternity.

Gaston Ramon and C. Zoeller of the Pasteur Institute in Paris are the first to immunize human beings against tetanus. Guinea-pigs for their vaccine, developed in 1923, are French soldiers.

FRINGE BENEFITS

Texan brothers John and Mack Rust invent a mechanical cotton-picker capable of harvesting a bale in a day. Widely marketed by 1949, it will put thousands out of work—producing a migration to northern cities that changes the face of US society.

Canada

France

Germany

Italy

Britain

Others

50,000   100,000   150,000   200,000

In the first demonstration of television in the USA, a large group of viewers sees Secretary Herbert C. Hoover in his Washington office. During the demonstration, Hoover's voice is transmitted over telephone wires to synchronize with the pictures on the screen. The main problem, which will seriously thwart television development, is that a frequency band of 4 million cycles is needed for a clear picture, compared with 400 cycles for clear sound on radio.

First on the line, inaugurating the new commercial two-way transatlantic telephone service, is the foreign editor of London's *Daily Mail*. Speaking from Fleet Street, he exchanges views with the paper's chief New York correspondent at a cost of £15 (about $75) for each three minutes. This new line is opened up by the British Post Office's new high-powered transmitter at Rugby, Warwickshire.

Negative feedback, the principle on which every hi-fi amplifier is based, is discovered in the USA by H.S. Black. By feeding some of the outgoing sound back into the amplifier, distortion is reduced.

Ford's now outdated Model T is replaced by the Model A. The three-geared car is built at Ford's River Rouge factory, the largest plant of its kind in the world, containing its own shipping berths, railway sidings, and blast furnaces. Despite the onset of the Depression, 4½ million Model As will be sold in four years.

Henry Segrave, driving a British twin-engined Sunbeam racing car, smashes the World Land Speed Record by reaching 203.79 mph (327.89 km/h) over one mile (1.609 km) at Daytona Beach, USA. He will be drowned only three years later after setting a new World Water Speed Record in his boat *Miss England II*.

Commuters travelling to New York from New Jersey can now drive to work, as the first alternative to the ferry boats, the Holland Tunnel, opens under the Hudson River.

The largest electrically powered shovel in the world comes into use at the open-cast coal mines of Illinois. It can dig out 24 tons of coal in one scoop.

Pumps operated by electricity are used in oil wells for the first time to raise small quantities of oil from deep wells in Kansas and Oklahoma.

An exploratory well, sunk in Orange County, California, reaches a depth of 8,000 ft (2,438 m) and becomes the deepest well in the world.

The first acrylic polymer is produced commercially by Rohm and Haas AG in Germany. Called polymethyl acrylate, it is a soft glass-like polymer which has potential uses as a lacquer and as an inter-layer for safety glass.

The first electrically powered, automatically controlled oil pipeline, the first of many, is built in California.

Two old vacuum cleaners and other bits and pieces are assembled to make the prototype iron-lung. Harvard professor Philip Drinker devises his Drinker respirator, an air-tight chamber that employs alternating low- and high-pressure pulsations to force air in and out of inert or failing lungs.

The effect of removing the adrenal glands, lodged on top of the kidneys, is certain death. But now, F.A. Hartman and his colleagues at the University of Buffalo produce an extract from the adrenal cortex, which keeps animals alive after their glands have been removed. This extract, which Hartman calls 'cortin', is of immediate value in the treatment of the once-fatal Addison's disease caused by underactivity of the adrenal glands.

James Leake of the US Hygiene Laboratory first describes the multiple pressure method of smallpox inoculation. Needle pressure is used through a film of vaccine lymph on a small area of skin, permitting the virus to grow in the superficial layers of the skin. This is less painful than the old scratch technique and gives maximum immunity.

Can openers are now wall-mounted in the kitchen for easy access.

Large-scale mass production boosts the number of motor vehicles built in the USA this year to almost 3½ million— 81% of world output. Of the remaining producing nations, Britain leads with 212,000, followed by France with 191,000 and Canada with 179,000.

In May Charles Lindbergh makes the first non-stop solo transatlantic flight in his modified Ryan monoplane, 'The Spirit of St Louis'. Without a radio during his 33-hr, 39-min flight, the 'Lone Eagle' had to rely on dead-reckoning navigation. He was also forced to use a periscope as his forward vision was blocked by the 451-gallon (2,029.5-l) fuel tank necessary for the 3,600-ml (5,760-km) journey from New York to Paris. The event, which earns Lindbergh a $25,000 prize, will be commemorated a year later by this airmail cover—complete with his signature and a 10-cent Lindbergh stamp.

COMMUNICATION AND INFORMATION

John Logie Baird designs the first video disc, half a century before its commercial introduction. His 78 rpm disc captures stills of faces, which can be reproduced as recognizable, though hazy, images when played on a gramophone connected to a Baird TV receiver. Several copies will be marketed by Selfridges, the famous London department store, during the thirties, but will disappear when the BBC drops Baird's mechanical TV system in 1936.

Full-colour home movies are now possible with the Eastman Kodak 16 mm colour film. The film works on a complex optical principle using an embossed film and special three-colour filters placed on the camera and projector. Colour quality is excellent, but the projected picture is too dim to be projected to any great size.

The Atlantic is spanned by television as viewers in New York receive pictures from Baird's London laboratories. First a doll's head, then Baird's own face appear faintly on the 2 in × 3 in (5 cm × 7.5 cm) screen.

Aiming to improve radio reception, Holst and Tellegen of Philips in Holland develop the five-electrode valve, the pentode. The valve proves popular for both high- and low-frequency amplification.

TRANSPORT AND WARFARE

The Pioneer Yelloway bus travels from California to New York, becoming the first transcontinental bus service; but it will sell out to Greyhound next year.

Snappy two-tone colour schemes are applied to cars by the young and rich Errett Lobban Cord who has owned the US Auburn Automobile Co since 1926. His advertising, too, breaks with conservative tradition: the powerful, seven-cylinder engines are illustrated by 115 stampeding horses to represent their horsepower.

ENERGY AND INDUSTRY

A great advance in electric motive power is made in Britain with the invention of the mercury arc rectifier, which converts alternating current (a.c.) to direct current (d.c.). Now, electric trains can have rectifiers and d.c. motors installed in them instead of a.c. motors, which are expensive to maintain.

A furnace is invented which makes steel by smelting iron ore electrically. Named after its Norwegian inventors, the Tysland-Hole furnace will become the most widely used electric iron-smelting furnace in the world.

The first electric shaver is designed by Jacob Schick, who capitalizes on the idea of a cutting surface that moves back and forth. In 1937, Philips in Holland, will produce the circular cutting head of the Philishave.

MEDICINE AND FOOD PRODUCTION

Harvey Cushing and W.T. Bowie cut time and risk in the operating theatre by introducing surgical diathermy. An electrified scalpel or probe is used to cauterize small blood vessels to prevent seepage at the site of incision.

The combine harvester is introduced into Britain—but only gradually. Despite its undoubted efficiency, few farms are large enough to make its use economical. Even in the USA as late as 1939, only about one farm in six will have any form of tractor or combine.

In honour of Wilhelm Roentgen, who discovered X-rays in 1895, the roentgen is established internationally as the unit of measurement for X-ray dosage.

FRINGE BENEFITS

The Louvre Museum, Paris, uses X-ray techniques to detect painting forgeries.

Alexander Fleming, a Scottish bacteriologist, discovers that the mould *Penicillium notatum* has the power to kill many different kinds of bacteria. He assumes the growth has produced an anti-bacterial substance, which he names penicillin without really knowing what it is. Although its potential is recognized, it will not be until World War II brings the need to treat soldiers' wounds that Howard Florey and Ernst Chain will successfully isolate it from the other toxic compounds in 1941. Its use will save many thousands of lives and, in 1945, Fleming, Florey and Chain will be awarded the Nobel Prize for Physiology and Medicine.

Timekeeping achieves a new accuracy when the quartz crystal clock is invented in the USA by J.W. Horton and W.A. Marrison. The clock uses the vibrations of a quartz crystal—not a pendulum—to drive a synchronized motor at a precise rate. Losing less than a thousandth of a second a day, it will be the heart of Britain's Greenwich time service between 1939 and 1964.

An improved Technicolor printing process, in which the coloured components of a picture are transferred by mechanical printing methods, is used for the first all-colour, all-talking movie musical, *On With The Show*.

Radio range, a system of radio tramlines which steers aircraft between two points, clear of high ground, is introduced to the USA. Armed with a radio, a map and a list of radio range stations and their frequencies, a pilot can fly all over the USA, as long as the weather does not cause radio interference. Any deviation from the set course produces Morse signals in an unsynchronized, not a steady, tone.

Pilots are no longer grounded by fog and heavy cloud. Using Sperry's artificial horizon, a gyroscopically stabilized line on the controls, they are provided with a way of checking their position relative to the horizon.

Nervous of renewed German hostilities, French War Minister André Maginot calls for massive fortifications and firepower to be built along the Franco-German border. The entire Maginot Line complex is either built underground or protected by concrete—to no avail; the German army will simply march round it through Belgium in 1940.

The shape of all single-decker public buses in the USA is established by the design of the Twin Coach motor bus. Drawing on their experience with the 1921 Safety Coach—the first purpose-built motor bus for passengers—Frank and William Fageol bring in low floors, driver-controlled pneumatic doors and engines mounted behind the front axle.

The French begin mass production of steel railway cars without chassis—an innovation copied from US subway cars in service more than 20 years before. The construction of cars as single units (without separate chassis) hugely reduces the chances of their breaking up in a collision.

By far the largest canal tunnel ever built opens in the south of France, making the port of Marseilles accessible to the water-borne traffic on the River Rhône. Called the Rove tunnel, it is 4.5 mls (7.25 km) long, and its dimensions—50 ft (15.24 m) high and 72 ft (21.9 m) wide—allow two 1,200-ton barges to pass each other at any point.

Adhesive tape is developed for the first time by Richard Drew, who works at the Minnesota Mining and Manufacturing Corporation. Manufactured in rolls of cellulose film coated with rubber glue, it is marketed as 'Scotch Tape'. It will be introduced into Britain, in 1937, under the brand name 'Sellotape'.

French engineer Eugène Freyssinet refines the techniques of pre-stressing concrete. A bridge, for instance, is subject to stresses such as traffic load, shrinkage and temperature change, which may cause it to crack. By inducing stress into the concrete before construction (with steel rods or wires), the usual stresses are counteracted before the bridge is built.

Hungarian-born Albert Szent-Györgyi, while investigating the function of the adrenal glands at Cambridge University, isolates a substance which he suspects is a vitamin. Although his suspicion is corroborated by the presence of the same substance in cabbages and oranges, he will be upstaged by Charles King who, in 1932, will isolate and identify the substance as vitamin C.

The correlation between ultraviolet radiation, present in sunlight, and skin cancer is confirmed by British scientist, G.M. Findlay, who produces the disease in mice by exposing them to intense ultraviolet light.

Greek-American George Papanicolau makes an important contribution to the diagnosis of uterine cancer, with a technique for recognizing malignancy in cells taken from the wall of the vagina. This technique is soon popularly known as the 'Pap' test.

The Royal Flying Doctor Service of N.W. Queensland, Australia, brings medical attention to isolated outback homes.

After 38 years as a specialist health food, peanut butter is improved and promoted nationwide in the USA.

The prototype Short S.8 Calcutta, moored at Westminster, awaits the blessing of British MPs. Considered the safest means of flying over water, the three-engined, metal-hulled Calcutta has been designed for the Mediterranean section of Imperial Airways' projected 'Empire' routes.

Rice Krispies are launched by the Kellogg cereal company. Energetic businessman Will Keith Kellogg has changed the eating habits of a generation by his vigorous promotion of the breakfast cereals made by the company he founded in 1906.

COMMUNICATION AND INFORMATION

Colour comes to television. With spectacularly good results, the first transmission is beamed between Washington and New York. The 50-line system used by the Bell Telephone Laboratories transmits the three primary colours—red, blue and green—along three separate channels. Later in the year, the basis of modern colour TV is laid down when several colour signals are transmitted over a single channel.

Music-while-you-drive goes on the road with the invention of the first car radio, the Motorola, by US engineer Paul Galvin. The size of a suitcase, the radio has a bulky speaker placed under the car floorboards which gives sound of doubtful quality.

On Christmas Day, Winston Churchill launches an appeal to provide every blind listener in Britain with a radio set equipped with braille dials and fittings.

To relieve congestion on the US airwaves, General Squier invents the Monophone. Now telephone wires can carry some of the radio signals, with minimum power consumption and without changing the receiver.

TRANSPORT AND WARFARE

Fuel levels in a car's tank can now be monitored by an electric gauge. Simple mechanical gauges are replaced, and so is the primitive manual method—the dipstick.

Following the success of the double-decker, horse-drawn railway car some 60 years before, Wales's Swansea and Mumbles railway (the first ever to carry passengers, in 1807) experiments with double-decker cars on its newly electrified rail system—a service that will survive until 1960.

The Cord L-29 is the first US car produced in large numbers to use front-wheel drive. Although its shape earns it the unflattering nickname 'coffin-nose Cord', the design provides unprecedented space and comfort for the car's occupants. But road-holding problems will delay general acceptance of front-wheel drive as a safe alternative to the usual rear-wheel drive, until the 1960 launch of Britain's Austin-Morris Mini.

ENERGY AND INDUSTRY

Electrical power is derived from the temperature variation in tropical oceans when Georges Claude exploits the difference in heat between the warm upper waters and cold lower waters at Mantanzas Bay, Cuba, and establishes the first ocean-thermal power plant.

An electric food waste disposer that fits into the kitchen sink outlet is invented by J. Powers of GEC in the USA.

MEDICINE AND FOOD PRODUCTION

German psychiatrist Hans Berger reports on his techniques of using electrodes, placed against the head, to record electrical events within the brain. His apparatus, the first electroencephalogram (EEG), soon becomes a useful tool in the diagnosis of some neurological disorders, particularly epilepsy. It also helps to locate brain tumours or areas of brain damage.

Austrian-born psychiatrist Manfred Sakel uses controlled overdoses of insulin to deliver a shock which modifies the behaviour of schizophrenics in the USA.

American biochemist Edward Doisy and German chemist Adolf Butenandt independently isolate estrone, the first sex hormone to be identified. Working in St Louis, Doisy and Edgar Allen have already shown that ovarian follicles contain this estrus-producing substance, while, in 1927, B. Zondek and S. Ascheim have shown that urine from pregnant women contains large quantities of it.

FRINGE BENEFITS

The starting-block helps athletes on their way.

A sunroof is devised for summer motoring.

Experiments with a wide variety of film formats are begun by the US film industry: they hope to improve quality and allow large-screen presentations in cinemas. The cinema owners, still recovering slowly from the cost of installing sound systems in a climate of economic depression, are not enthusiastic about incurring further expense. After a few feature films are made, wide-screen films are dropped, to be revived again in the fifties when the industry will need a fresh stimulant.

The 'Vacublitz', the first commercial flashbulb which is based on Vierkotter's 1925 patent, quickly replaces the erratic and dangerously explosive flash powders which have been in use for photography since the late 1880s. Safe, reliable, and easily synchronized with the camera shutter release, the new bulb revolutionizes action and press photography.

A new, improved magnetic tape recorder, developed in Britain by Louis Blattner and named the Blattnerphone, is used by the inventor to synchronize the sound tracks of his movies.

The number of telephones in the USA totals 20 million—more than twice as many as in the whole of the rest of the world. Most are wooden boxes hung on the wall, with cables to ring 'Central', but some are tube-like, and an increasing number are in the French style, with mouthpiece and receiver all in one.

Radiovisor, developed by C. Francis Jenkins, is the first home TV set in the USA.

Cadillac is the first company in the world to offer a car with a synchromesh gearbox to make gear changing smoother. Three years later Vauxhall and Rolls-Royce in Britain will follow Cadillac's example.

Professor Sir Melvill Jones publishes *The Streamline Aeroplane* in Britain. The paper's central thesis emphasizes the need for smooth airflow to obtain higher speeds without turbulence; he stresses the value of slotted wings to achieve this. Melvill Jones's theories inspire a series of experiments which will influence flight right up to the first supersonic jet aircraft.

US car production tops the five million mark—a peak that will not be equalled for 20 years. By 1932, the world Depression will have cut annual sales to just over one million.

German engineer Felix Wankel patents his revolutionary engine. It obtains power from a single rotating piston, or rotor, rather than from several pistons which fly up and down. But the problem of sealing the rotor against its casing at the high speeds and temperatures necessary to power a car, will delay commercial adoption of the rotary engine until Wankel enters into partnership with the German firm, NSU, in 1951.

The Dunlop Rubber Co produce foam rubber. Latex rubber is whipped with liquid soap to create a soft texture, full of air bubbles. The bubbles interconnect to form pores that allow the free passage of air, making foam rubber ideal for bathroom sponges, foam mattresses, pillows, cushions and insulation.

An ammonia factory at Leuna, Germany, is powered by the gas produced from coal—the first commercial application of the new technique of making gas from a fluidized bed of coal.

US physicist Robert Van de Graaff experiments with a silk ribbon and a motor to generate electrostatic lightning between two tin cans—and, two years later, builds a 10-million-volt model generator; its successor, standing over 7 ft (2.1 m) high, will be used to accelerate sub-atomic particles.

Berlin physician Werner Forssmann anticipates the technique known as cardiac catheterization by threading a fine tube through his own veins and into his heart. He watches its progress on an X-ray image on a fluoroscope which is reflected in a mirror.

Harvard physician Samuel Levine is the first to make the connection between high blood pressure (hypertension) and fatal heart disease.

Heparin, a complex organic acid which prevents blood clotting, has been known to doctors since 1916, but it is now used experimentally to prevent thrombosis occurring in the veins. In 1937, D.W. Gordon Murray will introduce heparin into general medical practice, and later it will be chosen as the anti-coagulant employed in kidney dialysis.

Although most British farmers still use horses on their farms, agricultural mechanization progresses with the first British-built combine harvester, produced by Clayton and Shuttleworth.

Pre-prepared baby foods appear in grocery stores.

The first do-it-yourself hair colouring, with 10 shades to choose from, is introduced.

The largest plane in the world to date, the Dornier Do.X makes its test flight carrying a record 169 people, including 9 stowaways. 12 air-cooled Jupiter engines, mounted on an auxiliary wing, burn 400 gallons (1800 l) of petrol at 110 mph (176 km/h). Equipped with a bar, smoking-, writing-, dining- and sitting-rooms, as well as bathrooms and sleeping quarters, the monster offers passenger comforts to rival that of the Zeppelins. However, the heyday of the flying boat is short: the public soon require speed rather than luxury, preferring the faster airliners.

This cake mixing machine plays a vital role in the early experiments by Dunlop in their search for a mouldable latex foam. By the end of the year, more conventional methods will whip the latex rubber, which is baked in a steam oven to emerge in batches 'like sponge cakes'.

COMMUNICATION AND INFORMATION

Leitz improve the versatility of the Leica camera by adding interchangeable lens features.

The computer makes its mark. The differential analyser devised in the USA by Vannevar Bush can, for example, solve a variety of differential equations, although its accuracy is impaired if it is run too slowly.

On 31 March, the BBC broadcasts the first television talkie with perfectly synchronized sight and sound. Spectators at Hendon, north London, see and hear a theatrical show transmitted from the Coliseum Theatre in London's West End, more than 10 mls (16 km) away.

The change-over to sound films is almost complete—at least in Hollywood where only 5% of production is now silent.

TRANSPORT AND WARFARE

The construction of the first bathysphere—a pressurised sphere lowered on a cable—enables Americans Otis Barton and William Beebe to make a record ocean dive to a depth of 1,400 ft (427 m).

Frank Whittle takes out patents on a gas-turbine jet engine, but will have to wait until Britain is on the brink of war before any financial backing to build it is forthcoming.

ENERGY AND INDUSTRY

Polystyrene, discovered in 1839, is commercially developed by I.G. Farbenindustrie in Germany. Resistant to many chemicals, this synthetic plastic will be used in electrical insulation, battery cases and toilet articles.

Whitney and Wedmore, working for the UK Electrical Research Association, invent the baffle switch for the oil-filled current breakers which break the high-voltage electrical mains circuits being installed all around Britain. The baffle switch will form the basis of most future designs for high-voltage oil circuit breakers.

The first domestic gas water heater to work efficiently is the Progas instantaneous water heater. In 1932 Bernard Friedman will introduce the heater into Britain, where it will be manufactured under the name 'Ascot'.

Poly vinyl chloride, a flexible plastic substitute for rubber, is discovered by W.L. Semon of the B.F. Goodrich Co, USA. He devises a new process for commercial manufacture, which will soon begin in the USA and Germany. After World War II the civilian market for PVC will be opened up—to insulate cables, as a leather textile, in packaging—until, together with polystyrene and polythene, PVC will become one of the three most widely used plastics.

MEDICINE AND FOOD PRODUCTION

Karl Menninger, son of the founder of the Menninger Clinic for the mentally ill, popularizes psychiatry with his book, *The Human Mind*. He states the case for psychiatry as a legitimate and relatively simple source of aid for the mentally disturbed.

US scientists crossbreed strains of corn (maize) to produce hybrids yielding up to 30% more than standard varieties. By 1949, these hybrids will account for 78% of US corn production.

FRINGE BENEFITS

Boeing Air Transport employ the first airline stewardess after an official sees the second pilot spill coffee over a passenger.

The Baird Televisor, the first factory-made television set ever to be retailed, goes on sale in Britain. Its 30-line scan produces flickering pictures from test transmissions (no real programmes are broadcast at this time). At a cost of 25 guineas (or 18 guineas for the do-it-yourself version), 1,000 sets are sold between 1930 and 1931. However, Scotsman John Logie Baird's mechanical system will soon be supplanted by electronic television with far clearer 405-line pictures.

Germany witnesses the introduction of the first tape recorder to use magnetized plastic—not steel—tape. Entire broadcasts, including Adolf Hitler's speeches, can be assembled from these tape recordings, and their sound reproduction is so faithful that they are indistinguishable from live transmissions.

The risks to which merchant vessels and lightships are exposed when they sail through icy waters are minimized by Professor N. Kamienski's ice telemeter. The actual distance of the vessel from an iceberg can be accurately read off a movable scale when the telemeter is aligned with both the ice and the apparent horizon.

Inspired by the rise of short wave radio, GEC in New York design a radio tube made of metal, not glass, as is usual. The heat-conducting and radiating properties of the metal improve short wave reception.

The largest production car ever built, the Bugatti Royale, is launched. Its Italian creator Ettore Bugatti has ambitions to build 25 in all, to represent the ultimate in spacious luxury; but, in the event, only six will be built and only three sold.

The 20 mph (32 km/h) speed limit on British roads, largely ignored during its 27-year life, is repealed by Parliament.

The first windshield washer for cars is devised by Briton Henry Derby: a simple manual pump sprays water through a nozzle on to the area of windshield covered by the wiper blade. It will not be bettered until 1936 when the US Trico Co devise a washer that sprays water automatically at the touch of a button.

Holes and cavities in metals can now be made by Wladimir Gusseff's new method of electrolytic erosion which, employing the same basic electrical process as batteries, will become important in the cutting and shaping of hardened metals and alloys.

The first electric kettle to be fitted with an automatic cut-out is available from the General Electric Co, England. The plug of this 'Magnet' kettle is fused; if the bottom of the kettle becomes too hot, the fuse melts and the current stops.

The first automatic factory in full production is the A.O. Smith Corporation at Milwaukee, Wisconsin. An automatic machine for making chassis frames for cars turns out one frame every six seconds. The machine inspects the stripped steel, rejecting any that is unsatisfactory, cleans, folds, drills and cold-rivets. All the material remains untouched by human hands throughout the operation.

High-speed aircraft and space capsules will eventually benefit from the research into the metal titanium which W.J. Kroll initiates in Luxemburg. Many further years of research will be required before titanium will be extracted by the Kroll process from its abundant, naturally occurring ore. It will be used to make strong, light alloys, crucial to the building of missiles, jet engines, metal-cutting machines and even artificial bones.

The first packaged frozen foods—meat, fish, vegetables and soft fruit—are sold in Springfield, Ma., by the Postum Company. Customers are at first reluctant to buy the new products because of high prices and poor shop display; but, within three years, 516 US shops will sell packaged frozen foods.

Spring chickens become a thing of the past. US poultry farmers build special sheds in which the young fowl can be reared intensively all the year round, making chicken dinners cheap and plentiful.

German research at last produces an iodine-containing substance which can be picked up in the bloodstream and concentrated in the kidneys. Called uroselectan, it is non-toxic and radio-opaque; thus the structure of the kidneys will show up on X-rays much in the same way as the stomach is revealed by barium meal.

Dry ice is now available to keep ice cream cool.

Sliced bread—the epitome of convenience food—is introduced.

Russian engineers devise the airsleigh to facilitate swift travel over snow-bound terrain during long bleak winters. An engine and propellor, mounted high above the ground to avoid large rocks and similar obstacles, are capable of driving the vehicle at high speeds across Russia's vast tundra.

COMMUNICATION AND INFORMATION

The velocity ribbon microphone improves musical broadcasts dramatically. The mike excludes background noise and reproduces sound so faithfully that within 4 years it is adopted as standard studio equipment.

The finish of the Derby, one of Britain's classic horse races, is transmitted by closed circuit television to a paying audience at London's Metropole cinema—and becomes the first ever outside broadcast. Now theatre pay-TV brings television within the means of the many who cannot afford to buy their own sets.

King George V accepts Britain's two millionth telephone for use at Buckingham Palace. London is now the telephonic centre of the world with daily calls made to distant parts of the globe.

TRANSPORT AND WARFARE

Britain wins the Schneider Trophy outright after three consecutive victories. The winning Supermarine S6B Seaplane is designed by R.J. Mitchell who will use the experience gained from his Schneider racers in the design of the Spitfire.

ENERGY AND INDUSTRY

The world's first cast-iron road is opened on a 100-yd (91-m) stretch of Romford Road, one of London's busiest thoroughfares. It is said to generate less traffic noise and vibration, prevent skidding and make renovation easy. The road is composed of triangular iron plates resting on bitumen with a concrete foundation, a method of building that its inventor, Frank Hough, claims is cheaper than granite and will last for 50 years.

Drilling for oil becomes more accurate as the Sperry Gyroscope Co start to use a device known as the gyroscopic clinograph to stabilize the drill.

Heavy water (deuterium oxide) is discovered by H. Urey of Columbia University, USA. Containing deuterium—an isotope of hydrogen—heavy water will be important to the Nazis in World War II, to produce fuel for their flying bombs, and later will be used in the production of power by nuclear reactors.

ICI succeed in producing gasoline from coal at Billingham, England. The equivalent of 9 tons of good-quality gasoline are made from 15 tons of coal in a process which will become fully commercial in 1935, producing 700–800 tons of gasoline daily.

MEDICINE AND FOOD PRODUCTION

Regulations relating to the British Therapeutic Substances Act of 1925 come into force. Their purpose is to control the purity, potency and quality of all antisera, toxoids and vaccines entering clinical use. The British standards, constantly under review, will prove acceptable internationally and will be taken up by the League of Nations and, much later, by the World Health Organization.

Three Boston surgeons use flanged nails for internal fixation of fractured femurs in place of various metal nails, which have been used up to now with only limited success.

The trouble with culturing viruses in the laboratory is that they cannot be grown in an ordinary culture-medium in the way that bacteria can: viruses need living cells in which to reproduce. Now a breakthrough in virological research comes when US pathologist Ernest Goodpasture has the idea of using live chick embryos in which to culture vaccinia virus, which is used as protection against smallpox.

FRINGE BENEFITS

The reassuring fizz of Alka-Seltzer, introduced by Miles Laboratories of Indiana, soothes hangovers, headaches and upset stomachs.

The Empire State Building, the tallest skyscraper in the world, is inaugurated by President Hoover. 1,248 ft (380.4 m) high, the 102-storey office building can accommodate about 25,000 tenants. Thanks to a special steel-cage framework, which locks tightly together, it can rock $1\frac{1}{2}$ ins either way in high winds.

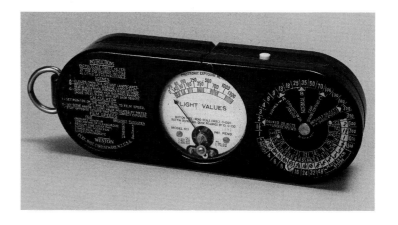

The introduction of 16 mm sound-on-film projectors in Britain, and their subsequent rapid development, greatly expands the use of film in education.

Marconi market the micro-ray radio which uses ultra short waves. One of the first customers is Pope Pius XI who uses the system to link the Vatican to the papal summer residence at Castel Gandolfo.

The first teleprinter exchange, prelude to the modern Telex system, goes into operation in London. It not only allows written conversations to take place but affords a permanent record of them.

In October, Moscow begins regular TV transmission. Viewers, all city-dwellers, use home-made receivers to pick up the broadcasts.

The USA's first regular TV broadcasts begin on 23 December from the West Coast station W6XAO and consist of one hour's transmission of movies each day. The station is the first to use an all-electronic televising system and one of the first to operate on VHF.

Anti-rolling devices have been used on a number of liners but now, for the first time, an Atlantic liner has a gyro stabilizer. The new Italian liner *Conti di Savoia* is fitted with a British-built Sperry plant which incorporates three gyroscopes that limit the roll of the ship to 3° on each side of the vertical.

A heat-resisting alloy—the first to be made from nickel and chromium—is produced by the International Nickel Co, Huntingdon, USA. Called Inconel, this wrought super-alloy will be developed into Inconel X-750 and used extensively in the X-15 rocket aircraft.

The needs of the refrigeration industry for a non-flammable, non-toxic, low-boiling liquid refrigerant—handling previous refrigerants had sometimes led to fatal accidents—are met when the Kinetic Chemical Corporation commercially produce Freons. Once industrially available, Freons will be used in aerosol sprays and will cause controversy by being held responsible for the deterioration of the atmosphere's protective ozone layer.

A new synthetic rubber, Neoprene, is developed by W. H. Carothers at Du Pont de Nemours, Wilmington, Del. Because of its resistance to abrasion and heat, it will be used as a gasketing material, and, as a result of its strength, it will be important for making adhesives and rubber cements.

New Jersey is linked to New York City when the George Washington Bridge opens over the Hudson River. This suspension bridge has a 3,500-ft (1,066-m) span—double the previous record—with towers 635 ft (194 m) high.

The first report of penicillin being used in clinical practice comes from a hospital in Sheffield, England, where it is used to treat gonococcal ophthalmitis in two children who have contracted gonorrhea from their mothers at birth. But no real attempt to pursue the treatment potential of penicillin will be made for another decade.

British researcher L.S. Penrose reports that, while the origins of mongolism are still unknown, there are certain characteristics associated with the condition. Most obvious are the oriental facial features, the hair texture and mental retardation. But Penrose also reports abnormal creases on the palm of the hand: instead of the usual three, mongol children are distinguished by having only two.

First catch your virus...English bacteriologist William J. Elford succeeds in trapping some viruses in a filter with very fine pores, proving that these minute agents of disease are material particles of some kind. This is an important first step towards identifying these mystery organisms, which parasitize plants and animals.

A 'refillable' toothbrush with removable bristles and made of colourful moulded plastic comes on the market.

Bouillon cubes imported from Europe provide short cuts in US kitchens.

The Weston Universal Model 617, manufactured by the Weston Electrical Instrument Co of Newark, New Jersey, is the first photoelectric exposure meter to be sold in any numbers. Two selenium photocells operate a needle gauge, the readings on which can be converted to exposure settings, using rotating scales.

For the first time a radio broadcast is received by listeners in an aircraft in flight: passengers hear a running commentary on the Oxford and Cambridge boat race as they watch its progress along the River Thames. Fliers' needs have precipitated the development of radio for navigational purposes, but now even its entertainment value can be appreciated in mid-air. The receiver is a McMichael Duplex Four, one of the higher-quality, suitcase-portable sets of the thirties, tuned to a specific frequency (TRF) transmitted from a radio station in Croydon.

COMMUNICATION AND INFORMATION

Using the deaf speaker invented in Britain by Professor Bedell, many deaf people can hear for the first time. A receiver held against the teeth or cheekbones carries sound vibrations directly to the inner ear via the bones and teeth, so by-passing the defective middle ear. The loudness or frequency of the sound is adjusted in the device, and the sound is received in the inner ear.

Walt Disney adopts a new three-colour Technicolor process for his Silly Symphony cartoon *Flowers and Trees.* It is a huge success, and from now on Disney works exclusively in colour.

To make home movies less expensive, Eastman Kodak introduce a new 8 mm format. A 16 mm film is run through the camera twice, and the two rows of pictures are separated after processing by splitting the film in half longitudinally.

Annual sales of radios in the USA soar to 4 million—now more than half of all homes own a set. In the same year, 1½ million sets are sold in Britain.

TRANSPORT AND WARFARE

Three diesel-electric shunting locomotives, built for Ford UK, feature double bogies and cabs at both ends—progressive design features which other manufacturers will introduce over the next 30 years. They will remain in service until 1968.

The shape of railway locomotives to come is laid down by Dr Tietjens of the US Westinghouse Electric Corp. He discovers that by streamlining a train's outline, wind resistance can be cut by over 60%.

Britain's first electrically-powered milk floats go into service with the Express Dairy in London. Although electric cars have practically died out since their peak of popularity at the turn of the century, the milk floats, with short journeys at low speeds, are ideally suited to electric power and will become the emblem of the early morning milk round.

ENERGY AND INDUSTRY

A high-grade gasoline is made from cotton seed by Dr Egloff, a Chicago chemist. While 50% of the yield is gasoline, the remainder contains important by-products which can be used in the manufacture of a heavy fuel for diesel engines, coke, 13 different gases—some of which are commercially profitable—and a type of alcohol. Although not commercially viable in the West, this gasoline may be of value to certain Third World countries where oil is expensive.

American nuclear physicist E.O. Lawrence builds the first practical cyclotron, which accelerates atomic particles in spiral paths. It will be used to help discover what an atom is composed of, how it behaves, and how its energy can be tapped.

Dual water immersion heaters—heating enough water to fill a bath, or a smaller amount for use in sinks—are introduced by such companies as Hotpoint, Backer and Bray. The model's design and the type of element used will be popular for the next 50 years.

The first practical dishwasher comes on the market in the USA. Even though 68 minutes per household per day is the average time spent in the kitchen drudgery of washing dishes, the dishwasher will be surprisingly slow to catch on.

MEDICINE AND FOOD PRODUCTION

A revolutionary advance in orthopaedics comes with the introduction of a non-corrosive metal, vitallium, into joint surgery. It is first used in the USA by Venable and Stuck on the suggestion of a dentist who has found it useful in his own field. Vitallium will be used for joint repair and replacement—most notably for the artificial hip.

Smith, Klein and French introduce the Benzedrine Inhaler as a nasal decongestant. With amphetamine as the active ingredient, it will also be used to treat obesity and, paradoxically, to calm down hyper-active children.

FRINGE BENEFITS

The flexible rubber ice tray is invented in the USA.

Sydney Harbour Bridge opens for road and rail traffic after seven years' construction. To demonstrate that it is 'the world's strongest bridge' 81 locomotives are parked on it for eight days. But its steel span of 1,650 ft (503 m) is not the world's longest: New York's Bayonne Bridge, opened four months earlier, has 25 in more.

'The Times' of London of 3 October is printed in the Times New Roman typeface for the first time. The face, prepared under the supervision of Stanley Morrison, is cut in small sizes of $5\frac{1}{2}$, 7 and 9 point specifically to meet the paper's needs. It makes the paper easier to read—especially by the many thousands of train commuters.

To rival the Leica, Zeiss Ikon of Germany launch the Contax 35 mm camera, with interchangeable lenses and an accurate coupled range-finder.

A lapel microphone, only $\frac{1}{2}$ in (1.25 cm) across, weighing a mere 1 lb (450 g) and with a 30-in (75-cm) cord attached, helps solve the problem of sound blocking created by gesticulating speakers using conventional microphones. The new mike also affords greater freedom of movement.

The Varityper, an office composing machine introduced in the USA, is the latest word in business equipment. Providing commerce with a cheap method of printing by composing cold type on to an offset litho printing plate, it is an overnight success. The Varityper's compact dimensions will make it invaluable in World War II, and it will eventually compose the Instrument of Surrender signed by the Japanese on board the US battleship *Missouri*.

The first diesel-powered lifeboat goes into service in Britain with the Royal National Lifeboat Institution. Diesel engines will replace gasoline engines in most lifeboats from now on.

The pride of the French merchant marine, the *Normandie*, is launched. The first transatlantic liner to exceed 1,000 ft (304.8 m) in length, the *Normandie* is powered by a turbo-electric plant comprising four independent sets of Zoelly impulse turbines, each connected to a 6,000 V alternator. The current generated is passed to four 40,000 hp motors, each of which is coupled to a propeller shaft.

Commodore Garwood is the first man to travel at 2 mls/min on water when his four-engined boat *Miss America X* reaches a speed of 124.86 mph (200.89 km/h).

Cotton, linen and artificial silk fabrics can now be made crease-resistant by a process announced by the Tootal Broadhurst Co, a British textile firm. A major non-mechanical advance within the textile industry, the novelty of the invention is that a synthetic resin, formed inside the fabric, imparts its elasticity to the fabric, making it crease-resistant.

The atom is split for the first time by John Cockcroft and Ernest Walton, atomic physicists working in Britain. By accelerating the positively charged subatomic particles called protons to very high velocities, they successfully bombard and split atoms of lithium and release large amounts of energy. This demonstrates the existence of a vast new power source—nuclear energy.

James Chadwick, the British physicist, discovers the neutron, a particle found in all atomic nuclei (except hydrogen). Having no electric charge, the neutron can readily penetrate the strong electric field of the atom and disrupt its nucleus. This makes it an important factor in nuclear fission—a reaction by which an atomic nucleus splits into roughly two halves—and, therefore, in atomic bombs and nuclear reactors.

Lane Wells invents an electric gun for perforating the casing in an oil well and thereby releasing neighbouring, but previously inaccessible, sources of oil.

Examination of some internal organs by direct viewing has been practised for many years, but now gastro-intestinal diagnosis is improved with the introduction of the semi-flexible gastroscope by Rudolf Schindler. Safer than its rigid predecessors, this viewing device is more easily passed into the stomach and is less uncomfortable than previous devices.

The first satisfactory and ultra-short-acting intravenous anaesthetic is hexobarbitone sodium (Evipan), used by Weese and Scharpff in Germany. However, it will be eclipsed in two years time by intermittent administration of thiopental sodium, which will remain the most favoured drug.

Allis-Chalmers in the USA market the first mass-produced tractor with pneumatic tyres. Farmers welcome the greater grip and fuel economy offered by the Firestone tyres and also the fact that the soil becomes less compacted under the wheels. Allis-Chalmers will capture 14% of the US market by 1935, rising to 95% in 1940.

Synthetic plastic tables and chairs appear on Paris pavements—durable furniture for eating and drinking al fresco.

Auguste Piccard, Swiss-born physicist, enters the stratosphere in his sealed aluminium shell, lifted by a balloon. He climbs to 53,153 ft (16,201 m). After the war, Piccard will establish more records—in a bathyscaphe for deep-sea diving.

London's Piccadilly Circus lights up with flashing advertisements—12 years after Georges Claud first demonstrated neon lighting at the Paris Motor Show.

COMMUNICATION AND INFORMATION

The BBC adopts the immediate playback method of disc recording. Developed by musician Cecil Watts, the system will be incorporated into the BBC's first mobile recording unit in 1935 and installed at the BBC's music studios in Maida Vale, London.

A new movement named Technocracy, founded in the USA, reflects the power and promise of technology. Its members advocate that engineers should run a country and that energy certificates should replace pay packets.

Frequency modulation, the greatest improvement in radio since the introduction of short wave transmission in 1921, is perfected by US scientist Edwin Armstrong. Although it will take 20 years to be accepted commercially, FM overcomes the problem of natural—and many forms of man-made—radio interference.

TRANSPORT AND WARFARE

Britain's first significant length of electrified railway track opens on the 60-ml (96.5-km) route between London and Brighton. Trains draw low voltage (660 V) direct current from a special third rail, instead of drawing high-voltage current from cables, placed overhead to avoid endangering the life of any trespasser on the track.

ENERGY AND INDUSTRY

A three-and-a-half-ton truck carrying 12 men is suspended from a sheet of Pilkington armourplate glass to test its strength. Only 1 in (2.54 cm) thick, the glass withstands the weight until a thirteenth man is added. This toughened glass will be marketed in 1941 and used for the cladding of buildings and for swing doors. Apart from its strength, its chief merit is that it does not splinter on breaking, but falls harmlessly into a pile of roughly cubic pieces.

A synthetic rubber, styrene/butadiene rubber (SBR), is invented by the German firm I.G. Farbenindustrie. It will soon be made so cheaply and on such a large scale that it will virtually sweep the board in the manufacture of automobile tyres.

The technique of directional drilling is developed to reach lucrative oil and gas deposits situated in inaccessible places. One drilling-site, for example on rugged terrain, near exclusive real estate or adjoining engineering projects, is used to bore many holes; the drill stems can even be inclined to drill horizontally. In this way, holes will be drilled underneath Los Angeles harbor, the Corpus Christi Ship Channel, and even under the San Andreas Fault.

MEDICINE AND FOOD PRODUCTION

In Britain, H.L. Marriott and A. Kekwick recommend a continuous drip technique for transfusing large quantities of blood. To gain access to the patient's circulation, a cannula, or large needle, is introduced into a vein and the drip is started with saline solution. The bottle of blood is fixed on an overhead stand and then allowed to drip into the vein at a steady rate of about 40 drops a minute.

European surgeons have already pioneered the operation known as pneumonectomy (removal of a diseased lung). Now Evarts Graham performs the first successful pneumonectomy on a patient with lung cancer.

Potentially serious middle-ear inflammation is often a complication of infectious diseases. Now, in a massive study of almost 15,000 cases of scarlet fever, H.J. Williams of Philadelphia finds that here, too, there are complications in the ear: 10.8% of patients have otitis media (about a third of these in both ears). Just over 1% require surgery for mastoids, and post-operative mortality is over 10%.

FRINGE BENEFITS

The 10-volume Oxford English Dictionary, published over a 45-year period, is reissued in 12 volumes.

Lithiated lemon is promoted as a 'mixer' drink in the USA under the new, catchier name of 7-Up.

The Boeing 247, the first 'modern' airliner, incorporates such innovations as retractable landing-gear, variable-pitch propellers and an automatic pilot. It is also the first to be fitted with rubber de-icer 'boots' on the leading edges of the wing and tail surfaces to prevent the accumulation of ice—until now a major hazard of long-distance flying. Fast and safe, the 247 can cruise at a comfortable 189 mph (304 km/h) and is the first twin-engined aircraft capable of climbing with one engine inoperative.

US President F.D. Roosevelt's radio 'fireside' chats, inaugurated in this year, epitomize the growing political awareness of the power of mass communications.

The Gasparacolor process, introduced in the USA by Dr Bela Gaspar, introduces multi-layer colour print film for colour movies. It is used almost exclusively for cartoon and puppet movies.

US astronomer Karl Jansky invents the new science of radio astronomy, a novel way of 'seeing' distant events optically obscured by interstellar material. While trying to pinpoint the source of radio interference, Jansky detects a strong cosmic hiss, identified as radio waves from Earth's own galaxy, the Milky Way. In so doing he opens up investigation of the billions of galaxies in the universe.

The speaking clock, invented by M. Escalangon of the Paris Observatory, is adopted in France's capital to provide an accurate recorded time message over the telephone.

The British Alvis car company, renowned for the manufacture of high-quality, high-performance cars, offers its new Firefly model with a synchromesh gearbox, following the introduction of the improved gearbox to Britain in the previous year.

Europe's first high-speed diesel locomotive, the 'Flying Hamburger', enters regular service between Berlin and Hamburg. The 'Hamburger's' average speed of 77 mph (124 km/h) owes much to its advanced streamlining as well as to its powerful engine. Nevertheless, European railways will tend to opt for the cheaper electric traction in the future.

Gas produced by burning charcoal is used to fuel tractors in Australia and makes the tractors 10 times cheaper and 25 times more efficient than those fuelled by the more common kerosene.

Imperfections in metals can now be detected by a device which produces high-frequency sound waves and beams them at the metals. Developed by O. Millhauser, the instrument will be widely used in the forties to detect hairline cracks in railway lines, to test the welding of pipelines and boilers, and even to measure the amounts of fat and lean in livestock.

The first all-electric automatic teamaker—the Teasmade—is introduced by Goblin of Leatherhead, England. Invented by Brenner Thornton in 1932, it incorporates an electric light and electric clock.

The Tennessee Valley Authority is established, in the midst of the USA's Great Depression, to develop the Valley. In one of the biggest engineering projects in the world, 42 dams and eight hydroelectric power plants will be built, natural erosion of the land will be reversed, and some 3 million acres restored to cultivation.

Ventricular fibrillation is a rapid, chaotic twitching of the heart which quickly proves fatal. Now Baltimore electrical engineer William Kouwenhoven and physician O.R. Langworthy introduce a device to overcome this during surgery. Attaching electrodes directly to the heart, they deliver a short, sharp shock to restore the heartbeat. Much later, this prototype defibrillator will be followed by an external version, to be used on the closed chest.

Thomas Hunt Morgan, zoologist turned pioneer geneticist, receives the Nobel Prize for Physiology and Medicine for establishing that it is the chromosomes which carry hereditary traits.

Doctors have no answer to influenza. Often a winter killer, it is sometimes catastrophically virulent: the flu pandemic which swept the world in 1918/19 killed nearly 20 million people (far more than perished in World War I). Now, following an epidemic in London, Smith, Andrews and Laidlaw succeed in isolating a virus from throat swabs of flu victims—an important prelude to the development of influenza vaccines.

The London School of Economics, part of London University, imports a US robot book-carrier for its library.

The British Museum, London, uses infrared photography to decipher illegible Egyptian texts.

The familiar outline of London's Battersea Power Station now houses the largest turbo-alternator in Europe. 120 ft (36.6 m) long, this huge machine is capable of generating 105 MW of electricity—enough to supply the needs of about 650,000 people. It provides a much-needed addition to the output of the two original alternators, which began providing the capital's power in 1928.

COMMUNICATION AND INFORMATION

The opening of the world's first commercial micro-ray radio service between the civil airports of Lymphe, Kent and St Inglevert, France speeds the transmission of weather and traffic information. Micro-rays also allow simultaneous telephone and teleprinter transmission.

For the first time, a mobile television unit is used daily to record sequences for an evening news programme. The unit belongs to Berlin's Reichs Rundfunk television station and the programme it records for is *Spiegel des Tages*—Mirror of the Days.

TRANSPORT AND WARFARE

Werner von Braun, working for the Weapons Development Branch of the German Army, fires a liquid fuel rocket to a height of $1\frac{1}{2}$ mls (2.4 km) in the course of a 16-sec flight. The Army is sufficiently impressed to give him 11 million Deutsche Marks for rocket research.

The British Gloster Gladiator makes its first flight. One of the last biplanes to see active service, it is typical of thirties' fighters—fabric-covered and armed, like World War I fighters, with machine-guns. By the beginning of World War II, stressed-skin monoplanes carrying heavy armament will have largely superseded the Gladiator, although it will still see action: in 1940, for instance, three Sea Gladiators, called 'Faith', 'Hope' and 'Charity', will defend Malta for 18 days until the arrival of British Hurricane fighters.

ENERGY AND INDUSTRY

The world's largest piece of glass, 200 in (508 cm) in diameter and 26 in (66 cm) thick, is installed in the reflecting telescope at Mount Palomar Observatory, California. This huge glass slab—it weighs 20 tons—has taken 12 months to perfect. It is made from high-quality borosilicate glass, first introduced commercially in 1915, which is also used to make thermometers and heat-resistant cooking ware.

The world's longest underwater tunnel is opened beneath the River Mersey, England. Over a million tons of sandstone had to be excavated before the four-lane Mersey Tunnel could be completed.

An extractor fan—the first to be made as a self-contained unit and to be fitted into a window pane—is designed by Vent-Axia of Crawley, England. Made from plastic, the 'Axia Six' is in two sections: an external cowl and an internal impeller, powered by an electric motor.

MEDICINE AND FOOD PRODUCTION

French physicist Frédéric Joliot-Curie and his wife Irène discover artificial radioactivity when they create radioactive phosphorus out of natural aluminium. Hundreds of radio-isotopes will eventually be made and widely used—for example, in radiation therapy and body scanning techniques.

J.S. Lundy popularizes intravenous anaesthetics with the introduction of sodium pentothal. When injected, the drug induces sleep quickly, without distressing the patient who may then be given ether.

FRINGE BENEFITS

The first utility car is so called after its shape which allows a family to travel in front, and goods or livestock in the rear open space.

Durex contraceptives for men are manufactured.

The train known as the 'Flying Scotsman', hauled by a steam locomotive of the same name, unofficially tops 100 mph (161 km/h) on a trial run between London and Leeds. The famous service, started in 1862, has left London's King's Cross Station for Edinburgh—a distance of 392.7 mls (633 km)—at 10 o'clock every weekday morning since, except in times of war or national emergency. In 1928 the train introduced the first non-stop service over the $8\frac{1}{4}$-hr journey, carrying two crews who change over at the half-way point. From 1961, the 'Flying Scotsman' will be hauled by diesel-electric locomotives which complete the journey in just over $5\frac{1}{2}$-hrs.

The 'Scotsman' newspaper introduces teletypesetting (TTS) to link its Edinburgh and London offices. Using this system, the operator of a Linotype or similar machine can set type which, only seconds later, is then set in identical form on a machine in another city. *The Times* also adopts TTS for setting its Parliamentary reports. They are transmitted by keyboard from the Houses of Parliament direct to the composing rooms in London's Printing House Square.

In an experiment in Czechoslovakia, light from the moon and stars is translated into sound by an electric cell contained within a telescope.

Live-action film using three-colour Technicolor makes its public début with the showing of the short *La Cucaracha*. The high quality of the Technicolor process is universally admired. The first feature film to use it—*Becky Sharp* in 1935—establishes Technicolor as the standard by which all its competitors are judged.

Rigid, four-axle trucks which can carry loads of up to 15 tons are introduced to Britain. The eight-wheelers are a natural evolution of the six-wheeled trucks developed after World War I; the additional axle further increases the load-bearing capacity.

The Chrysler Airflow is the first streamlined car to go into mass production—26,000 are made between 1934 and 1937—although other manufacturers have already experimented with aerodynamic styling. Radical features of the car's construction include a welded chassis and body, and headlamps mounted flush with the wings. The original, bold styling will be toned down from 1935 onwards because of lukewarm customer response.

Chrysler is the first US company to feature automatic overdrive on their cars. Engine performance and fuel consumption at high speeds are dramatically improved by adding the extra fifth gear, which automatically comes into operation when the gear ratio in fourth (previously the top gear) is too low for optimum performance.

Perspex is commercially produced by Imperial Chemical Industries (ICI) in Britain. A product of research carried out in 1931 by R. Hill, who discovered the polymer, it is a clear glass-like material which is light, unbreakable and weatherproof. Until 1945, the sheet output of Perspex will be used almost exclusively by the Royal Air Force for aircraft windows. Its optical properties will be used later in display signs, light fittings, dental prostheses and automobile finishes.

A machine which can both cut coal and load it on to conveyor belts at the coal face is installed at a Lancashire colliery. The Meco-Moore machine is the first effective cutter-loader to be used at a coal face.

The first coiled-coil electric light bulb is introduced in the USA. A filament of tungsten is coiled and then coiled again on itself: the arrangement traps some of the gas in the bulb in the filament, and this increases the amount of light radiated. The coiled-coil bulb is still the main type of domestic lamp in use in the eighties.

A Canadian woman gives birth to five girls who, as the Dionne quins, will go down in history as the first recorded case of viable quintuplets.

When a Wisconsin farmer seeks advice over his cattle, who are bleeding to death from trivial cuts, biochemist J.P. Lent detects an anticoagulant in spoiled clover. He develops Dicoumarol—a drug which reduces the level of prothrombin, the clotting agent in blood, and which will be used to treat thrombosis.

A Danish doctor, Følling, describes a metabolic disease which develops in infancy and leads to mental retardation. Later it is learned that this disease (which comes to be known as phenylketonuria) can be detected in new-born children by a blood test, and successfully treated.

Monopoly—a game of high finance and property deals—brightens the Depression.

The first ever launderette opens in Texas.

After a four-year suspended work programme due to the Depression, the Queen Mary's hull is launched on the Clyde by her namesake. Like her later companion, the Queen Elizabeth, she is designed for the Atlantic crossing. Both will serve as troop-ships in the war, and then give a further 25 years service as liners.

The world's most powerful magnifying instrument—the electron microscope—reveals the inner architecture of cells: Belgian physicist L. Marton develops the necessary techniques to enable it to be used in biology. By 1945, the microscope—used here at Brown Firth's metallurgy laboratory in Sheffield to study steel—will be showing the surface structure of metals. German engineers Ernst Ruska and Max Knoll built the first crude instrument, with a magnifying power of 400 ×, in 1932; by the early sixties, microscopes magnifying over 200,000 × will be displaying the atomic structure of elements.

Spare parts for the body

New faces for old, comfort for the crippled, hope for the handicapped—even life for the dying—are no longer mere medical pipe-dreams. Using his sophisticated skills in concert with materials tailor-made to suit the living environment of the human frame, the modern surgeon can operate to improve the quality and span of life for his patients.

Replacement surgery is now so diverse that the list of possibilities reads like a page from a body-builder's catalogue. Kidneys, heart, blood, bone marrow, liver, pancreas and the cornea of the eye can all be transplanted from one person to another—albeit with varying degrees of success—and skin and bone can be grafted and persuaded to grow perfectly well in new body sites.

The list of available artificial spare parts is still longer, and still growing. Even the heart, whose failure was traditionally considered un-treatable, can now be fixed up with artificial valves or an electronic pacemaker powered by mercury batteries or nuclear energy.

Spare-part surgery is nothing new. The Phoenicians were the first to make dentures of gold and amber, while wooden legs strapped to limb stumps have been a solution for amputees since Biblical times. Renaissance prosthetics came up with intricate artificial arms which moved at the elbow, and elegant hands able to flex at the touch of a button. And the sixteenth century French army surgeon Ambroise Paré made not only false limbs but also artificial eyes of gold, craftily enamelled to match their real equivalents.

Triggered by the movements of remaining muscles, and the electrical impulses these movements generate, today's false arm is po-wered by an electric motor. As well as allowing its owner a wide range of movements, it can also operate several plug-in attachments such as a knife and fork and a toothbrush.

Gadgets such as these offer crucial ad-vantages to victims of accident and disease but, in biological terms, are relatively simple: the real headache begins when an internal body organ or tissue needs replacing. So ingenious are the body's natural defences that any foreign matter entering it—from a bacterium to a donor heart—will stimulate the manufacture of protective antibodies and be rejected. This immunological response is enormously suc-cessful in fighting disease, but also presents a huge stumbling block to transplant and spare-part surgery.

The first successful tissue transplants ever made were blood transfusions (blood is a fluid tissue), and were made possible by Karl Landsteiner's identification of the A, B and O blood groups at the turn of the century—transfused blood with the correct group or signature is accepted as 'belonging'. Since these early days, the system has been refined by

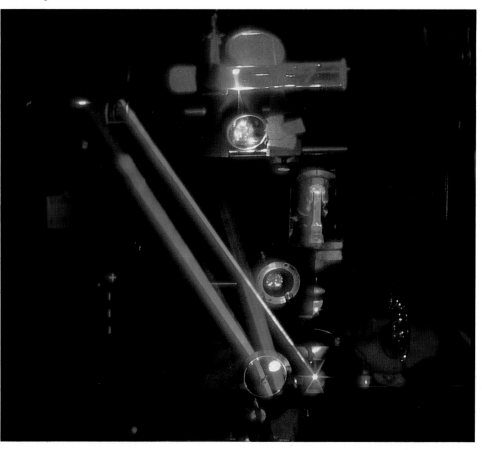

A versatile 'light knife' that never grows dull can now be numbered among the surgeon's tools. The searing blue-green beam of this argon laser is most effective in eye surgery because the eye's fluid does not absorb the energy of the beam, which can therefore penetrate through to a detached retina and reconnect it, or burn away the overgrown blood vessels that block normal fluid drainage and cause glaucoma.

The inventory of spare parts for the body, *right*, available to the modern surgeon would even impress Frankenstein. The problems of spare-part surgery lie less with the parts than with the body—it tends to reject parts that do not belong to it. Only powerful immunosuppressive drugs for transplanted organs such as hearts, and new inert plastics and metals for limbs and bones, can overcome the body's natural fastidiousness.

the discovery of more than a dozen different blood groups, and extended to comprise a worldwide collection of blood banks.

Unlike blood, other body organs cannot be so rigidly analyzed and typed, which explains many of the difficulties of organ transplants. The first kidney transplant was carried out in 1954 between identical twins, and worked largely because such twins beat the system by having identical tissue types. The first heart transplant came in 1967. The recipient, after surviving both the operation and the glare of worldwide publicity, lived 18 days.

The techniques of transplant surgery are not complicated. What is difficult is the prevention of rejection. Only immunosuppressive drugs, chemicals able to knock out the body's defence mechanisms, have endowed such surgery with any measure of success. The problem is ex-acerbated by a shortage of donors. In the USA, for example, fewer than 50 heart transplants

are performed each year while some 750,000 Americans die of heart disease.

In the realm of bioengineering, the develop-ment of biologically inert materials designed to evade the body's defence systems proceeds apace. For arthritics, one of the best ortho-pedic operations involves the replacement of hip joints; knees, elbows and shoulders are also being made from plastics and alloys of titanium and cobalt, each part being cemented to its recipient bones with acrylic glue.

Since the fifties, a whole family of spare-part silicones has been born, ranging from a fluid that can be injected beneath the skin to make a replacement breast, to tough plastics fashioned into new jawbones, knuckles, ears, noses and testicles. For the future, whole replacement organs such as tiny transistorized hearts or kidneys may be possible, or eyes able to see through miniature television lenses: the poten-tial is as vast as man's inventiveness.

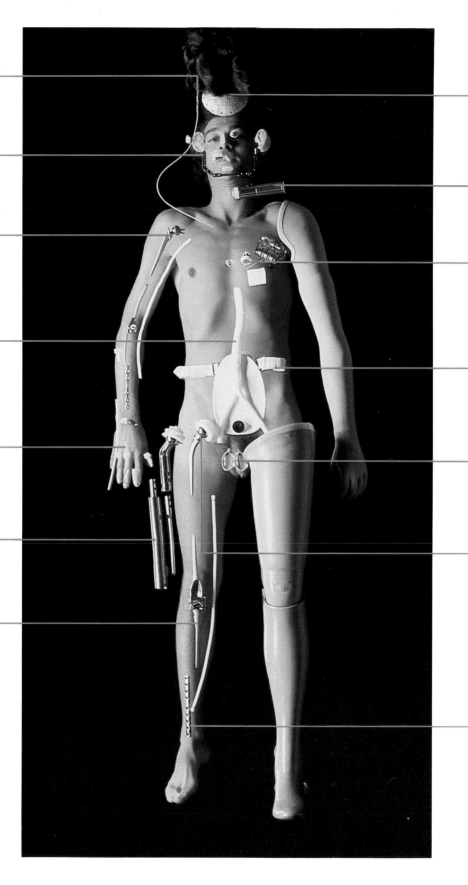

A Holtzer valve syphons and controls the 'water on the brain' in hydrocephalic children.

A metal plate can totally replace a multiple-fractured jawbone.

The ball-and-socket shoulder joint and the hinged elbow joint can both be wholly replaced by metal and plastic parts.

Large bifurcating blood vessels, and other arteries such as those in arms and legs, are replaced by grafts of Dacron fibre.

Plastic wrist bones, fingers and thumbs, and artificial tendons and joints, can all repair the hand.

A titanium femur shaft enables an artificial thigh to be connected to a completely new knee.

Severe damage to the knee joint, due either to accident or arthritis, may occasion total replacement by a metal and plastic hinge device. But since the knee carries so much weight and stress, the artificial knee operation is rarely successful.

A surgical wig and a Vitallium skull plate may be worn after intensive surgery and chemotherapy.

The electronic larynx is an external speech aid fitted after removal of vocal chords.

Artificial valves, electronic pacemakers and Dacron fibres to patch up holes, all keep the heart working.

A plastic ileostomy bag collects waste from the large intestine after removal of the colon.

Testicles can be replaced by non-functioning plastic ones for cosmetic reasons only.

The ball-and-socket hip joint can be replaced after arthritis has rendered it immobile. The socket is made of high-density polyethylene, while the ball of the thigh bone is built out of biologically inert cobalt and chrome.

If the long bones of the body are shattered, they may need to have compression plates inserted to take over the bones' functions—a tricky operation which is not always successful.

COMMUNICATION AND INFORMATION

A single lens reflex roll-film camera, the Ihagee/Exakta model B, launched in Germany, is the first camera to incorporate synchronization for flash bulbs.

Top-secret, radio-location equipment—radar—is developed by British scientists, led by Robert Watson-Watt, to protect Britain from aerial attack. A moving dot on a cathode-ray screen will indicate the presence of aircraft up to 40 mls (64.4 km) away—a range soon to be increased.

The magnetophone, the first commercial tape-recorder to use plastic tape, is marketed. Its performance cannot match the Blattnerphone, but it is cheaper and will soon be highly popular.

At last users are convinced that the electric typewriter, available in some form since 1902, is safe to use. This change of heart is largely the result of IBM's investment of more than a million dollars in their new model.

TRANSPORT AND WARFARE

A car exceeds 300 mph for the first time when Malcolm Campbell of Britain reaches 301.13 mph (484.5 km/h) over a mile test track at Bonneville Salt Flats, Utah, in his Rolls-Royce 'Bluebird'. Later this year, his fellow countryman George Eyston will break the 24-hr car speed record by averaging 140.52 mph (226 km/h) in his 'Speed of the Wind'.

Plentiful supplies of oil, and ample space in stations and sidings, mean that diesel locomotives are more popular in the USA than in the more restricted conditions of Europe. The first diesels, built by General Motors, are often coupled together to haul heavy trains at even higher speeds. They will continue to grow in number until, by the fifties, they are the country's major source of railway traction.

Hitler approves plans for the battleship *Bismarck* as part of his large-scale rearmament policy. The ship will have a formidable combination of heavy armour and a wide range of fire-power. It will be sunk in 1941 by 3 British torpedoes.

ENERGY AND INDUSTRY

Electroslag welding, a method of welding together thick sections of steel, is invented in the USA by R.K. Hopkins. The new process stops impurities from entering the weld while the steel is molten, so preventing the formation of potential sources of weakness when the steel is used under extreme pressure. Electroslag welding will be crucial in the development of machines, such as modern aircraft engines, where a high degree of stress is inevitable.

The jointed black Anglepoise lamp becomes available commercially. Designed to pivot and remain in any position, it will remain largely unchanged into the eighties, except that a range of colours will be introduced.

The speed and accuracy of large welds along very long metal seams is greatly improved by the introduction of submerged welding. By covering the electric arc, welds can be closely controlled, speeding up the production of construction materials for large engineering structures such as bridges, industrial boilers and buildings.

MEDICINE AND FOOD PRODUCTION

Accuracy of electrocardiogram recording depends on good electrical contact between skin and electrodes and so the patient must remain quite still. Now, in Britain, the Cambridge Instrument Company produces an electrode jelly which gives a lower electrical resistance and a more accurate ECG reading.

At Massachusetts General Hospital, John Gibbon and his wife anticipate the potential of open-heart surgery. They devise the machine that will make this possible: a pump-oxygenator which takes over from the heart and lungs. This is the prototype of the heart-lung machine which will be used successfully in 1953.

FRINGE BENEFITS

Hot meals replace lunch boxes on Pan American Airways Clipper flights in the move towards greater passenger comfort.

Moscow's underground railway system begins services in May this year, with passengers enjoying the world's most stylish stations. Other subway networks have stations of standardized design; not Moscow's. Each one has been designed by a different and distinguished Russian architect, briefed to provide an airy, restful environment. Lofty walls, ceilings and pillars feature white, pink and black marble; spacious staircases link different lines at interchange stations, and lighting is soft and diffused, as in this entrance hall of Smolenski Square Station. By the eighties, the city's electrified trains will carry 2,000 million passengers a year, more than any other metropolitan network.

Kodachrome, the first of the modern multilayer colour camera films, is launched by Kodak—the culmination of years of research. This research was begun in the twenties by two professional musicians, Leo Mannes and Leo Godowsky. Having been noticed by Dr C.E.K. Mees, Director of Research for Eastman Kodak, the pair were invited to become full-time photographic chemists and to join the company. The new film realizes, at last, the possibilities foreseen by Fischer in 1912. The Kodachrome films are initially available in 16 mm movie format; 35 mm films for stills follow in 1936.

The Novachord, the first electronic organ to be commercially produced, is invented in the USA by M. Laurens Hammond. It has no reeds or pipes; instead, each key controls a rotating wheel which sets off electronic pulses. These pulses are amplified and fed into a loudspeaker. The 275-lb (125-kg) organ costs less than one cent an hour to operate.

Exposure setting is simplified in the Eumig C–2 camera for 9.5 mm movie film. The camera is the first to incorporate a photoelectric exposure meter coupled to the lens adjustment. The camera is initially marketed in Austria.

Britain reacts to the growing threat of the German Luftwaffe by putting the Hawker Hurricane into the air. The first modern, eight-gun monoplane fighter will be used primarily for bomber interception, but sees service in a variety of roles. Over 14,500 of all models will be built.

A Heyford heavy bomber, flying over Daventry, England, is picked up by Watson-Watt's radar equipment as a green blob which expands and shrinks. The range is only 10 mls (16 km), but the first proof that radar really works has been obtained.

Boeing demonstrates the B-17—the first four-engined, all-metal, low-wing monoplane bomber. Designed originally for defensive anti-shipping operations, the B-17 will acquire heavier armaments, and the nickname 'Flying Fortress', and become the mainstay of US Air Force daylight raids on Germany during World War II.

Cheap imitation wool is manufactured commercially for the first time in response to increased demand and the spiralling costs of the real thing. The Italians produce Merinova, the first of the 'azlon' group of fibres to be spun from regenerated protein materials. Resistant to heat, acid, moths and mildew, but not as strong as wool, the easy-care characteristics will ensure the success of these fibres.

Six and a half million windmills have been erected in the USA during the past 15 years, either to pump water, run saw mills or generate small amounts of electricity.

Nylon is patented by W.H. Carothers and will be produced in 1938 by Du Pont de Nemours. One of a range of synthetic fibres, Nylon 66 will be used to make stockings, surgical sutures and gears.

Street lighting in the future will be orange, as a new improved version of the gas discharge lamp—the sodium-vapour lamp—is developed. Light is produced by an electric current passing between two electrodes in a tube that contains low-pressure sodium vapour. The lamps give more light than the white light of the 1930 high-pressure mercury lamps, and the orange hue is less dispersed by fog, mist and pollution.

Portuguese surgeon Antonio Moniz pioneers the operation known as leucotomy: partially severing the attachments which link the frontal lobes to the rest of the brain. Called lobotomy in the USA, it is intended to relieve the symptoms of severe mental disturbance. It brings improvements in some patients, but leaves others unchanged or downright lethargic.

A new generation of wonder drugs is ushered in with the introduction of Prontosil. The first of the sulfa drugs, this has been discovered by a German chemist, Gerhard Domagk, who has been working on the bactericidal properties of dyes, such as prontosil red, used in the textile industry.

Dr Chassar Moir and H.W. Dudley isolate ergometrine from the ergot fungus, *Claviceps purpurea*, and discover it to be far more potent than the ergotamine extracted 15 years earlier. Ergometrine is almost wholly responsible for the action of ergot in stimulating uterine contractions, treating migraine and causing temporary hypertension.

The synthetic resin 'Neoresit' replaces amber resin for use in medical apparatus.

A New Jersey firm market beer in easy-carry cans.

With a battery in one pocket, a small radio valve in another and a connecting lead to a comfortable earpiece, a deaf person can discreetly tune in to the surroundings. Previous hearing aids (on the right) collected sound through large horns and concentrated them through small earpieces. Twenty years later, transistors will allow almost invisible hearing aids.

The kitchen transformation

Fuelled by coal, lit by gas and cleaned by hard scrubbing, the 19th century kitchen, although warm and hospitable, was smoky, dark and hard work to run. But as the new century dawned, it brought with it a brand new power source that was to transform the kitchen out of all recognition. This was electrical power which, although still in its infancy, was gradually being introduced into homes—especially in Britain where the first power station had begun to generate electricity in 1881.

Initially, the high cost of domestic electricity meant that only rich families could afford the luxury, and even by 1910, only two per cent of British households were wired for it. And although the forerunners of many modern kitchen appliances, including electric cookers, toasters and kettles, were invented in the 1890s, they were regarded with scepticism and fear—and rightly, since they were neither efficient nor particularly safe.

Over the succeeding years, electricity was supplied to more and more homes and this coincided, particularly in Europe, with an increasing scarcity of servants following World War I. But while the reluctant Europeans viewed the convenience of novel electrical appliances as the harbinger of laziness, the Americans were quick to seize on the benefits.

During the first quarter of the century, kitchen illumination improved enormously with the advent of modern-style electric light bulbs, and the twenties witnessed a great many advances. The introduction of the Swan kettle in 1921, with its element totally immersed in water and not wastefully attached to the kettle base, made electric kettles a practical proposition. Dishwashers, electric mixer-beaters and pop-up toasters also made their débuts and began to play a part in kitchen life. The electric waste disposal unit, invented in 1929, was fitted to sink outlets.

By the mid-thirties electric blenders, liquidizers and can openers were available to those who could afford them. Clean, compact refrigerators became common and used new, more efficient refrigerants. Agitator and tumble-action washing machines were mass produced in the USA, and spin dryers were offered as an alternative to the wringer. The first practical dishwashers, although slow to catch on, were marketed, and electric immersion heaters were fitted to tanks above kitchen sinks. The thermostat arrived, bringing automatic control to oven heat at a time when more and more families were buying, rather than renting, electric cookers.

In 1940, production of all domestic appliances in Britain—and subsequently many other nations as well—stopped completely for the duration of World War II. This was the most powerful reason why, despite pre-war inventions and advances, it was not until the

Before its new electric cooker was installed, cooking in the kitchen of this 1937 London house was done on a cast iron range. On top of the cooker is an electric kettle with a totally immersed element. The refrigerator has a built-in motor compression chamber, a great advance on the motor compressors of early refrigerators. The 1948 Hoover washing machine, *below*, was the first compact British model. It has a hand wringer which, within 10 years, was to be made obsolete by the revival of the spin dryer. The multi-purpose kitchen unit, *centre*, was designed in the seventies as a complete, mobile, electric kitchen. When plugged in, supplied with water and switched on, it can be used in any room in the house.

fifties that many electrical appliances captured the imagination of an increasingly affluent public. Consumers were coaxed into buying the latest gadgetry for their ever more hygienic kitchens. Fitted cupboards and plastic laminated surfaces became the norm, while appliances made of new materials fell dramatically in price as they were mass produced. Kitchen design became increasingly important as every gadget and fixture required its own easily accessible place.

Of the many domestic inventions of the forties and fifties, microwave ovens, first made in 1947 but not popular until the seventies and eighties, were perhaps the most startling and are still viewed with suspicion by many cooks. Electric kettles, able to boil water at high speed, then switch themselves off, arrived in 1955—the same year in which domestic deep freezers made their début. Twin tub washing machines—one tub for washing, one for spin drying—came on the market in 1957. A new ceramic material was invented in 1966 which could replace metal on a cooker hob and heat pots and pans more efficiently, but was not popular because it was difficult to clean.

Now the kitchen has entered the computer age. Refrigerators have automatic defrost, cookers can switch themselves on and microchips control a washing machine's cycle.

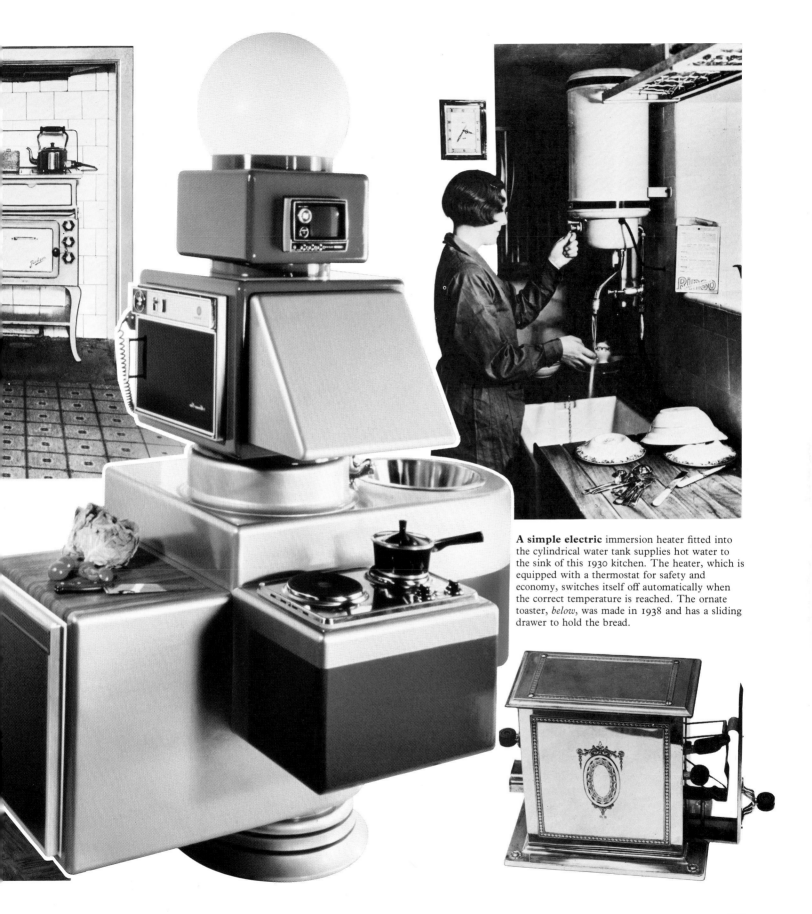

A simple electric immersion heater fitted into the cylindrical water tank supplies hot water to the sink of this 1930 kitchen. The heater, which is equipped with a thermostat for safety and economy, switches itself off automatically when the correct temperature is reached. The ornate toaster, *below*, was made in 1938 and has a sliding drawer to hold the bread.

COMMUNICATION AND INFORMATION

In Germany, Agfa introduce the Agfacolor Neue film. It uses the three-layer construction and incorporates the colour-forming materials proposed by Fischer in 1912. The film is available in both 35 mm still and 16 mm movie film sizes.

In Germany, TV viewers see live transmissions of the Berlin Olympic Games.

A life-saving telephone system, exclusively for emergency calls, is invented in France. Activated by a push button or—in case of fire—by a thermostat, the Signophone automatically dials the appropriate emergency number and transmits a pre-recorded $3\frac{1}{2}$-min message giving the rescue services all the essential information they need.

TRANSPORT AND WARFARE

The 'Super Chief' deluxe train begins a weekly service between Chicago and Los Angeles. It is hauled by a double diesel locomotive—the form of railway traction considered the most modern and prestigious alternative to steam. The train resembles a high-class hotel on wheels, giving rise to the advertising slogan: 'Extra fast, extra fine and extra fare'.

The Short 'C' class flying-boat enters service with Imperial Airways to carry airmail throughout the British Empire. The 24-passenger, all-metal monoplanes will eventually fly all major routes to Africa, India and Australia.

The Focke-Achgelis Fa 61 is the first practical helicopter to fly. Designed by German Professor Heinrich Focke, the twin-rotor Fa 61 V1 prototype, powered by a 160 hp engine, makes its first free flight on 26 June. Within two years, it will break all distance, endurance, altitude and speed records for its class.

ENERGY AND INDUSTRY

'Monastral Fast Blue B5' is ICI's name for their new blue pigment—the first to be discovered for over 100 years. More brilliant than other blues, it also possesses greater holding qualities, so that everything from paints and inks to wallpaper will retain its colour.

The problem of maintaining the pressure of oil in a well, so as to control the amount extracted, is overcome when engineers inject water into an oil reservoir shortly after it has first been drilled. As a result of these trials at the East Texas oil field, water injection will become an accepted engineering technique by 1950.

A new process for deriving gasoline from crude oil is introduced in the USA by the Sun Oil Co and the Socony-Vacuum Co. It employs a re-usable bauxite catalyst and a lower temperature to produce more high-grade gasoline.

Hoover Ltd, England, market their new upright vacuum cleaner which, according to the advertising slogan, 'Beats as it sweeps as it cleans'. The suction head contains a 'beater' which bangs down the carpet pile to raise dust and grit as well as a rotating cylinder with bristles which sweep everything up.

MEDICINE AND FOOD PRODUCTION

Mechanization spreads to thousands of small US farms when an inexpensive 'baby' combine harvester is marketed by Allis-Chalmers. Similar machines will reach Britain and Europe over the next 10 years, making crop harvesting cheaper and more efficient.

Collaborating with US aviator Charles A. Lindbergh, transplant pioneer Alexis Carrel invents the first artificial heart. This mechanical pump circulates blood to organs being kept alive outside the body while they are being operated upon.

FRINGE BENEFITS

A music chart for US best-sellers is published by New York's *Billboard* magazine.

Commercial tampons are now available.

Butlin's first holiday camp at Skegness, England, accommodates 1,000 people.

The Boulder (later Hoover) Dam on the Colorado River is completed. A system of cooling tubes ensures that the great mass of concrete sets (it would otherwise take about 100 years). Able to provide power to $1\frac{1}{2}$ million people, the dam impounds the world's largest reservoir, Lake Mead, and irrigates over a million acres of land.

PENGUIN BOOKS

A SAFETY MATCH

IAN HAY

THE BODLEY HEAD

The vocoder or voice coder—the first machine to recognize the human voice—is developed at the Bell Telephone Laboratories in New York. The US government later adopts the system to transmit secret information in coded form.

A news report on Britain's Jarrow march—a protest against a million unemployed—launches the world's first high-definition electronic television system from Alexandra Palace, London. Using EMI's sophisticated system, which incorporates a new form of camera tube named the Emitron, the BBC produces 25 unflickering pictures a second on a 405-line system which replaces Baird's 240-line mechanical system.

The first single lens reflex camera to use 35 mm film is the Ihagee Kine Exakta. After World War II the 35 mm SLR will become the most popular design with amateurs and professionals alike.

Train ferries between Britain and Europe carry road vehicles for the first time. These early 'Ro-Ro' (Roll on—Roll off) facilities reflect the expansion of road traffic between Britain and the Continent.

The Mercedes 260D is the first diesel-engined production car, and Mercedes-Benz the first company to offer the diesel engine as an alternative to the gasoline engine for most of their models. Although the diesel engine is economical to run, it costs more to make—and is noisier—than its gasoline equivalent, so that other car companies are reluctant to adopt it.

The Supermarine Spitfire, a single-seat, single-engine fighter-interceptor, makes its maiden flight. Derided by the German Air Attaché as a 'toy aeroplane', the Spitfire's small, neat shape belies its toughness—gracefully pointed wings house eight machine-guns. It will be produced continuously throughout World War II and, by 1945, it will have twice the power and heavier armament.

Electric clocks can now be operated by mains electricity in Britain without being more than a few seconds out from Greenwich Mean Time. The Central Electricity Board co-ordinates all supplies in the country to a uniform alternating current of 50 Hz.

The first fluorescent tube is produced by passing an electric current through mercury vapour in a glass tube, coated inside with a substance which fluoresces to produce light. It is the prototype of all future non-filament strip lighting and fluorescent tubes, and is capable of giving at least five times as much light as filament bulbs, lasting 15 times as long. A thousand million tubes will be made annually in the seventies, accounting for about 80% of the world's artificial light.

Ironing clothes becomes easier, with less danger of scorching the fabric, as the first electric iron to be controlled by a thermostat goes on sale in the USA. One of five different temperature settings can be selected according to the kind of fabric to be ironed.

The huge Bay Bridge, linking San Francisco to Oakland, opens in California after three years of construction. Consisting of two suspension bridges which share a common anchorage on the island of Yerba Buena, it is a product of the development of wire cable technology. Each bridge has two suspended cantilever spans—those of the West Bay Bridge are 2,310 ft (704 m) long, those of the East Bay Bridge 1,400 ft (427 m). The total length of the entire bridge is a staggering 43,500 ft (13,253 m).

Livestock breeding is revolutionized by the establishment, in Denmark, of western Europe's first artificial insemination association. Pioneered in the twenties by Russian scientist I.J. Ivanov, artificial insemination of animals allows a pedigree male to impregnate far more females than would be possible with normal mating.

There is renewed interest in oxygen therapy in general, and oxygen tents in particular. Now experience with an oxygen tent at St Bartholomew's Hospital in London encourages other hospitals to invest in this equipment. Simple to operate, it does not hinder nursing and has advantages in cases, such as pneumonia, where oxygen therapy is necessary.

The first vitamin pill to come on the US market is Vitamin Plus. Sold through both retail and mail-order outlets, it includes liver and iron supplements.

The 'night train' begins services between Britain and France—evening departures from London reach Paris the next morning, via a steamer crossing between Dover and Dunkirk.

Polaroid sunglasses, introduced by Land Wheelwright laboratories, give extra protection against glare.

Penguin Books, in its début year, has produced 60 titles. Its 'paperbacks', an innovation in English language publishing, are printed on cheap paper (but use good typography), have simple, eye-catching covers and cost only sixpence—which puts them within range of a much broader market.

Destined to become by far the most important aircraft in the history of civil aviation, the Douglas DC-3 begins production. Able to carry 21 passengers over 1,500 mls (2,414 km) with ease, the twin-engined Dakota (its military designation) proves so popular that, within a bare five years, over 10,000 will be built—and half a century later there will still be several hundred in service.

Sights and sounds on tape

Magnetic tape recording has revolutionized the entertainment industry. From classical concerts to comedy shows, nearly all the broadcasts put out by today's radio and television stations are prerecorded on audio or video tape. Words and music on tape can be heard at home, in the car, in the office or telephone dictating machine, or can even be played direct into a jogger's ear. Pictures plus sounds on tape are the software of the video industry, the commercial bonanza of the eighties.

The tape-recorder was born in Denmark in 1898 when Valdemar Poulsen made a recording on a steel wire. The wire was magnetized by being wound past an electromagnet attached to a microphone. To play back, the wire was rewound and then passed in front of the magnet once again. The resulting electrical currents were then used to create sound in a set of headphones. The idea was not exploited fully until the thirties, when the BBC made a series of recordings on steel wire for broadcast at different times.

The more familiar, flexible form of tape was also developed in the thirties. In Germany, Fritz Pfleumer took out a patent in 1929 for a flexible insulated tape coated with a magnetic material. A few years later, the idea was adopted by the German companies AEG and I.G.Farben, who in 1935 came up with a plastic tape coated with magnetic iron dioxide. Recording and playing back were performed by a Magnetophone, a machine used extensively in Germany during World War II.

Details of this 'secret weapon' were only revealed when the Allies captured German tapes and players, but British and American companies were quick to exploit their booty. Reel-to-reel recorders became available in the fifties and were followed in the sixties by cartridge and then cassette versions. In all these modern machines, recording begins with

Reel-to-reel recorders, such as this 1958 Grundig, were the type marketed in the post-war rise of magnetic tape recorders. The tape, $\frac{1}{4}$ in (5 mm) wide, was made of plastic with an iron oxide coating. The greatest disadvantages of this system were that the tapes had to be threaded by hand and so were easily damaged. They were also bulky and inconvenient to store. So, despite the growing popularity of tape, it was the gramophone that still held market domination.

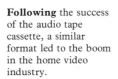

Following the success of the audio tape cassette, a similar format led to the boom in the home video industry.

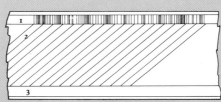

The cassette, in which the audio tape is housed on two reels in a protective plastic case, played a major role in the tape explosion that began in the sixties. As well as being easy to use, the tape had a long life and could be bought ready recorded. Only 0.15 in (3.8 mm) wide, audio cassette tape runs at 1.875 in (4.88 cm) a second and gives high fidelity results.

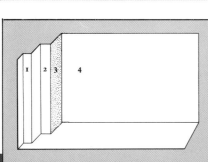

Video tape starts its life as tough, flexible polyester (2). One side of this base tape is then coated with carbon (1), to prevent the build-up of static during play. The other side is coated with metal oxide (3) to store the recorded magnetic fields. This is polished (4) to maximize recording and playback qualities.

The sound track (1) of a video tape is recorded in a strip along the side. The video message is recorded diagonally along the tape centre (2). The control track (3) consists of recorded pulses which act like the sprocket holes in 35 mm film to ensure that the tape is recorded and played back at an even speed.

a tape being passed in front of an erase head which 'muddles up' the magnetic particles. Sound fed in via a microphone is then used to energize a record/replay head which distributes and orientates the particles according to the wave forms of the sound signal. After rewinding, the tape is played back over the record/replay head and an electric current is generated according to the qualities of the magnetic particles. This is amplified and used to produce sound in a loudspeaker.

The need for a visual equivalent of audio tape was born with the success of the television industry. The first video tapes, made in the late forties, were produced in exactly the same way as their audio-only predecessors, except that the magnetic imprint incorporated information about vision as well as sound. These tapes not only suffered from poor quality but were also enormously bulky and difficult to play.

It was the Californian company Ampex that first came up with an elegant solution to the problem. In 1956 they invented a system of four moving heads able to record and replay the visual information in transverse parallel tracks in the centre of the tape while the audio and speed control signals were recorded in strips along the sides of the tape.

The Ampex system was—and still is with modifications and sophistications—ideal for commercial video recording, but proved impossible to adapt to the domestic market. Home video, the craze of the eighties, was made possible by the invention of a means of cutting down the number of record/replay heads to one or two. This was done by arranging for the tape to move through the recorder in a helix.

Such recording was achieved in the fifties, but it was only in the early seventies, when video tapes could be packaged in cassettes, that home video really began to boom.

As video becomes more versatile, so consumers have come to expect more and more refinements in their video systems—in addition to high quality reproduction. Among these are fast-search and freeze-frame facilities, and slow motion—a feature that has proved particularly popular with sports lovers. A tape counter in the recorder adds accuracy to tape search. As well as extending the entertainment value of video, such features are also proving vital to video's growing success in the educational sphere.

In the early days of sound recording, players such as the 1898 Edison, *above*, used a wax-coated cylinder played by a sapphire stylus. Only two years later, the flat disc was invented and soon displaced the cylinder for ever, but not until after World War II did the making of new plastic allow the birth of the LP. The latest form of disc is the video version. Etched with minute holes, the Philips LaserVision disc is read by a laser beam and the signals fed into a television monitor.

Latest weapon in the mounting video war is Sony's SL–C6 UB. For both recording and playback, the tape is loaded into the front of the machine. Timing devices ensure recording of the correct broadcast, even if the owner is watching another channel. Unlike many earlier models, it also incorporates a socket for a video camera.

COMMUNICATION AND INFORMATION

The Super Kodak Six–20, a camera for roll film, is the first to have a fully automatic exposure control system over a range of shutter speeds: a photo cell sets the lens aperture as the shutter release is pressed.

P.C. Smethurst of Britain patents the 'incident light' principle of exposure measurement, in which the meter measures the light falling on a subject rather than the light reflected from it. The concept, first embodied in the Avo-Smethurst Highlight meter and especially suitable for colour photography, will not be universally adopted until the fifties and sixties.

In the USA, engineer Howard Aitken begins work on digital computers. By 1944 he produces Mark I, the first fully automatic computer for mathematical calculations.

TRANSPORT AND WARFARE

Changing gear while driving becomes automatic. General Motors install their Hydromatic transmisson system on the Oldsmobile, to give drivers automatic transition through the forward gears. Most US car-makers will be quick to adopt the labour-saving innovation.

A new fashion in British motorbikes is set by Triumph's Model T. Known as the 'Speed Twin', it is the first popular bike to have its twin cylinders arranged vertically instead of in the more usual 'V' shape.

A lifetime of brightness is claimed for a British car headlamp. The secret is in the sealing: the filament in the sealed bulb is fixed to a glass reflector which is sealed to the front glass—the whole unit then being filled with inert gas. The undimmable, if costly, headlamp will be developed by GEC in the USA.

ENERGY AND INDUSTRY

A new synthetic rubber, butyl rubber, is invented by R. Thomas and W. Sparks of Standard Oil Co, New Jersey. Because it is almost impermeable to gas, butyl rubber will be used widely to make inner tubes for tyres. Only the advent of the tubeless tyre after World War II will oust butyl rubber, and even then it will remain in use for tyre linings.

Hydrogen is now widely used to cool the large turbo-alternators that generate electricity in power stations throughout the USA. Originally tested for this purpose in 1926, hydrogen will be first introduced as a coolant in Britain's Littlebrook Power Station in 1949.

MEDICINE AND FOOD PRODUCTION

An allergic reaction occurs when the body produces histamine in response to some outside stimulus. This can result in anything from itchy hives to life-threatening shock (anaphylaxis). Daniel Bovet, an Italian pharmacologist, produces the first drug to lessen the severity of these reactions. He discovers a prototype antihistamine which has the effect of blocking the production of histamine in the body.

Frederick Foley's latex catheter for draining the bladder replaces earlier rubber models. An inflatable balloon secures the catheter in the bladder, preventing it from coming adrift.

US immunologists develop the 17D yellow fever vaccine. Prepared from attenuated living yellow fever viruses grown in chick embryos, it gives complete immunity against the disease.

Conrad Elvehjem, a US biochemist, identifies nicotinic acid as the substance effective in treating pellagra, already recognised as a dietary-deficiency disease. To avoid confusion with nicotine, this substance (which is part of the B complex of vitamins) will later be renamed niacin.

FRINGE BENEFITS

Cellulose tape is introduced into Britain under the brand name 'Sellotape'.

A new plastic laminate—Micarta—is used to coat the blades of this electric fan. Fan blades surfaced with Micarta are quieter than the blades of the conventional fan, and have the further advantages that they do not corrode or warp. Made from mica and melamine formaldehyde, and developed by the Westinghouse Electrical and Manufacturing Co, Micarta will be widely used as a surfacing material because of its durability, attractiveness and versatility.

The Coronation of Britain's King George VI on 12 May marks the most complex outside broadcast yet attempted. Radio listeners can hear the service in London's Westminster Abbey and TV viewers can watch the procession, which is transmitted from TV cameras linked to vans placed at strategic points along the route.

The intensity of daylight in a room can now be measured using a factor meter. The device is used extensively by authorities involved in slum clearance schemes, particularly in Glasgow, Scotland. Here, some slums show a daylight factor of 0.003%, compared with a recommended minimum for working conditions of 0.2%.

The Minox, made in Latvia by Valsts Electrotechniska Fabrika is the first precision sub-miniature camera and, unlike its predecessors, can produce adequate results from small negatives. Tiny 'spy' cameras now appear.

The lightweight 'lip' microphone, designed by the BBC, becomes a hallmark of sports broadcasts. Held close to the commentator's mouth, it blocks out loud background noise, but allows the user to move about freely.

The Japanese Navy's specifications for a new fighter plane will produce the A6M Zero-Sen. It will soon gain a fearsome reputation, not just for its speed and handling but also for its long-range capability of up to 2,000 mls (3,218 km) on a round mission. Between 1941 and 1942, A6Ms will materialize uncannily over the Pacific Ocean and South-East Asia—hundreds of miles from their nearest bases—to blast surprised Allied pilots out of the skies.

The end of the airship as a commercial vehicle is signalled by the destruction of the 'Hindenburg' by fire. Britain has already cancelled her airship projects after 48 people died in the 1930 R101 crash; and both Italy and the USA have followed suit after similar tragedies in the mid-thirties.

There are now over three-quarters of a million route miles of railway track in the world.

The Raleigh Cycle Company patent an improved hub dynamo for bicycles in Britain. It promises to provide bicycle lamps with a much steadier light, even when the cycle is travelling at low speed.

The basic ingredient of Milk of Magnesia is successfully extracted from another mineral called dolomite, and also from sea water, by British scientists. The magnesia is important not only in curing indigestion, but also as a vital constituent of the linings for refractory furnaces used to produce steel, cement or ceramics.

The first commercial convector heater to be equipped with an electric fan is introduced in the USA by Belling, although it originates from an idea Robert Gordon had eight years ago. Though noisy, the installation of the fan enables the heater to be smaller than previous convector heaters, and because the fan increases the flow of warm air, the heater is highly efficient.

Asparagus is the first packaged frozen food sold in Britain, followed swiftly by strawberries, peas, raspberries, and green beans. G.W. Smedley has developed a food freezing process for Wisbech Produce Canners, after visiting the USA and studying freezing installations there. But a dearth of home refrigerators—there are only about 3,000 in the whole of Britain—will at first inhibit sales.

British surgeon R. Cooke regards the patella (knee-cap) as 'a morphological remnant which is tending to undergo reduction and to disappear.' Now he begins treating fracture of the patella by removing it altogether. He reports excellent results, claiming that removal of the patella actually increases both the strength and speed of movement of the knee joint.

Two Italian doctors, Ugo Cerletti and Lucio Bini, pioneer electro-convulsive treatment (ECT) for the relief of symptoms in schizophrenia. Although ECT (which involves passing an electric current across the temples) is to remain controversial, it soon becomes standard therapy for schizophrenia in Europe. Later, it will also be used to relieve some forms of depression.

A dog whistle, almost inaudible to humans but clearly heard by man's best friend, is developed.

Britain pioneers the use of a three-digit number for emergency telephone calls.

The Golden Gate Bridge across the entrance to San Francisco Bay opens to traffic and sets new records. It will be 27 years before another suspension bridge is built with a longer span than the Golden Gate's 4,200 ft (1,280 m); its towers too, at 746 ft (227.4 m) are taller than any such previously built. The bridge was exceptionally difficult to design and construct as it spans what is very nearly open sea, with tidal currents up to $7\frac{1}{2}$ knots. A magnificent feat of technological ingenuity, the Golden Gate may however one day suffer earthquake damage, as the south pier had to be built on a layer of serpentine clay that could be unstable in the event of an earth tremor.

The first photocopier is demonstrated by Chester Carlson, a New York law student. Years of research have gone into devising a system, cheaper than photostats and clearer than carbons, which could give an unlimited number of copies. Carlson came up with electrostatic dry copying, or xerography (*xeros* = dry).

Seeing inside the body

Medicine entered the twentieth century equipped with a powerful tool for seeing inside the body: the X-ray. Until its discovery by Wilhelm Röntgen in 1895, the only way doctors could examine the internal anatomy of their patients was to cut them open and look for themselves. The amazing penetration of X-rays enabled nearly all the tissues of the body to be exposed and accurate diagnoses to be made. Any abnormality, deformity or malfunction of the body's anatomy, it seemed, could be revealed safely and painlessly.

But although X-rays were particularly good for detecting early signs of tuberculosis by displaying shadows on the lungs, or scrutinizing fractured bones and arthritic joints, their ability to represent soft tissues like arteries, stomachs and hearts was limited. In 1908, a patient with a gastric ulcer was given barium sulphate to swallow. This was the first radio-opaque substance—it enabled the ulcer to be shown up on the X-ray—and from then on, soft tissue deformities such as ulcers became visible. The barium meal X-ray technique was often supplemented by the gastroscope, a long rigid tube inserted down the throat to afford a direct, if hazy, view of an ulcer. It remained a hit-and-miss affair until the Japanese, who are prone to stomach cancer, developed the gastro-duodeno-scope in the early sixties. An optical glass-fibre instrument, it is flexible, manoeuverable and provides such good illumination that ulcers and other abnormalities of the upper gut can not only be identified, but photographed as well.

Accurate information about the site and cause of bleeding, which may be obscured by internal haemorrhage, can also be obtained by injecting radio-opaque dyes through a catheter inserted into the blood vessel, and then taking a rapid series of X-rays. The combined process, known as cineangiography, has revealed many of the secrets of the heart and of blood circulation. Following the flow of blood through the coronary blood vessels, for example, may indicate hypertension in its early stages; and now that such continuous film study techniques have been applied to bones and joints, it is comparatively easy to detect malfunctions of knee cartilage and shoulder tendons, and to identify hip displacements in newborn children.

While the X-ray remains the most common and flexible means of seeing inside the body, other methods for charting and recording the body's internal events have been invented and developed throughout the twentieth century. The electrocardiograph is probably the best known: it amplifies the tiny electric currents generated by the beating heart, and records it on a continuously moving sheet of paper. Any disorder in the heart's rhythm immediately becomes apparent. The EEG, or electro-encephalograph, works in an analogous way, recording the brain's electrical activity via electrodes attached to the scalp.

More useful for diagnosis are the patterns of heat emanating from the skin. These can now be detected by the technique of infrared thermography—the infrared camera is so sensitive to heat that it can record temperature differences of only one or two degrees centigrade. Thus cancerous tumours which are hotter than normal, will show up red on the film, while arthritic joints are colder, registering as bluish.

Until very recently, the only way to detect the amount of a specific substance in the body has been to take a tissue sample and then to measure it very accurately in a laboratory. Now it is possible to examine the chemistry of cells in their natural state. Topical magnetic resonance (TMR) is a technique of 'interrogating' the body's atoms and molecules directly, while still involved, as it were, in the metabolic act, so

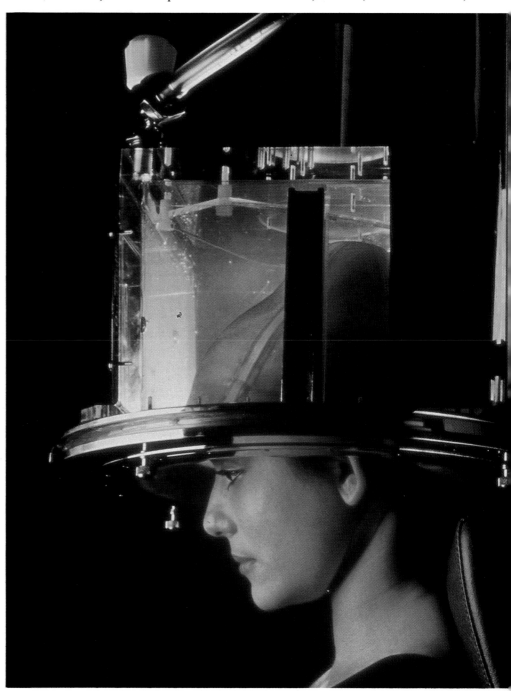

that a deeper understanding of physiological functioning can be gained—it has already upset textbook theories of how glucose is broken down to give the body energy. TMR is being used to diagnose and monitor the progress of such diseases as muscular dystrophy.

By the end of 1982, a whole-body TMR machine will be installed at John Radcliffe Hospital, Oxford, initially to detect signs of rejection after kidney transplantation, and later to monitor the progress of treatment.

Obstetricians in maternity hospitals use sound waves at frequencies beyond the range of the human ear to chart the course of a developing foetus. The different densities of its tissues reflect sound waves to varying degrees. These waves can then be translated into an image on a TV screen. This ultrasonic technique is the most accurate known for assessing the age of a foetus, the position of the placenta, the existence of a multiple pregnancy and the early presence of abnormalities, such as spina bifida and hydrocephalus.

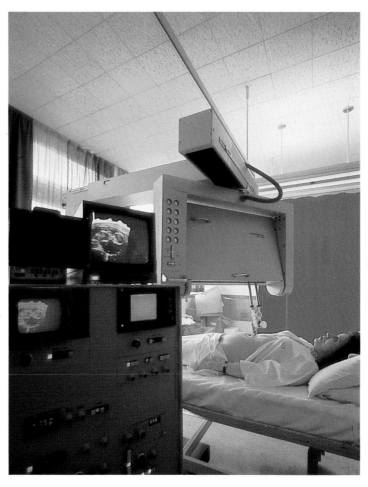

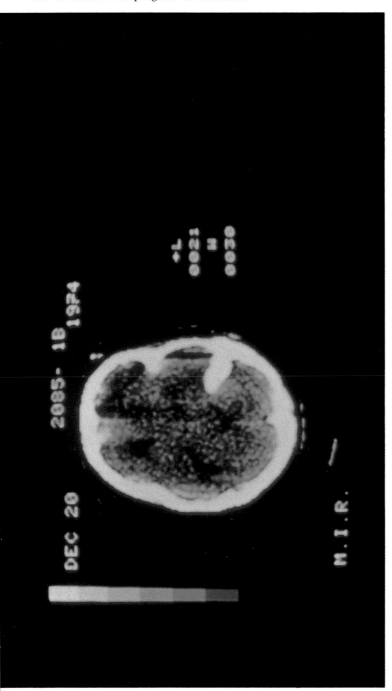

The brainscanner reveals more of the living human brain than any other instrument. Developed by EMI in Britain and used clinically for the first time in 1972, it builds up a cross-sectional image of the brain by passing a narrow beam of X-rays through the skull and coding areas of different density, displaying the image on a screen. The strange headset is moved up and down in a carefully measured way to take the brainscans. They enable surgeons to locate precisely many previously inaccessible structural abnormalities, such as tumours, haemorrhages, blood-clots and lesions.

COMMUNICATION AND INFORMATION

Gee navigation, which will help Allied bombers to pinpoint the great armament factories in the Ruhr Valley during World War II, greatly improves the accuracy of bombing. The system uses guiding radar pulses from three stations. The pilot calculates the distance of his target by plotting the station readings on a specially devised grid.

US engineer T. Ross constructs the first machine able to 'learn' from experience. The machine, based on the principle of feedback memory, can find its way out of a maze by trial and error. Later, more refined versions will become industrial robots, capable of adjusting their actions to adapt to new situations.

TRANSPORT AND WARFARE

The Boeing 307 Stratoliner is the first aircraft in airline service to provide the luxury of a pressurized cabin for its 35 passengers and 5 crew. Its cruising speed of 220 mph (354 km/h) immediately cuts flight times across the USA, but the plane will soon be requisitioned for war work.

The Czech-designed Bren gun, probably the most popular light machine-gun ever, enters service, first with the British Army, who have held manufacturing rights since 1935, and then with the free forces of Poland, China and France.

ENERGY AND INDUSTRY

Non-stick frying pans and saucepans will, in the future, make cooking and dish-washing easier as a new polymer, from which Teflon will be made, is accidentally discovered by Roy Plunkett of Du Pont. Known as PTFE (polytetrafluoro-ethylene), it resists most corrosive agents, remains uncharred by heat to 752°F (400°C), and is unaffected by sunlight and water.

The first non-stretch rayon fibre to remain strong when wet, begins life in Japan under the name of Toramomen. But the fibre is ignored for 20 years, when it resurfaces in Europe as Zantrel Polynosic.

The glass fibre industry is born when the Owens-Corning Fiberglas Corp is formed to produce the material on a large scale. Used initially for thermal insulation, glass fibre is so fine that it can be spun into yarn or woven into fabrics. Glass fibre is also strong and resists corrosion, and in the future its biggest single use will be in reinforced plastics, applied to boat hulls, car bodies and pipes.

MEDICINE AND FOOD PRODUCTION

In the USA, H.H. Merritt and T.J. Putnam describe an effective treatment for epilepsy to replace the former bromide remedy. They use a new anticonvulsant drug, Epanutin, prescribed in conjunction with phenobarbitone.

Surgery brings relief for an important cause of deafness—the hereditary condition known as otosclerosis. This is due to an overgrowth of bone gradually immobilizing the stapes, one of the tiny bones which transmits sounds to the inner ear. Now Julius Lempert in New York introduces a procedure called fenestration—cutting a window in the overgrown layers—to improve the hearing of sufferers who would otherwise need hearing aids.

Harold Cox of the US Public Health Service grows the rickettsiae microbes of typhus in the yolk sacs of laboratory chick embryos. Suitably treated, this culture yields the vaccine which, manufactured on a large scale, will give the Allied forces protection against typhus throughout World War II.

In the north of England, Reckitt and Colman begin to seek an acceptable form of soluble aspirin; but 10 years will elapse before Disprin comes on the market. Disprin Junior—quarter-strength tablets—will be introduced in 1955.

FRINGE BENEFITS

US police bring in the 'drinkometer' to test the breath of party-loving motorists.

Impressed by the quick-drying properties of printers' ink, Hungarian Lazlo Biro applied the principle to writing and invented the ball-point pen in the mid-thirties. Although patents are taken out this year, Biro works on the design for another 5 years. In 1944 the pen, which still resembles a conventional fountain pen, will become an unlikely war weapon when it is offered to British and US bomber crews—for the first time navigators have a pen that will not blot or leak at high altitudes.

John Logie Baird demonstrates high-definition colour TV on a 9 × 12 ft (2.7 × 3.6 m) screen erected in London's Dominion Theatre, and less than a fortnight later transmits live action in colour from Crystal Palace. But commercial development of colour TV in Britain is blocked by Baird's refusal to consider electronic rather than mechanical scanning systems.

The shadow mask colour TV tube—it will become universally popular—is conceived in Germany by W. Fleichsig.

Radio broadcasts can now be cut and edited on tape. WQWR Interstate Broadcasting Co, New York, are first in the field with a 15-min broadcast made from a total of 1,000 ft (33 m) of tape.

US mathematician Claude Shannon shows how an abstract algebraic system can be applied to logical problems. This will lead, a decade later, to his 'information theory' which presents communication in terms of statistics and information in terms of measured quantities, and will bring about a fundamentally new approach to computer programming.

The British 'Mallard' steam engine, pulling a seven-car train, reaches 126 mph (202 km/h)—a record speed. The engine features a streamlined shape quite unlike the traditional 'face' of a steam engine, and incorporates the best of current railway locomotive design.

After seven years' hard labour, the trans-Iranian railway is completed, reflecting the trend of less industrialized countries to establish long-distance rail links. Running through many mountainous areas, the railway has, at one point, to wind for 41 mls to cover 22 as the crow flies.

John Garrand's MI rifle is adopted by the US Army as their standard service automatic rifle. The first weapon to arm all members of a country's fighting force, the MI is called, by General Patton, 'the best battle implement ever devised'. Four million will be made by 1945.

Otto Hahn, a German atomic physicist, first splits atoms of uranium. The reaction—known as nuclear fission—releases not only vast amounts of energy but also neutrons, which themselves can split further atoms of uranium. This huge energy source will be tapped in the future to make atomic bombs and to generate electricity.

The heat of a domestic electric oven is thermostatically controlled for the first time. Made by the Simplex Electric Co, England, the thermostat is fitted to a Creda cooker.

Sixty-five per cent of British households—8.7 million homes—are now wired for electricity, compared with 1.1 million (12%) in 1921. Of these, 27% own a vacuum cleaner, 3% a washing machine, 18% a cooker, and 3% a refrigerator. By 1961, 96% of all households will have electricity.

A pressure cooker which has an interlocking pan and lid, to replace the bolts that held the lid down on previous models, is designed by Chicago draughtsman Alfred Vischer. With its saucepan-type handle and a replaceable rubber seal between pan and lid, Vischer's design sets the style for all later pressure cookers.

Surgeons are seeking ways to bring relief for painful and immobilized joints—in particular hip joints eroded by osteo-arthritis. Now Philip Wiles, a London orthopaedic surgeon, pioneers total hip replacement, operating on both hips of one disabled young patient. But the replacement parts he uses—made of stainless steel—do not last long, and two decades or more are to pass before materials are developed to the point where total hip replacement becomes standard.

In Britain, Edward Dodds develops stilboestrol, a synthetic estrogen (the female reproductive hormone) which will relieve menopausal problems, inhibit lactation and alleviate breast cancer.

German electrical engineer Ernsk Ruska—co-builder of the first crude electron microscope in 1932—and his colleague Bodo von Borries are the first to use the instrument to take photographs of viruses. With a magnifying power of up to about 7,000 ×, these electron photomicrographs show far more detail than that previously attained.

Eight years of Swiss research produces Nescafé instant coffee.

Cheap, hard-wearing and hygenic, new nylon-bristle toothbrushes are favoured by dentists and patients.

A prototype 'people's car', forerunner of the Volkswagen, is one of sixty made by German engineer Ferdinand Porsche before World War II. The engine exemplifies compact reliability: two pairs of horizontal cylinders are cooled by an engine-driven fan—a system used virtually unchanged 40 years later in the 'Beetle'.

In March, 10 years after his published thesis on the gas turbine as a power source for aircraft, Frank Whittle is given a contract by the British Government to build a jet engine. He was the first to combine the gas turbine with the principle of jet propulsion—filing patents in 1930—but received little help until officials saw the prototype turbojet running in 1937.

The surge of the jets

Early aviators dreamed that their aircraft would unite nations and bring about world peace. Ironically, however, it has been military demands that have dictated the pace of aviation technology. The jet age began in 1939, in a Germany preparing for war, with the flight of a Heinkel 178 powered by a gas turbine engine. Jet fighters appeared before the end of hostilities, but after 1945 it was the old piston-engined planes that enabled commercial airlines to recover at a time when the safety and efficiency of air travel had been proved.

In 1952, when BOAC boldly introduced the first scheduled jet passenger service—with the de Havilland Comet 1—most airlines felt this to be premature, and even in 1957 BOAC were still introducing new, slower turboprops. But passengers were quick to respond to the faster, more comfortable flights, at 'over the weather' altitudes, that jet flight had to offer. During their first year of service, Comet 1s operated at 80 per cent loads, but in 1953 a Comet 1 broke up in flight and, after two more crashes, they were withdrawn.

By 1958, when the Comet 4 entered service, commercial initiative had passed to US airlines. During the short, spectacular career of the Comet, US aircraft builders had continued their own research and development. In July 1954, Boeing flew their first jet prototype, the 387–80, later known to the world as the 707. The first of the 'big' jets, the 707 carried 179 passengers compared to the Comet's 36. It

Pioneering international air travel, Louis Blériot flew the English Channel in 1909 in a type XI monoplane of his own design. Regular London to Paris services did not begin until 1919, but Blériot's flight epitomized the commercial potential of the new mode of transport.

The jet engine, able to generate continuous rotational power and transmit it without the need for moving parts, has proved far more efficient than its predecessor, the piston engine. The axial compressor (1) sucks in, compresses and heats air, delivering it to a combustion chamber (2) where it is used to burn fuel. The turbine extracts only enough of the resulting hot gases to drive the compressor; the rest is forced out of the exhaust nozzle (3), propelling the plane forward. In 1952 BOAC flew the first scheduled jet passenger flights, and in 1958 began the first North Atlantic service with the Comet 4, *below*, the modified replacement of the Comet 1.

Frank Whittle's jet engine, designed in Britain as part of the war effort, carried this Gloster prototype aloft in 1941. Two years earlier, parallel research in Germany had resulted in the Heinkel 178. By 1944, both countries had jet fighters in service, and Gloster Meteors proved particularly successful against the V-1 flying bombs. The jet engine revolutionized aerial combat: by 1945, fighters were flying 200 mph (320 km/h) faster than any aircraft used in 1939.

spawned a whole family of passenger and cargo models and, eventually, the medium-range 727 and short-range 737. McDonnell Douglas also built their DC–8 in the fifties and the British Vickers VC–10 was introduced in 1964.

Excessive noise and fuel consumption, the twin problems of early jets, were solved with the aid of US technology. In 1958, Pratt and Whitney decided to rebuild their JT3 turbojet as a turbofan, and created an engine incorporating all the best features of its jet predecessors. American Airlines' decision to convert their entire Boeing fleet to the JT3 in 1959 led the way to faster, quieter jet travel.

In the sixties, jet passenger travel increased rapidly—between 1960 and 1966 the number of air travellers almost doubled from 106 to 200 million. Boeing responded by building the 747, the first wide-bodied 'jumbo' jet, which was double the capacity of existing aircraft.

To meet the requirements of those airlines that needed large-capacity aircraft, but could not fill the massive 747, McDonnell Douglas and Lockheed built smaller wide-bodied jets. The DC–10 seated 270 and flew over a range of 4,000 miles (6,400 km) in direct competition with TriStar, whose luxurious interiors proved that jet travel could be speedy and stylish. The latest wide-bodied airliner, the Airbus, represents Europe's attempt to break the US monopoly. Quieter than jets a tenth its size, it also boasts the lowest fuel consumption of any jet in history.

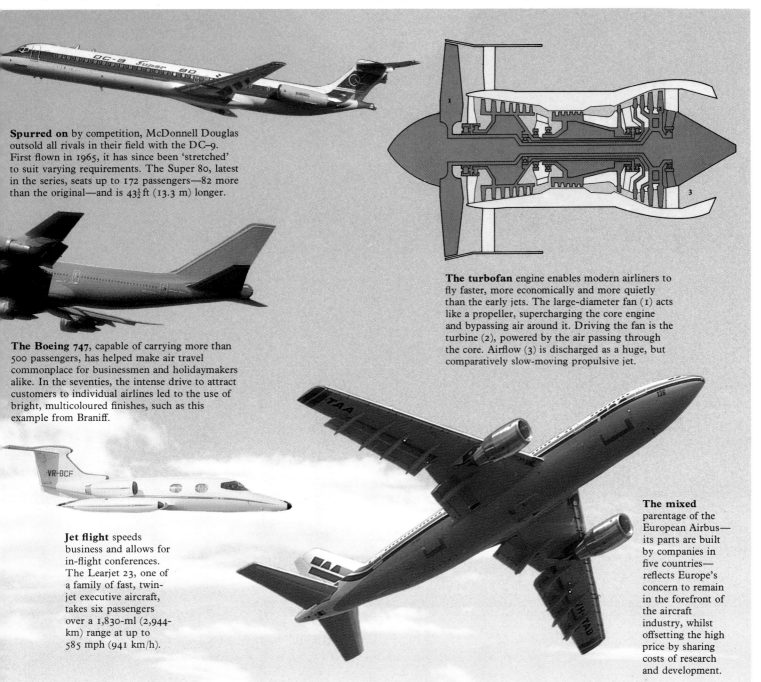

Spurred on by competition, McDonnell Douglas outsold all rivals in their field with the DC–9. First flown in 1965, it has since been 'stretched' to suit varying requirements. The Super 80, latest in the series, seats up to 172 passengers—82 more than the original—and is 43½ ft (13.3 m) longer.

The Boeing 747, capable of carrying more than 500 passengers, has helped make air travel commonplace for businessmen and holidaymakers alike. In the seventies, the intense drive to attract customers to individual airlines led to the use of bright, multicoloured finishes, such as this example from Braniff.

The turbofan engine enables modern airliners to fly faster, more economically and more quietly than the early jets. The large-diameter fan (1) acts like a propeller, supercharging the core engine and bypassing air around it. Driving the fan is the turbine (2), powered by the air passing through the core. Airflow (3) is discharged as a huge, but comparatively slow-moving propulsive jet.

Jet flight speeds business and allows for in-flight conferences. The Learjet 23, one of a family of fast, twin-jet executive aircraft, takes six passengers over a 1,830-ml (2,944-km) range at up to 585 mph (941 km/h).

The mixed parentage of the European Airbus—its parts are built by companies in five countries—reflects Europe's concern to remain in the forefront of the aircraft industry, whilst offsetting the high price by sharing costs of research and development.

COMMUNICATION AND INFORMATION

The military need for a high-powered microwave transmitter which can produce sharply defined radio and radar signals spurs J.T. Randall and H.A.H. Boot of Birmingham University, England, to invent the cavity magnetron. The new machine not only generates powerful radar pulses but its transmissions can be picked up by small receivers sited in cramped aircraft and ships. The Klystron, developed simultaneously in the USA by D.C. Hahn and the Varian brothers, serves the same purpose, but eventually proves more useful in the invention of the microwave cooker.

At New York's World's Fair, Electro and Sparks, a robot man and dog, demonstrate the art of robotics. Electro's 26 actions include smoking cigarettes, counting up to 10 on his fingers and reciting a speech. Sparks can beg, bark and wag his tail.

War correspondents can record eye-witness reports using the Midget disc recorder. Portable and easy to operate, the machine is used to produce a permanent record of many incidents of historical significance.

Professor Fischer of the Swiss Federal Institute of Technology develops the first large-screen TV projector, the Eidophor, and is among the many who believe that television theatres will head the future of the new entertainment medium.

TRANSPORT AND WARFARE

A small refrigerator in the ventilating airstream forms the first air conditioning system for cars. The US Nash Motor Co add to the comfort afforded by their 'Weather Eye' air cooling units by fitting seats that can convert into a bed.

Huge subsidies from the Germany Army have paid for the experimental rocket station at Peenemünde, on the Baltic, where the V-2s, or 'vengeance weapons', will be made. Their successful flights in 1942 prompt a German general to remark: 'We have proved rocket propulsion practicable for space travel.'

ENERGY AND INDUSTRY

French scientists Frédéric Joliot-Curie and his wife Irène, daughter of Marie Curie, show that the fission of the uranium atom by bombarding it with neutrons—particles from the atomic nuclei—releases more neutrons than are required to initiate the reaction. This indicates the possibility of a chain, or self-sustaining, nuclear reaction. Controlled, this will power the nuclear reactor which produces nuclear energy; uncontrolled, it will become the atomic bomb.

A hand-held electric slicing knife is marketed in the USA. An improvement on the fixed position slicer employing a rotating blade, it has two electrically powered serrated blades which move, side by side, to carve the meat.

The Massachusetts Institute of Technology builds a solar house in one of the first attempts to measure scientifically the domestic value of solar power. A one-storey, two-roomed building, its roof is fitted with a 410 sq ft (38 sq m) solar panel, tilted south towards the sun, which heats water stored in a tank. At the end of the first summer of the experiment, the temperature in the tank is 195°F (90.6°C).

MEDICINE AND FOOD PRODUCTION

Bacteriologist René Dubos, working at the Rockefeller Institute, isolates *Bacillus brevis* from the soil and extracts from it gramicidin. The first commercially produced compound in a group later named antibiotics, it kills some of the bacteria which cause infection, and reawakens interest in penicillin.

A miraculous addition to the armoury of chemical defences against insect vectors of disease is DDT, developed by Swiss chemist Paul Müller. But growing fears surrounding its long-term use (as well as that of other destructive chemicals) will crystallize with the publication of Rachel Carson's *Silent Spring* in 1962.

FRINGE BENEFITS

British Citizens' Advice Bureaux offer easy-access information.

'Catseyes'—reflecting studs to be set in roads—are approved for use by Britain's Ministry of Transport. They were invented by Percy Shaw, who got the idea after being saved from going off the road in thick fog by seeing the reflection of a real cat's eyes. Shaw, a Yorkshireman born in poverty, patented the idea in 1934 and went on to make a fortune from it. Each 'eye' is a prism backed by an aluminium mirror and set in pairs within a rubber pad. Each time a vehicle passes over and depresses a stud, the prisms are wiped clean by the stud's casing.

In the USA, more than 45 million radio sets are now in use. Compared with a figure of 10 million in 1929, 27.5 million US families now have a set.

Declaration of war against Germany on 3 September impels the BBC to close its television service: the reason is to prevent transmitters serving as navigational beacons for the enemy. But in the seven years before national broadcasts begin again, research and development continue on a modest scale.

Typesetting by photographic means is progressing apace. In the USA, William C. Heubner introduces a photocomposing machine in which the characters are arranged round a circular plate. When the operator moves the disc into position for a particular character, he can press a key which projects that character through a system of lenses on to a photographic film.

The radio altimeter, by which a pilot can calculate his height above the ground, is developed in the USA at the Bell Laboratories. The altimeter bounces signals off the Earth and measures the time they take to return to the aircraft. The pilot then uses a calibrated indicator to translate this figure—the relative altitude—into a figure giving his absolute altitude.

In Britain the print run of the National Registration Identity card is 45 million.

Degaussing is developed by the British Navy to protect ships against magnetic mines laid by U-boats. A ship's natural magnetism, which explodes the mines, is neutralized by current-carrying coils wound round the hull, or by 'wiping' (a process similar to the wiping clean of a magnetic tape).

Pan Am's Boeing B314, the 'Yankee Clipper' flying-boat, carries 17 passengers and the mail from Washington, USA to Southampton, England, to inaugurate the first regular commercial transatlantic service. Powered by four 1,500 hp Wright Double Cyclone engines, and with a range of 3,100 mls, the 314 will maintain this service throughout World War II.

The first jet aircraft, simply called the He 178, flies on 27 August in Germany. Ernst Heinkel's financial support enables Pabst von Ohain to develop his gas turbine engine more quickly than the dilatory British, who are slow to realize the potential of Frank Whittle's jet engine, patented some nine years earlier.

The manufacture of nylon starts at the Du Pont de Nemours factory. The first nylon stockings—nylons, as they will be called—are made and sold to Du Pont's employees. The first man-made fibre to be made exclusively from mineral sources, nylon is extremely strong, elastic, mothproof, does not absorb moisture and is not degradable by biological agents. It will be an ideal material for ropes, parachutes and sails, as well as for waterproof fabrics and drip-dry cloth.

The solar house, built by Dr Maria Telkes, proves that flat metal plates, painted black and covered with glass or plastic glazing, will successfully heat air. The transfer of the heat from metal to air is much improved if the plates are corrugated, since the corrugations give a greater surface area to be heated.

Polythene is made commercially by ICI in England. This plastic polymer is tough, chemically inert, and does not conduct electricity. It will soon transform the manufacture of electric cables and will have so many industrial and domestic uses—from packaging to unbreakable bottles—that it will become one of the most important of all plastics.

Two biochemists, Henrik Dam of Copenhagen University and Edward Doisy of St Louis, isolate pure vitamin K, which is essential for normal clotting of blood. Later in the year, Louis Fieser will synthesize it in the laboratory.

At the Children's Hospital in Boston, Mass., Robert Gross performs a pioneering feat in paracardiac surgery. He operates on a child to tie off a connection—a remnant of foetal circulation—between the great blood vessels entering and leaving the heart.

Chicago surgeon Charles Huggins develops a two-stage treatment for prostate cancer. After removal of the testes, his treatment using the female sex hormone estrogen demonstrates how a major cancer can be controlled by purely chemical means.

Precooked frozen foods are on sale for the first time, under the Birds Eye label.

US President Franklin D. Roosevelt appoints an Advisory Committee on Uranium after Albert Einstein informs him of the potential of atomic fission for military ends. Einstein and other scientists are alert to the Germans' possible use of radioactive materials to make bombs, as German research is in advance of American.

The Parker Dam, on the Colorado River at the border between Arizona and California, begins to provide water for Los Angeles and other West Coast cities. Standing 320 ft (98 m) high and 856 ft (261 m) long, it was equipped with a hydroelectric power plant with an output of 120 MW—enough to supply the needs of about 150,000 people.

Arming the superpowers

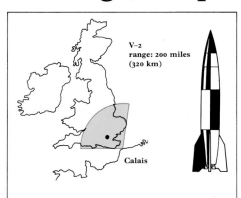

The German V–2, launched on London in 1944, was used to equally devastating effect against Paris and Antwerp. At the war's end, plans were discovered for a version intended to attack the USA.

In the aftermath of World War II, as relations between East and West became ever more frigid, both America and Russia began work to refine an ultimate weapon. If launched, this weapon would be able to reduce nations to rubble at the touch of a button but it would, by its truly terrible power, also act to deter war. One such weapon of devastation is the inter-continental ballistic missile (ICBM) which is able to travel thousands of miles to its target. Among the latest Soviet ICBMs is one with a device whose explosive power is 2,500 times that of the Hiroshima atomic bomb.

Missile technology had its origins in Nazi Germany, home of the V–2 long-range rockets which delivered one-ton warheads at speeds of up to 3,500 mph (5,600 km/h). The V–2 was to be the precursor of both ICBMs and space rockets. After the armistice, America and Russia welcomed German scientists with their rocketry and guided weapons expertise.

Initial American work on post-war weapons was closely linked to the development of nuclear power and to the twin doctrines of potential retaliation and deterrence. But by 1949 a Russian fission device had been exploded and eight years later the Soviet SS–6, the world's initial ICBM, scored a second success as it launched Sputnik, the first satellite, into space. The arms race had begun.

The early ICBMs were weapons of threat and last resort. Even second generation ICBMs were little more refined. The US Titan II of 1963, for example, had a huge 10-megaton warhead (one megaton has the equi-

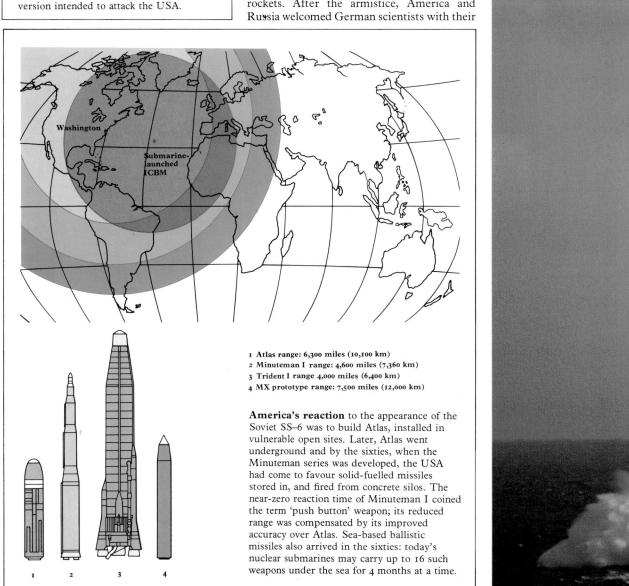

1 **Atlas** range: 6,300 miles (10,100 km)
2 **Minuteman I** range: 4,600 miles (7,360 km)
3 **Trident I** range 4,000 miles (6,400 km)
4 **MX prototype** range: 7,500 miles (12,000 km)

America's reaction to the appearance of the Soviet SS–6 was to build Atlas, installed in vulnerable open sites. Later, Atlas went underground and by the sixties, when the Minuteman series was developed, the USA had come to favour solid-fuelled missiles stored in, and fired from concrete silos. The near-zero reaction time of Minuteman I coined the term 'push button' weapon; its reduced range was compensated by its improved accuracy over Atlas. Sea-based ballistic missiles also arrived in the sixties: today's nuclear submarines may carry up to 16 such weapons under the sea for 4 months at a time.

valent explosive power of a million tons of TNT) so inaccurate that it was little more than a blunt instrument capable only of flattening cities. This was despite its increased range—nearly double that of its predecessors—and improved guidance system.

As the sixties progressed, the policy of potential retaliation gave way to one of mutual deterrence. As the superpowers became in-

creasingly aware of the possibility of holocaust by accident, they initiated arms limitation treaties. At the same time, however, they also began work on improving the quality and quantity of their ICBM forces, including ballistic missiles launched from submarines, to strengthen their negotiating position.

During these years, America built up a force of small, accurate missiles which could be kept at instant and indefinite readiness inside hardened underground silos. Minuteman II, which first flew in 1964, incorporated new guidance systems and penetration aids, or 'penaids'. These included 'chaff'—clouds of aluminium foil designed to deter enemy radar. Minuteman III carried the first multiple independently targeted reentry vehicle (MIRV) in which individual warheads were grouped together in one cone. By this time, accuracy had reached an astonishing 380 yards (350 m)

over a range of 8,062 miles (12,900 km).

The USSR meanwhile had developed the giant SS–9—potentially the most destructive of any mass-produced weapon in history, dispensing a 25–megaton warhead over 7,500 miles (12,000 km). Between 1975 and 1980 these weapons were largely replaced by SS–17s, 18s and 19s. Cold-launched from a silo of novel design, the SS–18 has been described as a 'monster with cataclysmic power' and its eight 2–megaton MIRVs have an incredible accuracy of 195 yards (180 m).

Faced with a constantly improving Soviet ICBM force, the Americans have been compelled to press for modernization of their missile force and to develop their new MX system. As each side moves cautiously toward the conference table, there may eventually come a better use for the deadly power each holds—as an instrument of peace.

The US Trident missile is pictured in its first flight, *below*, as it is fired from the nuclear submarine USS *Ohio* in January 1982. Such submerged firing sites are increasingly preferred to more vulnerable land sites.

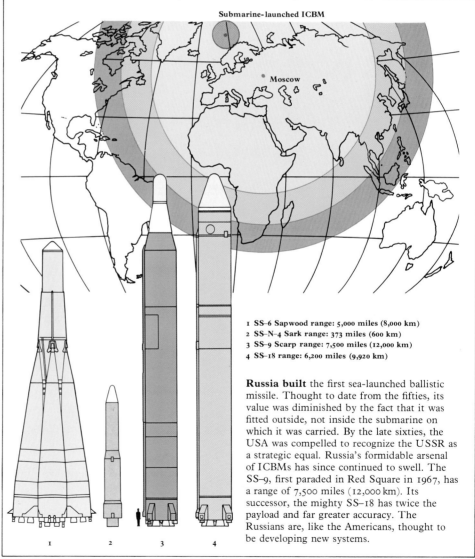

Submarine-launched ICBM

1 SS–6 Sapwood range: 5,000 miles (8,000 km)
2 SS–N–4 Sark range: 373 miles (600 km)
3 SS–9 Scarp range: 7,500 miles (12,000 km)
4 SS–18 range: 6,200 miles (9,920 km)

Russia built the first sea-launched ballistic missile. Thought to date from the fifties, its value was diminished by the fact that it was fitted outside, not inside the submarine on which it was carried. By the late sixties, the USA was compelled to recognize the USSR as a strategic equal. Russia's formidable arsenal of ICBMs has since continued to swell. The SS–9, first paraded in Red Square in 1967, has a range of 7,500 miles (12,000 km). Its successor, the mighty SS–18 has twice the payload and far greater accuracy. The Russians are, like the Americans, thought to be developing new systems.

COMMUNICATION AND INFORMATION

Broadcasting speech, using the system of pulse modulation as an alternative to frequency modulation (FM) or amplitude modulation (AM), has the immediate advantages of low cost, low distortion and low background noise. Future applications of the system include long-distance sound and vision communications—even from outer space.

The Plan Position Indicator (PPI), is developed in Britain and will arrive in the USA in time for her entry into the war. As an aircraft is detected by radar echo, it appears on the circular screen as a pattern of fast-moving dots against a cartographic background. After successful tests aboard USS *Semmes*, the PPI is used for anti-submarine patrol and blind bombing.

TRANSPORT AND WARFARE

Following Blitzkrieg victories in Poland and the Low Countries, the Luftwaffe confronts the Royal Air Force in what is soon called 'The Battle of Britain'—and fails. Encountering a 'modern' air force for the first time, the Luftwaffe loses many experienced pilots and, by September, the RAF has the upper hand, averting the threat of a German invasion of Britain.

The US Air Force P-51 Mustang is a single-seat, single-engined, long-range fighter and fighter-bomber. Designed to an RAF specification, and fitted with an American-built Rolls-Royce Merlin engine, Mustangs will destroy 4,950 enemy aircraft in the European war zone alone.

ENERGY AND INDUSTRY

Scientists Peierls and Frisch draw attention to the huge explosive power in a small amount of uranium 235, and to the effect of the radiation that would be released.

Tyres of rubber made from such surprising materials as potatoes, grain, petroleum and coal tar are made by the B.F. Goodrich Co, USA. By 1955 the company will produce a million tons annually—more than all the natural and reclaimed rubber produced in that year.

Walls, floors and ceilings will soon be covered by blocks of foam glass, an excellent heat-insulating material, which is produced for the first time by aerating ordinary molten glass.

Cheap, long-lasting underground electrical cables are made. Layers of paper, steel tape and jute protect cables from the dual menace of corrosion and rodents.

The first gas-powered turbine in the world to generate electricity for public use begins operating at a power station in Neuchatel, Switzerland.

MEDICINE AND FOOD PRODUCTION

Freeze drying, first used to store biological material such as penicillin, is adapted for food preservation in the USA. Frozen food is placed in a heated chamber to dry—a process later accelerated by the use of a vacuum pump to aid the removal of the food's water vapour. The freeze-dried food reconstitutes swiftly, with little loss of flavour or aroma.

Harvard University's Edwin Cohn separates the albumin, globulin and fibrin fractions of blood plasma. Albumin will be used to treat shock, globulin to treat infection and fibrin to halt bleeding.

In Britain D.D. Woods and Sir Paul Fildes explain the way in which the sulfa drugs successfully combat bacterial diseases such as pneumonia, meningitis and venereal disease. But even these drugs (which work by depriving bacteria of nutrients) will soon be eclipsed by far more potent antibacterial agents: the antibiotics.

FRINGE BENEFITS

The Jeep, designed by US engineer Karl Pabst, is a general-purpose (GP) vehicle. Lightweight but sturdy, it can ride over rough terrain, climb 60% gradients and ford shallow streams. It is used for a variety of military tasks: as a command or reconnaissance car, or for the carriage of weapons. Some Jeeps will be armoured for combat misssions, others given waterproof hulls and propellers. Over 600,000 will be built by 1945, peak production rate at one factory reaching one every 80 seconds.

In an experimental broadcast in the USA, high-definition colour TV is demonstrated. The system, developed by Dr Peter Goldmark of CBS, is similar to—but more successful than—the one demonstrated in Britain by Baird two years before. The transmissions can even be picked up on monochrome (black and white) sets.

The Kodatron Speedlamp brings the pioneering work of Dr Harold Edgerton at MIT to professional photography. It creates a brief, high-intensity flash which allows the novel photography of action shots in a studio.

'Oboe', a high-precision method of radar navigation, aids bomber pilots in locating targets and timing attacks. 'Cat-and-mouse' ground stations, up to 150 mls (240 km) from the target, provide guidance information through earphones and effect an automatic bomb release once on target. Bombs can be dropped from 30,000 ft (9,000 m) to within 150 yds (130 m) of the target.

Glider-borne German troops, their craft towed by Ju-52 transport planes, drift silently on to the 'impregnable' Belgian fort of Eben Emael and begin to destroy it. Parachute troops add reinforcements at daybreak, the 1,000-man garrison surrenders, and the Belgian front is broken.

Commercial airlines in the USA complete a whole year of operations—from March 1939 to March 1940—for the first time without suffering a single fatal accident.

Named after the initials of its designers, A.I. Mikoyan and M.I. Gurevich, the deadly Russian MiG-1 is equally at home with guns and rocket projectiles—acting as a fighter-interceptor—as it is with 440 lbs (199.6 kg) of bombs.

The rare, light isotope of uranium, known as uranium 235, is isolated for the first time from the common, heavier isotope uranium 238. A team at Columbia University, New York, shows that the light isotope is more fissionable than the heavier one and will release the immense amount of energy required for nuclear weapons and nuclear power stations.

The Tacoma Narrows suspension bridge, with a span of 2,800 ft (853 m) and a width of only 39 ft (11.8 m), opens over Puget Sound, Washington, USA. While graceful and slender, the bridge is susceptible to undulations caused by the wind, so much so that it becomes affectionately known as 'Galloping Gertie'. In four months' time the bridge will start to vibrate and twist and will eventually collapse. The disaster will lead civil engineers to test all later bridges for their aerodynamic stability, and to intensify research into the effects of the wind on large structures.

A breakthrough in finding a metal suitable for gas turbine blades is made after intensive research results in nickel-chromium alloys: about 3% aluminium and 30% titanium added to a nickel-chrome base produce the new alloys, called Nimonics. They resist any creep that might arise from a centrifugal force working at high temperatures and they are not subject to fatigue.

In Britain, E.P. Abraham and E. Chain discover germs which are resistant to the new wonder drug, penicillin. The germs contain an enzyme called penicillinase, which negates the effect of penicillin. The discovery of these resistant bacteria prompts the search for further antibiotics which will not succumb to this disruptive enzyme.

Dutch doctors recognize that coeliac disease—the small intestine fails to absorb food, particularly fats—can be caused by sensitivity to gluten, the major protein of wheat and rye. This discovery comes about fortuitously when the occupying German forces requisition all supplies of wheat and rye flour, after which coeliac patients in Dutch hospitals begin to show improvement.

Karl Landsteiner and a team at the Rockefeller Institute discover the Rhesus factor in blood (so called because it was first identified in rhesus monkeys). Rh factors will later be linked to haemolytic disease of the newborn—the result of an Rh-negative mother developing antibodies when blood from her Rh-positive foetus enters her circulation. In subsequent pregnancies these antibodies invade the foetal blood, causing severe jaundice, brain damage or still-birth.

The 'larger than life' quality of Walt Disney's *Fantasia*, an animated visualization of musical classics, is enhanced by the use of stereophonic sound. This is the first time a film sound-track has been recorded in multi-dimensional sound, created via a three-channel stereophonic system.

Igor Sikorksy is pictured at the controls of his prototype VS–300 helicopter which makes its first free flight on 13 May. The Russian-born inventor—who built his first helicopter in 1909 and the world's first multi-engined plane in 1912—has worked in the USA since 1923. In May 1941 the VS–300, the world's first practical single-rotor helicopter, will establish a world helicopter endurance record by remaining airborne for over $1\frac{1}{2}$ hrs.

COMMUNICATION AND INFORMATION

Forces' mail is sent by 'Airgraph', a microfilm airmail service based on the Recordak microfilm system. Letters written on special forms are photographed on 16 mm films. These are flown to depots all over the world, where enlarged copies are made. The bulk and weight of the mail are thus greatly reduced and morale—both at the front and at home—boosted immeasurably. When the USA enters the war, the same method will be used for GI mail under the name 'V-mail'.

The proximity radio fuse lessens the need for pinpoint marksmanship by fighter pilots. A tiny radio transmitter fitted into a shell emits radio waves which are reflected back from the target to a receiver. When the return time falls below a certain value, the shell is near enough to its target and explodes. US scientists will take over the development of the device from its British inventor, W.S. Butement.

In a Moscow cinema, S.P. Ivanov installs a stereo movie system: its screen gives a 3–D effect without the audience having to wear special spectacles. Only the limited number and arrangement of seats restrict the system's commercial scope.

TRANSPORT AND WARFARE

The Owen 9 mm Parabellum sub-machine-gun becomes the official weapon of the Australian Army. Designed by one of its own soldiers, Lt Evelyn Owen, some 45,000 will be made before production ends in 1944.

W1, the jet engine designed by Frank Whittle, is used to power the Gloster E28/29, an experimental aircraft built especially for the tests. Though the W1 performs successfully, Whittle decides that a bigger, more powerful engine should be designed for mass production. Unfortunately, the W2 runs into development difficulties which delay the introduction of the Allies' first jet, the Gloster Meteor, until 1944.

ENERGY AND INDUSTRY

Polyurethanes, a class of polymers, are commercially produced by the German company I.G. Farbenindustrie. First discovered between 1937–9 by Otto Bayer, their properties mean they can be used as plastics and fibres, though later research will extend their usefulness, and they will become ingredients of adhesives, hard surface coatings and rigid foams.

Polyester fibre is discovered by E. Whinfield, working at the laboratory of the Calico Printers Association in Accrington, England. The new fibre, which follows closely on the heels of nylon, is tough, resists both wear and sunlight, and does not stretch easily. It will be marketed as Dacron in the USA and as Terylene in Britain.

MEDICINE AND FOOD PRODUCTION

An Australian eye specialist, Norman Gregg, sounds the first alert over German measles (rubella) in early pregnancy. He finds eye cataracts in babies whose mothers have had rubella while pregnant. Later, other congenital abnormalities are reported, including blindness, deafness, heart disease and mental subnormality.

In the USA, Albert Coons devises immunofluorescence to track down unidentified disease organisms. He labels antibodies of lobar pneumonia with a dye that fluoresces under ultraviolet light, and traces their progress after they contact the bacillus.

FRINGE BENEFITS

Johannes Croning's shell moulding process enables metals to be shaped more accurately, with a smoother surface. The use of a thin form, made of sand held together by resin, revolutionizes metal casting. Moulds can now be made on automatic machines, and products—from needles to propellers—have a better finish.

Lithography becomes the first printing process to move into the age of plastics. The first plastic litho plates are followed, later in the year, by pre-sensitized plates coated with a solution which does not lose its sensitivity during storage. The plates prove ideal for producing maps and charts for use in the front line.

Using radar television (H_2S), Allied bomber pilots no longer need visual sitings of targets. Very short radio waves, which can penetrate darkness, cloud, smoke and fog, present geographical elements, such as soil, stone and water, as different shadings on a screen in the cockpit. The outline of a city, such as Berlin or Hamburg, appears despite the murky atmosphere. The newly acquired ability to detect metallic objects at sea helps contain the U-boat menace. The first plane to fly with H_2S equipment on board is the British Halifax V9977 bomber.

Two radical advances in computer design are incorporated into German scientist Konrad Zuse's Z2 computer. Electromagnetic relays, replacing clumsy mechanical switches, significantly improve the machine's speed and reliability, and a punched tape system is used as an input device instead of a keyboard. In 1943, Zuse will found the first computer company, Zuse Apparatebau, to produce a radio-controlled flying bomb, but all the equipment is destined to be destroyed in an air raid.

The world's first gas turbine railway locomotives, are introduced by the Swiss Federal Railways, and eight years later by Britain's Great Western. At first, their inefficiency and high running cost at variable speeds cause both countries to abandon them. But, by the sixties, Britain and France will revive the gas turbine, to power prototypes of the APT (Advanced Passenger Train) and TGV (*Train Grande Vitesse*).

The Russian Il-2 dive bomber, known as the Stormovik, flies. The heavily armoured two-seater is used for low-level attack, diving at high speed to drop high-explosive bombs and to fire guns and rockets at tanks. The first aircraft equipped with air-to-ground rockets, the Il-2 proves more than a match for even the heavy German tanks, breaking up many ground operations before they start.

A large windmill is built on Grandpa's Knob, Vermont, USA and delivers 1.25 MW of electricity directly to the grid system, so producing the first synchronous generation of electric power by the wind. The wind generator will remain in use until 1945, when one of its blades will break and it will be dismantled.

The Grand Coulee Dam opens on the Columbia River, Washington, USA. Built for electricity generation and irrigation purposes, this feat of engineering impounds a 150-ml (241-km) stretch of water and has 21 turbine generators to produce vast amounts of electricity. Twelve electrically driven pumps raise water from the dam to be distributed by canals to irrigate 1,200,000 acres of dry, barren land, thus providing farmland for 75,000 people.

Plutonium is isolated at Berkeley, California, by E. Seaborg and E. McMillan, who show that the element would be better than uranium as a fuel for nuclear reactors because of its higher energy yield. It will be used in the US atomic bombs dropped on Japan in 1945.

Penicillin enters clinical use 13 years after its discovery by Alexander Fleming. The drug has been isolated from the *Penicillium notatum* mould by an Australian pathologist, Howard Florey, and German-born biochemist Ernst Chain, working together at Oxford, England.

In Britain, David Evans of the Medical Research Council reports that a third dose of tetanus toxoid, administered 10 months after the original two doses, rapidly yields much greater amounts of antitoxin in the bloodstream than have been noted up to now. This leads to the introduction of booster anti-tetanus injections.

Recalling the work of Werner Forssmann, who performed cardiac catheterization on himself in 1929, Dickinson Richards and French-born André Cournand develop the procedure on patients at New York's Bellevue Hospital. This is an important advance in the diagnosis of heart disease.

Robert Watson-Watt's team of scientists, working in the greatest secrecy, developed radio-location equipment—radar—in the thirties. In 1937, construction began on a chain of radar stations along Britain's coastline, to provide the first early-warning system. The latest equipment has made it even more effective.

The aerosol is developed by research chemist L.D. Goodhue and entomologist W.N. Sullivan as a means of countering the high mortality rate of US troops serving in the Pacific—in 1942 more soldiers will die of infection and disease than in battle. Goodhue and Sullivan's device sprays a fog of insecticide to control the disease-bearing pests of the tropics; 50 million will be manufactured and distributed to the US forces overseas, who christen them 'bug bombs'.

COMMUNICATION AND INFORMATION

LORAN (Long Range Air Navigation), which marks the world's air and sea lanes like streets, goes into operation at four stations between the Chesapeake Capes and Nova Scotia. LORAN, a natural successor to the GEE system developed in Britain and given to the USA in 1940, can at long range, give an aircraft pilot or ship's captain his position to within a few hundred yards. The LORAN receiver, developed at MIT, picks up radio signals as pairs of 'pips' on a screen; when the pips intersect, the position is indicated.

Snapshots go coloured as Eastman Kodak launch Kodacolor roll film. A multi-layer colour negative film is used to make prints on paper and is sensitive enough to be used in simple cameras—at least in good light.

TRANSPORT AND WARFARE

The USA's first jet plane, the XP-59, makes its maiden flight on 1 October, powered by two General Electric 1-A turbojets based on Whittle's W2B design. Intended as a fighter, its poor performance makes it fit only to train pilots for the Lockheed P-80.

'Bazooka' is the nickname of a rocket-launcher tested by the US Army for the first time in May. Developed as a short-range anti-tank weapon, the 5-ft (1.5-m) smooth-bore tube is shoulder-held, to fire a 19 in (48.3 cm) long rocket containing an armour-penetrating explosive. The rocket's low velocity makes the bazooka inaccurate, even at close range, but improved models will appear late in the war.

Napalm is developed by a Harvard chemist, Louis Fieser. Used in flame-throwers and bombs by the US forces, the jelly-like mixture, inexpensively made of gasoline and palm oils, sticks to its target until it is burned out.

ENERGY AND INDUSTRY

Natural gas is liquefied for the first time in Cleveland, Ohio, where small quantities of the gas—mainly methane—are cooled to −162°C. A fatal explosion in 1944 will delay its development as a means of transporting and storing the fuel.

MEDICINE AND FOOD PRODUCTION

Prompted by the exigencies of war, the British Government agrees to the Lend-Lease arrangement, an Anglo-American venture in which US agricultural machines are shipped to Britain to replace horses and old or inefficient implements. Lend-Lease, combined with the ploughing up of five and a half million acres of old grassland for arable crops, will, by 1945, produce a British agricultural industry receptive to widespread mechanization.

S. Hertz and A. Roberts pioneer a safer treatment for hyperthyroidism, using radioactive iodine. Instead of being surgically removed, diseased tissues in an over-active thyroid gland are killed by radiation.

Leishmaniasis (named after William Leishman, the English pathologist who discovered the causative parasite in 1900) is a group of diseases, including Kala-azar ('black' fever) and tropical sore, found in the Near and Far East, Africa and South America. Only now is the insect carrier discovered—one species of sandfly, *Phlebotomus argentipes*.

FRINGE BENEFITS

An inflatable armchair set on a timber or metal frame is made by Elliott Equipment, specialists in aircraft dinghies.

Coming into use in North Africa with the British Army, the Bailey Bridge will eventually find civilian applications as well as military. Made of braced panels, Bailey Bridges can be erected quickly by an army on the move as anything from a simple, lightweight bridge, to one capable of carrying heavy armour—the British Army in Africa, for example, constructs bridges up to 220 ft (68 m) with load capacities up to 100 tons. Extra strength is easily gained by doubling or trebling the panels in each section. Civilian use will be mainly in cases of flood or accident, but the Bailey Bridge will see service in any context in which rapid or temporary bridging is required.

John Logie Baird comes a step closer to a complete imitation of reality with his 3–D colour TV. Images, corresponding alternately to the inputs for left and right eyes, create nerve impulses which blend in the human brain to produce an illusion of depth and solidity. Only one person can view the experimental pictures at a time, but Baird has high hopes for the future of stereoscopic TV.

The USA enters the war and bans the manufacture of TV stations and receivers.

Wartime tape-recording strides forward, following the innovations of Martin Camras, a young US engineer. Improved coating for magnetic tapes and the skilful reduction of sound distortion from the tape itself, are soon adopted worldwide.

The Avro Lancaster is a heavy, four-engined bomber, described by the chief of RAF's Bomber Command as the greatest single factor in winning the war. Its load-carrying ability and excellent performance put it into massive production immediately. Modified Lancasters carry out some of the most famous raids of the war: breaking the Möhne and Eder dams in 1943, sinking the German battleship *Tirpitz* in 1944 and destroying the Bielefeld viaduct with 22,000-lb (9,988-kg) 'Grand Slam' bombs in 1945.

X-ray pictures of munition castings and welding illuminate flaws more quickly and speed up vital wartime production. The X-ray tube, developed at the US Westinghouse Lamp Division Laboratories, can also take high-speed X-ray pictures at a millionth of a second.

A 10,000-ton cargo ship is built in an amazing 10 days and delivered, ready for sea, only five days later. Under the direction of Henry J. Kaiser, 2,770 'Liberty' ships will be built in US shipyards by 1945 to replace vessels lost through enemy action.

US Army engineers construct the Alaska-Canadian Highway in 8 months, at an estimated cost of $135 million. Planned since 1930, the 1,523-ml (2,450.5-km) all-weather road is only now built at such huge cost because Alaska has become a strategically important area.

The world's first controlled, self-sustaining nuclear chain reaction is achieved by Enrico Fermi and others in a modified squash court at the University of Chicago. Using what is the first experimental nuclear reactor, they complete the groundwork necessary for the inception of the 'Manhattan Project', established to produce the atomic bomb.

Selman Waksman, a microbiologist at Rutgers University, N.J., discovers and isolates streptomycin from a microscopic soil fungus. The first real cure for tuberculosis, it banishes forever the human fear of this dreaded disease. He also introduces the word 'antibiotic' to embrace the new, active compounds being found in the soil.

Although unconscious and unaware of pain, a patient's body still reacts to painful stimuli, and so muscle spasms are one of the problems facing the surgeon. H.R. Griffith and Enid Johnson of Montreal introduce curare (the poison used by South American Indians) as a relaxant.

Diabetics will benefit from André Loubatière's discovery that sulfa drugs are closely related to a substance in the vitamin B complex, which has the effect of reducing blood-sugar levels.

As British potato acreage increases significantly because of quotas levied by the Government to feed the nation during wartime, the Packman potato harvester speeds up production of the crop. The new machine lifts the potatoes from the soil and carries them to bags or a trailer, but stones and clods still have to be sorted from the crop by hand.

The lightweight nylon parachute is developed by a firm in Manchester, England.

Heinz go into battle. The self-heating can proves to be a blessing on the battlefield, where conventional heating may not be available, and in situations—such as undercover missions—where lighting a fire has to be avoided. The lifeboat service, too, finds self-heating cans useful and will continue to do so for more than a quarter of a century, until production costs become too high. The heat source is housed in a vertical tube through the middle of the can. The cap is peeled off to reveal the fuse, which in turn ignites the main heating mixture. In four or five minutes the contents of the can are evenly heated.

The biggest gun of all time shells Sevastopol. 'Gustav' fires 5-ton shells 30 mls, is mounted on railway tracks and weighs more than 1,350 tons. Its total staff and operating crew number 1,420, 500 of whom are engaged in the actual firing. One of the mysteries at the end of the war will be the complete disappearance of this vast German gun.

COMMUNICATION AND INFORMATION

The Colossus decoding machine gives the Allies a direct line to the German high command. The machine works fast enough to test all possible code combinations before the information becomes outdated, and accurately decodes the crucial Enigma messages until the end of the war.

TRANSPORT AND WARFARE

Designed in 1939 as a civil airliner, the Lockheed Constellation is commandeered as a military transport, the C-69. Back in commercial service by 1946, the 'Connie' cruises at 300 mph (483 km/h)—80 mph (129 km/h) faster than its rival, the Douglas DC-4. Throughout the fifties, Lockheed and Douglas piston-engined planes will compete fiercely until the jets take over.

A Goblin turbojet, one of the first British jet engines to be produced in large numbers, powers the de Havilland Vampire to speeds of 531 mph (854 km/h); in 1945, it will become the first jet to operate from an aircraft carrier's deck.

Russia's most successful woman fighter pilot, Lt Lydia Litviak of the 73rd Guards Fighter Air Regiment, is killed in action on 1 August. She scored 18 confirmed victories.

ENERGY AND INDUSTRY

Electric cables filled with pressurized gas as a means of insulation are tested by the Central Electricity Board. Because the gas insulation takes up little space, three cores—separate metal conductors—can be put into one cable, which can carry the vast amount of 132,000 V. The CEB installs $1\frac{1}{4}$ mls (2 km) of the high-power cable at Burford in Oxfordshire, England—the first such installation.

Very tough materials, such as hardened steel and Nimonic alloys, can now be cut and shaped easily by a new process that employs an electric impulse to cut through the metal. Known as electro-discharge machining, or spark erosion, the technique will be used extensively in manufacturing machine tools and dies.

Wartime shortage of rubber stimulates the development of plasticized PVC for use in electrical insulation and vehicle tyres. It proves so versatile that it will also be used for piping, upholstery and shoes.

MEDICINE AND FOOD PRODUCTION

Swiss chemist Albert Hofmann discovers the hallucinogenic qualities of LSD when he accidentally swallows a few crystals of a derivative of ergot. The effects wear off after two hours, but the episode becomes sufficiently notorious to alert pharmaceutical companies to the possibilities of 'mind-expanding' drugs.

DDT reaches the USA. The pesticide is hailed as a boon to farmers because of its effectiveness against crop pests, and will be manufactured and used in large quantities.

Chemists at the University of Stockholm produce xylocaine for use as a local anaesthetic. Safer than compounds in the cocaine-procaine group, it will first be used at the Karolinska Hospital and will soon gain worldwide recognition.

FRINGE BENEFITS

Matchbox cameras are made for wartime intelligence use.

Relief for kidney patients comes with a new machine, built by Wilhelm Kolff, a Dutch doctor. Essentially a sophisticated pump, the machine moves dialysing fluid from a tank, where it is prepared and brought to the right temperature, to a cellophane filter, where it removes poisons from the patient's blood. The cleansed or dialysed blood is then circulated back into the sufferer's body. Designed to offer temporary relief to patients while damaged kidneys recover, the machine will be updated to form part of this 'Diakhron-80' machine which will become operative in the sixties.

Long distance telephone calls are transformed from 'snap, crackle and pop' into coherent sound with the insertion of telephone repeaters into the lines at regular intervals, to amplify two-way sound. After five years of experimental work, the first submarine cable to be fitted with such repeaters is laid between Anglesey in Wales and the Isle of Man off NW England.

In a raid on Hamburg on the night of 24/25 July, RAF Bomber Command aircraft drop thin strips of metal foil to confuse German radar. The device—known as 'window'—succeeds in disorientating the defenders, and only 12 aircraft from a force of 700 are lost to enemy guns and night fighters.

Code-named 'Mammut', or Mammoth, the super-heavy German Maus tank weighs in at 188 tons and is intended to out-gun and outlast any Allied opposition. Protected by $9\frac{1}{2}$ in (24.13 cm) thick frontal armour and heavy guns, the Maus has also to be fully submersible, since no bridge can take its weight. Although the prototype is tested, it never goes into production: by 1944, German industry is taking all material available for conventional weapons.

The 'Dambusters', the RAF's 617 squadron, successfully bomb the German Möhne and Eder dams on 17 May. Their Lancaster Special B MKIIIs are adapted to carry the spinning drum bomb developed by Dr Barnes Wallis to reach a dam face protected by torpedo netting. The huge drum is spun by an engine in the bomber's fuselage just before release; when it hits the water, it bounces over the netting and, striking the dam wall just below the waterline, explodes.

Steel is cast continuously for the first time by S. Junghans in Germany, using a machine developed in 1933 for continuously casting copper alloys. Junghans' machine will be the prototype of later industrial-scale steel plants.

The world's first operational nuclear reactor is constructed and activated at Oak Ridge, Tennessee, USA. This, and the first water-cooled reactor built at Hanford, Washington, provide plutonium for the 'Manhattan Project'.

Silicones are manufactured commercially by the new Dow Corning Corp, USA. Discovered in 1904 by F. Kipping, they are a large family of chemicals composed chiefly of silicon, oxygen and carbon. Their technological advantage lies in their reluctance to be affected by any other substances. They are the prime material of spare parts for the human body, from artificial hearts and valves to the cosmetic augmentation of a breast or a jaw.

Two friends, Paul Burkholder at Yale and research chemist Oliver Kamm, begin their quest for the first broad-spectrum antibiotic—a compound derived from the soil which will prove to be effective on a number of diseases. The men will sift through more than 7,000 samples from around the world, and, in 1947, they will isolate chloramphenicol from Venuzuelan soil. This drug will combat a number of disease microbes, including the rickettsiae.

Diabetes insipidus is a disorder characterized by a failure to form concentrated urine. Sufferers urinate frequently and experience continual thirst. Control of the disease is much improved by the vasopressin treatment developed in Britain by Court and Taylor. This antidiuretic hormone from the pituitary gland stimulates the kidneys to retain water.

Hepatitis is found to be two distinct diseases with many similar features, but different causative agents (both viruses). P.O. McCallum and G.M. Findlay conclude that hepatitis A, with a short incubation period, is infectious. But hepatitis B, with an incubation period of up to six months, is not an epidemic disease and is transmitted by the blood serum—found for example on contaminated hypodermic needles.

The British pre-stamped aerogramme, or air letter service, is extended to civilians.

B–29 'Superfortresses' alter the course of war in the Pacific. Their range is enormous—up to 3,250 mls (5,230 km), which means they can be used to bomb the Japanese mainland. Indeed, it is B–29s that will drop the atom bombs on Hiroshima and Nagasaki that end the war in 1945. A very advanced aircraft, the Superfortress takes its name from the amount of weaponry it carries, much of it remotely controlled. In 1945 the Russians will profit by the research that has gone into the B–29 when they take apart Superfortresses forced down in Manchuria and Eastern Siberia. Two years later their Tu–4 strategic bomber, an exact copy of the B–29, will be in production.

Speeding up coal output is critical to the war effort. This mining machine can cut out a 6-ft (2-m) depth of coal and load it immediately, as its two horizontal cutting jibs and vertical shearing jib slice through the coal face, transferring the cut coal to the conveyor belt at the rear of the machine. Such mechanization of coal mining will proceed apace after the war is over, to modernize the industry and to try and make coal competitive as an industrial fuel with oil from the Middle East.

COMMUNICATION AND INFORMATION

IBM engineers—after eight years of research—develop the first typewriter to have proportional spacing. The system allows 2–5 units of space per letter, and can produce typescripts which look like printed pages. The first IBM 'Executive' is presented to US President F.D. Roosevelt and his personal letters are typed on it: one such letter is to Winston Churchill who replies that although he realizes that their correspondence is very important, there is no need to have it printed.

The Association for Scientific Photography is set up in Britain to promote the development of photography of all kinds, including radiography, photomicrography and kinematography.

The British Government introduces a wartime domestic radio—the Utility set—and sales quickly top the quarter-million mark. Apart from its low cost, the success of this unbranded set, with a public hungry for news of the war, is hastened by the decay of old receivers and the shortage of spare parts.

TRANSPORT AND WARFARE

The car population explosion prompts the US Government to pass the Federal and Highway Act which, quite simply, authorizes the most ambitious road-building scheme ever seen. Forty thousand miles of highway are planned to link the nation's cities and industrial centres; and, by 1975, over 37,000 mls (59,533 km) will have been completed to give the USA the world's finest inter-city road network.

German 'Anzio Annie' guns are used against the advancing Allies after the Anzio landings on 22 January. The 240-ton railroad guns fire conventional 561-lb (254.7-kg) shells, and also rocket-assisted, arrow-like projectiles.

The V-1 flying bomb is powered by a single pulse jet engine and controlled by an autopilot. Used against London and the invasion ports, the V-1's effect on morale is considerable, and great efforts are made to destroy its launch-sites.

ENERGY AND INDUSTRY

A machine for making precise threads on screws—the centreless thread-grinding machine—is patented by A. Scrivener in Britain. When manufactured by the Landis Machine Co, USA, in 1947, it will produce headless, hardened-steel screws for such uses as the tappet clearance adjustment in the rockers of car engines.

MEDICINE AND FOOD PRODUCTION

Typhus epidemics are worst in winter, when clothes infested with the disease-carrying lice are least likely to be shed. Now for the first time, a winter epidemic of typhus is brought to a halt: DDT is used to spray the population of Naples, quickly ridding the city of lice—and of the disease. Antibiotics, still not widely available, will later prove effective against rickettsial diseases like typhus.

After a temporary standstill caused by the war, artificial insemination (AI) of livestock spreads in Europe and the USA. In England, the Milk Marketing Board opens its first cattle breeding station, which will expand into the largest AI centre in the world.

In Britain, the sunflower is developed as an oil-producing crop; when crushed, the flower's seeds produce oil which can be used in the making of margarine and other foods.

At the Rockefeller Institute, a team led by Oswald Avery isolates from bacteria the basic material of heredity—deoxyribonucleic acid (DNA)—and indicates the underlying chemical mechanism of inheritance.

FRINGE BENEFITS

Time measurement is revolutionized on a world scale when the Greenwich Royal Observatory in London installs a quartz clock. The crystal that forms the nucleus of this high-precision, electrically powered clock vibrates 100,000 times a sec, giving an accuracy of a second gained or lost every $2\frac{1}{2}$ years, compared with the 3-month span of accuracy of a pendulum clock.

Facsimile telegraphy plays an essential part in the war effort—in the handling of train orders. The system is extremely accurate and, unlike radio, can operate through high levels of interference. To use the system, the operator dials one of the automatic recorders placed at selected stations along the line, indicates the number of copies requested, and drops the order into the machine. The printed message rolls out of the receiver, even if there is no one there to witness its arrival.

Air accidents caused by navigational error will be significantly reduced thanks to the Gyro Flux Gate compass system introduced in the USA. The compass is kept horizontal, despite the movement of the aircraft, by a gyroscope and by the Earth's magnetic field. More sensitive than an ordinary compass and, unlike it, operational close to the Earth's magnetic poles, the new system is also reliable under varying atmospheric conditions.

The Gloster Meteor becomes the world's first fully operational Allied jet fighter when it enters the RAF's 616 Squadron in July. It destroys its first German V-1 flying bombs in August, but never meets its German counterpart, the Messerschmitt Me 262, in combat.

'Vengeance Weapon Two', or V-2, is a German liquid-fuelled rocket, carrying a one-ton warhead at supersonic speeds. Developed as a ballistic missile, and first launched against England in September, it burns 9 tons of fuel in 60 secs, reaching an altitude of 50 mls (80.4 km) before its 1,500 mph (2,413.5 km/h) dive. England will be hit by 1,115 V-2s in the last months of World War II, but because of their inaccuracy, their chief value will be psychological—as terror weapons.

The first and only rocket-powered plane to see service, the German Me 163B-1 Komet, shoots to a height of 39,700 ft (12,100 km) in around $3\frac{1}{2}$ mins under 3,750 lb of rocket thrust. Designed to intercept the American daylight bomber formations, it is more dangerous in theory than practice: both ineffective in the air and vulnerable on the ground, it is also liable to sudden, spontaneous explosion.

In their search for oil, surveyors explore the rocks beneath the Gulf of Mexico, using the technique of seismic profiling: small controlled explosions of compressed air are detonated on the sea bed and the shock waves are picked up as they bounce back from the rocks beneath.

The Delaware aqueduct is completed. Built to supply water to New York City, it is the world's longest tunnel. A total of 105 mls (168.9 km) long, it is a deep-pressure tunnel in five parts, each connected by shafts and valves that control the water flow.

US physiologists Joseph Erlanger and Herbert Gasser are awarded the Nobel Prize for Physiology and Medicine for their contribution to the understanding of nervous transmission. They show that nerve bundles contain fibres of varying sizes, serving different functions, and that different nerve fibres conduct electrical impulses at variable rates.

Benjamin Duggar and his colleagues in the USA isolate aureomycin, first in the group of broad-spectrum antibiotics known as tetracyclines because of their distinctive molecular structure. Soon soil compounds like aureomycin (which will become commercially available in 1948) will be running second only to penicillin as the drugs most commonly prescribed to combat infection.

British biochemist A.J.P. Martin and R.L.M. Synge develop the laboratory technique of paper chromatography, for which they will be awarded the 1952 Nobel Prize for Chemistry. The constituent amino acids of a protein can be separated and identified after the solvent they are dissolved in carries each one to a specific height on a vertical sheet of filter paper.

The first automatic, general purpose digital computer—Mark I—goes into operation at Harvard University. Designed and built by Howard Aitken and a team of IBM engineers, with financial backing from IBM and the US Navy, the machine weighs 5 tons, stands 8 ft (2.4 m) tall, is 51 ft (15.3 m) long and contains 500 mls (800 km) of wiring. Instructions are fed in on punched paper tape. The machine will produce answers to relatively simple calculation problems in a few seconds, but has an unfortunate tendency to break down.

The Messerschmitt 262 starts flying with the German Luftwaffe and becomes the first jet aircraft to go into service. Over 1,000 Me262s will be built before the end of the war; and, if Hitler had not insisted that Messerschmitt should first develop a jet-engined bomber, the Me262 fighter could have been ready sooner.

129

COMMUNICATION AND INFORMATION

Radio tells the world that the war is over. Count Scheverin von Krosingk broadcasts the unconditional surrender of Germany from Flensburg.

DECCA, internationally regarded as the best navigation system, undergoes crucial tests during the Allies' D–Day landings on the Normandy beaches. Developed by William O'Brien and Harvey Schwartz, in London and Hollywood, DECCA indicates on cockpit dials the position of an aircraft in three dimensions—latitude, longitude and altitude—and is accurate to within a few yards. Waves of radio signals, emitted from two transmitters, collide and are picked up in phase.

TRANSPORT AND WARFARE

The world's first atomic bomb is detonated in the New Mexico desert on 16 July, in an explosion code-named Trinity. Developed by scientists working on the Manhattan Project, a $2,000 million programme to develop nuclear weapons, the bomb uses energy created by nuclear fission. It is much more powerful than a conventional bomb of the same size, producing blast, light, heat and lethal radiation.

Designed to compete with the heavy German tanks, the British Centurion is produced for trials just too late for World War II. The well-armoured, wide-bodied tank will be developed and upgunned, during 20 years of service with tank forces throughout the world.

ENERGY AND INDUSTRY

Clothes washed 'whiter than white' are now possible as detergent manufacturers add brightening agents to their washing powders. First noticed by a German chemist in 1929, these fluorescent substances were patented for use in detergents in 1941 by I.G. Farbenindustrie. Now, white clothes will, in sunshine or in ultraviolet light, look whiter than they really are.

MEDICINE AND FOOD PRODUCTION

During the war, John Enders of Harvard has worked on the problem of immunization against mumps, in collaboration with Joseph Stokes of the University of Pennsylvania. Now a preliminary vaccine is used successfully—first in monkeys, later in man. A further breakthrough comes when Enders succeeds in growing the mumps virus in the laboratory. This leads to the development of the vaccines which will appear on the market in the fifties.

Prompted by the Japanese occupation of the Dutch East Indies—the source of world quinine supplies—ICI chemists discover paludrine, which proves effective as an anti-malarial drug.

Arnold Gessell, in the USA, publishes *How a Baby Grows*. This seminal book on paediatric practice deals with aspects of development—feeding behaviour, for instance—in normal children.

The powerful herbicide, 2,4–D (a phenoxyacetic acid which inhibits plant growth) is patented in the USA after being developed as a possible biological weapon. In 1979, a closely related herbicide, 2,4,5–T, will be banned in the USA after it is linked with an increase in miscarriages in areas where it is used.

FRINGE BENEFITS

Injection-moulded bugles of cellulose acetate butyrate, weighing only 10 oz, are made for the US army.

Simple de-salting boxes are issued to the Eastern Air Command, SE Asia, for use by 'ditched' airmen.

To house families made homeless by bombing raids during the war, the British Ministry of Supply orders thousands of prefabricated aluminium houses as temporary accommodation. The first houses in the world to be entirely factory-built, they consist of only four sections (here the kitchen section is being lowered into place) and are thus very quick to erect. In all, 54,000 such 'prefabs' will be built in the two years after the war and some will be occupied for many years longer than their 'temporary' designation implies.

With a storage capacity of 512 words, an adding time of 32 microsecs and a multiplication time of one millisec, the Pilot ACE (Automatic Computing Engine) is the world's most powerful and advanced computer to date, and for the first time, information can be extracted at random. Designed by Alan Turing at the National Physical Laboratory in Middlesex, England, ACE is adapted for commercial development by the English Electric Co.

Science fiction writer Arthur C. Clarke proposes the use of geostationary satellites for communications between distant parts of the Earth. He thus lays the intellectual foundation for nearly all modern space communications systems.

Post-war radio broadcasting is established in Britain with the opening of the BBC's Home Service and Light Programmes, giving listeners a clear choice between current affairs and light entertainment. The Third Programme, with a mix of more serious arts and entertainment, is opened in the following year.

No 'au revoir' for the pilots of Japan's Yokosuka MXY-7—it is a rocket-driven suicide plane, first flown successfully off Okinawa, where it damages the battleship USS *West Virginia*. Affectionately called Ohka (Cherry Blossom)—possibly a reference to its transience—it is known to the Allies as Baka (Fool).

Three days after the horror of Hiroshima, 'Fat Man', a plutonium-core atomic bomb, is dropped by a USAF B-29 over Nagasaki, killing 39,000. Thousands more are injured or left dying slowly from burns and radiation sickness; but, as Japan sues for peace the following day, it is obvious that US atomic power has ended the war.

While the Canadians are drilling their first offshore oil well in the Gulf of the St Lawrence, off Prince Edward Island, mining engineers in Saudi Arabia discover the onshore section of the large Qatif oilfield. The field has reserves of 8.5 billion barrels of oil and, in 1974, will produce 100,000 barrels a day.

The first Russian nuclear chain reaction is achieved by the physicist Igor Kurchatov, giving the Russians the potential to build their own atomic bombs.

The Food and Agricultural Organisation (FAO), an autonomous United Nations Agency, is founded. Its aims are to improve the production and distribution of food and agricultural products, and to raise nutritional levels, particularly in poor countries.

A simple but useful invention, the twist-lock syringe, is introduced in Britain. Made of metal and glass, it is modified so that the plunger can lock at any point along the barrel. This enables drugs to be introduced into the body at an intermittent rate.

In Britain, the Wellcome Foundation produces a vaccine against scrub typhus, a rickettsial disease which has troubled troops in South-east Asia.

Fluoridation of water is tentatively introdced in the USA after dental researchers find that people who live in areas where the water is naturally high in fluorides have healthier teeth.

The quality and expectancy of life for 'blue babies' is greatly improved when two Americans, cardiologist Helen Taussig and surgeon Alfred Blalock, pioneer an operation which increases oxygenation of the blood. The 'blueness' is due to cyanosis, a condition in which much of the blood circulating through the body does so without first passing through the lungs. The operation diverts more blood through the lungs and relieves the cyanosis.

Wax pencils, for writing on cold, wet glass, are developed.

Butane-gas cigarette lighters are manufactured.

Tupperware Corp is founded; its plastic containers with special seals can be stored in any position.

Latest War News
3¢ DAILY TIMES
BARE SECRET WEAPON
'ATOM' BOMB JAPAN
Most destructive force in universe

'Little Boy' devastates Hiroshima on 6 August, the first time an atomic bomb has been used in anger. The bomb, dropped from US Air Force B–29 'Enola Gay', effectively flattens 4 sq mls and kills close to 80,000 people. Eight days later, another atom bomb is dropped on Nagasaki.

The portable gramophone comes ever closer to hi-fidelity. Full frequency range recording—a consequence of wartime advances in microphones and amplifiers—gives better records; building tweeters, woofers into the speaker and tone compensation into the volume control gives gramophones a truer, more pleasing, sound quality.

COMMUNICATION AND INFORMATION

Broken discs become a thing of the past as RCA release *Til Eulenspiegel* on the first practical unbreakable disc of vinylite. When LPs arrive two years later, vinylite—the USA's first PVC, made in 1928—will begin to oust shellac completely.

TV reasserts itself as the US ban on TV manufacture is lifted. Meanwhile, in Britain, the BBC resumes its TV service.

TRANSPORT AND WARFARE

Among the many trends in car design set by the US Kaiser-Frazer Co, not the least is the look of their first model: a smooth, uninterrupted side body line, finished with a rounded fender, owes much to the technique of constructing body and chassis in one piece. The newly created company will go on to score further successes with novel car designs, notably with the concave radiator grilles that will give a distinctive look to their 1954 Manhattans.

The post-war vogue in Britain for touring Europe by car is enhanced by a new ferry service: the Forde 'Ro-Ro' vessel is the first to be specially built for ferrying road vehicles across the English Channel.

The Vespa motor scooter, produced by former aircraft maker Dr Enrico Piaggio, is an immediate hit with an Italian public looking for a means of travel more convenient than a motor bike but cheaper than a car. The scooter's step-on design, platform and protective front panels mean it can be ridden without the paraphernalia of special clothing and footwear. One million Vespas—the name is Italian for 'wasp' and well suited to its exhaust noise—will be sold in 1955.

ENERGY AND INDUSTRY

The risk of coal-mining shafts collapsing is greatly reduced when a new type of roof support—the Dowty hydraulic pit prop—is introduced. Originally a simple prop which had its own manual pump, it now makes use of a new range of safe, synthetic, non-flammable hydraulic fluids, first developed for the aircraft industry, to pump the prop up to support the roof.

MEDICINE AND FOOD PRODUCTION

Swedish physiologist Ulf von Euler isolates noradrenalin, a substance closely related to the 'fight-or-flight' hormone adrenalin. Both are chemical transmitters of the autonomic nervous system which quicken heartbeat.

In the USA, J.L. Jacobson and colleagues discover how nitrogen mustards—encountered in World War I as mustard gas—can help to treat Hodgkins disease. The treatment brings remission for up to 18 months, but rarely cures the disease.

Benadryl (diphenhydramine) becomes freely available, offering ready relief from the symptoms of hay fever. It is the first oral antihistamine to be sold over the counter.

Fishermen use ultrasonic equipment to help them detect shoals of fish. In the twenties and thirties, the echo-sounder has been used experimentally for this purpose; now, more sensitive instruments, developed in World War II, enable skilled fishermen to distinguish different species from variations in the ultrasonic signals received.

FRINGE BENEFITS

Time is money—Chicago has the first drive-in bank.

The cheap, mass-produced Timex watch is introduced and soon dominates the market.

The jukebox boom begins. The Chicago Automatic Machine and Tool Co made the first, rather rudimentary jukebox 40 years before and the US began large-scale production in the late thirties; but now the war is over people in the USA and Britain have gone jukebox crazy.

Professor Frank Willard Libby, an American chemist, presents a new technique for dating objects up to 35,000 years old with a high degree of accuracy. Radiocarbon dating measures the level of radiation from carbon-14 atoms, which are present in all organic material.

Eastman Kodak introduce Ektachrome, colour film which can be processed by the user. The new film immediately makes colour popular with professional photographers.

A wholly new automatic electronic digital computer, built at the University of Pennsylvania to compute firing and ballistic tables for the US Defense Department, begins a revolution in industrial technology. Using electronic pulses in 18,000 radio tubes, ENIAC (Electronic Numerical Integrator and Calculator) can complete 5,000 additions a sec. But ENIAC's power consumption is so huge that every time the machine is switched on, the lights in the nearby town fail. It also takes hours of manual rewriting to change the programme.

US newspaper reporters are the first to take full advantage of car telephones, introduced commercially by the Bell Telephone Co; businessmen soon follow suit.

Bikini Atoll in the Pacific Marshall Islands is used by the US Navy as an atomic testing ground in the experiment called 'Operation Crossroads'. One atomic bomb is exploded over the lagoon and another is detonated 90 ft (27.4 m) below the water's surface, sending up a mile-high, hollow column of water, which falls back as a storm of waves, steam, debris and radioactivity. Although both bombs are the same size, each releasing energy equivalent to 20,000 tons of TNT, the second is far more dangerous since its products have been mixed with water, and intense radiation levels remain for days.

Blackpool, the only British city to have completely modernized its tram fleet since the twenties, introduces Vambac equipment which automatically controls braking and acceleration to provide a swifter, smoother ride. But the difficulty of combining the rapid tram services with the old, slower ones will lead to the new equipment being withdrawn in the fifties.

Arguably the best steam locomotive ever built, André Chapelon's 242A1 goes into service with the French railways—a bold move in face of the growing popularity of electric trains (which will supersede it in 1960). But even electric locomotives will rarely equal the 242A1's power, which is greater than any other steam engine of its size and weight.

The Martin-Baker ejection seat is used for the first time, at 301 mph (484 km/h), giving military jet crews the prospect of high-speed deliverance to parachuted survival.

The textile industry sees the inception of a new shimmering metallic yarn when the Dow Chemical Co produce Lurex, an aluminium-based yarn protected by a clear plastic film. Because of its cheapness, Lurex offers an economical alternative to traditional metallic yarns, such as lamé.

Ceramic magnets are produced by Philips Research Laboratories, Eindhoven, Holland. Secretly developed by Dutch scientists during World War II, these magnetic ferrites—a mixture of oxides of iron and other metals—will have an immense influence on the development of microwave and radar technology.

Radioautography enables Canadian anatomist Charles Leblond to study protein synthesis. Developing the technique first used by Lacassagne in 1925, Leblond attaches radioactive labels to amino acids. Following their path, he discovers where proteins are built up in the body and how they migrate to other sites.

The Instant Milk Co of America patents an agglomeration process which greatly improves dried, skimmed milk. By re-wetting dried milk particles, and agitating them so that they stick together to form bigger granules, the company produces a milk which reconstitutes more easily. This agglomeration process will soon be applied to many other dried products, such as coffee.

While serving in the wartime US Navy medical corps, New York psychiatrist Benjamin Spock has written *The Common-sense Book of Baby and Child Care*, advocating selected child-rearing methods along broadly permissive lines. Retitled *Baby and Child Care*, it soon becomes an all-time best-seller.

The 'bikini' swimsuit is modelled four days after the bomb test on Bikini Atoll in the Pacific Ocean.

Rotary clothes hoists, invented in Australia, let washing catch the breeze.

HMS 'Eagle', the first British aircraft carrier to be built since the war, is launched. At 36,800 tons when complete, she and her companion ship, the *Ark Royal*, will be the largest carriers ever to fly the White Ensign. Her armament too will be formidable: apart from a force of up to 110 aircraft, she carries 16 4.5 in guns and no fewer than 58 of the smaller 40 mm. *Eagle* will not in fact be finished until 1951 as her completion programme is halted after the launch, to be set in train again as Cold War tensions mount in the late forties.

COMMUNICATION AND INFORMATION

The Fairchild Scan-a-Graver, destined to be the forerunner of all scanning print systems, is the first printing machine electronically to create a printing surface for illustrations. The original picture is placed in a rotating drum and is scanned by a photocell. This then transmits a signal to a cutting head which engraves a reversed copy of the illustration on a printing surface.

The Aircraft Radio Laboratories at Wright Field, USA, have developed radar techniques for predicting weather patterns. Reconnaissance weather planes can detect storms up to 100 mls (320 km) away, from the radar screen which shows images of cloud formations. Ground radar can detect wind speed and direction by following the movements of balloon-borne metal foil reflectors.

Radio set manufacture is simplified and speeded up by the introduction of printed radio circuits by British electronics expert John A. Sargrove. His electronic circuit-making equipment (ECME) automates the production of electronic apparatus.

TRANSPORT AND WARFARE

Two swept-wing fighters, the US F-86 Sabre and its Russian counterpart, the MiG-15, meet in combat over Korea. The final score of 792 MiGs lost to 78 Sabres belies the strength of the Russian plane, whose acceleration and rate of climb is the best there is. The Sabres' success is attributed simply to their pilots—with a little help from their superior, radar gun-sights.

A Napier Railton is the first car to travel at over 400 mph. Driven by Englishman John Cobb, the car sets an official mile record of 394.2 mph (634.3 km/h) and, on one run, reaches 403 mph (648 km/h).

The 'Stratojet' or B-47, America's first strategic bomber, benefits from German wartime research into wing design—they are thinner and swept back to an angle of 35° to minimize drag. Powered by six engines and an extra take-off thrust from 18 rocket units, the B-47s will proliferate during the Korean war; in all, over 2,000 will take to the skies.

ENERGY AND INDUSTRY

A new type of cast iron, which is twice as strong and three times as resistant to shock as others, is announced in Britain by Harold Hartley. He added small amounts of titanium to an iron-graphite mixture to produce this extra strength. The new cast iron is described as the biggest advance in cast-iron metallurgy this century.

An experimental solar house, the first to be designed by George Löf, is constructed at Boulder, Colorado, USA. Solar panels on the roof heat air, which is channelled from under the roof to be stored in 8.3 tons of rock; the hot air provides 23% of the heating needs of the house.

MEDICINE AND FOOD PRODUCTION

A blocked artery can lead to a stroke, a heart attack and death—blood clots and a breakdown of the inside artery walls are two common causes. Portuguese surgeon J.C. dos Santos performs the first endarterectomy: by making an incision in the affected blood vessel to remove a clot, he saves his patient's life.

Methadone is introduced in Britain as a pain killer, equal in strength to morphine. Its main advantage is that it can be taken orally with only moderate sedative and hypnotic effects. Later it will be discovered to be addictive, although it will still be used to treat morphine and heroin addicts.

FRINGE BENEFITS

An infrared trap is devised to snare burglars.

The first microwave cooker goes on sale in the USA. A spin-off from the development of radar, and using the same principles, the radarange is designed for commercial use. Domestic microwave cookers will go on sale in the USA in 1965 and in Britain seven years later.

In November the Remembrance Day Service at the Cenotaph in London's Whitehall is the occasion of the first non-experimental, high-definition TV recording. Film made by the outside broadcast unit of the BBC is transmitted to viewers from Alexandra Palace, with the help of a synchronized camera.

EDSAC (Electronic Delayed Storage Automatic Computer), built under the direction of Maurice Wilkie at Cambridge University, England, is much more flexible than its predecessors. By storing both its programme and its working data together, the computer can modify its own programmes as it operates. The capacity of the programme is increased by dual ultrasonic storage tanks. EDSAC is less bulky than ENIAC and its like, since it has only 3,000 valves.

At the University of Pennsylvania, von Neumann designs and builds the EDVAC (Electronic Discrete Variable Automatic Computer) for the US Government's Ballistic Research Laboratory. It is the first machine capable of storing a flexible programme which can be changed without revising the computer circuits.

The diesel-electric locomotive arrives on British mainline railways. The idea is to combine the simplicity of the diesel engine—it requires no extra equipment such as overhead cables—with the close control over varying speeds provided by electric traction. The diesel engine drives an electric generator that powers the motor to drive the train.

The favourite weapon of later freedom fighters, the Kalashnikov assault rifle is introduced to Soviet forces. In an age of increasing weapon size and range, the Kalashnikov is designed with a deliberate reduction of power: it fires lower velocity bullets over a shorter range, but carries and fires more ammunition.

The first tubeless car tyre is made by the US Goodrich company. The tyre seals itself when punctured.

The first warship to be propelled by a gas turbine goes on trial. Originally a triple-screw motor gunboat, MGB2009 was at first fitted with three Packard gasoline engines; but once the central engine was replaced with a propulsion gas turbine—developed from Whittle's aircraft jet engine—the suitability of gas turbines for naval high-speed craft is proved.

A new, exceedingly bright electric bulb, is invented. A type of gas discharge lamp which is filled with the inert gas xenon, it will be employed in lighthouses since its light can be seen 20 mls (32 km) away.

The continuous coal-cutting machine, now marketed by the Joy Manufacturing Co, will come to dominate coal production. Originally developed in 1940 by the Consolidation Coal Co, the machine moves at 500 ft (152.4 m) per min and can dig out a series of vertical, 18-in (45.7-cm) slices of coal, or bore a tunnel up to 18 ft (5.49 m) wide.

Britain's first atomic reactor is activated at Harwell, Oxfordshire. Called Gleep—Graphite Low Energy Experimental Pile—it will be used to make plutonium for use in the nuclear energy industry.

The 'Fairfree', an experimental freezer trawler owned by the Salvesen of Leith Whaling Co in Britain, pioneers the stern ramp. Traditionally, nets are lowered and hauled in over the side, and the catch sorted on the open deck; the *Fairfree* follows whaling practice, whereby the catch is hauled up a ramp on the ship's stern to position the fish more efficiently for freezing.

Flanders Dunbar publishes *Mind and Body: Psychosomatic Medicine*, in which psychosomatic illness is extensively documented for the first time.

A Chinese typewriter with 5,400 characters enables a typist to work 3 or 4 times faster than a traditional clerk with an ink brush.

Pioneering the offshore oil industry, this drilling platform goes into place in the Gulf of Mexico. The search for new oilfields had not been neglected during the war years, partly because of a predicted increasing world demand for oil in the long term, and partly in response to the immediate needs of wartime production. Exploration revealed that a high proportion of usable oil available to US companies lay under the ocean, and it was not long before the Kerr-McGee Corporation solved the initial technical problems of offshore drilling and were able to put this platform into production.

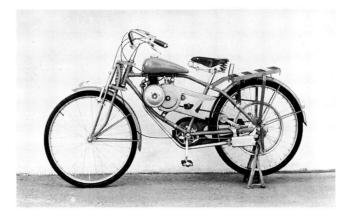

Soichiro Honda adds army surplus engines to push-bikes to make his first batch of 500 motor cycles. From these modest beginnings, the Honda company will go on to be the largest motor cycle maker in the world by 1970. Honda's success will be due to allying astute design and marketing with Japanese mass-production know-how.

COMMUNICATION AND INFORMATION

Dr Edwin Land, American inventor of Polaroid (a cheap polarizing material) in the thirties, launches a revolutionary photographic process in which a picture exposed in the camera is processed in the space of a minute—inside the camera itself.

The highly flammable cellulose nitrate film, in general use since the 1890s, is at last replaced by improved safety film made from cellulose trinitrate.

In the USA, Dr Peter Goldmark develops a fine-grooved vinyl disc which becomes the first long-playing record.

The first transistor—a piece of germanium crystal shorter than a matchstick and not much thicker—is developed by Bell Laboratories in the USA as an amplifying device.

The atomic clock, accurate to a second in 1,000 years, heralds a new era in timekeeping.

In Sweden, Victor Hasselblad markets the first Hasselblad single-lens roll-film camera.

TRANSPORT AND WARFARE

The Morris Minor, designed by Alec Issigonis, is the first British car to capture the imagination of Europe. Its distinctive shape, independent front suspension and responsive steering give its handling an edge over similar European models. When its uninspired engine is replaced in 1952, the improved Minor goes on to become Britain's first car to sell over a million.

Auguste Piccard's deep diving 'bathyscaphe' is sent down to a depth of 4,600 ft (1,402 m). In 1953, Piccard and his son will man the *Trieste*, descending to a depth of 10,395 ft (3,168 m).

A vehicle for tackling the roughest terrain is brought out by Rover in Britain. Somewhere between a truck and a car, the Land Rover can handle almost any surface owing to its four-wheeled drive, adopted from the US Jeep. The Land Rover will be the most successful vehicle of its kind; and, in 1970, a luxury version, the Range Rover, will add speed to versatility—it can reach 100 mph (160.9 km/h).

ENERGY AND INDUSTRY

Teflon, the familiar coating of non-stick saucepans, is first produced commercially by Du Pont. ICI will introduce it into Britain in 1959, under the trade name Fluon, and both materials, derived from the PTFE material discovered by Roy Plunkett in 1938, will be widely used for electrical insulation, to coat machine parts, and to rebuild bones and tissues of the body.

Pure titanium is produced on a commercial scale for the first time. Because of its lightness, and great strength at high temperatures, the metal will be vital in aircraft construction.

The electronic comparator is introduced into machine tool shops. It can measure ten times more accurately than its mechanical precursors.

Plastics and rubber will be made increasingly from ethylene, the main by-product of ICI's newly opened refinery for breaking down naphtha.

MEDICINE AND FOOD PRODUCTION

Working independently of each other, E.L. Smith in Britain and E.L. Rickes in the USA succeed in isolating vitamin B12. In 1949, sufferers from pernicious anaemia will benefit from B12 treatment, when monthly injections are introduced to replace the usual diet of raw liver.

In Britain, John Gillies pioneers hypotensive anaesthesia by which drugs are introduced into the spinal cord, lowering the blood pressure and thus controlling blood-loss, particularly during brain surgery.

Britain introduces its National Health Service, and the United Nations establishes the World Health Organisation—with headquarters in Geneva—to monitor and advise on world health problems.

US chemist Percy Julian discovers a cheap way of making cortisone, a drug which dramatically alleviates arthritis. Julian's discovery will make cortisone widely available—and secure him a personal fortune.

FRINGE BENEFITS

Britain's first full-sized supermarket is opened in North London.

Britain's first regular TV broadcast, the BBC Newsreel, begins.

RCA in the USA introduce a 35 mm magnetic film recorder for movie sound tracks.

The BBC's radio coverage of this year's Olympic Games is the most extensive ever given to any world event. Reports from 239 commentators will go out in 40 languages, and a specially built radio centre—dubbed the 'Tower of Babel'— will be able to handle 32 simultaneous broadcasts.

RCA introduce the first 7 in (17.5 cm) disc to play at 45 rpm.

Agfacolor negative films for colour prints on paper go on sale.

Zeiss of West Germany introduce the Contax S, the first single lens reflex camera to have a pentaprism—an optical device which permits the camera to be used at eye level and corrects the reversed image seen in an ordinary reflex camera.

Radio-telephony is used to control railway shunting for the first time at a Cambridgeshire, England, goods yard. Uncoupling orders to train drivers are transmitted from a control tower via two-way, VHF radio telephones—a system soon to become commonplace in Europe and the USA.

EMI installs the first permanent closed-circuit TV system at Guy's Hospital, London, enabling large groups of medical students to witness experiments and surgical operations.

Commercial colour TV, developed by Pye engineers, goes on public view at London's Olympia.

Whirlwind, the first computer system to simulate the performance of an aircraft, is completed in the USA at MIT.

The production of a 'demand valve', designed by Emile Gagua, enables Commander Jacques-Yves Cousteau to make a self-contained, light-weight breathing apparatus—the aqualung—which allows a diver freedom of movement.

The USSR becomes the second country to explode a nuclear fission device. No reports are given—the first evidence comes when a US Air Force plane picks up radioactive debris while flying over the Pacific.

Only a crew's endurance now limits the range of a bomber or fighter. A US B-50 bomber, *Lucky Lady II*, flies non-stop round the world, at an average speed of 235 mph (378.1 km/h). It refuels four times in flight.

Disc brakes on a production line car are offered for the first time by the US Chrysler company, 47 years after they were patented by the British designer Frederick William Lanchester. When the brake pedal is pressed, two pads grip a revolving disc attached to each wheel hub.

A record height of 244 mls (393 km) is attained by a US two-stage rocket, launched from White Sands, New Mexico; its first stage is a captured German V-2 weapon.

Tufted carpet is made for the first time in the USA on a machine which works on a principle similar to that of a sewing-machine, except that there is a row of closely spaced needles, not just one. The length of the loop stitched is adjustable and the loop can be cut or uncut. The tufted carpet industry will account for 70% of US carpet production by 1963.

Russia discovers its first offshore oil field in the Caspian Sea; and the first fixed, purpose-built drilling rig starts operations in 20 ft (6 m) of water in the Gulf of Mexico.

Scientists at Harwell in Oxfordshire, successfully operate the largest cyclotron in Europe at its first trial. The success of the new cyclotron, which makes atomic particles travel at 95,000 mls/s (153,000 km/s), and in so doing split the nuclei of most atoms, gives nuclear research a great boost.

The first synchrotron for medical research is demonstrated in London. The machine produces rays which are far more penetrating than X-rays and will be used to treat cancer. Also, investigators at Ohio State University report success using Cobalt-60 to treat cancer in 25 patients on whom all other treatments have failed.

In the USA, Philip Hench and Edward Kendall's report on the relief cortisone brings to rheumatoid arthritis sufferers, begins a new era of 'wonder drugs', based on cortisone and related steroids.

In Canada, Murray Barr identifies the tiny black dots (later called 'Barr bodies') found in the cell nuclei of females. Used as a cellular diagnosis of sex, the Barr test will later determine the sex of some athletes.

A breakthrough in the struggle against paralytic poliomyelitis comes when David Bodian of Johns Hopkins discovers that there is not just one strain of the virus but three: protection against one strain does not necessarily ward off the other two. This stimulates work on the first really effective weapon against polio—the trivalent Salk vaccine—which arrives five years later.

Manchester University's MADM is the first computer capable of playing a complete game of chess.

The Haloid Co markets the first xerographic duplicating machine, the Model A 'Ox Box'.

Prepared cake mixes, introduced by General Mills & Pillsbury in the USA, join the growing list of convenience foods.

The low-priced Citroën 2CV is an immediate popular success in France due to its tough, no-frills bodywork coupled with technical sophistication—including hydraulic brakes, improved suspension and a hard-wearing air-cooled engine. A roll-top roof and easily removed doors also enable it to carry large or unwieldy loads. Five million will be sold by 1976.

COMMUNICATION AND INFORMATION

The Vidicon, the first TV camera tube to use the principle of photoconductivity by which light of different intensities produces a change in electrical activity, is devised in the USA by RCA. After further developments, the Vidicon proves significantly more adaptable, more sensitive—and cheaper—than previous TV cameras.

Colour movies can now be shot with conventional cameras, not just with Technicolor cameras, as Eastman colour negative and positive materials are introduced.

Europe's first electronic flight simulator is introduced in Britain by Rediffusion. It is used to train pilots to fly BOAC Stratocruisers.

An hour-long CBS colorcast, featuring Ed Sullivan and Arthur Godfrey, heralds the start of regular commercial colour TV transmissions in the USA.

Early warning and height detecting Marconi radar systems are introduced at London's Heathrow airport.

On the centenary of the sending of the first cross-channel telegraph cable, France and Britain are linked by TV for the first time.

TRANSPORT AND WARFARE

Rolls-Royce engineers scale up the supercharger of a piston engine to make a compressor and add a combustion chamber, turbine and gearbox. The result is the Dart, one of the most successful aero-engines of all times, which will still be in production in the eighties. Its immediate triumph is the powering of the first turboprop airliner—four Darts drive the four constant-speed propellers of the Type 630 prototype of the Vicker's Viscount.

President Truman directs the US Atomic Energy Commission to work on the development of all types of nuclear weapons, after the Russian atomic explosion in 1949 ends the US monopoly on nuclear fission.

After 50 years, the British Army replaces .303 in (7.7 mm) calibre small arms by .280 in (7 mm) calibre guns. The basic weapon of the new calibre is the EM-2, a self-loading rifle which is lighter than previous self-loaders, such as the US Garand MI, and fires almost twice as many rounds a minute.

ENERGY AND INDUSTRY

The textile industry sees the inception of modern automatic looms as Sulzer weaving machines start to be produced commercially. These shuttleless looms weave one colour of weft by rapidly propelling the yarn across the warp threads. Machines which weave two colours will be made in 1950, four-colour machines in 1959.

Auto-reclosing circuit breakers are successfully tested in Britain to cut off the electricity supply as soon as a fault occurs and to reconnect it once the fault has been corrected.

For the first time in the western world, gas is produced from coal, while it is still underground in the coal seam, at a colliery at Newman Spinney, England. An important source of fuel should oil reserves be depleted or imports restricted by war, Russia has had a large-scale installation working at full capacity for the past 15 years.

MEDICINE AND FOOD PRODUCTION

Tractors outnumber horses on British farms for the first time. By 1980, the farm labour force will have been cut by two-thirds, but food production will be up 50%.

J.P. Link, the discoverer of Warfarin (a substance which is widely used for rodent control), urges that this anti-coagulant should be used on man. Tested in the USA next year, it will prove more effective than dicoumarol (from which it was developed) in the prevention of thrombosis.

The first calf born to a virgin cow is reared at the University of Wisconsin, after a fertilized egg is transplanted from one cow to another.

Despite the development of intensive systems of poultry and pig farming, most of the world's livestock is still cared for extensively—in open fields.

FRINGE BENEFITS

Cyclamate-based artificial sweeteners are introduced for the weight-conscious.

The first credit card, Diner's Club, heralds the 'cashless' society.

Aircall Inc of New York inaugurate the first radio paging service, with a call to a doctor on a golf course.

JET 1 takes to the road. The first jet-powered ordinary passenger car has been developed by the Rover company in Britain and has very impressive performance—151.9 mph (224.5 km/h) over a kilometre will be recorded in 1951. Fuel comsumption is so high, however, that the prototype will not go into production.

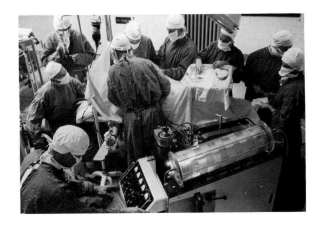

A computer predicts victory for Dwight D. Eisenhower in the 1953 US Presidental election, and arouses public interest in the computer 'brain'. Remington Rand's UNIVAC I makes its début at the US Census Bureau, becomes the first computer to be commercially produced for business organizations, and sets the trend for using magnetic tape in place of cards or paper.

Ferranti build their Mark I, the first commercial computer in Britain. This follows an order for seven such machines from Britain's National Research and Development Corporation.

The gradual miniaturization of flashbulbs culminates in the AG1 bulb which is so small that it enables cameras to be designed with built-in flash guns.

At the Festival of Britain, the Telekinema revives interest in stereoscopic movies. Viewers use polarizing spectacles to see colour films, which generate great interest—especially amongst film makers searching for ways to attract audiences away from the growing medium of TV.

'Operation Greenhouse' is mounted by the USA in the Pacific Marshall Islands, where nuclear bombs are set off. It is believed that one is an atomic bomb being tested for its ability to 'trigger' the high-temperature reaction required for an H-bomb (Hydrogen bomb) explosion; but US officials are non-committal.

Worthy of her namesake in size alone, the first great superliner, *United States*, is floated out of her construction dock. On her maiden voyage from New York she proves to be no slouch: the 51,985-ton liner crosses the Atlantic in just under $3\frac{1}{2}$ days at an average speed of 35.59 knots, making her the world's fastest passenger liner.

Power-assisted steering comes to the aid of US drivers, coping with ever larger cars. But the Chrysler model which is the first to have it, is not a commercial success: it is unimaginatively styled in an era when good looks are crucial.

Tests take place with a gas turbine for marine commercial operations. The 12,000-ton tanker *Auris* is fitted with a gas turbine unit in place of one of her four diesel engines; and after trials, the *Auris* will cross the Atlantic next year.

Britain's primary plant for separating plutonium from uranium is opened at Windscale in Cumbria. The efficiency of the process, which separates irradiated fuel from re-usable nuclear fuel, reaches 99%.

A pure white light from fluorescent tubes will result from Peter Ranby's discovery of the first fluorescent halophosphate, which can 'convert' mainly invisible ultraviolet light into visible light.

Du Pont manufacture the first garments made from Orlon, the trade name given to new acrylic fibre yarns. Orlon answers the need for a synthetic fibre that feels soft and can be spun into yarns from which clothing can be knitted.

The first useful electric power to come from atomic energy is produced at the national reactor testing station at Arco, Idaho, USA. Molten metal draws heat from the experimental breeder reactor—EBRI—which breeds more fuel than it uses and, by creating steam to drive turbines, generates enough electricity to operate lights, pumps and other domestic equipment.

The flying spot microscope, developed at University College, London, by Young and Roberts, uses a scanning device similar to that of a TV receiver to project an image 3 ft (90 cm) square on a screen. In one second it can magnify, measure and count up to a million cells.

Frederick Heaf's Multiple Puncture Test for diagnosing tuberculosis is introduced in Britain.

Drugs are first used in transplant surgery when Sir Peter Medawar in Britain shows that treatment with cortisone prolongs the life of skin grafts.

In Hong Kong Dr Li introduces Methotrexate, a drug to treat chorion carcinoma—a form of uterine cancer, common in young women.

Conspicuous black and white striped 'zebra' crossings contribute to British road safety.

Tape-recorders are used in an early 'language lab' at a US university.

A transistorized hearing aid is launched by Raytheon in the USA.

Open-heart surgery becomes a practical possibility with the invention by American doctor John Gibbon of the world's first heart-lung machine. Before operating on the inside of the heart, surgeons must arrest its action and isolate it from the circulatory system without arresting the circulation itself. This machine bypasses the heart–lung complex and both oxygenates the patient's blood and pumps it round the body long enough for the operation to be performed. Using the machine, Gibbon will perform the first successful open-heart operation in 1953 and Christian Barnard will achieve the first heart transplant in 1967.

Electronics make train control simpler, safer and quicker. Just one operator, replacing several signalmen, can oversee the movement of traffic on a large and complex track system with the aid of this illuminated track diagram, installed in a signal centre at York in England.

COMMUNICATION AND INFORMATION

The high purity—and thus the effectiveness—of silicon and germanium crystals, upon which the whole future of microelectronics depends, is largely due to two techniques developed in the USA by William G. Pfann. The first is a simple method of freezing and melting, which avoids any handling of the material; the second is zone refining, a means of distributing impurities evenly within each crystal.

The first pocket-sized TV camera—it allows cameramen to squeeze into the tightest corners—is tested in France and the USA and proves a huge success. The zoom lens is highly effective for shooting in streets and sports arenas.

The first high-definition video recording on magnetic tape is made in the USA by the electronics division of Bing Crosby Enterprises. Images are recorded on the tape, which is then rewound and played through a standard monitor to produce a perfect picture. A tape 1 in (2.5 cm) wide, with 12 tracks (one for sound and 11 for pictures), is used and proves three times cheaper than a comparable photographic recording process.

TRANSPORT AND WARFARE

Chinese scientists allege the use of germ warfare by the USA in Korea. Deadly successors to the chemical weapons developed in World War I, countless biological agents will, in fact, be manufactured, but not used, partly because they are so difficult to control. Careless handling of an ounce of *Botulinus* toxin, for instance, could kill 240 million people.

HMS 'Plym' is vaporized as Britain detonates its first ship-borne atomic bomb in the Monte Bello Islands, off the west coast of Australia. Masterminded by W.G. Penney, who has worked on the US atomic research programme at Los Alamos, the British nuclear project coincides with the first plutonium deliveries from the Windscale production reactors.

ENERGY AND INDUSTRY

Marking the beginning of a new era, steel is made for the first time by the new oxygen steel-making process, which Linz-Donawitz, a firm of Austrian steel-makers, have spent three years perfecting. The mill produces 30 tons of steel using the new method, by which oxygen is injected through the roof of the furnace to purify the molten iron before it is converted into steel. By 1966 the USA will have installed equipment capable of making 40 million tons of steel a year.

The discovery of Acrilan, one of the acrylic fibres which will be used in the manufacture of cloth, is announced by the Chemstrand Corp, USA.

The world's first major accident at a nuclear reactor occurs at the Chalk River heavy water research reactor in Canada. A technician accidentally opens some valves and this triggers off a series of events, including the leakage of an estimated 140,000 cu ft of radioactive water and an explosion that destroys the core—the central part of the reactor that contains the nuclear fuel.

MEDICINE AND FOOD PRODUCTION

An American soldier becomes the first person to have a 'sex-change operation'. George—later Christine—Jorgensen has already been living under a female identity. Now Dr Karl Hamburger at the Serum Institute in Copenhagen completes the transformation, endowing 'George' with a female physique through hormone therapy and plastic surgery.

The death rate from bronchitis in London, which has increased significantly owing to the city's 'smog', precipitates the Clean Air Act (1954) for controlling environmental pollution.

FRINGE BENEFITS

Radio broadcasting takes to the ocean as the US Navy cargo ship *Courier* begins Voice of America transmissions off the coast of Colombia, South America.

Actor Gig Young throws a 3–D punch from the screen that has audiences recoiling in fear. Hollywood goes big on 3–D movies after their success at the Festival of Britain, and will produce at least 60 in the next couple of years. But audiences do not like them once the novelty wears off, complaining of eyestrain and headaches.

The ultra-wide screen, an alternative to 3–D cinema, fills the viewer's field of vision and makes him feel part of the action. The first wide-screen process is Ed Waller's Cinerama, an extension of the experimental system developed during the war as a gunnery training device. It uses three films, shot simultaneously to embrace a wide horizontal angle, and projected on a very wide, deeply curved screen. Audio accompaniment is seven-track stereophonic sound on a separate magnetic film.

The first pocket-sized transistor radio is marketed by the Japanese company Sony. After some teething problems, the number of defective sets is cut from 95% to 2% and, when mass production begins, the cost is reduced from $6 to $1.

Geoffrey Dummer of Britain's Royal Radar Establishment puts forward the concept of an integrated circuit in an address to a symposium in Washington, DC. His ideas are not adopted until 1958 when Jock Kilby of Texas Instruments in the USA makes the first working circuit.

An agreement on the sharing of VHF (very high frequency) wavebands is made by 21 European countries. This co-operation clears the way for more widespread use of VHF as an alternative to the heavily congested medium wavelengths.

BOAC's (British Overseas Airways Corporation) de Havilland Comets fly the world's first regular jet airliner service, from London to Johannesburg. The Comets are soon speeding to the Far East, reaching Singapore in 25 hrs instead of 2½ days and reducing flight times to Tokyo by 53 hrs. Within two years, disaster will strike when three Comets break up in flight, forcing the withdrawal of the fleet from airline service.

Ten years' work by US scientist Edward Teller ends in the explosion—code-named Ivy-Mike—of an H-bomb in the Eniwetok Atoll. The 10-megaton bomb (equivalent to 10 million tons of TNT) owes its huge power to the thermonuclear fusion of deuterium (an isotope of hydrogen) as an energy source.

The spread of nuclear energy means a world rush for uranium. Aircraft, developed in Britain, are equipped with batteries of Geiger counters—detectors of radioactivity—which can locate a source from 500 ft (152 m) up. A plant for the extraction of uranium from its natural ore is built at the West Rand Consolidated Mine in South Africa. Prospectors flock to Uranium City in Canada hoping to stake claims in the rich Athabasca fields.

Proof against ice, snow and condensation, a new 'electric' glass is made at the National Physical Laboratory in England. A thin deposit of tin on the glass, with a gentle electric current passing through it, keeps the temperature high enough to retain visibility through windshields and shop windows even in the severest weather.

In the USSR, a huge new project involves the opening of a 60-ml (96.6-km) canal which connects the two great rivers, the Volga and the Don, a reservoir at one point raising the Don by 90 ft (27.4 m). The world's largest hydroelectric power station will be built at Kuibyshev; a reservoir on the Dnieper will irrigate more than 8 million acres of land; eight new forest zones will hold rain and prevent soil erosion. The entire development will totally transform the lives of many Russians.

In Britain Douglas Bevis develops the technique of amniocentesis—drawing off amniotic fluid from a pregnant mother's womb to test for inherited disease or abnormality in the developing foetus. If the screening test reveals an abnormality the mother may be offered an abortion.

US biochemists discover a new anti-tubercular drug, isoniazid, for the long-term treatment of TB patients.

The first time a patient's circulation is stopped is when John Lewis, a University of Minnesota Hospital surgeon, operates to close a hole in the wall of the heart. To prevent brain damage during the vital seven minutes without oxygen, he lowers the patient's temperature to about 84°F (29°C).

At Georgetown University, in the USA, Charles Hufnagel develops an artificial device to replace diseased aortic valves in the heart.

Banknote scales that weigh bundles of money relieve the tedium of counting each note individually.

Scrabble, a crossword game played with single-letter counters, is produced by a Long Island firm. It soon rivals Monopoly.

The huge hydroelectric power station of Donzère-Mondragon comes into operation to help meet France's growing electricity needs. Situated at Genissiat in the Rhône valley, near Geneva, the station takes advantage of the flow of water off the Alps and is one of the largest hydroelectric power plants in Europe. With power lines to Paris and Lyon, the station's output is 300 MW—enough to supply the needs of more than a third of a million people.

The first commercial application of the transistor proves a blessing to numerous small children who have impaired hearing. The transistorized miniature hearing aid is expensive at $150, but its smallness, lightness and longevity help to compensate for its initial cost.

141

COMMUNICATION AND INFORMATION

TV viewers in the USA can now receive colour transmissions on monochrome sets. This follows the development of compatible technical standards for colour and black and white by the NTSC (National Television Systems Committee). NBC are the first to respond, with a colour transmission of the New Year's Day Tournament of Roses Parade in Pasadena, California.

The discovery of the MASER (microwave amplification by stimulated emission of radiation), which can be used to amplify very low noise in radio and satellite communications and to test accurate timekeepers, is announced by C.H. Townes of the USA. A feverish search now begins for an optical equivalent—it will soon be found in the laser.

TRANSPORT AND WARFARE

Pratt and Whitney, US aircraft engine builders, fit their J57 to the F-100A Super Sabre and create the world's first supersonic combat fighter, flying at Mach 1.3 over a range of 1,300 ml (2,092 km).

The fastest diesel-electric locomotive in the world is produced for British Railways by the English Electric Company. The prototype Deltic locomotive, named after the 'delta' shape of its two diesel engines, will begin a service between London and Scotland in 1961, regularly reaching a speed of 100 mph (161 km/h).

Nike-Ajax becomes the first operational SAM (surface-to-air-missile). Both missile and target are tracked on a radar screen so that, guided by a computer, Nike-Ajax can seek out, intercept and destroy enemy aircraft.

ENERGY AND INDUSTRY

Polyester fibre, described as the workhorse of the textile industry, comes on the market for the first time, under its trade name, Dacron. Produced by Du Pont, it was developed by British scientists at ICI, although the British version of the same polyester, known as Terylene, will not be available until 1955. It will be used to make curtains, dress fabrics and 'drip-dry' men's shirts.

Wind power comes to Britain as its first large wind generator runs at full capacity at Costa Head, Orkney. Developed by the North of Scotland Hydro-Electric Board, it generates 100 kW in experiments.

The noise made by the fans in convector heaters is virtually silenced when Bruno Eck of Cologne designs a small, quiet fan. By placing the light, tubular, electric fan behind the heating element, Eck creates the forerunner of the compact fan heater which, in five years' time, will become the most popular electric heater in the world.

MEDICINE AND FOOD PRODUCTION

The world's first successful open-heart operation using a heart-lung machine is performed at Jefferson Medical College, Philadelphia. The machine takes over from the heart and lungs for 26 mins while its inventor, surgeon John Gibbon, repairs a hole in the heart of an 18-year-old girl.

US anaesthesiologist John Krantz develops a new fluorine-based anaesthetic, Fluormar. Chemically more stable than other anaesthetics, its other advantages include a rapid rate of expulsion from the body.

FRINGE BENEFITS

'Solid dot' printing provides cheaper Braille books that are easier to use.

Underwater explorer Jacques-Yves Cousteau, here with a cup brought up from an ancient Greek wreck, brings experience of the ocean depths to millions using new, sophisticated underwater TV cameras. In a few years, high-quality pictures of submarine life and of sub-ocean archaeology will become commonplace to home audiences. Remotely controlled underwater TV cameras have already found other uses, such as identifying the lost US submarine *Affrey*, and such cameras will in future be used widely in salvage operations.

Cybernetics, defined by US mathematician Norbert Wiener as 'the study of control and communication in the animal and the machine' is born; its parents are electronic computers with feedback mechanisms. The new science explores the connection between the function of the human brain and nervous system and the equivalent programming and switching systems in computers.

Icebergs are detected by radar during experiments in Hudson Bay, and radar soon becomes an indispensible aid to ships navigating in icy waters. In calm seas it can detect large icebergs at a distance of 15–20 mls (24–32 km).

Young patients at the Great Ormond Street Hospital for children in London see the Coronation of Queen Elizabeth II on colour TV. This first public showing of colour TV in Britain is a special BBC outside broadcast.

After a slow start, IBM realize the potential of computers in industry and launch their IBM 701, to be followed in two years time by the 752. Both compare well with Remington Rand's UNIVAC I, and IBM will increase its share of the world market to more than 70% within the next decade.

'Atomic Annie', a long-range piece of heavy artillery, fires its first atomic shell in the Nevada Desert. The 11 in (280 mm) gun's design predates the use of nuclear warheads, but is the first to be based on the shape of the shells it will fire.

Russian press reports intimate that the USSR now has the hydrogen bomb. Evidence follows in the form of an explosion, known to involve both fission and fusion reactions. By 1961, the USSR will claim to have detonated the highest explosive of all time—a 58-megaton bomb (equivalent to 58 million tons of TNT).

The US Chevrolet Corvette is the first production car whose bodywork is made from fibreglass-reinforced plastic. Although not quite as strong as steel, the fibreglass bodywork is light and less likely to corrode. Later in the fifties, Citrëon and Lotus will use it for their high-performance cars.

Both Michelin in France and Pirelli in Italy introduce radial-ply tyres to improve cars' roadholding. Cross-ply tyres, with cord plies running at 45° to the central line of the tyre, have been in use since 1903; the new tyre's plies are set radially—at 90° to the tyre's edge—to give a better grip on the road.

The American Electric Power Co commissions a 345,000 V electricity supply network that will interconnect the system of seven states. This reduces the costs of transmitting power since it uses only as many power stations as are required by the load, and sends the power over long distances, rather than allowing all the stations to work at less than full capacity.

A cheaper process for producing polythene starts a new era of low-cost plastics. Invented by Karl Ziegler, it uses atmospheric pressure instead of the expensive, specially created pressures of previous methods.

A milestone in nuclear research and development is reached when the breeding of atomic fuel is achieved at the nuclear reactor at Arco, Idaho, USA. The reactor splits atoms of the isotope uranium-235 to produce energy and changes the isotope uranium-238 into plutonium. Uranium-235 and plutonium are the fuels needed for nuclear reactors, and since uranium-238 is 140 times more plentiful than uranium-235, future supplies of atomic fuel are assured.

A Paris surgeon performs the first human transplant involving an organ from a live donor: the transfer of a kidney from mother to son. The kidney functions normally for 21 days but then begins to fail, due to rejection, and the young man dies.

One of the century's most important biological discoveries comes when English physicist Francis Crick and US biochemist James Watson present their double-helix model for the structure of the DNA molecule. The model explains how genetic information can be stored, and how chromosomes duplicate themselves in the process of cell division.

Low-cost aerosol cans come into daily use after the invention of a simple plastic valve mechanism.

The first collapsible polythene tube comes on the market—it contains sun-tanning lotion.

In CinemaScope—*Demetrius and the Gladiators*: 20th Century Fox launch CinemaScope in response to the challenge presented by Cinerama—the first wide-screen process. Using Chrétien's anamorphic 'hypergonar' lenses of the twenties, CinemaScope squeezes a wide field of view on to a standard film. In projection, the process is reversed, to give the wide picture that will become near standard for Hollywood movies. With the sound track distributed from speakers all round the auditorium, the experience of going to the movies will be much more dramatic than it was in front of a square screen with sound coming from the front only.

COMMUNICATION AND INFORMATION

Eurovision, the European TV community, begins experimental transmissions linking Belgium, Denmark, France, W. Germany, Italy, the Netherlands, Switzerland and Britain. Two years later, E. Germany and Czechoslovakia broadcast Eurovision's first coverage of the Olympic ice hockey games, but in 1960 the Eastern Bloc forms its own system, named Intervision.

In the area of California that will be known as Silicon Valley, Texas Instruments sire a new generation of transistors, using silicon in place of germanium. Silicon is able to withstand higher temperatures than germanium, but it will be well into the sixties before the silicon version is ready to supplant germanium as the heart of the 'chip'.

The world's total of radio sets outnumbers the newspapers printed every day, for the first time.

TRANSPORT AND WARFARE

The US Army Signal Corps sets up a camera on a bluff at Atlantic Highlands, New Jersey, and demonstrates its long-range, infrared capability. Not only do cars in New York, 25 mls (40.2 km) away, show up clearly, but they can be photographed through haze and fog.

The Dutch Fokker company build the twin-engined F27 Friendship, designed for short-range 'city-hopping'. The type will still be in production in the eighties, making it the most successful turboprop ever built.

ENERGY AND INDUSTRY

The Russians claim to have built the world's first nuclear power station. However, the APS-1 at Obninsk has only a small electrical output of 5 MW—enough to power a small town of about 6,000 people—whereas England's Calder Hall will have an output 10 times as large.

Dissimilar metals such as aluminium and brass can now be successfully joined together by friction welding, a new technique invented by Soviet engineers. By putting huge pressure on the two metals and then sliding or rubbing them together, enough friction and heat are generated to bind them rigidly.

The island of Gotland is linked to mainland Sweden by a 60-ml (96.5-km) electricity transmission cable—the world's first successful commercial use of high-voltage direct current as opposed to alternating current.

A new plastic, polypropylene, is invented in Milan by Dr Natta. As a fibre, the material will rival nylon in quality, but will cost less. A by-product of petroleum, it will replace jute and hemp in string, rope, sacks and carpet backing, and will be commercially produced in 1957.

MEDICINE AND FOOD PRODUCTION

Hybrid wheats which are more resistant to disease and drought, become possible thanks to progress made in wheat genetics by US scientist Ernest Robert Sears. He demonstrates that specific chromosomes can be substituted for others, to change and improve varieties of wheat.

Boston surgeons carry out the first successful kidney transplant using a living donor. Their decision to operate is influenced by the fact that donor and recipient are identical twins, which avoids the rejection problem associated with organ transplants.

FRINGE BENEFITS

Livingstone Electronics of New York introduce home stereo tape-recording outfits.

The US Navy's *Nautilus* is the first vehicle of any kind to have a nuclear power source. Capable of staying submerged for months at a time and of operating at high speeds almost indefinitely, this will be the prototype of all the hunter-killer submarines that will transform the world's major navies over the coming decades.

The Regency, the first commercial transistor radio, reaches the US market—and opens the flood gates to mass-produced transistors for car and home radios, TV sets and, before long, computers.

To counteract the effects of over-enlargement in wide-screen cinemas, Paramount develop VistaVision, a hi-fi movie process. This uses a large negative during filming, which is reduced to the standard format for cinema presentation. *White Christmas*, the first VistaVision film, clearly shows the improved definition and quality of the new process.

A method of etching printing plates which is four times faster than its predecessors, and also cleaner and less harmful to health, is introduced in the USA by the Dow Chemical Co. The first metal used for the plates is magnesium (rumour has it that this is due to a glut of the metal, following the post-war fall-off in aircraft production), but the system is also developed for etching copper and zinc, the two metals most commonly used for printing plates.

Early excitement over the potential of atomic power leads physicists at the University of Utah to design an atomic railway locomotive. But the projected reactor, needing a huge 80 ft (24 m) long steel container, will never be built.

A radioactive cloud, 114,000 ft (34,732 m) high, spreading fallout from Bikini Atoll across the Pacific Ocean, signals the explosion of a US 15-megaton device—750 times more powerful than the bombs of 'Operation Crossroads' eight years earlier. The contamination of nearby Rongelap Atoll, as well as the crew of a Japanese fishing vessel, receives worldwide publicity and prompts the Japanese to investigate radiation levels in the area.

The British government decides to follow the lead of the USA and USSR by including thermonuclear weapons in its nuclear deterrent policy.

Scientists Chapin, Fuller and Pearson, working at the Bell Telephone Co in the USA, develop the silicon photovoltaic cell, which converts sunlight directly into electricity. The efficiency of conversion is 6%—about 10 times higher than previously achieved. The cell depends on the abundant element silicon, but the silicon must be exceptionally pure, making the cells expensive—it costs more than $1 million to make enough to generate 1 kW.

'Mr Charlie', a submersible drilling unit operated by Odeco Inc, goes into service in the Gulf of Mexico. It is the first mobile drilling unit designed for offshore operations.

The shape of things to come in production engineering can be seen as the first electronically programmed milling machine—it makes machine parts and removes metal—is introduced by the Massachusetts Institute of Technology. This so-called numerical control automatically programmes the machine so that specific operations, such as changes in directions and dimensions of cuts and cutting speeds, are carried out accurately.

US microbiologists John Enders, Thomas Weller and Frederick Robbins receive the Nobel Prize for Physiology and Medicine for work on culturing polio viruses.

Bryan Brooke, professor of surgery at London's St George's Hospital, improves the ileostomy operation: joining the lower end of the small intestine to an outlet in the abdominal wall, he creates an alternative outlet for body waste. Patients who have undergone removal of the bowel can now once again lead normal lives.

US biochemist Vincent du Vigneaud succeeds in synthesizing two pituitary hormones, vasopressin (which raises blood pressure and stimulates the kidney to retain water) and oxytocin (which causes the uterine muscles to contract in childbirth).

A new method of detecting fingerprints is investigated—it uses sensitive chemical reagents, activated by perspiration, to show up evidence.

Fast food takes off as the first TV dinners are introduced in the USA.

The anti-polio vaccine developed by American microbiologist Jonas Salk in 1952 will all but eradicate one of the most damaging of childhood diseases. The first programme for the mass vaccination of schoolchildren is set up in Pittsburgh, Pennsylvania, and by 1956 such programmes will be established in Britain as well.

'Dash 80' as the prototype Boeing 707 is known, is the result of a $20 million investment programme; but the 707 will not enter regular service with an airline for another four years, when Pan Am will start to fly them. Differing most noticeably from its rival, the Comet, in having its engines suspended from its elegantly swept wings rather than built into them, the production 707 will beat the opposition by flying faster and farther on less fuel. 'Dash 80' will go through many test-bed conversions, including, as here, the mounting of a fifth engine towards the tail to test rear-mounting of power plants for the projected Boeing 727.

The advance of computers

In less than a millionth of a second, the vast computer of an international airline can simultaneously accept 500 booking enquiries, and search its 40 million memory units for appropriate replies. It takes only another split second for the requested information to be flashed up on 500 separate monitors, which may be hundreds of miles apart. Such is the power of the modern mainframe computer.

The computer is, in essence, a high-speed calculator with an electronic memory. Instructions (the programme) are fed in using computer languages imprinted on magnetic tape. This reaches a control unit which converts it into a series of stepwise arithmetical operations, which are performed by the arithmetical logic unit. To complete its tasks, it may draw on information stored in a read-only memory unit or transfer data to a random access memory unit for use later on in the calculation. The final result is then 'translated' into mathematical symbols, numerals, letters or graphics, and either printed out on paper or displayed on a monitor.

The 'brain' of a computer of the eighties is housed on a silicon chip. The larger a computer, the bigger and better its memory and calculating power, and the more chips it has. Thanks to the silicon chip, computers are now so ubiquitous that they are used in some way by about 40 per cent of the total work force of the western world.

The power of the computer for scientific and social change can never have been envisaged by British inventor and 'father' of the computer, Charles Babbage. In 1834, Babbage sketched the first plans for an engine which would, with the help of a memory stored on punched cards, work as a calculating machine. This punched card idea (with the holes read by feelers) was used by US statistician Herman Hollerith for analyzing the results of the 1890 Census.

Not for nearly half a century were any more real strides made. But experiments in the thirties used machines with mechanical parts driven by electrical input to make calculations. More significant was the incorporation of thermionic valves into calculating machines. These were used to allow the passage of electric currents generated to be equivalent to numerals. Banks of valves, plugged in by hand, were needed to do even simple arithmetic.

Further refinements of the forties included the invention of the binary code—the representation of numbers in sequences of 0 and 1—which meant that the values could be operated simply by transmitting or not transmitting current, and by advances in the design of memory stores. As computers first entered business as payroll calculators in the fifties, their everyday applications were becoming more and more obvious. But it was the transistor that was destined, in the sixties, to breed

The first fully electronic computers, such as the ENIAC (Electronic Numerical Integrator and Calculator) built in 1945, were massive machines equipped with more than 18,000 thermionic valves, *above*. The purpose of these valves was to permit the flow of an electric current which corresponded to any particular number. The valves were plugged in manually to programme the computer, which could complete 5,000 calculations a second but occupied 1,500 sq ft (138 sq m) of floor space.

Without computers, units such as NASA's Jet Propulsion Laboratory would not exist. The many mathematical calculations required to propel men and machines into space, and keep them there, are so complex that only a computer can complete them in a realistic time. And it is the speed of computer calculation that also puts space flight within the bounds of safety: as craft power through space, or when emergencies arise, only computers can make the correcting sums quickly enough to ensure the correct in-flight responses.

the second generation of computers.

By using transistors instead of valves to conduct electricity, computers became smaller, cheaper and more reliable overnight. So fast was progress in electronics that by 1965 a third generation of computers was born—this time using silicon chips in place of transistors. Now millions of calculations and memorizations could be made on a thin slice of silicon only $\frac{1}{4}$ inch (5 mm) square.

Home computers, using an ordinary television set as a display unit, are now available at increasingly low cost. At the other end of the scale, today's largest computers have 'bubble' memories made of garnet which can store a million bits of information.

A glance backward into time, shows that the computer has changed the whole tenor of industrial society. Yet the power of the computer remains the same: it is that of the programme fed in by its human operator.

The visual display unit is vital to many modern computer tasks. In the design of drugs, for example, the configuration of a possible new formulation is shown up on the screen. To arrive at this solution, the computer is fed information about a huge range of existing drugs and their actions, good and bad, upon the body. To investigate further, the scientists then interact with the computer by feeding in additional data and instructions through the control panel.

Even shoes can now be made with the help of computers. A shoe last can now be described mathematically, or digitized, and this description is fed into the computer. Next, the stylist draws up a coloured, three dimensional design on a screen and this, too, is entered into the data store. On command, the computer then prints out the various patterns for the leather or material. Once the design has been tested and proved satisfactory on the foot, the computer prints out as many templates as are needed.

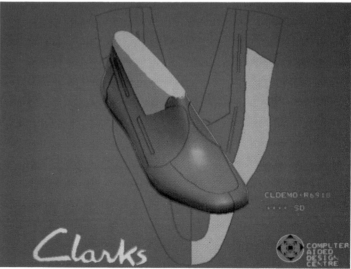

COMMUNICATION AND INFORMATION

World powers are beginning to realize the potential of computers in defence. The US Government is using SAGE air defence computers to monitor and process radar information and to guide interception weapons.

High-contrast photographic film has replaced glass wet-collodion plate for printing, and now new types of process cameras are available. Two such cameras, the Rotadon and the Chemco, both have focusing scales, electrically controlled shutters and support the film on a vacuum base board. Together with high-contrast photographic film, the cameras have increased the output of negative production by more than 20%.

In the USA, Les Paul and his wife popularize multi-track recording by taping the guitar and voice parts of songs separately. Within five years the technique will be standard.

TRANSPORT AND WARFARE

Americans now own 52 million private cars. The numbers have swelled from 28 million in 1946 and 40 million in 1950.

Christopher Cockerell's 'hovercraft' rides across the water on a cushion of air. The practical outcome of years of experimentation, his device follows 18th and 19th century efforts to reduce friction by interposing a layer of air between the bottom of a ship and the surface of the water.

ENERGY AND INDUSTRY

An automatic kettle with a thermostat that automatically switches off the kettle as soon as the water reaches boiling-point is marketed. This soon makes obsolete all other warning devices like buzzers, whistles and flashing lights.

The first domestic deep freezers capable of freezing fresh food appear on the US market and will go on sale in Britain in 1956. A substantial improvement on the 1950 version, they can maintain a temperature of $-27.8°F$ $(-18°C)$.

Atmospheric disturbances, such as lightning, and switching operations set in motion by electrical engineers, create huge voltage surges in electricity cables. To test the insulation and strength of these cables the National Physical Laboratory in Britain install a large impulse generator, designed by Ferranti and capable of punching out 3.2 million V. Such generators will be used later by the electricity industry to test large transformers and transmission line insulators, as well as high-voltage cables.

Artificial diamond, to be used in cutting tools and drills, is made for the first time by a team at GEC in New York. By subjecting graphite to ultra-high pressure, the atoms change into the configuration that characterizes diamond.

MEDICINE AND FOOD PRODUCTION

Hydrocephalus is a congenital condition where the infant's head becomes progressively enlarged due to the build-up of fluid in the ventricles of the brain. Now the Holtzer Shunt is invented which, implanted in the head, drains off some of the unwanted fluid. The shunt will save thousands of infants from premature death or gross abnormality and retardation.

Blindness in children, caused by retrolental fibroplasia and noted since about 1940, is traced to the practice of treating premature babies with high doses of oxygen.

FRINGE BENEFITS

Wimpy bars bring the hamburger to British high streets.

Sony's transistor radio, cheap and eminently portable, sets the pattern for the future. Within a very few years the bulky cabinet radios of the thirties and forties will be a thing of the past, ordinary families will possess several radios and in-car entertainment will become commonplace.

Steam irons for all. At the Vienna Spring Fair, Josef Scherner's new steam sole is shown. Attached to the base of an ordinary electric iron, the sole is filled with water. The iron heats the water to steaming point, and the chore of damping clothes before pressing is eliminated.

In his Todd-AO process, first seen in the movie *Oklahoma*, Mike Todd Jr revives the 1930 idea of wide film to improve screen quality. A 65 mm camera film is used to make prints on 70 mm film; soundtracks are stereophonic and magnetic. The same format will remain in use for large-scale cinema presentations well into the eighties.

Almost 20 years after VHF TV transmissions began in the USA, regular VHF radio broadcasts begin in Britain from a station in Kent, serving London and SE England.

The BBC's monopoly of British TV broadcasting ends with the opening of the commercial channel ITV (Independent Television) to serve an audience of 12 million. Britain's first TV advertisement is for toothpaste.

The US Navy introduces NORC (Naval Ordinance Research Computer) and reflects the increasing use of electronic computers for weather forecasting. Working at a rate of 15,000 mathematical calculations a second, NORC can process the information needed for a 24-hour forecast and calculate a 30 day forecast over one hemisphere of the globe in a mere 5 seconds—a task that previously took a whole year for an unaided human.

Two French electric trains break the world speed record by reaching 205 mph (329.9 km/h) on a short stretch of line. But such speeds are ruled out for regular service unless existing track is straightened and strengthened, or an entirely new track built without tight curves. A third option, eventually tested by Britain, is to design a new type of train, which can tilt to adapt to sharp bends in the track.

Sud-Aviation's Caravelle follows Comet's design but mounts the engines on either side of the rear fuselage—a style which later short-range jets will copy—instead of in the roots of the wings.

The French Citroën DS19 features a revolutionary gas suspension system that keeps the car level even if it is unevenly loaded, or if one wheel goes over a large bump. Its brakes, transmission and steering are all power-assisted, which makes it too expensive to sell well; so Citroën develop the ID19 without power assistance, but retaining the suspension system.

The first jack-up oil drilling rig is designed and constructed in the USA for operations in shallow water, usually less than 360 ft (110 m) deep. Such rigs will eventually make up nearly half the world's fleet of offshore oil installations.

Triacetate fibres, such as the Celanese Company's Arnel, now give synthetic textiles the luxurious feel and appearance of high-quality clothes at a cost within the price-range of the average American.

Optical fibres are invented as a result of research at Imperial College, University of London, by Dr Narinder Kapary. He draws out long fibres of optical glass until they are as thin as human hair, then shines a light down one end. The light does not escape from the sides of the fibre even when it is curved or looped, but emerges intact at the other end. Fibre optics is born, and will first be used by physicians to see deep inside the body, and later by telecommunications engineers to transmit telephone, telex, television and computer signals.

Electricity generated by atomic energy is formally inaugurated in the USA when the normal public supply lines of the Niagara-Mohawk Power Corporation are fed with electricity from a generator powered by an atomic reactor. A similar, larger reactor is used to power the nuclear submarine *Sea Wolf*.

Hormones are present in the body in such small quantities that they are hard to trace. In America, Solomon Berson and Rosalyn Yalow introduce radio immuno-assay, a technique for measuring these elusive chemicals by tagging them with radio-isotopes. This brings greater precision to the diagnosis and assessment of hormonal disorders.

A group of Nobel prize-winners issue a warning after meeting at Lake Constance: modern weapons of war may contaminate the world with radioactivity to such an extent that entire nations may be wiped out. Also this summer, Bertrand Russell issues his famous anti-nuclear statement, signed by eight internationally known scientists, including Albert Einstein.

In the USA Dr Gregory Pincus reports successful results of the first clinical trials with oral contraceptives.

The simple Velcro fastener is patented. Hundreds of tiny hooks on each surface of the fastener lock and hold fast when pressed together.

A bubble car comes home first in its category in the Mille Miglia, the 1,000-ml road race that will be abandoned two years later. A major advance in cheap, popular transport, the tiny two-seater Isetta boasts hydraulic brakes and a four-speed plus reverse gearbox. The diminutive air-cooled engine is rear-mounted and the whole of the front swings open to allow access for driver and passenger. When Isetta cease to build the car, BMW in Germany will take it over, producing their own version right up to 1962.

149

The nucleus of power

In 1945, the atomic bombs that devastated Hiroshima and Nagasaki ended a war and illustrated to horrific effect the enormous energy stores locked up inside atoms. From the ashes of conflict has arisen the phoenix of peace, in the form of nuclear power generated simply for the purpose of making electricity.

What the Americans really unleashed in their attack were uncontrolled chain reactions involving the splitting, or fission, of nuclei of uranium and plutonium. By bombarding these nuclei with neutrons—subatomic particles which are the real currency of nuclear power—the nuclei split, releasing more neutrons which split more nuclei, and so on, until all the uranium and plutonium were destroyed in a split-second radioactive holocaust.

For nuclear engineers, the challenge has been to develop the technology for controlling this chain reaction both safely and efficiently, and to convert the fantastic amounts of heat generated in the process into electricity. The art of this control lay in understanding the behaviour of the all-important neutron which is an integral part of the nucleus of all atoms.

Neutrons involved in the chain reaction can move at different speeds, but it is only the slow-moving ones that can split uranium nuclei. At the heart of a nuclear reactor, graphite—the same material employed as the 'lead' in pencils—is widely used to moderate or slow down the fast-moving, unproductive neutrons. All nuclear power stations, from the world's first at Calder Hall in Britain, to one of the latest at Three Mile Island, Penn., use moderators to control neutron speed.

Notable exceptions to this rule are fast-breeder reactors such as those at Dounreay in Scotland and Marcolle in France. Here, fast-moving neutrons emitted from uranium and plutonium fission are used to 'breed' yet more plutonium. This method generates nearly 60 times as much energy as a conventional 'thermal' reactor, and has the added advantage of being able to make good use of the spent fuel from a thermal reactor.

In a nuclear power station, sophisticated engineering techniques are used to assemble the fuel rods and the control rods which, because of their ability to absorb neutrons, provide the necessary fine tuning of the chain reaction. Made of boron or cadmium, control rods slow down the reaction by swallowing neutrons, and if necessary, can stop it completely. The intense heat generated by the fuel elements is rapidly removed by a coolant, then this heat is used, as in a power station burning fossil fuels, to produce steam to drive the turbines which generate electricity.

The variety of nuclear reactors stems from the use of different fuels combined with different coolants. British engineers, who designed the first commercial power station, used carbon dioxide gas as a coolant. Worldwide, the most common sort of reactor is now the American pressurized water reactor which uses ordinary water under high pressure as a coolant. The Canadian CANDU reactor uses heavy water, the Dounreay, liquid sodium.

The pressurized water reactor (PWR) is fuelled by uranium dioxide and cooled by water under high pressure. The water, which in the process becomes highly radioactive, is also heated and carries its heat from the reactor's core to the steam generator where it boils water in a separate circuit. The steam drives a turbine in the electricity generating plant. Like all other thermal nuclear reactors, the core of the PWR contains a moderator —in this case, its water coolant—to slow down the neutrons released in the fission reaction.

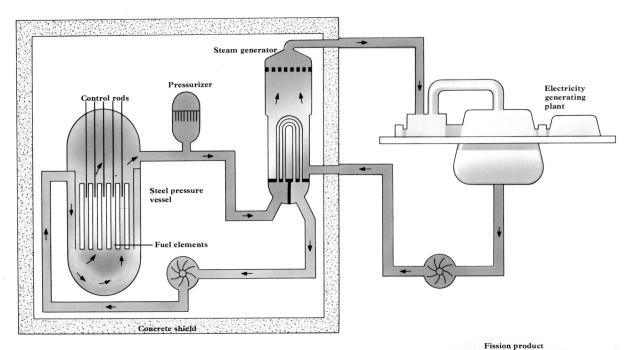

Steam generator

Pressurizer

Control rods

Steel pressure vessel

Fuel elements

Concrete shield

Electricity generating plant

Vast amounts of energy are released when the nucleus of a uranium–235 atom is split into two by a slow-moving neutron. Yet more neutrons— electrically neutral particles—are released and, if moving slowly enough, will split further uranium–235 atoms, so triggering a powerful chain reaction. This nuclear fission, the basis of all thermal reactors, gradually leads to the build-up of radioactive products such as strontium, xenon, iodine and krypton. These increasingly hinder the reaction by poisoning the fuel, but when extracted, are put to good use in medical radiation therapy and in scientific research.

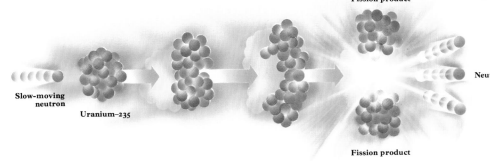

Fission product

Slow-moving neutron

Uranium–235

Neutro

Fission product

The shape of nuclear power stations to come will—for 50 years at least—be much as today. A combination of thermal and fast breeder reactors is expected to provide at least half the nuclear nations' electricity needs by the year 2000. But during that time, completely new fusion reactors may be developed, using the same energy that explodes from a hydrogen bomb—the energy generated by the fusion or combination of atoms. It is fusion power that fuels the sun, and fusion reactors could become a reality if engineers could invent a means of maintaining the 100 million °C it takes to fuse the atoms of deuterium, tritium or lithium.

Fusion power could answer man's energy problems for ever, since the deuterium atoms needed to fuel a fusion reactor come from water, the cheapest and most abundant of Earth's natural resources. Nuclear fusion has already been achieved experimentally by high-powered lasers focussed on to atoms to create energy a million times greater than the power of all man-made machinery.

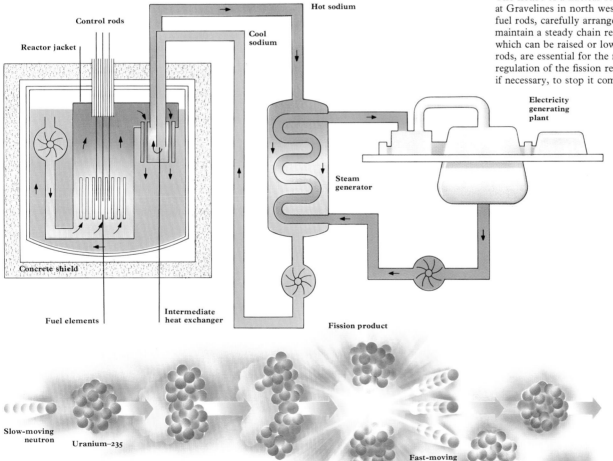

Control rods

Reactor jacket

Hot sodium

Cool sodium

Electricity generating plant

Steam generator

Concrete shield

Fuel elements

Intermediate heat exchanger

Fission product

The heart of a nuclear reactor, such as this one at Gravelines in north west France, is a pile of fuel rods, carefully arranged by engineers to maintain a steady chain reaction. Control rods, which can be raised or lowered between the fuel rods, are essential for the minute-by-minute regulation of the fission reaction and can be used, if necessary, to stop it completely.

Fast breeder reactors use plutonium and uranium fuel and are cooled by liquid sodium. This transfers heat from the core to more sodium in a secondary circuit which boils water in a steam generator; the steam drives a turbine coupled to an electricity generator. The reactor uses the fast-moving neutrons to breed more plutonium fuel from uranium contained in a 'blanket' of steel cans around the core.

Unlike a thermal reactor, a fast breeder has no moderator to slow down the neutrons released as nuclei are split. Fast-moving neutrons make uranium–238 atoms decay into plutonium, which is extracted, and also release beta radiation.

Slow-moving neutron

Uranium–235

Fission product

Fast-moving neutron

Uranium–238

Plutonium

COMMUNICATION AND INFORMATION

The first desk-sized computer, the Burroughs E-101 is made in Philadelphia and demonstrated in Paris and London. The 'baby brain' is designed to fill the gap between mechanical adding machines and large electronic computers, and is intended for use by mathematicians and scientists, rather than by businessmen and accountants.

Improvements in the design of the quartz crystal mean that six times as many short wave radio channels are now available—the stable frequency given by the crystal allows radio channels to be more closely spaced.

An electronic watch is perfected at the Lip factory in France. Lighter than an ordinary mechanical watch, and less sensitive to changes in atmospheric pressure, it does not tick—instead its mechanism pulses silently three times a second. The watch runs on a two-cell battery and the makers claim that a million watches can be run on the power consumed by a 100 candle-power lamp.

TRANSPORT AND WARFARE

A motorcycle exceeds 200 mph for the first time when German Wilhelm Herz, riding a 499 cc NSU, reaches 211.40 mph (338.092 km/h) at Bonneville, USA.

The world airspeed record tops the 1,000 mph (1,609 km/h) mark for the first time on 10 March, when test pilot Peter Twiss reaches 1,132 mph (1,821.4 km/h) in a Fairey Delta II research aircraft over the south coast of England.

ENERGY AND INDUSTRY

An electricity turbo-alternator, installed at a power station near St Helens, England, is the first in the world to be cooled by water. This distilled water flows over the stator bars (the fixed parts of the generator which house the rotors), allowing the generator to carry three times as much current as generators cooled by the previously used, less efficient hydrogen. The total output of the station is 30,000 kW, enough to power a town of 36,000 people.

Liquefied natural gas is produced on an industrial scale for the first time in Louisiana, USA. It will be transported to Britain in 1959 when the vessel *Methane Pioneer* carries its first load of 2,000 cu m. By 1977, 21,500 million cu m of natural gas will be liquefied annually, and six countries will be exporting it.

MEDICINE AND FOOD PRODUCTION

In the USA, J.D. Hardy and W.R. Webb experiment with heart transplants on dogs, new-born calves, monkeys and human cadavers.

M. Johnstone of the Manchester Royal Infirmary, England, introduces halothane to the field of anaesthesia. Marketed under the trade-name 'Fluothane', its potent, manageable and non-flammable qualities will make it the most important new inhalation anaesthetic since chloroform.

FRINGE BENEFITS

The FORTRAN computer language is invented for scientific and engineering problems.

The go-kart, a scaled-down racing car for kids, hits the tracks in the USA.

After 30 years, during which calls were transmitted by radio, the TAT 1 cable comes into service on 25 September. No longer subject to atmospheric interference, telephone calls across the Atlantic will be clear regardless of weather conditions. Within 20 years, cable capacity will have to be increased 100-fold.

The video era begins: Alexander Poniatoff demonstrates his Ampex video tape-recorder in Chicago and produces a picture almost indistinguishable from that of 'live' TV. In November the first video recording is aired by CBS-Hollywood to the Pacific Coast TV network.

A sight-sound visual telephone is introduced in the USA by the Bell Telephone Co and tested between New York and Los Angeles. Pictures of the speaker are carried along telephone cables. But since one image takes up the same space as 125 telephone connections, the idea is abandoned.

Bell Telephone Laboratories in New York, the place where the transistor was invented in 1947, builds the Leprachaun, the first experimental transistorized computer. The on-off switching transistor fathers a new breed of more reliable, more economical machines. IBM, Philco and General Electric quickly follow suit with 'second generation' computers.

Dectra, a long-range navigational aid, allows airline pilots 10-ml (16-km) 'vision' at night and greatly increases the accuracy of flying at approaches to airports. With the increased potential for accidents—75 aircraft are in the air over the North Atlantic at any one time, and there are 3,000 transatlantic crossings a month—Dectra promises to be a life-saver for the future.

Dracones, flexible tubular floating containers for carrying liquids lighter than water, are invented. Made of woven nylon, with inner and outer surfaces proofed, dracones carry petroleum products through rough seas better than ordinary barges.

The US Atomic Energy Commission is responsible for the explosion of the world's first airborne hydrogen bomb, in a new series of nuclear tests in the Pacific.

The prototype B-58 Hustler, the first supersonic bomber, takes off in the USA. Its innovations include fuel and armament pods, which are carried beneath the fuselage to save interior space, and jettisoned when empty to make the plane aerodynamically 'clean'. It is constructed of glass-fibre, aluminium and stainless-steel honeycomb, to resist the heat and stress of Mach 2 flight. Each of the three-man crew has his own escape capsule.

The first full range of brightly coloured, wash-fast dyes to be successfully used on cellulose fibres are made commercially available by ICI. Until the advent of these Procion dyes, cellulose fabrics, such as artificial silk, Celanese and Tricel, could be dyed in only a limited range of colours.

Calder Hall, the world's first nuclear power station, opens in Cumbria, England.

Two large ocean-thermal power plants are built by the French off the Ivory Coast. Electricity is produced by exploiting the large temperature difference between the warm upper waters and the cold deeper levels, to operate turbines.

The world of nuclear technology looks on as a new, very powerful nuclear reactor, called DIDO, is inaugurated at Harwell nuclear research station in England. The reactor's ability to generate neutrons is 40 times greater than previously, enabling research scientists to complete fission experiments in weeks instead of years.

Major progress in the diagnosis of intestinal disease comes when Dr Margot Shiner, of London's Hammersmith Hospital, perfects a biopsy capsule which can be fed through the mouth and correctly positioned in the gut with the aid of X-ray equipment. The capsule collects tissue from the intestine which is then examined.

US physicians pioneer haemodialysis—cleansing the blood on an artificial kidney machine—to save patients with severe barbiturate poisoning. The technique removes up to 40% of the drug from the blood and speeds a return to consciousness. It succeeds in serious cases where conventional methods of detoxification fail.

St Thomas's Hospital in London installs the first British radio paging system to contact doctors instantly.

Long-life stainless steel razor blades are produced by the British firm of Wilkinson Sword.

Automation in banking begins in the USA where a computer handles 32,000 accounts for the Bank of America.

Birth control pills go on mass trial in Puerto Rico. The success of the trials, directed by obstetrician John Rock and biologist Gregory Pincus, will lead to the marketing in the USA of the first oral contraceptive, Enovid–10, in 1960. One year later the Pill will be available in Britain.

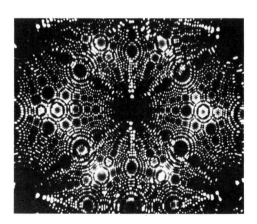

Atoms become visible for the first time. This is how a tungsten crystal appears through the new field ion microscope. The magnification is 2,700,000 × and the microscope is the most powerful in existence. The invention of German-American physicist Erwin Wilhelm Mueller, this revolutionary microscope will be used most often to study imperfections in metals—minute cracks and signs of fatigue. Later, Mueller will modify it, producing an 'atom probe', with which the chemical identities of atoms can be established.

Flightpath to supersonic

Ever since the Wright Brothers first conquered the air at Kitty Hawk in 1903, the race has been on to achieve ever higher speeds. At the first aviation meeting, held at Reims, France, in 1909, the speed prize was won by US flying-boat pioneer Glenn Curtiss, with a stunning 46 mph (75 km/h). Four years later, the Schneider Trophy began. The first real speed event, it attracted global interest as designers grappled with engine and airframe problems to produce faster, more streamlined aircraft.

By 1940, supersonic speeds were in sight: the RAF Spitfire was capable of reaching 0.9 of the speed of sound in a power dive. The simultaneous development of the jet engine suggested that even higher speeds were possible. Aircraft began to carry Mach meters—Mach 1 is the accepted measurement for the speed of sound—and serious research into the so-called sound barrier began.

In 1947, a three-year project at the Bell Aircraft Corporation gave birth to the Bell X–1. The rocket-powered plane, air-launched from a B–29 bomber to conserve fuel, broke the sound barrier with Capt 'Chuck' Yeager at the controls. The X–1's supersonic speed was 670 mph (1,078 km/h). A bare 15 years later, a distant cousin—the X–15—would fly higher and faster than any other manned plane. Its speed would reach 5,434 mph (7,295 km/h), almost seven times that of sound.

After World War II, the jet engine made supersonic flights commonplace, but exclusively military. Fighters and reconnaissance planes in particular quickly proliferated. In 1954, the US F–100 Super Sabre claimed a special place in history: at a speed of 850 mph (1,368 km/h), it became the first fighter to break the sound barrier in level flight. As aircraft production costs escalated, a new family of more versatile military aircraft was called for. The Russians built the MiG–25

The Lockheed SR–71 has been called the ultimate spy-plane. Built out of costly titanium to withstand the heat generated at Mach 3, 80,000 ft up, its smooth lines and anti-radar black paint make it almost undetectable to radar.

The unmistakable face of Concorde, *right*, shows its 'droop snoot', lowered 15° at landing to improve the pilot's view. The wings' leading edges are shaped so that the air swirls over them, creating a powerful vortex to increase lift.

fighter, capable of short dashes at Mach 3.2 on reconnaissance missions; the Americans countered with the F–15 Eagle, which can carry bombs as well as missiles for fighter interception, at speeds of Mach 2.5.

In 1974, a remarkable black object was sighted over London—the Lockheed SR–71, known as the Blackbird, had flown from New York in less than two hours. But, significantly, its astonishing speed and shape are matched in technological sophistication by its powers of reconnaissance: a battery of cameras, radars and infrared sensors enable it to survey 100,000 square miles (259,000 sq km) an hour. Electronic gadgetry is now as important to aerial warfare as the jet engine.

In 1962, the Anglo-French Supersonic Treaty brought faster-than-sound flight a step closer for civilians. Years of intensive research and over 5,000 hours of wind-tunnel tests proved that a long, streamlined fuselage and slender, ogival delta wings reconciled good control at low speeds, with low drag at speeds up to Mach 2.2.

The aircraft was christened Concorde, and commercial services began in 1976. At last it was possible, if you could afford it, to cross the Atlantic ocean in less than three hours—a far cry from the days of Charles Lindbergh some 50 years before. His non-stop flight took more than ten times as long.

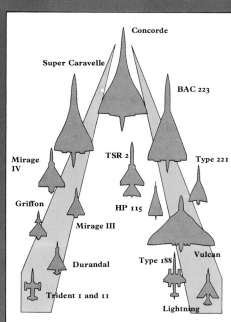

The creation of Concorde was the culmination of two historical strands of civil and military aeronautical technology, one French and one British. About 50,000 people in 10 locations around France and Britain were directly involved in its development.

Mach 0.5 (around 330 mph)   Mach 0.9 (around 600 mph)   Mach 2 (around 1,300 mph)

Shockwave

As a supersonic aircraft approaches the speed of sound—Mach 1—pressure waves caused by its passage through the air are so compressed that they form a vertical shockwave. At speeds beyond Mach 1, this wave forms a cone with the aircraft at the vertex, 'towing' it along. The cone expands, reaching ground level as a 'sonic boom'. Supersonic transports, such as Concorde and the Russian Tu–144, are designed to fit snugly inside the shockwave cone, minimizing air resistance.

COMMUNICATION AND INFORMATION

In the USA, Marconi market their Doppler navigation system for civil aviation through RCA. It is the first navigational system not to rely on outside aids, and works by bouncing electromagnetic waves from the aircraft to the ground. The frequency of waves returning to the aircraft indicates the pilot's position, air speed and ETA. Unfailingly accurate, this self-sufficient system also allows all the equipment to be carried in the aircraft—but it does not solve the long-standing problem of informing ground control of the aircraft's position.

The first surgical operation to be televised in colour is shown to 300 British and French viewers at St Bartholemew's Hospital, London. Every detail of the thyroid operation is seen on the 8 × 6 ft (2.4 × 1.8 m) screen.

SUBSET, a high-speed telex capable of transmitting 1,000 words a minute, is introduced by the Bell Telephone Co in the USA.

The first electronic calculator to have a memory is installed at the British Atomic Energy Authority laboratories. Its storage drum allows a series of problems to be worked out in a single run or to be interrupted for accumulating totals.

TRANSPORT, WARFARE AND SPACE EXPLORATION

The first turbine-powered aircraft to run a transatlantic service is the Bristol Britannia 102. But manufacturing problems—to say nothing of competition from US jets—seriously shorten the lifespan of the potentially excellent turboprop airliner.

The first man-made satellite of planet Earth, Sputnik 1, is launched by a Russian intercontinental ballistic missile (ICBM) to measure the density and temperature of Earth's upper atmosphere. A month later, Sputnik 2 is launched with a dog—Laika—on board, and instruments to monitor her body's reactions to space flight.

ENERGY AND INDUSTRY

The core of nuclear power stations, which contains the nuclear fuel, will become stronger and safer as a new electron beam technique for welding metals is introduced by J.A. Stohr of the French Atomic Energy Commission. Performed in a vacuum to achieve a pure weld, electron beam welding means that metals such as titanium and tungsten, which are difficult or impossible to weld by other means, can now be safely joined and used to construct nuclear fuel rods. Such welding will be used later to construct aircraft and rockets.

Hoover make the spin dryer accessible to housewives, adding it to the same cabinet that holds the washing drum to create a new style in washing machines—the 'twin tub'.

The nuclear reactor at Shippingport, Pennsylvania, is activated, so becoming the first large nuclear power station in the USA to be used for commercial purposes. The world's first pressurized water reactor (PWR), it is a scaled-up version of the one that powered the *Nautilus*.

A new dry cell battery, the first to be developed for 50 years, is sold by P.R. Mallory & Co. The mercury cell lasts several times longer than previous dry cell batteries.

MEDICINE AND FOOD PRODUCTION

The lightweight high-speed dental drill is demonstrated at a conference in Rome. Developed in the USA, it is water-cooled and emits a high-pitched whine.

The final triumph in the polio campaign comes when Albert B. Sabin of the Children's Hospital, Cincinnati, produces a live vaccine which is very safe. Taken orally, the Sabin vaccine quickly multiplies in the gut, gives complete immunity and, by the mid-sixties, will supplant the Salk vaccine.

FRINGE BENEFITS

A shredder marketed by Karl Zysset takes the effort out of vegetable preparation.

Reports confirm that wool can be moth-proofed 'on the hoof', using insecticide in sheep-dip.

Radioactive materials can be handled at Britain's nuclear research centre at Harwell. Five chambers with 30-ton doors made of steel-shot concrete, have just been completed, in which radioactive material can be safely studied. Items are handled sensitively by fully shielded workers using master–slave manipulators.

Dangerously radioactive materials are closely examined for the first time, using a remote control microscope. The microscope head and lighting, encased in a 14-ft (4.2-m) shield, are operated by both mechanical and electrical controls.

In their Pentax camera, Asahi of Japan overcome the problem that has bugged 35 mm single lens reflex cameras—the disappearance of the image in the viewfinder at the point of exposure. An instant return mirror in the Pentax restores the image immediately.

Phototypesetting, which will speed printing enormously, breaks into commerce. In Britain, the Penguin edition of Eric Linklater's *Private Angelo* is the first book to be entirely photoset. The phototypesetting process makes it possible to produce offset-litho plates direct from photocomposed film without the intervention of metal setting.

The 'canals' of Mars reach the TV screen. Dr E.C. Slipher of the Lowell Observatory takes 1,450 pictures of Mars through the new televisor, which enlarges and brightens the images to eliminate distortion caused by the atmosphere.

Philips introduce the Plumbicon TV camera tube, a greatly improved version of its predecessor, the Vidicon. In Britain the BBC bases all its plans for the development of colour TV on the new tube, which soon becomes universal in colour TV camera design.

Despite strong protests, Britain tests thermonuclear bombs in the Christmas Islands in the Pacific. The US government attempts to allay fears of increased atmospheric radioactivity by introducing the concept of the 'clean' H-bomb— one that gives a high percentage of explosive power without associated radioactivity—and implies that the British bomb is like this. Immediate fall-out is reduced by exploding the bombs, dropped by RAF Valiant jet bombers, at high altitudes.

Atlas, the USA's first intercontinental ballistic missile (ICBM), is tested two months after the Russians launch Sputnik 1 with an ICBM of their own. ICBMs are designed to travel hundreds of miles to their target—the farthest weapon range in World War II was 75 mls (120.7 km)—and Russian progress on similar weapons pushes the Atlas project to the highest military priority.

An important new light source which produces a golden-white light—the high-pressure sodium lamp—is developed by Maurice Cayless and others for future use in street lighting, workshops, factories and swimming baths.

Ovenproof pyro-ceram domestic cooking ware has its origins in the accidental discovery of a new crystalline ceramic: a particular type of glass called Foto-form is left overnight in an oven for heat treatment, but the thermostat fails, the oven overheats, and a new class of ceramic-like materials is born, which can be made and shaped like glassware and changed into a ceramic by heat treatment.

The fusion of atoms comes one step closer to realization when the British Atomic Energy Authority's experimental apparatus, called ZETA, begins operating at Harwell. ZETA is concerned with deriving energy from the fusion of atoms, unlike all the nuclear reactors in operation which obtain energy from splitting atoms. If ZETA can show that the fusion of heavy hydrogen atoms is possible, then the oceans of the world could be tapped to provide an inexhaustible supply of fuel.

Trawlers can stay at sea longer and bring back larger catches, thanks to a quick-freezing plant developed by a Scottish scientific research station. Compact, simple to operate, and able to withstand the buffeting from gales, it keeps the fish fresh without removing their original flavour.

British biochemist Alick Isaacs and colleagues discover and name the anti-viral protein, interferon. Though costly to produce, it gives hope for treating a wide range of drug-resistant viral diseases.

Frank Berger, a Czech chemist working in the USA, accidentally discovers the tranquillizer meprobamate, while looking for penicillin preservatives.

An ultrasonic generator foams bottled and canned beer in the USA, removing the air bubbles which will eventually give the beer a cloudy look.

Spray taps, installed in a London office building, are shown to save water and fuel.

The Lotus Elite, a new British sports car, is shown with its designer, Colin Chapman. The car is unique in having a glass-fibre body and can be bought in kit form, to be built by a keen amateur.

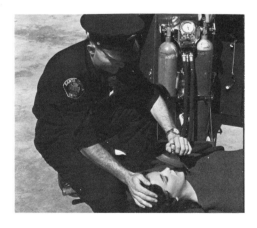

Resuscitation of people who are suffocating takes a step forward. With this new portable resuscitator (being demonstrated by a Santa Monica, California, fireman) oxygen can be given on the spot, instead of waiting until the victim has been taken to a hospital.

157

The giant leap into space

On 12 April 1961, Soviet spaceman Yuri Gagarin indelibly entered his name into the annals of human history as he blasted off into Earth orbit. Swathed in a bulky spacesuit and strapped into a capsule only 7½ ft (2.3 m) across, his life lay in the balance. Would he survive the massive acceleration forces generated as his craft reached the 25,000 mph (40,000 km/h) necessary to escape the pull of Earth's gravity? And would his capsule provide adequate protection against a merciless environment in which objects are bombarded by absolute cold on one side and solar radiation on the other?

To the joy and amazement of the world, the flight was a triumphant success—the first in a series of ever more ambitious missions that were to take man to the moon and lead, only 20 years later, to the launch of orbiting space stations in which astronauts and scientists could live and work in comfort.

Not least among the concerns surrounding the early space flights was the effect that weightlessness, or zero gravity, might have on the body. Only in 1973, when NASA launched its orbiting space laboratory, Skylab, did western scientists have the chance to make an exhaustive monitoring of the physiological effects of prolonged space flight.

The Skylab mission demonstrated conclusively the incredible adaptability of the human body. Even periods of weightlessness lasting 84 days induced no permanent ill effects. All the astronauts temporarily grew at least an inch

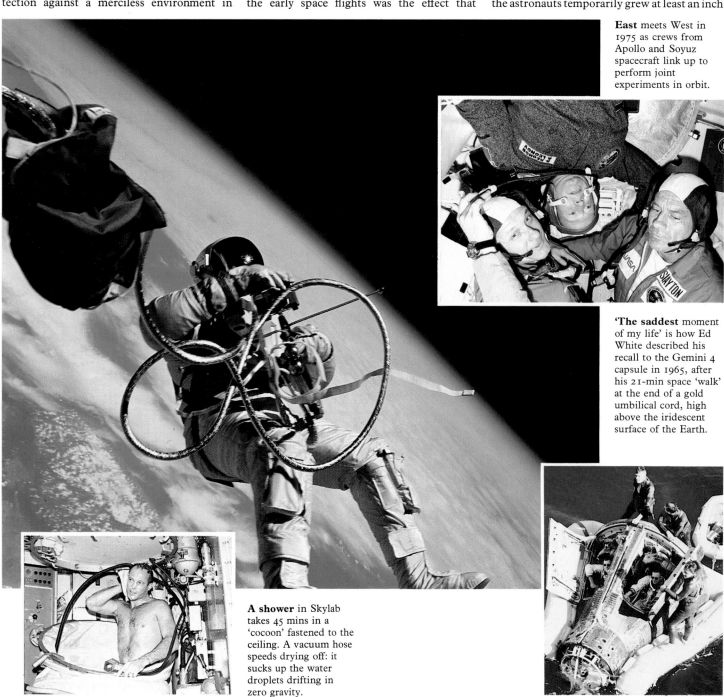

East meets West in 1975 as crews from Apollo and Soyuz spacecraft link up to perform joint experiments in orbit.

'The saddest moment of my life' is how Ed White described his recall to the Gemini 4 capsule in 1965, after his 21-min space 'walk' at the end of a gold umbilical cord, high above the iridescent surface of the Earth.

A shower in Skylab takes 45 mins in a 'cocoon' fastened to the ceiling. A vacuum hose speeds drying off: it sucks up the water droplets drifting in zero gravity.

as their backbones lengthened, and their faces got fatter as body fluid migrated upward. The men's hearts shrank by 3%, and 14% of red blood cells were lost—changes that prompted scientists to devise new means of exercising in space to keep the heart in good trim.

Between May 1973 and February 1974, three crews visited Skylab. They were the first US astronauts ever to live anything approaching a 'normal' life in space. Instead of popping food pills, for instance, they dined on menus that included prime ribs of beef. 'Waste management' was greatly improved by means of a suction operated fecal/urine collector.

Encouraged by Skylab's success, NASA went on to develop its orbiting Space Shuttle, the first re-usable 'commuter' spacecraft, which was launched on 12 April 1981—20 years to the day after Yuri Gagarin made man's first orbital flight. Like its Soviet equivalent, the Salyut space station, the Shuttle offers the experience of spaceflight to astronautical novices and aims to explore the potential of space science to the full.

By the beginning of the eighties, more than 100 men and just one woman had travelled in space. Now that the first space frontier has been crossed, a bright future beckons, which may include space factories, orbiting power stations to harness solar energy and space bases to launch missions beyond our solar system. Fantastic perhaps; but so, only 25 years ago, was manned space flight.

Gemini 8 astronauts Scott and Armstrong, *left*, are released from the confinement of their capsule after an aborted mission and an emergency landing in the Pacific in 1966.

The Space Shuttle is a strange hybrid: it needs a huge rocket to launch its 99 tons into orbit, but it handles like an aircraft and lands like a glider.

159

COMMUNICATION, INFORMATION AND SPACE APPLICATIONS

An automatic camera microscope, the Ultraphot, is developed by Zeiss in West Germany to improve quality control and trace the source of difficulties in the manufacture of materials. At the press of a button, the machine automatically selects the correct exposure time, light level and speed of film to produce high-quality photographs of microscopic samples.

Stereophonic radio transmissions, outside normal broadcasting hours, are begun in Britain as an experiment by the BBC.

Vanguard 1, the second satellite launched by the USA, weighs only 3.25 lb (1.47 kg), and is derided in the Soviet press as a 'grapefruit'. Vanguard 1's scientific achievements are, however, impressive, providing valuable information about the Earth's shape and atmosphere.

TRANSPORT, WARFARE AND SPACE EXPLORATION

The new-look Comet 4, with redesigned fuselage and extra fuel tanks, successfully operates the first London-New York jet service. The non-stop flight takes just over 6 hrs. But already the shadow of the US aircraft giants, Boeing and Douglas, has fallen over the British aviation industry, and the Comets will not be able to compete for long.

The nuclear-powered *Nautilus*, voyaging from the Pacific to the Atlantic, is the first submarine to pass under the North polar ice cap.

Britain opens her first motorway, the 8½-ml Preston by-pass. Reluctance to pay the large sums of money needed has put Britain's motorway programme far behind that of the USA and most European countries, although, as early as 1920, there had been a proposal for a London-Birmingham link similar to the M1, whose first section will finally open in 1959.

ENERGY AND INDUSTRY

The first offshore oil surveys in Italy are carried out in the Adriatic Sea; and the first semi-submersible drilling rig—whose submerged floats keep the drilling platform above the water—is constructed in the USA.

Lycra, a man-made elastic, is sold by Du Pont, the first of a succession of so-called Spandex fibres which are stronger and last longer than rubber.

Domestic tumble dryers are marketed by Parnell after their use in coin-operated laundromats proves their popularity. Hot air, whose temperature can be regulated, is blown into the rotating drum to dry the washing.

MEDICINE AND FOOD PRODUCTION

Dr Ian Donald of Glasgow, Scotland, pioneers the use of high-frequency sound waves to examine the unborn child. First used in gynaecology to detect tumours, diagnostic ultrasound produces a clear outline of the foetus, measures the size of the foetal skull—an indication of development—and provides pictures of soft tissues and blood-flow in the placenta.

John Enders at Harvard, a man who has had major successes with polio, mumps, chickenpox and other virus research, now succeeds in preparing an effective vaccine against measles. Mass vaccination will prove especially beneficial in parts of the world where measles is still a killer disease.

FRINGE BENEFITS

The Universe can be surveyed in comfort at the newly opened Planetarium in London.

A fire alarm, unaffected by hot sun or industrial work-shop temperatures, is developed.

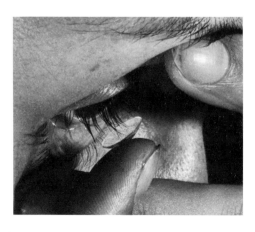

The first bifocal contact lenses appear on the market, twenty years after the appearance of the modern plastic lens. Recent developments have included the corneal lens which only covers that part of the eye and floats on the tears, allowing much longer wear without discomfort.

This Jupiter C rocket lifts the first US satellite, Explorer 1, into orbit. The data sent back by this small—31 lb (14 kg)—package of delicate research instrumentation leads to the discovery of the Van Allen belts—girdles of radiation from the solar wind, trapped above the atmosphere by the Earth's magnetic field.

The first colour videotape is made in the USA. The 'Betty Freezor Show', recorded at 11 am is transmitted 2 hrs later by WB TV of Charlotte, North Carolina. The broadcast is recorded on $\frac{1}{2}$-in (1.25-cm) tape with only a slight loss of definition.

President Dwight D. Eisenhower's Christmas message to the US nation is broadcast from outer space. In a prelude to satellite communications, the tape recording is transmitted from a rocket circling the Earth.

Radar with a 20-min memory is devised by Ferranti in Britain. Immediate or remembered images to be displayed are selected using a special phosphor; then the screen is immediately cleared so that it can show fresh impressions of aircraft or ship movements.

The introduction of the STD (subscriber trunk dialling) system, enables British telephone users to dial long distance direct, using a coded prefix. Queen Elizabeth II makes the first STD trunk call from Bristol to Edinburgh, but the system will not be complete nationwide for nearly 20 years.

IBM announces its electronic 'brain', named the Perceptron. When fully developed, this IBM 704 computer will be able to read, write, recognize faces, translate a variety of languages and talk. Its inventor, Dr Frank Rosenblatt, also predicts that it will be able to replicate itself.

NASA (The National Aeronautics and Space Administration) is formally inaugurated in the USA. It immediately approves the Mercury project, which aims to send a man into orbit and return him safely to earth.

Following an agreement between the USA and USSR, negotiations begin on a treaty banning tests of nuclear weapons. A moratorium on testing is declared for the duration of the talks.

General Motors develop an aluminium car engine which is 30% lighter than one made of cast-iron. This will enable GM to build a lighter and more economical car—a trend begun 10 years previously in Europe with the introduction of the Volkswagen, the Citroën 2CV, and the Morris Minor. Their research also shows that engine parts made of aluminium alloys are more resistant to wear.

London taxi-drivers testing the new British Perkins diesel engine find that it achieves an average of 36 mls per gallon (58 km per 4.56 l), double the mileage obtained from gasoline engines.

Parisian engineer Mark Grégoire begins manufacturing non-stick frying pans coated with PTFE, the material Roy Plunkett discovered in 1938, and markets them under the brand name Tefal.

An automatic all-in-one machine tool is introduced by Kearney and Trecker, so that complete operations can be carried out by one instead of several machines. This machining centre is numerically controlled by feeding in programmes which inform the machine of the desired shape and size of the finished component. Such a modern type of control increases the flexibility and usefulness of the machine tool, and saves time, money and labour.

Vanguard I is the first satellite to use electrical power from solar cells. Its radio transmitter is powered by six solar batteries and will continue sending signals back to Earth for another six years.

The most spectacular windmill-type electrical generator in Europe is built in France. It has a single three-blade propeller with a diameter of 102 ft (31 m).

East German physicist Professor von Ardenne invents a miniature radio transmitter for gastro-intestinal investigations. The encapsulated transmitter is swallowed and, for 24 hours, sends out information on levels of acidity and pressure in the digestive tract.

Doctors worldwide are beginning to recognize the damage to human tissue caused by exposure to radioactivity over many years. The cumulative effects of even low-level radiation is responsible for the degeneration of the reproductive organs. As a result, women over the age of 40 run a great risk of giving birth to children with such congenital malformations as Down's syndrome.

Massey-Ferguson demonstrate their new sugar cane harvester to Australian farmers. It eliminates back-breaking labour by severing the cane at ground level, removing the leafy tops, and chopping the cane into pieces of manageable size. By the eighties, similar machines will be in use throughout the world.

Woollen clothes can now be given permanent creases and pleats through a chemical treatment developed in Australia.

US and European fast food manufacturers show great interest in dehydrated potato flakes, which, when water is added, turn into mashed potato.

As steam power is slowly phased out of the railways of western Europe, the French have diesel locomotives specially designed for the new Trans-Europ-Express network. Capable of cruising speeds of up to 90 mph (140 km/h) they are also able to run on all continental rails. The TEE network, set up by France, Belgium, the Netherlands, Luxembourg, Italy, Switzerland and West Germany, will carry first-class passengers only and connect 70 major European cities.

The boats that fly

Since before the Stone Age, mankind has built water-going craft and used them to travel the world's waters. But the ever-increasing desire for speed was restricted by an inability to overcome some basic laws of physics. These dictate that while a craft is buoyed up by the water, it is also subject to the 'drag' of the water—and air—through which it travels.

So, unless a ship raises itself up out of the water, like a speedboat, it can never attain speeds much over 35 knots (40 mph). The solution—in theory at least—is a simple one. If the craft is lifted up on wing-like foils or a cushion of air, then the drag will disappear and speeds will increase.

Not until the twentieth century was the theory put into practice. The idea of the hovercraft, or air cushion vehicle (ACV), was first propounded as long ago as 1716 by Swedish philosopher Emanuel Swedenborg. Although theoretically correct, he was unable to provide an energy source capable of fulfilling his requirements. Nearly two centuries later, Austrian engineer Dagobert Muller von Thomamhul built what is reliably recorded as the first operational hovercraft; but it was not until 1959 that the idea of a working hovercraft really caught the public imagination.

The scientist responsible for this breakthrough was Briton Christopher Cockerell. After experiments involving such everyday items as kitchen scales, a vacuum cleaner and some empty coffee cans, he came up with a model in which a vehicle sat on a cushion of compressed air injected forward from its base. Unlike earlier designs, in which the air was allowed to escape, the hovercraft's continuous air jets 'sealed' the air cushion and resulted in the generation of a strong upward force.

Following a brief spell on the British Government's secret list, the experimental SRN 1 made its maiden Channel crossing between Calais and Dover. The reports took an unsuspecting public by storm. Within 10 years, hovercraft modified by the introduction of an inflated 'skirt' were in commercial operation between Britain and France.

Chief architects of the plane-like hydrofoil were, perhaps not surprisingly, pioneers in aviation. The first successful hydrofoil, with wing-like foils connected to the hull by struts, was designed and built by the Italian airship expert, Enrico Forlanini, and demonstrated in the years 1905–11. This first hydrofoil worked because the curved upper surfaces of the foils created a faster water flow above than beneath and, exactly as in an aircraft wing, caused a pressure difference which lifted the craft out of the water.

Only in the fifties was the first commercial passenger transport hydrofoil opened—

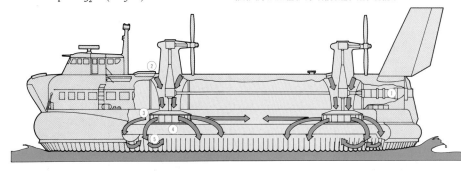

The inauguration of a regular cross-Channel service in 1968 was a notable first in the story of the hovercraft. The addition of the skirt has transformed the SRN 1 of 1959 from a craft able to rise above 18-in (45-cm) waves and 9-in (22.5-cm) land obstacles, into a vessel capable of coping with 7-ft (2.15-m) waves and land outcrops of $3\frac{1}{2}$ ft (1.05 m). The cross-Channel SRN 4, first introduced in 1969, was powered by four turbine engines (1). The airflow from the intakes (2) is pumped by lift fans (3) geared to propellers, and enters an expandable plenum ('full') chamber (4) within the flexible skirt. Air is then fed through jets which turn it inward to form the cushion (5) and downward to stabilize the craft.

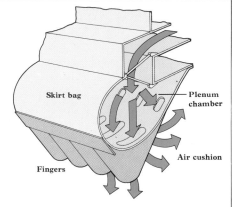

Skirt bag

Plenum chamber

Air cushion

Fingers

The hovercraft's skirt, made of pliable rubberized fabric, suspends it and enables the craft to maintain high speeds whilst crossing rough surfaces. Pressure losses are minimized by the action of the skirt's flexible 'fingers'.

between Locarno and Arona on Lake Maggiore—and even then it was soon to be overshadowed by the dramatic success of the hovercraft. In the eighties, the hydrofoil and hovercraft have both proved their long-term value. Although restricted to aqueous environments, the world's 1,000 or so hydrofoils carry more than 25 million commuters and tourists a year; the more versatile hovercraft has found a wide range of military uses.

Boeing's Jetfoil, a high-speed waterjet-propelled passenger ferry, is designed to cruise at 43 knots (50 mph). The result of a 12-year development plan, with useful spin-offs from US military efforts, the jetfoil is intended to provide competitive commercial transport on inshore and open waters. It gives a fast but comfortable ride while retaining full manoeuvrability in heavy seas.

Lifting itself above the surface over which it speeds, the hovercraft is ideal for covering difficult terrain. Even in the fifties, this suggested great military potential, and by 1966 three converted British Hovercraft Corporation SRN 5 vehicles were being used on patrol search and rescue missions by the US Marines in the swampy Mekong delta of Vietnam. On water, they have the added advantage of being invulnerable to attack from submerged mines and torpedoes.

Faster than anything afloat—apart from some speedboats—hydrofoils, *right*, can offer passenger travelling times comparable with both buses and trains. Hydrofoils are used as ferries the world over, but the largest fleet—70% of the world's total—is in Russia. Here, hydrofoils are used to exploit to the full the country's system of rivers, lakes and inland seas. Hydrofoils have also proved their worth in countries, such as Norway and Japan, with massively indented coastlines which restrict land links.

COMMUNICATION, INFORMATION AND SPACE APPLICATIONS

The planar process for integrated circuits, for creating transistors on the surface of a wafer of silicon, is invented by US scientist Hoeni, and changes microelectronics from a dream into reality. The concept, developed by Fairchild Superconductors in 'Silicon Valley' triggers scientists and engineers to start a feverish search for ever smaller and more complex circuits. First applied to defence and space equipment, integrated circuits will find their way into computers by the mid-sixties.

The Xerox 914, the first convenient office plain paper copier, is unveiled—21 years after the invention of xerography. It can make copies at the touch of a button (and is the first to do so) without ink, spirits or chemicals.

The RCA 501, the world's first fully transistorized computer, is introduced by the Radio Corporation of America and starts work in the offices of the New York Life Insurance company. RCA then begin work on the smaller 301 computer which will become a hot competitor with IBM and Sperry Rand in the growing data-processing race.

TRANSPORT, WARFARE AND SPACE EXPLORATION

Nike-Zeus, a US anti-missile missile is test-fired at White Sands, New Mexico. The USA will spend billions of dollars developing an anti-ballistic missile (ABM) system called Safeguard, which uses Nike-Zeus and its successor Nike-X, only to dismantle it in 1976.

The first non-military nuclear vessel, the Russian ice-breaker *Lenin*, makes her maiden voyage. Her nuclear power plant has three pressurized water reactors to provide, through heat exchangers, steam for four 44,000 hp turbo-generators. The *Lenin* can break through 8 ft thick pack ice, and refuelling is only required every 18 months.

The 42,000-ton liner *Oriana* is built with side propulsion units in tunnels at the bow and stern. They enable the vessel to be moved sideways when docking or manoeuvring in harbours, thus reducing the need for tugs.

ENERGY AND INDUSTRY

Seven years of intensive research at Pilkington Brothers in Britain results in the manufacture of float glass, which combines the flatness and lack of distortion of plate glass with the brilliant fire-polished finish and cheapness of sheet glass.

Mexico's first offshore oilfield, the Santa Ana, is discovered in the Gulf of Mexico. It is small, with deposits of only 10 million barrels, but there is an associated gas field.

The New Zealand Electricity Department install a large generating plant at Wairakei that becomes the world's first geothermal power station to be fuelled by steam from hot rocks. Built by Italian engineers, it differs from the earlier geothermal power station at Lardarello, Italy, because the rocks that supply the heat are non-volcanic.

MEDICINE AND FOOD PRODUCTION

Workers at the Sloan-Kettering Institute in New York isolate DNA, the basic material of heredity, from a virus known to cause malignant tumours in mice. They are startled to find that the DNA on its own can cause cancer just as the virus does.

At Harwell, Oxfordshire, Charles Ford devises a way of making human chromosomes visible and sorting them into pairs to establish both normal and abnormal karyotypes. This enables him to show that certain congenital conditions, such as Down's syndrome, can be traced to errors in chromosome make-up.

FRINGE BENEFITS

COBOL, the computer language, is invented specifically for business purposes.

The Identikit, a method of building up the facial features of a suspect, is first used to catch a criminal.

The Polaris Intermediate Range Ballistic Missile is fitted to an Italian warship, the *Garibaldi*. Polaris has already been in service with the US Navy for three years, and is now being made available to the fleets of NATO allies. The Americans have built special submarines to carry Polaris anywhere in the world without having to surface and capable of launching their missiles with great accuracy while still submerged at considerable depths. Fitting Polaris as a deck weapon to the *Garibaldi* is an experiment that turns out to be unsuccessful: exposure to the elements upsets the missiles' delicate mechanisms, but Polaris will continue to be deployed as a submarine weapon for more than two decades.

Enlarged copies of documents can be obtained from microfilm in 5–10 secs with the Thermo-Fax unit, introduced by the Minnesota Mining and Manufacturing Co.

Audio tapes now have a long-playing capacity, thanks to a new type of plastic film. This film is so thin that it can be wound twice round a normal spool, yet it remains strong enough to operate properly, since it has been stretched widthways, not lengthways.

Europe's smallest digital computer, the Ferranti Sirius, which is about the size of a refrigerator, makes full use of the latest transistorized techniques. Although not fast, its makers believe that its reasonable cost, easy method of programming and convenient size will attract many customers.

The IBM Stretch computer can make half a million decisions a second—reputedly 100 times the speed of any other general purpose machine. One section of the computer resembles a telephone exchange and allows simultaneous communication between input and output units and the computer memory.

Sony market the first commercial transistorized TV. This year's portable black-and-white set will be followed in 1960 by the colour version.

The St Lawrence Seaway, a deep water channel connecting the St Lawrence River with the Great Lakes, is opened. The Seaway makes it possible for sea-going ships to sail all the way from the Atlantic to Fort William, at the head of Lake Superior.

Three Luna spacecraft put the USSR ahead in the space race. Luna 1, the first craft to escape the Earth's gravitational pull, passes within 3,700 mls (5,955 km) of the moon, and goes on to orbit the sun. Luna 2 actually reaches the surface of the moon, while Luna 3 flies around it, taking pictures of 70% of the moon's 'dark side'.

The US X-15 rocket-powered research plane begins test flights which will be higher and faster than those of any other manned plane. At altitudes of 100 ml (161 km), speeds approaching seven times that of sound will be made possible by an air frame made of Iconel X, an alloy able to withstand the temperatures of 1,200°F (649°C) generated at 4,534 mph (7,295 km/h).

Heavily armed with 5 in (12.7 cm) guns, surface-to-air launchers and torpedoes, the USS *Long Beach* is the first guided-missile cruiser to be driven by nuclear power, which enables it to cruise for six years before refuelling.

The exact measurements of large complex objects, such as whole motor vehicles, can now be taken with a device developed at Ferranti in Britain. What is known as an electronic coordinate measuring machine probes all the points on the object, giving a precise digital read-out of each of its three dimensions.

Large reserves of natural gas are discovered offshore at Slochteren in the Netherlands, raising the possibility that other natural gas fields exist in the North Sea.

The first cargo of liquefied natural gas is transported from the USA to Britain, to be stored in the specially constructed terminal at Canvey Island in Essex.

The experimental fast breeder nuclear reactor at Dounreay, Scotland, reaches its designated output of energy and feeds 15 MW of electricity into the national grid. The reactor successfully demonstrates the effectiveness of fast breeder reactors in breeding more plutonium fuel, and also gives valuable experience in the use of liquid metals for cooling purposes.

In Britain, scientists at the Sir William Dunn School of Pathology succeed in isolating a new antibiotic, Cephalosporin C, which is effective against penicillin-resistant bacteria. Unlike penicillin, this new drug is not rendered inactive by penicillinase, the destructive enzyme produced by some bacteria.

A group of Yugoslav scientists, who have been exposed to a lethal dose of radiation in a reactor accident, are now well again following treatment with bone-marrow cells. The success of this therapy prompts the Vienna Cancer Institute to inaugurate the world's first bone-marrow bank.

Hollow clay bricks provide thermal insulation.

A metallized fabric is patented. This aluminized clothing keeps heat in or out—its first use may be for firemen.

Small, cheap and fun, the Morris Mini-Minor will have an enormous influence on car design. Given its start here on a Mediterranean trial by top racing driver Jack Brabham, it will prove a zesty competitor as a saloon racing car and will sell millions as an all-purpose runabout, unbeatable in city traffic. Designers all over the world will follow the lead set by Alec Issigonis with the Mini, and start mounting engines transversely to power the front wheels. The combination of space-saving, road-holding and manoeuvrability is highly effective. The car's strikingly unusual appearance outrages some but delights millions, who will buy Britain's best-selling car ever for many years to come.

The SRN 1 Hovercraft sits on a Calais dockside prior to attempting a crossing of the English Channel. On the 50th anniversary of Blériot's first cross-Channel flight, the 7-ton craft will complete the trip in just over two hours. Its inventor, Christopher Cockerell, patented the plans for a vehicle riding on a cushion of compressed air in 1955. In 1962, hovercraft will acquire rubber 'skirts', giving them greater clearance and allowing them to operate over waves up to 7 ft high. Six years later a regular cross-Channel hovercraft ferry service will be launched, using craft of enormously increased size and power and taking only one-third the time needed by Cockerell's prototype.

Lasers, the light revolution

Of all the new techniques of illumination that modern science has brought, none seizes the imagination more than Light Amplification by Stimulated Emission of Radiation: the laser. A laser beam is so razor-sharp and so dense that it can be focused by a lens on a spot no bigger than a micrometre (one millionth of a metre) or even smaller. Colour is determined by its wavelength—a laser is a concentrated beam of monochromatic light—and the result is a purity of hue unknown in nature.

The principles which underlie the laser are as complicated as the nature of light itself, but the apparatus is relatively simple. A laser amplifies light waves, rather in the way that it is possible to amplify sound. But the problem with light is that it is naturally chaotic; sunlight, electric or candle-light scatters a mixture of wavelengths in all directions, in a way that is described as incoherent. Laser light is coherent, a single pulse of such intensity that it will emerge from a prism exactly as it went in.

The first laser was created in 1960 when scientists in a Californian laboratory produced a blinding pulse of light which, when focused, could drill a hole through a diamond. The medium they used was a rod of synthetic ruby, soon to be replaced by a hollow tube filled with gas which produces a continuous beam rather than a series of flashes.

Both these types of laser consist of sealed tubes in which the internal ends are reflective, one end only partially, like a two-way mirror. The atoms in the laser medium, gas or solid, are then stimulated by an outside power source—bursts of light from a flash tube, for instance, similar to those used in 'strobe' lighting. This causes the atoms to emit photons of light which are unable to escape randomly as they do, for example, in a conventional incandescent bulb or fluorescent tube. Instead, they bounce backwards and forwards between the reflecting ends until they fall into a regular or coherent wavelength of great intensity. This is emitted through the partially mirrored end of the tube either in the vivid flashes of the pulse laser or in an even beam from a gas laser.

The heat and brightness of such a beam has boundless potential. Surgical 'light knives', or carbon dioxide lasers, can be used in operations to cut and cauterize delicate parts of the body at one go, reducing the risk of infection. In neurosurgery, lasers can remove tissues next to vital organs and burn a way through to tumours which would normally be inaccessible. In gynaecology, they can unblock Fallopian tubes so that women can become fertile.

Since light has a far higher frequency than radio waves, a laser beam could carry millions of TV or other signals through fibre optic cables, which allow the beam to bend around corners. The secretive Lawrence Livermore Laboratory in California is developing a laser system called NOVA, which is aimed at achieving nuclear fusion: 10 laser beams will focus their full force on to a pellet of deuterium and tritium. The rise in temperature caused by the enormous compression should be enough to spark fusion reactions.

Bar coding, which is now common on goods in stores, works together with a low-intensity laser to check out purchases: the pencil-thin beam can detect changes in the light reflected from the bar code as it is passed over the checkout counter 'window'. Laser lights have also become enormously popular for prestigious civic displays and even for rock concerts. But more intriguing, and potentially more valuable, is their use in the art of holography.

From the Greek word *holos* meaning 'whole', holograms are three-dimensional photographs you can actually walk around without being able to tell the difference between the real object and the image—until you put your hand through it. The principle has been known since the late forties but no light source was powerful enough to produce one until the advent of the laser.

The burst of power from a pulsed laser can be used to punch holes in metal as fine as 0.01 mm in diameter. The UK Atomic Energy Authority uses such lasers to cut open spent fuel rods from nuclear reactors: a 2 kW laser can slice through materials, up to half a centimetre thick, faster than almost any other technique. There is no contamination and no question, naturally, of breaking any drill 'bit'. Industry is rapidly realizing the advantages of lasers for cutting anything from ceramics to rubber to cloth: in 1981, the laser equipment market grew by 40%, whereas the conventional machine tool market remained practically static.

Einstein worked out the theory of the laser in 1917, but the world had to wait 43 years before it was put into practice; it was immediately dubbed 'the invention with no use'. But its potential soon became clear—for surveying, welding, surgery, optical communications and even nuclear fusion. It can also be fun; this coloured light display owes its particular brilliance to the superluminous, almost solid, appearance of laser light.

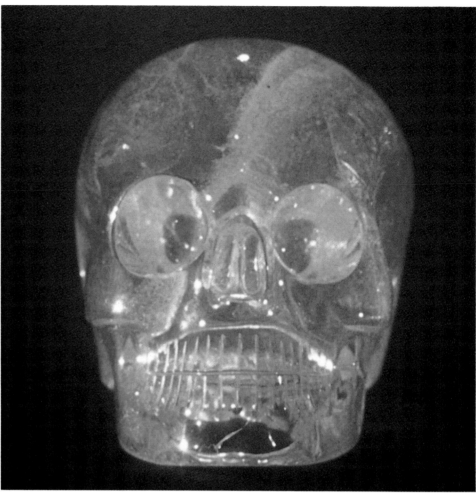

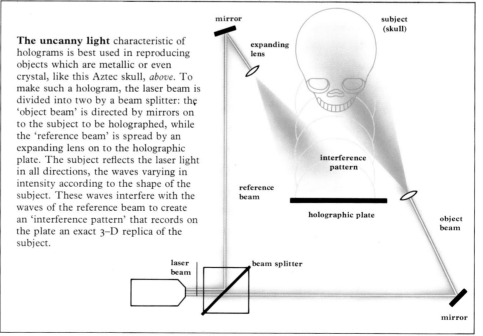

The uncanny light characteristic of holograms is best used in reproducing objects which are metallic or even crystal, like this Aztec skull, *above*. To make such a hologram, the laser beam is divided into two by a beam splitter: the 'object beam' is directed by mirrors on to the subject to be holographed, while the 'reference beam' is spread by an expanding lens on to the holographic plate. The subject reflects the laser light in all directions, the waves varying in intensity according to the shape of the subject. These waves interfere with the waves of the reference beam to create an 'interference pattern' that records on the plate an exact 3–D replica of the subject.

mirror

subject (skull)

expanding lens

interference pattern

reference beam

holographic plate

object beam

laser beam

beam splitter

mirror

COMMUNICATION, INFORMATION AND SPACE APPLICATIONS

The first automated post office opens at Providence, Rhode Island, and will handle mail and parcels for the entire state. More than a million addresses are read by electronic eyes and sorted into destination bins. Britain's first automatic letter sorter follows 6 years later.

The world's first weather satellite is launched by the USA on 1 April. For three months, Tiros 1's twin TV cameras return pictures of the Earth's surface which can be usefully employed to monitor the weather. Nine more Tiros satellites will be launched between 1960 and 1965.

The Gorky Educational Institute in the USSR produces a machine for teaching foreign languages. Programmed to deliver a lesson, and then to test the pupil's spoken and written assimilation of the material, the machine is the forerunner of the language laboratory.

The USA launches Echo 1, a plastic balloon 100 ft (30 m) in diameter, whose shiny surface reflects radio waves linking Earth stations thousands of miles apart. Echo 1 proves conclusively that satellites can be used for worldwide communications, but this type of passive satellite will soon be abandoned in favour of active versions which can transmit signals, not merely reflect them.

TRANSPORT, WARFARE AND SPACE EXPLORATION

Blandly named the Utility-2, to disguise its real nature, the US Lockheed surveillance plane, equipped with sophisticated photographic equipment, is capable of high and fast, long-distance cruising. When U-2 prints appear to reveal an advanced missile base in the USSR, a further U-2, piloted by Gary Powers, is sent to check. The plane is shot down, Powers bails out and is captured. At his trial, the photographic range of the U-2 is revealed, embarrassing the US government.

Private car ownership reaches an all-time high, with one car for every 31 people in the world, one for every 22 in Europe and one for every 3 in the USA, where 15% of families have more than one car.

All previous depth records are broken by the bathyscaphe *Trieste*, operated by the US Navy. The bathyscaphe descends nearly 7 mls (11.3 km) to the greatest known ocean depth at the bottom of the Challenger Deep in the Pacific. The important discovery that life exists at these great depths militates against the depositing of radioactive waste on the seabed.

ENERGY AND INDUSTRY

Gas can now be produced from any type of coal in the new pressurized gasifier being developed by John Brown Ltd of England. The gas, a mixture of carbon monoxide and hydrogen, can be fed into a town's gas supply and may also be useful for making industrial chemicals.

OPEC, the Organization of Petroleum Exporting Countries, is formed. Iran discovers its first offshore oil field in the Persian Gulf, and Italy its first offshore gas field in the Adriatic.

MEDICINE AND FOOD PRODUCTION

The synthesis of chlorophyll—the green pigment which absorbs sunlight to provide the energy necessary for plant photosynthesis—is achieved independently by German Martin Strell and US chemist Robert Burns Woodward. They use different methods to construct the complex, 140-atom molecule. Chemists now hope that this development may lead to the synthetic formation of carbohydrates, and hence the artificial production of food.

FRINGE BENEFITS

Astroturf synthetic turf is laid in the Astrodome in Houston, Texas

Pentel, the first felt-tip pen, is introduced.

The 'Evening Star', Britain's last steam locomotive, goes into service but will run for only a few years before becoming a museum piece. Most of the railway track in Europe and North America is now worked by diesel or electric trains; but steam traction is still a popular option in parts of Africa, Asia and South America.

The light-emitting diode, destined to become the most popular digital display in pocket calculators and electronic watches, is invented by Nick Holonyak Jr in the USA. The diode contains gallium arsenide phosphide, a chemical compound which glows when conducting an electric current. Although it consumes more power than liquid crystals, it is more reliable, and is luminous in the dark.

The first pulse of laser light, created through the medium of a synthetic ruby rod, is beamed by US scientists over a distance of 25 mls (40 km) and has a spread of only 8 ft (2.43 m) per mile. A million times brighter than sunlight, the light waves are almost on a single wavelength—which suggest that they can, like radio waves, be modulated to carry communications signals.

An electronic telephone exchange, faster, smaller, more reliable and more economical than its predecessors, is the latest experiment by the Bell Telephone Co in the USA.

The first robot able to imitate the grasping motion of the human hand is employed in a US nuclear plant. Handyman's 9-ft (2.7-m) arms, which are operated by remote control, can perform 10 basic movements.

Smell-O-Vision introduced in the USA by Mike Todd Jr, adds another dimension to the movies. A complex mechanism, synchronized with his film, *Scent of Mystery*, delivers odours, via dusts, to each seat position.

An iron ore mine in arctic Sweden is the setting for a new electronic breakthrough: 16 electric trains are entirely controlled by a computer, saving human discomfort in the sub-zero temperatures.

A transistorized device in the driving cab stops the trains of Leningrad's new underground railway system within one foot (0.3 m) of the desired point. Similar electronic systems to control the speed and stopping point of trains will be introduced to most of the world's new subways during the next two decades.

A sophisticated union between nuclear submarines, inertial navigation systems and ballistic missiles produces the deadly USS *George Washington*, the first submarine to carry a full complement of 16 Polaris missiles.

Around the world in 84 days—without ever surfacing. The epic underwater voyage is completed by the American nuclear submarine *Triton*. New electronic systems monitor all movements and speeds in relation to the sub's starting point so that 'inertial navigation' allows its position to be located at any time.

Geothermal electric power begins production in the USA at a dry steam field at The Geysers near San Francisco.

The first nuclear power station to use a boiling water reactor begins generating electricity for commercial use at Dresden, Illinois, USA. The nuclear core heats water under pressure to produce the steam that drives the generator. By 1981, there will be 57 boiling water reactors throughout the world.

In their search for ever stronger rayon fibres, the American Viscose Corp comes up with Avron, a fibre which is toughened by stretching it in hot water until it is ready for blending with nylons and such polyesters as Dacron (Terylene).

Ultrasound proves a major breakthrough in the diagnosis of brain damage from disease and trauma. Dr A. Jefferson and Dr D. Gordon produce echoencephalograms (pictures made by patterns of radio waves), by which blood clots and tumours can be detected.

Bell Telephone Laboratories report the development of an artificial voice-box to replace vocal cords damaged by disease or injury. When held against the throat, this transistorized electronic larynx replaces the vocal cords by producing sound waves. Words can be formed by moving the tongue and lips as usual. There are two models, one with a deep pitch for men and one with a higher pitch for women.

Artificial tanning creams promise a permanent suntan.

Belka and Strelka survive 17 orbits of the Earth in Sputnik 5. Put into space by the Russians to prove that living creatures can be launched into space and recovered safely, with no apparent ill effects, the two dogs are part of preparations for the first manned space flight. The Americans, behind in the space race, plan to use monkeys for the same purpose.

Hawker Siddeley's P1127—later to be known as the Hawker Harrier—proves that the concept of a vertical take-off jet fighter is viable. By directing the thrust downwards, the pilot can also land the plane vertically or keep it hovering. A highly versatile and effective military aircraft, the Harrier will become operational with the RAF in 1969.

COMMUNICATION, INFORMATION AND SPACE APPLICATIONS

Work begins on London's Post Office Tower, a communications centre 620 ft (189 m) tall and 54 ft (16 m) wide that will dominate the city's landscape. Tall enough to rise above interference from surrounding buildings, it will control radio stations and transmitters, provide 40 TV channels and link them with the satellite station at Goonhilly, Cornwall. The tower will also supply thousands of telephone connections to link Britain's capital to all parts of the country.

Communication by light waves seems possible with Bell Laboratories' successful production of the first maser (microwave amplification by stimulated emission of radiation) to give out coherent infrared light. The 40-in (1-m) gas tube achieves this by 'beating' together twin light waves with very close frequencies. Since the light waves have a frequency millions of times greater than that of radio waves, they can carry much more data.

The first computer to be designed by another computer is completed in the USA. Destined for the US Army's Nike-Zeus anti-missile system, the computer is the brainchild of the Bell Laboratories.

TRANSPORT, WARFARE AND SPACE EXPLORATION

An ingenious double-decker car transporter arrives on British railways: cars are lowered on to an extra deck between the wheels of the bogies. Double the number of cars can be carried without contravening height restrictions.

Permanent markings, which promise to be more hard-wearing, visible and skid-resistant than those currently used on European roads, are made by a manufacturing process devised in West Germany. The markings consist of blocks which are embedded in the road surface. They are constructed from layers of granite fragments set in cement and hydraulically moulded at high pressure to give them a pore-free surface that will not absorb dirt. Fluorescent particles are added to the top layer to improve visibility.

Britain's first nuclear submarine, *Dreadnought*, is launched. Designed to hunt and destroy submarines, *Dreadnought* is powered by US-built propulsion machinery and a nuclear reactor.

The USA's giant aircraft carrier, *Enterprise*, is commissioned for service. Her eight nuclear reactors enable her to operate for three years and 200,000 mls (320,000 km) without refuelling.

ENERGY AND INDUSTRY

The electrical grid systems of Britain and France are connected by a cable submerged under the English Channel. Carrying up to 160 MW of direct current electricity, the cable link enables the two countries to exchange power, and for one national system to support the other should the need arise.

The quartz-iodine lamp is introduced and immediately used as the light source in film projectors. Though small, this compact lamp is half as bright again as other filament lamps because quartz, with iodine (or bromine) vapour inside the bulb, can withstand the high temperatures needed to generate powerful beams of light. A type of tungsten-halogen lamp, it will also be used in car headlights, floodlights and display lighting.

Silicon chips will be incorporated into integrated circuits faster and more efficiently as high-voltage electron beam welding is made commercially viable by Zeiss.

MEDICINE AND FOOD PRODUCTION

Three Dutch doctors discover that gas gangrene can be successfully treated with oxygen under pressure. This is because the causative organisms are unable to survive in the presence of oxygen. The Dutch technique is later widely adopted throughout the world.

In Britain, Roy Calne and J.E. Murray report on an immuno-suppressant, azathioprine (Imuran), which prevents rejection of transplanted organs. Often combined with steroids, it will be used for transplant cases, replacing the dangerous method of treating the whole body with radiation.

FRINGE BENEFITS

The self-wringing mop whose flat sponge can be wrung by a lever on the shaft, is patented in the USA.

Soviet astronaut Yuri Gagarin makes history as the first man to travel in space, spending 1 hr 48 mins in flight and completing a single orbit of the Earth. From the Vostok ('East') 1, Gagarin can distinguish large rivers, lakes and coastlines on Earth and can keep check on the equipment monitoring the flight. He enjoys the sensation of weightlessness and returns to Earth without suffering any ill effects.

Computers are used to assess the acoustics of concert halls at the design stage. A digital pattern of a sample piece of music, and the detailed dimensions of the proposed hall, are fed into a computer programmed to calculate the paths the sound waves will follow and the length of time they take to bounce back to their source. The computer plays out the sound over several loudspeakers in an echo-less room and—so the makers claim—accurately synthesizes the quality of sound that will be created in the finished hall.

ATLAS, the world's largest and Europe's fastest ever computer—it can make a million additions a second—is installed at Britain's Atomic Research Establishment at Harwell, Oxfordshire, to aid atomic research and weather forecasting.

Half the BBC's radio broadcasts are now recorded before being transmitted—on 58,000 discs and 122,000 reels of magnetic tape.

The IBM 'golf ball' typewriter is destined to set a new trend in office equipment. Instead of the traditional moving carriage, and type set on bars, the golf ball typewriter has its letters mounted on a sphere, set on a small carriage which runs along a cylindrical metal bar.

The hydrofoil *Sputnik*, capable of carrying 300 passengers, enters service between Gorki and Moscow. In Russia, hydrofoils carry some three million passengers a year on lakes and rivers, and development of such craft is given high priority.

Alan B. Shepard becomes the first American in space. Shepard's 15-min suborbital flight, the first of a series of space shots destined to develop into the Apollo moon exploration programme, demonstrates that man can think clearly and perform useful tasks under conditions of weightlessness. Later in the year, American Virgil Grissom completes a similar mission which is successful until his space capsule sinks at splashdown, forcing Grissom to swim from the craft. He is picked up safely within minutes.

Herman Titov is the first man to spend a whole day in space as he completes 17 orbits of the Earth in the Soviet spaceship Vostok 2 launched on 6 August. Titov travels 435,000 mls (700,000 km)—as far as to the moon and back—and is reported to have eaten and slept during the 25 hr 18 min flight.

A heat-resistant plastic is made by Du Pont at Wilmington, Del., USA. Called SP (super-polymer), the plastic has great strength, both mechanically and as an electrical insulator. It will be developed into the Kapton film, a thin clear orange film so resistant to heat that electronic circuits can be soldered to its surface simply by immersing the film in molten solder. It can also be made into fire-proof magnetic tapes.

Freezers with a front-opening door appear on the domestic market. They are smaller, and therefore more suitable for modern kitchens, than the earlier chests with top-lifting lids. In a year's time English Electric will market their 'Fresh 'n' Freeze' model, which combines both a freezer and a refrigerator.

Steels up to ten times stronger than normal steel are developed by the International Nickel Co and made commercially available. Known as maraging steels, they acquire their extreme strength through the addition of certain elements to iron. A high-strength maraging steel has up to 19% nickel, 9% cobalt, 5% molybdenum and about 0.5% titanium. These steels will be used for the bodies of rockets and missiles.

The incidence of once-fatal haemolytic disease of the newborn—previously treated by exchange transfusion of babies' blood—is further reduced by injections of anti-rhesus serum for Rhesus-negative mothers, following delivery of a first baby. This cancels out any harmful antibodies built up during pregnancy.

Lloyd Williams and Maxwell Cade work out the clinical requirements for the Pyroscan thermographic camera at the Middlesex Hospital, London. Thermography uses a person's body-heat, emitted in varying intensity by parts of the body, to produce a thermal image. Tumours, for example, are often hotter than normal tissue, and breast cancer can be detected as a 'hot-spot'.

In Britain, three Medical Research Council scientists volunteer to live for 40 days on food containing strontium-90—grain grown on contaminated land, for instance, and milk from cows grazed in areas of nuclear fallout. The body is found to absorb about 5% of the strontium ingested with food.

The 'hoverbed', introduced by British surgeon John Scales, uses jets of air to support burns cases.

With a successful track record in many European countries, the first fully automatic level crossing in Britain goes into service in Staffordshire. As a train nears, flashing red lights and two-tone gongs warn all those approaching while barriers are lowered across the oncoming lanes of traffic.

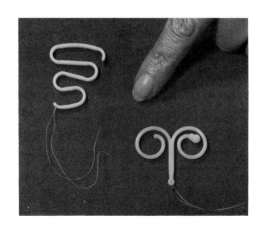

The contraceptive action of the intra-uterine device (IUD), known since Ernest Grafenburg's first use of a simple silver ring in the thirties, has been largely ignored until Jack Lippes produces his loop of inert plastic. The loop, and Ralph Robinson's similar T-spiral, prove less likely to irritate the uterus or be rejected by the body, and their flexibility eases insertion. Although it will remain unclear by what mechanism the IUD creates an environment in the uterus that is unfavourable to conception, its convenience will make it popular. However, sporadic increases in pelvic infections and ectopic pregnancies—the foetus lodging in the Fallopian tube—will periodically cause its safety to be questioned.

COMMUNICATION, INFORMATION AND SPACE APPLICATIONS

The era of live transatlantic TV broadcasting arrives as Telstar, the first active communications satellite, is launched. A 3-ft (90-cm) sphere powered by solar cells, Telstar follows a low orbit. It links the USA and Europe for periods of up to 20 mins at a time, during which TV pictures are clearly transmitted. During the same periods, up to 60 simultaneous telephone conversations can also be relayed.

An atomic clock, a supertimekeeper 100 times more precise than any previous clock—it will remain accurate for 100,000 years—is made at Harvard, using stable hydrogen atoms in place of ammonia molecules.

Japanese engineers build an analog computer to help control water levels at hydro-electric power plants. Within 30 mins of being put into operation, the system provides information about water flow from one station to another, prevents overflow, and divides the loading economically between stations.

TRANSPORT, WARFARE AND SPACE EXPLORATION

British inventor Alex Moulton patents the world's first substantially new bicycle design for 50 years. Small wheels give the bicycle a low centre of gravity, making it stable to ride and excellent for carrying small loads such as shopping.

John Glenn becomes the first American to orbit the Earth. He makes three orbits in the spaceship Friendship 7, during which his heartbeat, blood pressure, reaction to weightlessness and his ability to control the capsule are monitored. Two dozen ships, 126 aircraft and 26,000 personnel make up the forces ensuring his safe recovery. Glenn's only injury is a set of bruised knuckles from punching the detonator button to blow off the hatch after the capsule has been hauled aboard a recovery destroyer.

The de Havilland Trident airliner makes its maiden flight. The first rear-engined trijet is built to a BEA specification for a short-range jet—a design later adopted by Boeing for their 727.

ENERGY AND INDUSTRY

A new dishwasher, using neither soap nor water, is demonstrated by Kelvinator in Seattle, USA. The machine is not developed because of its high cost, but its technique of cleaning dishes with high-frequency sound waves may one day be revived.

The first advanced gas-cooled reactor (AGR) fuelled by enriched uranium is built as a small prototype at Windscale in Cumbria, England.

Professor E.R. Laithwaite of Manchester University, England, demonstrates his updated version of the linear motor—it has no moving parts—which was used originally to catapult planes from aircraft carriers in World War II. A commercial version will be developed by Herbert Morris Ltd in 1966 and will be used for the traversing of cranes and, experimentally, for the propulsion of trains.

Electricity, independently generated by the waste heat of domestic fires and central heating systems, may soon be available in the home. Scientists at Plessey's Caswell laboratories in England discover another iron disilicide, a cheap material which produces electricity from small amounts of heat. Moulded into discs and stacked together, it will form the heart of a new thermo-electric generator which can also be widely used in industry.

MEDICINE AND FOOD PRODUCTION

US orthopaedic surgeon Dr Harrington, develops an operation for the correction of severe scoliosis (curvature of the spine) in young people. He realigns the spine by embedding two long metal rods into the adjacent muscle.

In the USA, Thomas Weller succeeds in culturing the virus of rubella, or German measles. This leads to the development of live vaccines which come to eclipse the 'rubella tea-parties' held to expose young girls to an infection which could harm the foetus if contracted in early pregnancy.

FRINGE BENEFITS

The omnifocal lens ousts the split bi-focal by allowing the bespectacled to see close-up and far-away without disruption.

A moulded car seat with its own safety belt is designed for children.

The world's largest sea-going passenger hydrofoil, the Russian *Vikhr* ('Whirlwind') undergoes trials on the Black Sea. It will soon go into service there, operating from the port of Odessa. Vikhr's design includes an extra foil amidships, to increase its stability and ensure safety in winds up to force 5.

Bell Telephone Laboratories in the USA direct a laser beam at the moon's surface and receive its reflection 2½ secs later; the inference is that this may be a possible form of future long-distance communication. More than 10 years earlier, in 1951, the moon has been used to reflect telegraph and teleprinter signals transmitted by radio telescope facilities from Britain to Australia.

The first wide hot-strip steel mill to have an integrated computer system is the one at the Richard Thomas and Baldwin Co in Britain. As well as controlling processing, the system also orders production planning.

Cheaper and smaller electronic gadgets can be made now that the MOS (metal oxide semicondenser) integrated circuit has been perfected. Developed by scientists at RCA, it allows more circuits to be crammed into one chip.

An 'electronic brain', smaller than a man's head and capable of making many million basic decisions a second, is destined to be used in rail, road and air traffic control, in language translation and in weather forecasting.

The market for integrated circuits widens as the US Government places a contract with Texas Instruments for 300,000 circuits for the Minuteman Missile programme.

Seacat, a British surface-to-air guided missile, is tested from HMS *Decoy*. Developed as an anti-aircraft missile to replace the obsolete Bofors gun, the short-range weapon will be adopted by 15 of the world's navies.

The pilotless plane, the US Model 147, makes its first flight. A tactical RPV (remotely piloted vehicle) developed for reconnaissance work, it is expendable over enemy territory and so will hopefully avoid the embarrassment of a second U–2 incident.

Britain's first commercial hovercraft service, intended to evaluate the Vickers VA 3 as a passenger carrier, is used between Rhyll in North Wales and Wallasey in Cheshire.

Mariner 2, a small US unmanned spacecraft weighing only 446 lb (202 kg), achieves the first fly-past of another planet. It sends back valuable data from Venus during its 109-day journey.

Vostok 3, carrying astronaut Andrian Nikolayev, blasts off and completes 64 Earth orbits in 94 hrs 27 mins. Pavel Popovich, launched 24 hrs later in Vostok 4, completes 48 orbits. The public marvels at the first TV transmissions from space, and millions watch the cosmonauts exercising, singing and talking to each other.

Isambard Brunel's famous suspension-bridge spans on the railway bridge across the River Wye at Chepstow, England, are replaced by the world's first welded and trussed box girders. Welding instead of riveting has made the box girder's development possible and accounts for its immense strength. The box girder will be used in the future in nearly every new bridge built to carry either rail or road.

The first industrial robot is marketed by the US company Unimation. Once programmed, the robot can pick things up and move them continuously and reliably. By the seventies, more flexible robots will be used in industry, particularly for welding.

The first two commercial nuclear power stations in Britain begin generating electricity for the Central Electricity Generating Board at Bradwell in Essex and at Berkeley in Gloucestershire. They use a fuel of natural uranium in a reactor made from a special magnesium alloy (Magnox). The reactor is cooled by carbon dioxide gas, the steam produced being used to drive the generators.

Only 20 years after Fermi successfully operated the world's first nuclear reactor, the USA has more than 200 atomic reactors; Britain and the USSR have 39 each.

A solar furnace is completed under the direction of Dr Felix Trombe at Mont Louis in the French Pyrenees. The furnace generates 50 kW of heat via a system of mirrors and reflectors, and is used as an industrial smelter and for further solar research.

The limitations of broad-spectrum antibiotics appear after 20 years of use. Already, indiscriminate treatment with 'wonder' drugs has resulted in the evolution of resistant strains of disease-causing microbes. Long-term treatment with streptomycin may damage hearing and balance. Now, chloramphenicol is sometimes found to destroy bone-marrow.

In Tennessee, Donald Pinkel pioneers a three-stage 'total therapy' for children with leukaemia: steroids and vincristine to prevent further damage to body tissues; radiation to kill obstinate leukaemic cells lurking in the nervous system; and regular doses of anti-leukaemic drugs for up to three years.

George Hitchings, a biochemist at the Burroughs Wellcome Laboratories, provides an answer to the agonies of gout. Allopurinol, derived from an anti-rejection drug also discovered by Hitchings, blocks the production of uric acid in the body and ends the painful inflammation of gout-ridden joints.

Instant orange juice is now available in powder form—just add cold water.

Sacs of silicone rubber gel replace sponge pads for breast implants.

The Braille system of printing and writing for the blind, which uses raised points or dots in 63 combinations, is successfully applied to a typewriter. By the late seventies, a speaking word-processor will also be developed, so that the sightless can even detect typing errors and make corrections.

Digital Equipment Inc gives birth to a third generation of computers. Their minicomputer, whose integrated circuits make it much smaller without loss of performance, is marketed in the USA at $15,000—a price that will decrease tenfold over the next decade.

COMMUNICATION, INFORMATION AND SPACE APPLICATIONS

The perplexing question of the true authorship of St Paul's epistles is tackled by a Mercury computer at Cambridge University, England, with the help of theological scholars. Using known sources to compare styles, the computer counts the frequency of certain words and phrases and concludes that St Paul wrote only four of the 15 epistles in the New Testament: the result is a fierce theological debate.

The compact cassette, introduced by Philips in the Netherlands, revolutionizes home tape recording.

Polaroid's Polacolor film makes prints available to the photographer within a minute of exposure. The new films are housed in a flat pack, which is much easier to load than the earlier rolls.

Loading a camera becomes child's play with the introduction of Kodak Instamatic cameras. The film is contained in a drop-in cartridge which will fit in only one position in the camera. More than 70 million Instamatics will be sold within the next few years.

TRANSPORT, WARFARE AND SPACE EXPLORATION

The Japanese plan the world's longest railway tunnel to connect the mainland with the island of Hokkaido. The 33.5-ml (54-km) Seikan undersea tunnel will open in the eighties, forming a vital link in Japan's rail network.

More than 100 countries will sign a treaty to ban nuclear weapons tests in the atmosphere, outer space and underwater. But despite this nominal agreement, tests continue covertly, underground.

In the latest shipyards, large sections of a ship are prefabricated in welding shops and taken to the construction dock on multi-wheel 'module' transporters capable of carrying loads of 500 tons. When it reaches the dockside, the module is lifted into its exact position by a giant crane. The subassemblies are then welded together to form the complete hull.

ENERGY AND INDUSTRY

Cheaper electricity and a more efficient use of fuel are ensured as the CANDU system of nuclear reactors is activated at a prototype station in Ontario, Canada. This new system uses natural uranium fuel, in pressure tubes surrounded by heavy water, which converts ordinary (light) water into steam to drive turbo-generators.

Hoover market their new steam-or-dry electric iron in Britain. A switch releases jets of steam from the ironing surface to moisten the garment. It anticipates an even more efficient model which sprays a fine mist of water as it irons.

The painting of car bodies by electro-coating methods comes into operation on a large scale. The paint is composed of tiny, electrically charged particles, suspended in water, which are especially attracted to unpainted or to thinly painted areas. The result is a coat of uniform thickness—even in corners and on inside areas.

The second experimental fast breeder reactor (EBR II) opens at Arco, Idaho, after five years of construction. It is an integrated nuclear facility which breeds and recycles fuel.

MEDICINE AND FOOD PRODUCTION

After experiments on dogs, F.D. Moore and T.E. Starzl are the first to perform liver transplants in man. Although initially the survival rate is less than a year, valuable knowledge is yielded on what could become the first effective treatment of hitherto fatal liver disease.

Houston surgeon Michael De Bakey pioneers the use of the artificial heart when, for the first time during cardiac surgery, one is employed to take over the pumping of the blood.

FRINGE BENEFITS

The visible man/woman, an educational model of human anatomy in a transparent skin, is marketed in the USA.

International subscriber dialling puts Britain in direct telephone contact with Europe.

Valentina Tereshkova becomes the first woman in space. Her craft, Vostok 6, is launched from Russia on 16 June and completes 48 orbits of the Earth in 70 hrs and 50 mins. She suffers some space sickness, but returns essentially unscathed after a successful mission. She will marry fellow cosmonaut Andrian Nikolayev and give birth to a healthy daughter, Yelena—the first child to be born of parents who have both travelled in space—who allays fears that spaceflight may expose human hereditary material to damaging radiation.

Seat reservations on transatlantic flights of BOAC (British Overseas Airways Corporation) are now being made by a computer, which can answer booking queries in as little as 4 secs.

A million pages of information can be stored on microfilm, and an enlargement of any particular page flashed on to a screen in 8 secs, using a system developed by the Recordak Corp, a subsidiary of Eastman Kodak.

Syncom 2 is the first communications satellite to be launched into synchronous (24-hour) orbit. With an orbit inclined to 28°, it appears to trace an elongated figure-of-eight track in relation to the Earth's surface.

A computer eases the frustration of Toronto traffic jams. The device controls the timing of traffic signals according to the number of passing vehicles, which it detects magnetically. The pilot scheme reports a 28% decrease in congestion, and the average rush-hour speed goes up by 3 mph (5.6 km/h). Following earlier tests of a similar machine in New York tunnels, the computer will also be used to relay information about unusual traffic patterns to the police.

Gordon Cooper, pilot of the ninth and final US Mercury mission, orbits the Earth 22 times in a flight lasting 34 hrs 20 mins. Cooper carries out experiments in guiding and manoeuvring the craft, which will prove valuable in the development of the Apollo programme. After his spaceship develops a fault, Cooper skilfully guides the craft through its re-entry into the atmosphere, landing only 4 mls (6.4 km) from the planned recovery point.

Japan's NSU Spyder two-seater is the world's first production car to feature a Wankel rotary engine. The car, and the Ro80 family saloon that follows it four years later, is quiet and comfortable to drive, although plagued by problems with the automatic clutch and the sealing of the rotary piston. Other manufacturers, notably Mazda and Citroën, will follow NSU's lead, and claim that the Wankel engine is potentially more efficient than conventional engines.

Pilot of the Soviet spaceship Vostok 5, Valerie Bykovsky, sets a new record by remaining in space for nearly five days. In this time he completes 81 Earth orbits.

Stronger than steel but only a quarter of the weight, carbon fibres are developed at the Royal Aircraft Establishment, England. They will mainly be used to reinforce materials which need to retain their strength at high temperatures. For example, in 1966, Rolls-Royce will announce that major parts of their new turbofan for aircraft—the RB178—are composed of carbon-fibre reinforced plastic.

A solar furnace using a 33-ft (10-m) parabolic reflector, starts operating in Japan and produces temperatures of over 9,300°F (3,400°C). The 70 kW furnace is used for research into the high-temperature properties of various materials.

Increased demand for electricity means the addition of higher voltage transmission cables to Britain's national grid system. Fortunately, the new 400,000 V cables fit into the existing system of 275,000 V cables and the earlier 132,000 V cables. Also, since fewer pylons are needed to carry these new cables, there is less intrusion on the environment.

In Russia, thermal springs each year produce the energy equivalent of over 100 million tons of fuel. The water of the world's largest subterranean lake, covering an area of 1.15 million sq mls (3 million sq km) in Western Siberia, is near boiling-point.

In the USA J.D. Hardy and his colleagues perform the first human lung transplant, using a cadaver organ. The donor lung begins to function immediately, and continues to do so until the patient's death from other causes, 18 days after the operation.

The Roche laboratories introduce Valium, which is soon more widely prescribed than Librium, an earlier tranquillizer from the same stable. Valium will also be used as a muscle-relaxant and anti-convulsant.

An electronic hospital 'watchdog', developed in the USA and named the body function recorder, uses transducers to record the respiration and pulse rates, blood pressure and temperature of up to 12 post-operative patients every two minutes.

Mechanized parcel-sorting is introduced by Britain's GPO in Worcester to serve a local mail-order company.

Photographic equipment aboard the US research ship *Atlantis II* supplies clear pictures of the dark ocean floor.

Technicians test one of the mobile outside-broadcast cameras bought specially for use by the BBC's new television service, BBC2. The channel will begin broadcasting on 30 April of the following year, transmitting (only to London and South East England at the outset) exclusively on UHF (ultra-high frequency) using 625 lines, in preparation for the introduction of colour broadcasting three years later. As the two other existing channels still broadcast on VHF (very high frequency) using only 405 lines, manufacturers have to supply dual-standard receivers operating on both systems.

COMMUNICATION, INFORMATION AND SPACE APPLICATIONS

The motions of an orbiting satellite are visualized with the help of computer-made films. The motion of a hypothetical satellite is predicted by an IBM 7090 digital computer and transferred to a magnetic recorder, which converts the digits into line drawings. These are then photographed by a motion picture camera.

The second BBC channel, BBC-2, begins broadcasting on 30 April, transmitting on 625 lines as opposed to the 425 lines of the existing high-definition channels (BBC-1 and ITV).

The third generation of computers reaches the market as IBM introduce 'chips' into their 360 system. The new technology, which paves the way for portable and desk-top computers, spreads like wildfire.

The opening ceremony of the Tokyo Olympic Games is broadcast live to the USA via the US communications satellite Syncom 3. The satellite is the first to be placed in the geostationary orbit first proposed by Arthur C. Clarke in 1945; because it remains in 24-hour orbit directly over a small region of the Earth's surface, close to the Equator, it can provide a totally uninterrupted communications service. Since Syncom 3, virtually all communications satellites, apart from those serving the poles, use geostationary orbits.

TRANSPORT, WARFARE AND SPACE EXPLORATION

China explodes her first atomic bomb in the Takla Makan desert. Claiming that the bomb lacks an effective delivery system, the Western powers are less impressed than neighbouring India.

The first three-man spacecraft, Voskhod (Sunrise) 1 is launched in October. The Soviet flight is unique in that the ship carries a spacecraft designer and a doctor as well as the pilot. In a radical departure from convention, the cosmonauts wear light grey sports suits and special space helmets instead of spacesuits.

More than 4,000 spectacular close-ups of the moon's surface are sent back to Earth by the US spacecraft Ranger 7. Rangers 8 and 9, launched the following year, will provide an additional 13,000 pictures and enable US scientists to press on with the development of the Apollo programme. The cost of the entire Ranger series is around $260 million.

ENERGY AND INDUSTRY

A new mothproofing agent—Sivin 55—is developed by the Fibre and Forest Products Institute of Israel to protect woollen clothes from the larvae of moths. This chemical agent retains its effectiveness even after the garments have been washed and dry-cleaned, and is cheaper than all previous mothproofing agents.

Generating electricity without using turbines is first achieved in Britain when scientists pass a rapidly moving stream of hot gas through a strong magnetic field—a process which produces an electric current. Called MHD (magnetohydrodynamic) generation, it could double the output of a nuclear power station once technical difficulties have been overcome.

A factory at Arzew, Algeria, begins liquefying natural gas from huge reservoirs, discovered in 1957 at Hassi R'Mel in the Sahara Desert. Purpose-built tankers will transport it to Britain later in the year.

MEDICINE AND FOOD PRODUCTION

New strains of 'miracle' rice are grown at the Philippines International Rice Research Institute. The most promising is IR-8 which matures swiftly and has a yield nearly double that of local strains. But large doses of nitrate fertilizer are needed, and its prolific foliage is prone to disease and insect pests.

Houston surgeon Michael De Bakey grafts a length of an artificial material—Dacron—to replace a diseased section of the aorta.

In New York, J.D. Hardy's team, which has been working on animal heart transplants, performs the first human heart transplant. The patient, already in shock from terminal heart disease, receives the heart of a chimpanzee but dies an hour later. The operation proves that a heart transplanted into a human body can resume an effective beat.

FRINGE BENEFITS

Electric knives take the strain out of carving the roast.

A computer controls biscuit-making in the Netherlands' Royal Verkade Factory.

The Sealab series of experiments gets under way. Sealab is an underwater research station designed to remain at considerable depths and to house teams of research workers. Its viability is confirmed when a team of American divers spends 11 days in Sealab at a depth of 192 ft (58.6 m), studying the effects of prolonged deep immersion on mind and body. The programme will move on rapidly. A year later, teams of divers will work in Sealab II at similar depths for periods of 15 days, and two members of one team will stay down for 30 days without suffering ill effects. Two years on, Sealab III, *left*, will be operational at three times these depths.

Direct calls between London and Australia become possible when the first transpacific telephone cable opens.

A 'mayday' radio transmitter—its magnesium and nickel battery is triggered only after immersion in seawater—is developed at the US Naval Research Laboratory in Washington.

Soviet scientists successfully bounce radar signals off the planet Jupiter. The signals, which perhaps form the embryo of a 'space spy' system, take 66 mins to complete the 770 million-ml (1,232 million-km) journey—four times the distance between Earth and sun. But because Jupiter's fast rotation deflects many waves away from the Earth, the return signals are weak.

Automatic, electronic map-making has been perfected at Oxford University. Compared with the months previously taken to draw maps by hand, they are now reproduced as photographic negatives in a few days.

Second thoughts about a phrase no longer means retyping a page. IBM's word processor stores typed material in coded form on magnetic tape. To correct, the operator types new words over the old, the tape incorporates the amendments and the typewriter automatically retypes the entire folio.

Intelsat, the International Telecommunications Satellite Organization, is formed by a group of nations including Britain and the USA. By 1980, its members will number 105.

The European Launcher Development Organization (ELDO) is born. Based on the use of the British Blue Streak rocket—originally built as her ballistic weapon—as the first stage, it has French, West German and Italian upper stages. Although Blue Streak works satisfactorily at each launch attempt (its first flight takes place this year), shortcomings in the upper stages lead to the termination of the project in 1973.

Bloodhound MK2, the RAF's land-based missile system for 'sniffing out' and destroying enemy aircraft, replaces the MK1 version of 1958 and will be deployed by NATO in West Germany.

Monorail train services open between Tokyo and Japan's international airport at Haneda. The Alweg system chosen is the one invented by Swedish industrialist Axel Wenner-Gren: the train straddles a concrete beam and is powered by electric lines running on each side.

Britain's second scientific satellite, Ariel 2, is launched from the USA and successfully placed in orbit on 27 March.

The world's first high-temperature gas-cooled nuclear reactor—the Dragon—is started up as part of an international experimental project at Winfrith, Dorset, England.

Electric motors can be stopped almost immediately when engineers at AEI in England devise a new, fast-braking technique for machine tools and heavy machinery. In one revolution they succeed in stopping a small motor revolving 1,500 times a minute.

A new mirror, shatterproof and very light, is announced by the British Aircraft Corp. It is made from polyester foil only 0.10005 in (0.012 mm) thick and coated with a thin film of aluminium. Mounted on moulded plastic or plywood, the mirror gives a clear, crisp image and prevents condensation. It will be used in aircraft and cars—and even for a shaving mirror which does not steam up.

The first pair of photochromic spectacles is invented by Dr Stookey at the Corning Glass works, New York. Made from ordinary silica, the glass has very small crystals of a silver compound scattered through it. These crystals absorb light and darken rapidly when exposed to bright light and then become clear again once the light dims. The glass darkens in seconds when exposed to sunlight, but takes minutes to lighten again.

Fertilizers, containing higher concentrations of nitrogen, are introduced to Europe and the USA. First of this new influx is ammonium nitrate with a 34.5% nitrogen content. It is followed by a liquid fertilizer containing 82% nitrogen, which, when injected into the soil, is absorbed more swiftly than granulated or powdered fertilizers.

Doctors in Boston and London introduce home dialysis for kidney patients. Equipment is expensive and bulky, but the patient—taught to dialyse himself in hospital—has more personal freedom.

In Holland, Voorhorst and his colleagues implicate the house dust mite (*Dermatophagoides pteronyssinus*) in provoking asthma attacks. Victims sensitive to this microscopic mite—always present in household dust—suffer most at night or early in the morning.

A talking typewriter developed at the US Westinghouse Research Laboratories is used as a teaching aid for language students and the blind.

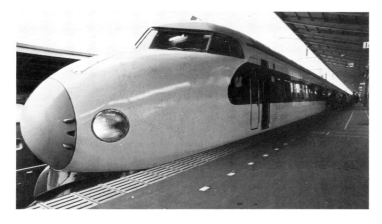

The New Tokaido Line is the world's most advanced inter-city rail link. Special railway track with no sharp bends allows the sleek, bullet-nosed electric trains to race between Osaka and Tokyo at speeds averaging in excess of 100 mph (161 km/h). The line, 322 mls (515 km) long, took a mere five and a half years to complete.

COMMUNICATION, INFORMATION AND SPACE APPLICATIONS

The first photographs of Mars are transmitted by the US Mariner 4. The probe's 21 pictures of the planet's surface detail numerous craters, but indicate that the possibility of life on the planet is unlikely.

The world's first electronic telephone exchange is installed in the small New Jersey town of Succasunna by ATT (Automatic Telephone & Telegraph Corp). Subscribers can use an abbreviated dialling code to connect them with frequently dialled numbers, bring a third person into a conversation, or transfer calls elsewhere.

A laser beam 2 mls (3.2 km) long is folded into a 10-ft (3-m) space by reflecting it between two mirrors more than 1,000 times. Since there is no overlap between the light waves, huge amounts of information can be stored in the beam and rapidly retrieved.

The brief silences in telephone conversations can be used to send coded information. Engineers at Standard Telecommunication Laboratories at Harlow, England, develop IDAST (interpolated data and speech transmission), a system that squeezes telegraphy messages or digital information for data processing into the silences in much the same way as TASI (time assignment speech interpolation) 'sardines' several simultaneous telephone conversations on to the same line. A magnetic storage tape can record the speech, delay it for a second then relay it without causing any disruption to the listener.

TRANSPORT, WARFARE AND SPACE EXPLORATION

Underground railway activity intensifies as European cities, from Munich and Milan to Brussels and Rotterdam, construct or enlarge their systems to help cut road traffic congestion caused by the post-war boom in car sales.

A magnetic highway, claimed to be a possible transport system of the future, is demonstrated in the USA. The magnetic suspension system works through the interaction of two sets of magnets, one on the underside of the vehicle, the other on the road beneath. The vehicle 'floats' $\frac{1}{4}$ in (5 mm) above the magnetic track and is propelled by an electric motor.

Man takes his first space 'walk' as Alexei Leonov passes through the airlock of the Soviet spaceship Voskhod 2 and, attached to the ship by an umbilical line, somersaults and floats in space for 10 mins. Leonov wears a spacesuit inflated to full atmospheric pressure, and experiences some difficulty in squeezing back into the ship's airlock. Although the craft returns safely to Earth, the pilot has to make a manual re-entry and landing—the first by a Soviet astronaut.

ENERGY AND INDUSTRY

Eighty per cent of total Neoprene production, accounting for 5% of the world's synthetic rubber, will by 1980 be made by the technique now developed by the Distillers Co, England. The manufacturing process involves using supplies of the chemical butadiene, which is now available very cheaply.

The UK Atomic Energy Authority develop the first radioisotope generator, which has a radioactive element as its source of power. The generator is used to provide the electricity to light a navigational beacon at sea.

The first electrical transmission lines in the world capable of carrying 700,000 V come into service in Canada. Built by the Quebec Hydro-Electric Commission, they carry power 226 mls (364 km) from dams on the Manicouagan River to Montreal. Two similar transmission lines are planned for construction in 1970.

MEDICINE AND FOOD PRODUCTION

Concern over the choice of site for the amputation of a limb affected by diabetic gangrene or vascular disease, causes L.H. Stalgren and M. Otteman of the Philadelphia General Hospital to redefine the criteria, so as to achieve uncomplicated wound healing.

US surgeon John Ochsner describes a new plastic mesh, Marlex, which can be used to bridge large defects in body tissue without risk of rejection. He uses it to 'patch' large wounds and to replace missing parts of the pericardium (the membranous sac surrounding the heart), the trachea and the abdominal wall.

FRINGE BENEFITS

A computer installed by the New York Stock Exchange gives spoken answers to telephone enquiries.

The first fully electric clock has no moving parts and a cathode-ray tube time display.

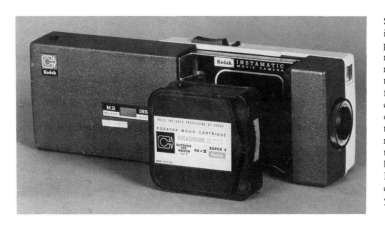

Super 8 gives a 50% increase in home movie picture size. Kodak's redesigned 8 mm movie film comes on to the market in cassette form for Instamatic cameras. The quality of the pictures is better than with the old 8 mm film, and the easy-to-use cartridges will be as popular as the Instamatic still cartridges were two years before.

The first Soviet Molniya ('Lightning') satellites follow elongated 12-hour orbits at large inclinations to the Earth, reaching their zenith over the Soviet Union at the busiest communications periods and giving good service to the polar regions.

Computer time-sharing speeds up theatre and airline bookings, improves warehouse stock control and brings computer technology within the reach of many more businesses. A central computer can present answers to several users simultaneously.

The US Army sets a record by successfully transmitting seven television channels (those normally broadcast separately from New York's Empire State Building) simultaneously along a single laser beam.

Intelsat–1, nicknamed Early Bird, the first Intelsat satellite is launched. It provides 240 telephone circuits or a single TV channel between Europe and North America. Although designed to operate for only 18 months, it will prove a remarkable success and stay in geostationary orbit for four years.

A demonstration of the MVR videodisc recorder in California reveals the machine's ability to record up to 600 single frames (or 20 secs of continuous TV action) on magnetic disc, to replay or erase any single frame and to play back pictures instantly.

Miniature TV arrives—and in colour. A set with a $7\frac{1}{2}$-in (19-cm) screen is developed in Japan, and has all the electronics packed into a set 10 in (25 cm) high. By using transistor circuits for most of the components, the power consumption is also cut to 10% of that used by an average TV.

The use of pre-packed containers for sea-borne trade booms following international agreement on the standards for container ships. Freight is packed into boxlike units to be transported by road or rail to a port where they are loaded by special cranes. A purpose-built container ship has internal cellular and deck stowage for hundreds of standard 20-ft (6-m) containers.

In the first space rendezvous, the US spacecraft Geminis 6 and 7 come within $6\frac{1}{2}$ ft (2 m) of each other. Gemini 7 also sets a new 14-day record for the longest space flight to date.

Traffic congestion in Chicago is eased by a computer installation which monitors and controls the flow of vehicles along 7 mls (11.2 km) of a major highway. The computer analyzes data fed to it from ultrasonic detectors on the road, then operates red or green lights at entrance points to the highway to stop vehicles or allow them to join the road, depending on traffic conditions. Similar traffic surveillance schemes are also operating in Detroit and New York City.

Scientist Yoshio Masuda invents a small navigational buoy which generates its own electricity to power a light. A column of water inside the buoy oscillates up and down as the waves pass, compressing air and driving a turbine. The Marine Science and Technology Centre in Japan will investigate the device, and, in 1979, will test a full-scale oscillating water column with a view to developing a major source of power from the waves.

The first commercial fast breeder nuclear reactor—the Enrico Fermi Fast Breeder Reactor—begins operating in the USA, but a fault in the cooling system, which will cause radioactivity to escape, will lead to its closure in 1966.

Deposits of natural gas are first discovered in the North Sea at the West Sole gas field. Located by British Petroleum, production will start in 1967.

Czechoslovakian engineers produce a totally new type of spinning machine which can spin natural and synthetic fibres up to six times faster than any previous machine. Known as a rotor spinning machine, it cleans, straightens and, using speeds of up to 60,000 revolutions per minute, spins the fibres into a groove, where they are twisted into yarn.

A machine which could revolutionize farming practice, by doing away with ploughing, goes on trial in Britain. After herbicides have destroyed unwanted vegetation, the machine cuts grooves about $\frac{1}{2}$ in (1.25 cm) wide in the soil. Seed and fertilizer are then dropped into the grooves at the correct depth.

After reports linking cigarette smoking with lung cancer and cardiovascular disease, Britain imposes a ban on cigarette advertising on TV.

The possibilities of surgery conducted outside the body become apparent when researchers at the University of Minnesota find that dogs' stomachs can be removed, kept in cold storage for several hours, operated upon, and then replaced—to resume normal functioning. Removal of organs in this way would also mean greater freedom in radiation or drug therapy for cancer.

Long-life milk that stays fresh in the unopened carton is developed.

A newly invented, partly permeable plastic may be used in future to make 'soft' contact lenses.

London Transport brings in automatic ticket barriers to cut queues and reduce evasion of fares due. Tickets are magnetically coded and checked by the new barriers. If the barrier does not 'approve' the ticket it will close, gently but firmly, trapping the passenger until a ticket inspector comes.

The first US astronaut to 'walk' in space, Ed White floats outside his ship, Gemini 4. White carries a rocket gun powered by compressed gas with which he manoeuvres himself during the 21 mins he remains outside the spacecraft, attached only by a thin 'umbilical cord'.

COMMUNICATION, INFORMATION AND SPACE APPLICATIONS

In Britain, computers make major inroads into industry. BOAC announce a massive scheme for computerizing design, administration, planning and control, while Shell UK install in a tanker a sophisticated remote control system which will eventually monitor the ship's machinery. ICI report that a computer is running an industrial alchohol plant.

Regular stereophonic broadcasts of live concerts on VHF begin in the London area.

Daily weather observations can be made worldwide following the launching of the first US ESSA (Environmental Science Service Administration) weather satellites. The satellites work in pairs: while one relays data to US Earth stations for processing and later transmission, its partner transmits TV pictures, showing cloud coverage and other weather conditions, direct to meteorological stations all over the globe.

An experimental laser telephone linking two Moscow districts, is put into operation.

TRANSPORT, WARFARE AND SPACE EXPLORATION

A quartet of astronauts practises the skills of walking in space: Eugene Cernan from Gemini 9; Michael Collins from Gemini 10; Richard Gordon from Gemini 11 and Buzz Aldrin from Gemini 12. The latter is the last in this highly successful series of US manned orbital spaceflights.

Francis Chichester sails single-handed non-stop from Plymouth to Sydney, Australia, in his yacht *Gipsy Moth IV*. He then completes the circumnavigation of the world in an overall time of 274 days.

American engineers take a tip from Chilean villagers and construct a 'broom' to clear fog-bound US highways. The Chileans convert dense fog into valuable water for irrigation by using stationary wooden frames strung with nylon threads to trap fog water droplets which then dribble into irrigation pipes. A rotating device built in New Jersey to the same principle will soon be tested to clear fog on state highways.

ENERGY AND INDUSTRY

One of the largest known gas deposits in the North Sea, and one of the largest offshore deposits in the world, is discovered 43 mls (69 km) north-east of Lowestoft, England. Called the Leman gas field, it has reserves of an estimated 10 million million cu ft (283,170 million cu m) of gas, nearly half of which will have been recovered by the beginning of 1980.

First developed in 1927, the contact grill is revised as a method of cooking food directly on two plates of heated metal. Known as the fast grill, it is used as a sandwich toaster.

A new type of street lighting—high-pressure sodium discharge lighting—is tested in London. It produces a great deal of light per watt, making it economical, and glows with a golden hue which penetrates further than the yellow light of the earlier low-pressure sodium lamps. The first of its kind in Europe, this street lighting will be installed in the City of London in 1967.

Oil is discovered in the Danish sector of the North Sea but as yet has no commercial value.

MEDICINE AND FOOD PRODUCTION

An elegant test for minute quantities of hormones is devised at The Radiochemical Centre at Amersham, England. The first radio immuno-assay kit measures insulin levels in diabetes: a labelled compound—a radioactively tagged substance—marks insulin and indicates its presence and concentration in the blood.

Although there have been occasional deaths from blocked arteries in women taking the contraceptive pill, the US Food and Drug Administration concludes that there are no adequate scientific grounds for declaring the pill unsafe for human use.

FRINGE BENEFITS

Corrosion testing for canned foods provides an accurate prediction of shelf-life.

Radar is used to measure ice thickness at the Poles.

The Severn Bridge is opened to provide a motorway link between England and South Wales, replacing a ferry route across the Severn which has been in operation since the 12th century. Some radical new design features have been incorporated to make the bridge stable, given the considerable length of its span and the force of the winds that blow up the Bristol Channel into the Severn estuary. The roadway, for example, is composed of aerodynamically shaped box sections and the suspender cables are fixed at an angle, not in the conventional vertical position.

An accurate aircraft radar apparatus, which can work when the ground beneath the plane is blanketed with ice—previously the cause of occasional false readings—is developed at Cambridge, England.

Lunar Orbiter 1 photographs some 2 million sq mls (5.18 million sq km) of the moon's surface. It is the first of five US spacecraft developed to orbit the moon and, in conjunction with the Surveyor probes, to investigate possible sites for an Apollo moon landing.

Computers are widely used to analyze the results of Britain's General Election. Programmed with data from previous elections, and then fed fresh results, the computers are able to forecast the final result, which is a win for the Labour Party, led by Harold Wilson.

Early warning for miners of impending methane gas explosions is possible with the electronic alarm developed by US Government scientists. The Methane Monitor burns any methane in the atmosphere and when this combustion raises the temperature sufficiently, an alarm is set off.

Fibre optics, in which the conventional copper wire in telephone cables is replaced with glass fibre, will revolutionize the science of telecommunications. New methods of measuring the way in which light waves travel through glass fibres take the research a stage nearer the day when between 1,000 and 2,000 telephone conversations, TV signals or computer data signals will be carried simultaneously on a single fibre.

The unmanned Soviet spacecraft Luna 9 is the first to make a successful soft landing on the Moon. On touch-down, the craft ejects an ingenious egg-shaped capsule which rolls into an upright position. Four petal-like panels open to form stabilizing legs and to reveal an antenna and TV camera which, for three days, relay the first TV transmissions from the moon's surface.

An electronic fuel injection system—it could replace the carburettor—is developed in Britain. A small computer analyses data on engine-operating conditions, then injects the correct amount of fuel into each cylinder. The result is improved fuel distribution, reduced fuel consumption and air pollution, and better performance. The system will soon be tested and installed in a range of Rover cars.

The dream of docking in space becomes a reality as Neil Armstrong and David Scott link their Gemini 8 spacecraft to an Agena target rocket.

The largest and most advanced atomic plant in the world for reprocessing nuclear fuels is built at Windscale in England. The reprocessing plant takes plutonium from the nine existing nuclear power stations in Britain and mixes it with natural uranium. This fuel 'factory' then prepares and packages the reprocessed nuclear fuel so that it can power the core of the prototype fast reactor at Dounreay in Scotland.

The first domestic electric cooker to have a ceramic hob—a totally flat surface consisting of both hotplates and their surrounds in the same material—is introduced. The ceramic, discovered accidentally at an American glassworks, is patterned into rings to indicate the position of the hotplates, which heat up when switched on by electric elements underneath.

The first superconducting motor is developed in Britain by the International Research and Development Co of Newcastle. The coils of an electromagnet are cooled to such low temperatures that they lose their resistance to electricity. Thus they can conduct very high direct currents which, in turn, can drive the powerful motor. A 1969 version—the largest in the world—will be built for Fawley power station, where it will pump thousands of gallons of water from the sea to cool the turbine condensers.

Chronic protein deficiency cannot be cured overnight: it results in generations of brain-damaged young. Studies at the University of Natal, South Africa, show that malnourished rats produce young with impaired mental processes. Even if the new-born rats are themselves well fed, the effects of starvation are still seen in their offspring.

In Britain, the first warnings are published of the toxic side-effects of the popular pain-killer, paracetamol. Even in quite small quantities, it can cause damage to the liver.

A high incidence of birth defects, following an epidemic of German measles (rubella) in the USA, alerts doctors to the risks associated with the disease in early pregnancy. This creates added interest in the safe vaccine against German measles developed by Paul Parkman and Harry Myer.

Biodegradable liquid detergents reduce polution.

Photography by flash becomes really easy. A small, throwaway unit containing four flash bulbs slots into the camera. It rotates automatically, meaning that pictures can be taken in rapid succession. Gone are the old, cumbersome flash holders, and gone too is the nuisance of removing sizzling hot, spent bulbs.

Grand National runners have their starting prices checked by computers used by British bookmakers. The computers say that the odds should have been shortened on the first three horses, but lengthened by up to 60% on the rest of the field. Bookmakers will now regularly use computers to calculate odds and reckon winnings.

COMMUNICATION, INFORMATION AND SPACE APPLICATIONS

A light-sensitive pen, a TV screen and a computer are the components used by IBM, New York, to create new computer-assisted circuit designs. Instead of re-drawing the whole circuit, any design changes can be made simply by manipulating the computer-generated images with the electronic pen.

A miniature TV camera, the size of a cine camera and able to transmit its own pictures, has been developed in the USA by RCA. The battery-powered, tubeless camera weighs only 2.2 lb (1 kg).

Background hiss, an everyday problem in audio recordings, is effectively eliminated by US scientist R.M. Dolby, whose system improves fidelity, boosts low sounds and masks sounds that have reached a predetermined level.

Communications systems, using laser beams to carry TV pictures from space probes to satellites, are under development in the USA. The huge capacity of the laser beam will allow more pictures to be sent back much faster than by radio.

TRANSPORT, WARFARE AND SPACE EXPLORATION

During a 94-min descent (before landing and abruptly ceasing transmission), a capsule from the Soviet spacecraft Venus 4 sends back information on the temperature, pressure density and composition of the Venusian atmosphere.

Tragedy mars space exploration: Soviet astronaut Vladimir Komarov perishes as the parachute of his Soyuz (Union) 1 fails to open. The crew of America's first manned Apollo mission are killed as fire rages through their craft as it sits atop a Saturn rocket on the launching pad.

The giant US Saturn 5 rocket makes its first successful flight in November, launching the unmanned Apollo 4 mission.

ENERGY AND INDUSTRY

North Sea gas begins to flow into Britain as the first commercial production gets under way from the West Sole gas field.

'Project Gasbuggy' employs a 24-kiloton nuclear explosion 4,000 ft (1,200 m) beneath New Mexico to release natural gas—the first US underground blasting experiment of its kind.

A solar house, with ponds of water on the roof to act as insulation, is constructed by H. Hay, who patented the idea, and J. Yellott, of the University of Arizona, USA. A movable slab of foam covers or exposes the ponds: when covered in summer the water cools the house; when uncovered, the winter sun warms the water and consequently the house. On a day when the outside temperature is 96.8°F (36°C), Hay finds he has to wear a sweater and a coat to keep warm indoors.

MEDICINE AND FOOD PRODUCTION

Scientists at the National Institute for Medical Research in Britain overcome the leprosy bacillus' reluctance to grow in the laboratory or to succumb to drug treatment. The elusive microorganism—close relative of the tubercule bacillus—is cultured in laboratory mice whose natural immune system has been suppressed. At the same time, large-scale trials in Uganda raise hopes that BCG, the tuberculosis vaccine, may effectively prevent leprosy.

Asthmatics gain some relief with the use of Intal, discovered in Britain by Roger Altounyan. This preventative treatment—a powder which, when inhaled, inhibits allergic reactions in the lining of the air-passages—is particularly effective against external allergens, such as pollen or dust.

US physician Irving Cooper introduces cryo-surgery—freezing a small part of the brain—as an alternative to prevailing operative techniques for the treatment of Parkinson's disease.

FRINGE BENEFITS

British and US troops use an electronic sentry which can pick up footsteps 40 yds away.

The transparent 'Blow Chair' designed in Milan, is the first totally inflatable chair.

Louis Washkansky receives the heart of a 24-year-old woman killed in a traffic accident in the first-ever human heart transplant. Performed by South African Surgeon Christiaan Barnard in Cape Town, the 5-hr operation is a success, although Washkansky dies 18 days later from post-operative complications.

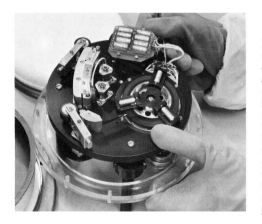

Britain's latest space satellite, Aerial 3, designed to investigate and monitor galactic radio signals, incorporates this tape-recorder—precision-built for the Space Research Council which administers the project. The recorder will collect data whilst in orbit and release it, on command, to ground stations.

Intelsat–II, the second of a new generation of satellites, vastly improves communications to the southern hemisphere. Its increased transmission power enables the operational costs to be cut enormously.

CBS introduces a means of watching pre-recorded movies or video tapes on home TV sets. With EVR (electronic video recording), a cartridge is inserted into an automatic player which, as well as producing normal pictures on the TV screen, has single frame, fast forward, skip motion and reverse facilities. EVR also promises a quality of colour reception and resolution comparable to that of 35 mm films shown on TV.

The BBC begins Britain's first regular colour TV service, in time for the Wimbledon mens' singles tennis final—it is won by John Newcombe of Australia who beats Wilhelm Bungert of West Germany. The system chosen by Britain is the PAL (phase alternation line) system, a West German modification of the NTSC system, used in the USA. In the same year, France and the USSR adopt the French SECAM system (*système electronique couleurs avec memoire*). By 1972, Turkey, Iran, Australia, Brazil and some Asian countries have adopted PAL and by 1978 it is the choice of more than 40 countries.

A battery-operated cordless telephone which, unlike a walkie-talkie, allows two-way conversations, is tested in the USA.

The field of view of a conventional light microscope is doubled by a lens attachment developed by Zeiss in West Germany.

The first automatic landing by a scheduled passenger airliner is made at London's Heathrow airport. Radio beams sent out by the airport's Instrument Landing System (ILS) guide the Trident to a safe touchdown.

Two Cosmos unmanned Soviet satellites complete the first automatic docking exercise, and the first docking of any kind, by Soviet spaceships. The craft fly together for $3\frac{1}{2}$ hrs.

A safer car bumper (fender), which absorbs some of the energy of an impact or collision, is developed in the USA by the Pontiac company. Made from a synthetic cushion backed by reinforcing steel, it will replace the usual, all-steel rigid front bumper of 1968 Pontiacs.

Dreamland add a safety device to their electric blankets after a series of accidents cause stricter standards to be enforced. Their monitoring system cuts off the electricity supply should the blanket overheat.

The amount of light and heat passing through glass can now be controlled by a new process for modifying the surface of clear ribbon glass. Known as the electro-float process, the quantity of metallic particles embedded in the glass is varied according to its application, whether in buildings with large windows, or in screens and windows of automobiles and aircraft.

The construction of the largest hydroelectric power station in the world is finished on the Yenisei River in Siberia. The Krasnoyansk Dam will generate three times as much power as the Grand Coulee Dam in the USA.

In Sri Lanka, A.E. Kulatilake gains a few hours' grace for transplant surgeons seeking to match donor and recipient. He finds a way of extending the usable life of cadaver kidneys from 3 to 14 hours by keeping them washed in whole fresh blood.

Rene Favaloro, cardiovascular surgeon at Ohio's Cleveland Clinic, develops the coronary bypass operation for conditions such as angina pectoris. A section of healthy vein, grafted from elsewhere in the body, bypasses a blocked coronary artery and provides an alternative route for the blood supply to the heart muscle itself.

To prevent stroke or sudden heart-attack, Sol Sobel, a New York heart surgeon, refines the technique of endarterectomy by injecting carbon dioxide gas into clogged arteries to loosen and remove fatty deposits. A powerful jet of gas is directed through the blood vessel by hypodermic syringe: the congealed deposits can then be removed with forceps. This life-saving procedure cleans even small branch arteries.

The British liner, Queen Elizabeth II, is fitted with the most advanced computer ever designed for a non-military ship.

The improved Frisbee or 'flying saucer' is patented with aerodynamic spoilers.

The world's first tidal power station is completed across the estuary of the River Rance at St Malo in north-west France. Turbines driven by the rise and fall of the Atlantic waters—the average tidal range is 27.56 ft (8.4 m)—generate a maximum electrical output of 240 MW. While sufficient to power a city of about 300,000 people, its supply is not continuous and its peak power output is governed by time and tide rather than demand.

COMMUNICATION, INFORMATION AND SPACE APPLICATIONS

Spying by laser is demonstrated by British glass manufacturer Dr Pilkington. By using the vibrations of the glass in the windows of a room as a microphone, the laser can pick up conversation perfectly. The best protection from such eavesdropping, argues Dr Pilkington, is to fit double glazing!

Using radar, astronomers at Cornell University have mapped a third of the surface of Venus.

The first computer to diagnose and cure its own faults is completed at the Jet Propulsion Laboratory in Pasadena for space programmes of the future. When, using its built-in error-detecting code, it notices a fault, it automatically switches power to a spare module while it tests the faulty one. It then requests a replacement module if necessary.

Science fiction becomes fact with the first ever colour TV transmission from space. Apollo 10 carries a compact field-sequential type camera in its orbital flight around the moon and sends back clear pictures.

TRANSPORT, WARFARE AND SPACE EXPLORATION

The 'Queen Elizabeth II', quickly nicknamed the QE2, is launched. Although smaller than the earlier 'Queens', her standard of passenger accommodation is said to be the highest ever provided in a liner. In 1982 she will see service in the South Atlantic, when she is requisitioned to carry troops by the British government and joins the task force sent to help recover the Falkland Islands, following their invasion by Argentina.

Surveyor 7, the last in a series of US lunar probes, soft lands successfully on the moon. Its TV camera, which can be focussed from 4 ft (1.2 m) to infinity, and take in narrow or wide-angled views, sends back 21,000 lunar photographs.

The deep-sea drilling ship *Glomar Challenger* goes into service. The vessel stays in a fixed position above the sea bed relative to a sonar beacon placed on the bottom, and any movement is automatically corrected by her side-propulsion units and the main propeller.

Zond 5 is the first spacecraft to travel around the moon and return safely to Earth. A second Soviet craft, Zond 6, repeats this achievement later this year, and both craft carry tortoises, insects and seeds on board to study the effects of spaceflight on behaviour and growth.

ENERGY AND INDUSTRY

Steel is made by a new technique when the experimental pilot plant of the Lancashire Steel Manufacturing Co opens in England. Molten iron, sprayed out in a number of directions, becomes atomized and rapidly turns into steel. Called spray steel-making, this high-pressure technique may be of future importance as the first continuous steel-making process.

An orbiting solar power station is proposed. The station, composed of an array of solar cells, would be put into a particular orbit. It would convert the abundant solar energy into electricity and beam it, via a microwave transmitter, to a point on the Earth. It is estimated that a solar panel 5 mls (13 km) square can generate 10,000 MW—enough to supply the 1973 power needs of a city the size of New York.

The new zinc-air battery is commercially manufactured for the first time by Energy Conversion, England. Giving a steady voltage for 12 hrs, the 12 V, 2.2-lb (1-kg) battery will be used in communications equipment.

MEDICINE AND FOOD PRODUCTION

A survey by researchers at the University of Sheffield, England, establishes that cigarette smoking by pregnant women has a harmful effect on their unborn babies.

The eruption of meningitis among American GIs triggers a frantic search for a vaccine. Malcolm Arnstein, a US Army virologist, cultures meningococci from throat swabs, isolates the substance that stimulates antibody production, and from it successfully develops a vaccine.

FRINGE BENEFITS

A partly transparent hole punch allows the user to position paper more precisely.

A computer wins the transatlantic yacht race—the *Sir Thomas Lipton* follows a course plotted daily by computer.

The largest reservoir of petroleum on the North American continent is discovered on Alaska's North Slope. Oil companies combine to establish the Trans-Alaska Pipeline System, running from Prudhoe Bay on the Beaufort Sea to the ice-free port of Valdez on the state's southern coast. When completed in 1977, the 4-ft (1.22-m) wide pipeline will be 807.8 mls (1,300 km) long and able to transport nearly 300,000 tons of crude oil a day. It will cross three mountain ranges, 800 rivers and streams, and three major earthquake zones. Climbing, in places, as high as 4,953 ft (1,400 m) above sea level, it will have to withstand temperatures ranging from 89.6°F (32°C) to −70.6°F (−57°C).

Six European nations submit designs for the first all-European TV satellite.

A deep-sea cable which can carry 720 simultaneous two-way telephone conversations is manufactured by Standard Telephones and Cables to link Florida with the Caribbean. The cable consists of 41 high-tensile steel wires twisted together and surrounded by polythene insulation and a copper outer conductor.

The smallest ever time measurement is made by scientists at the Bell Laboratories in the USA: the picosecond—a millionth of a millionth of a second—is measured by using single pulses from a laser.

Cyclops 3, a cheap but sophisticated machine for reading and identifying neat handwriting, is made in Britain by Plessey. Able to cope with variations in letter sizes and gaps in the ink flow, Cyclops will prove invaluable in processing forms.

A radar device developed at the University of Miami, Florida, to pinpoint lightning areas in storms, will reduce the threat of lightning strikes on forests and airliners. The detector uses 100 transistors to pick up radio noise emanating from electrical storms and translates them into arrow-like signals which shoot across a screen.

The first 250,000-ton tankers, known as VLCCs (very large crude carriers) are constructed. The worldwide increase in demand for oil, and the closures of the Suez Canal in 1956 and 1967, make these supertankers economic for bulk transportation of oil.

The Soviet Tupolev TU–144 becomes the first supersonic airliner in flight. Initially revealed in model form at the 1965 Paris Air Show—where it is destined to crash in spectacular fashion in 1973—it is dubbed 'Concordski' from its superficial similarities to Concorde.

Apollo 8, crewed by Frank Borman, James Lovell and William Anders, makes the first manned flight round the moon and back. The feat suggests that NASA is now ready to fulfil the avowed aim of the Apollo programme: a moon landing by men.

An automatic control system makes Berlin's underground railway safe. An insulated cable between the tracks relays information about other train movements to the driver's cab; stop and start signals sent directly to the motors make it impossible for two trains to enter the same track.

The world's largest hovercraft, the SRN4 starts a regular service across the English Channel. At 130 ft (39 m) long and 78 ft (23 m) wide, the SRN4 can carry 609 passengers at an average in-service speed of 55 knots.

A glass developed by Glaverbel of Belgium is as strong and flexible as some types of steel. Because it is also light and resistant to chipping, the manufacturers predict that it will be used to build glass domes, curved windows, cathode-ray tubes and light-bulbs.

The number of road accidents at busy junctions will be reduced as Shell UK perfect an anti-skid road dressing, called Shellgrip, which is composed of epoxy resin, bitumen and bauxite.

Washable wallpaper, manufactured by Du Pont's Textile Fibers Department in the USA, becomes popular. Made from polythene, it resists tearing but, while it can be printed normally, it requires special inks for high-precision printing. A flexible fabric version, using the same basic materials, is also made. Twice as strong as the wallpaper, this cannot be laundered or dry-cleaned and is therefore useful only for making into cheap, disposable garments, such as laboratory coats, nurses' aprons and underpants.

The hard metal beryllium is just beginning to be used in the manufacture of aircraft parts—the US aircraft builders Lockheed now use it instead of steel in the brake discs of their new C5 transport aeroplane. Five times as heat-resistant, and four times as light as steel, beryllium will also be used in missile and satellite heat shields—and in animal surgery, when a golden eagle in Scotland acquires an artificial leg made from beryllium.

In Britain, a Birmingham mother gives birth to sextuplets in a record-breaking example of multiple births arising from new fertility drugs.

New Mexican strains introduced to India by the Ford Foundation push the country's wheat production up by 50%. The project is one of many contributing to the so-called 'Green Revolution'—the enlistment of technological knowledge to increase food crop production in undeveloped areas of the world.

Record crop yields come from new 'miracle' rice strains introduced to the Philippines and other Asian countries by the International Rice Research Institute. However, it is unpopular: the Thais call it 'sticky rice', and poor Asian farmers complain that it needs more fertilizer, water and sophisticated cultivation than traditional varieties.

Britain's Football League fixture list is produced by computer.

Heart conditions can be diagnosed by telephone, using equipment developed for use in the home.

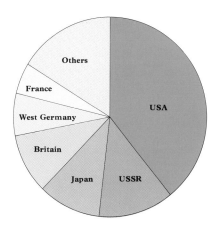

42 years after John Logie Baird's first demonstration of television in London, world TV ownership approaches the 200 million mark. There are 78 million sets in the USA, 25 million in the USSR, 20.5 million in Japan, 19 million in Britain, 13.5 million in West Germany and 10 million in France.

The first Poseidon C-3 submarine-launched strategic missile is fired from Cape Kennedy, Florida, in August. Each of these missiles has a warhead with a range of 2,875 mls (4,626 km) and twice the nuclear payload of the Polaris missile it replaces; but existing launch tubes can be used without radical modification. Testing of this weapons system will be fully completed by the 14th launch in 1969, and the missile will enter service with the US Navy in 1971.

COMMUNICATION, INFORMATION AND SPACE APPLICATIONS

Goonhilly 2, a new telephone and satellite TV antenna system, is built at the British Post Office's Goonhilly Earth station in Cornwall. The space bowl, which will operate through the Intelsat–III satellite, will carry up to 400 telephone circuits and a TV broadcast simultaneously—more than all the transatlantic cables and the previous Goonhilly antenna put together.

A single crystal of a new material, lithium niobate, records the complex interference patterns of light waves as semi-permanent changes. It can thus store 1,000 holograms which are used to 'memorize' information as well as to produce 3–D images. According to Bell Laboratories who researched the technique, information can easily be retrieved or erased from the crystal.

TRANSPORT, WARFARE AND SPACE EXPLORATION

SALT (Strategic Arms Limitation Talks) opens in Helsinki, Finland, after Russia states its willingness to discuss the limitation and reduction of strategic nuclear delivery systems.

Three manned spacecraft make history— Soyuz 6, 7 and 8, launched by the USSR on successive days, are all in orbit at the same time. To the surprise of western observers, there is no attempt to dock the craft, although a wide variety of rendezvous manoeuvres are practised. The two-man crew of Soyuz 6 conducts experiments in remote-control welding, a skill essential to the Russian objective of developing a space station within Earth's orbit.

LASH (the Lighter Aboard Ship) system is introduced as a variant on the established container trade. The LASH ship is equipped with a gantry crane capable of lifting and stowing on board up to 70 specially designed lighters. Unlike conventional container ships, the LASH does not need a dockside discharge berth or a large dock marshalling area—given sufficient depth of water it can be loaded or unloaded anywhere.

Concorde, the supersonic airliner developed jointly by Britain and France, makes its maiden flight from Toulouse.

ENERGY AND INDUSTRY

The first electronically controlled industrial knitting machine is marketed by Franz Morat. It can digitally record and store infinitely complex patterns, which are then transmitted for manufacture at the flick of a switch. In 1970, the machine will be controlled by a computer, making knitwear design and production almost totally automated.

Huge underground reservoirs are built in frozen soil at Canvey Island in Essex, England, to accommodate 7,063,000 cu ft (200,000 cu m) of liquefied natural gas imported from Algeria.

The colour codes for electrical wiring are changed throughout Britain. Neutral changes from black to blue, live from red to brown, and earth from green to yellow and green stripes.

MEDICINE AND FOOD PRODUCTION

Dr Max Perutz of Cambridge, England, reports that haemoglobin is made up of four chains of molecules which reorganize themselves to pick up or release oxygen. By studying the changing configurations of the molecular chains, he hopes to learn how many genetic defects cause oxygen starvation because of abnormally-shaped red blood cells.

Five hundred million hectares of arable land and two-thirds of the world's original forest have been lost, mainly through short-sighted agricultural management and forest clearance. These findings are published in a report, entitled *Problems of the Human Environment*, commissioned by the United Nations.

FRINGE BENEFITS

A crossbred tick-resistant cow is bred for the tropics.

On 20 July Neil Armstrong becomes the first man to set foot on the moon, followed 18 mins later by Buzz Aldrin, *left*. Millions watching the Apollo 11 mission on television hear Armstrong's words as his left boot touches the lunar surface, 'That's one small step for a man, one giant leap for mankind.' The two practise moving around in the low gravity ($\frac{1}{6}$ that of Earth's) and then erect a US flag. They collect 9lb 12oz (21.75 kg) of rock and soil samples, and set up a laser reflector, a seismometer and an aluminium sheet to trap particles in the solar wind. The Eagle lunar module takes off again 21 hrs 37 mins later to dock with the Apollo command module, piloted by Michael Collins.

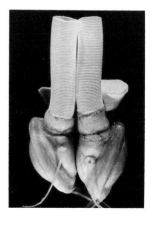

A waterproof telephone cable, whose units are encased in a mixture of petroleum jelly and plastic, is developed by Bell Laboratories. The cable promises improved reliability and reduced maintenance costs.

American astronauts Neil Armstrong and Edwin (Buzz) Aldrin become the first men to photograph another world. The astronauts use modified Hasselblad cameras to record their work on the moon, while the Kodak Lunar Surface camera provides stereoscopic close-ups.

The first successful flight model of the high-capacity Intelsat-III satellite is put into service.

A magnetic device, which stores information on tiny 'bubbles' of magnetism and allows any detail to be retrieved within 100 microseconds, improves the memory power of computers. Each chip contains hundreds of thousands of bubbles which retain data even if the power supply is cut off.

Preparing for a manned lunar landing, the crew of Apollo 9 practises separation and docking manoeuvres between the lunar module, which is to descend to the moon's surface, and the main Apollo craft—the command module. Two months later, the Apollo 10 mission takes the complete Apollo spacecraft into orbit round the moon for the first time. The lunar module descends to within 9 mls (14.5 km) of the moon's surface and sends back the first colour TV pictures from a space mission.

The turbofan engine sets new standards of power, fuel economy, quietness and reliability in airline engines. Four Pratt and Whitney JT9Ds, each with 43,500 lb of thrust, are fitted to the planned Boeing 747, the first of the turbofan aircraft to enter service.

A mini-motorcycle, small and light enough to be carried in a bag, is marketed by the German company Poppe. Frame and wheels made of aluminium alloy help keep the weight of this mechanical midget down to 54 lb (24 kg).

The Apollo 12 mission gets a spectacular send-off from the USA in November, when its Saturn 5 rocket is struck by lightning during the launch. After thorough checks, the spacecraft continues on the first of a series of six Apollo missions devoted to scientific study of the moon. The crew accomplishes an accurate landing, despite a fierce dust storm blown up by the descent engine. In $31\frac{1}{2}$ hrs on the lunar surface, Charles Conrad and Alan Bean collect 5 lb 5 oz (2.4 kg) of soil and rock samples and leave behind six nuclear-powered scientific experiments which will have a working life of at least a year.

The largest oil field in the North Sea—the Ekofisk—is discovered in Norwegian waters about 205 mls (330 km) south-west of Stavanger.

Computers begin to be used to control industrial processes as the Molins Machine Co in Britain show that computers can manufacture a variety of components in a relatively short time. At the same time, the Bunker-Ramo Corp in the USA take out a patent for the use of a central time-sharing computer, which can simultaneously control many industrial machines.

'As bright as a well-lit supermarket' is the way the new floodlighting is described at the West Ham soccer club in London. For the first time, compact source iodide (CSI) lamps are used—chiefly to provide a brighter light for the new outside-broadcast colour TV cameras. Pioneered by Thorn Lighting, each tiny lamp shines as brightly as 80 average domestic bulbs. Many scenes in future films like *Star Wars* and *Superman* will be filmed under CSI lamps.

Oil is discovered in the British sector of the North Sea, in the Montrose field, by the British Gas Corp/ Amoco group, who will announce in 1973 that the field is commercially viable.

Dr Robert Edwards at the Physiology Laboratory, Cambridge, England, succeeds in fertilizing the human egg outside the mother's body. He hopes that in bypassing damaged Fallopian tubes—a major cause of infertility in women—eggs fertilized in this way can be implanted directly in a uterus which has been prepared for pregnancy.

US life scientists Max Delbruck, Salvador Luria and Alfred Hershey receive the Nobel Prize for Physiology and Medicine for their research on the bacteriophage (bacteria-destroying) group of viruses.

A yoghurt maker for home use is marketed.

Decomposable material, which is activated by ultraviolet light, may help the litter problem.

Two surgeons in Houston, Texas, perform the first total replacement of a human heart. Denton Cooley and Domingo Liotta implant an artificial heart in 47-year-old Haskell Karp. The mechanical device, known as an Orthotopic Cardiac Prosthesis, is made from Dacron and silastic—a silicone rubber compound. The four-chambered apparatus is attached by tubes to a nearby power source and keeps Karp alive for nearly 3 days.

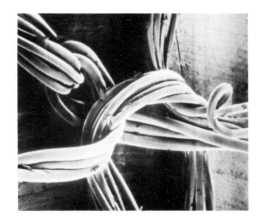

A magnified image of the fibres of a nylon stocking appears almost three-dimensional—captured by a unique scanning electron microscope which has taken almost 15 years to develop. Unlike the conventional electron microscope, which has achieved magnifications of over 1,000,000 ×, the Stereoscan has a maximum power of only 100,000 times. However, specimens to be examined by the former have to be sliced thinly to allow electrons to pass through them—producing an unsatisfactory, 'flat' image; this new device uses electrons to excite the specimens' own surface electrons, which are collected in order and reassembled to form an image.

COMMUNICATION, INFORMATION AND SPACE APPLICATIONS

Simultaneous transmission of two TV sound channels is pioneered in Japan. Using a Matsushita multiplex adaptor, an important movie can now be heard either in its original language or in Japanese.

Forerunner of the video disc systems of the eighties, the AEG Telefunken-Decca Teledec, demonstrated in West Berlin, gives excellent picture quality. The disc is a sheet of PVC 0.04 in (1 mm) thick, and the pick-up is a pressure-sensitive device driven mechanically over the minute grooves in the disc. Playing time is 5 mins for a 9-in (22.5-cm) disc and 12 mins for a 12-in (30-cm) disc.

Britain orders the largest computer in Europe to help improve her weather forecasting. The IBM System 360 Model 195 is designed to calculate the probable amount of rainfall up to a day ahead and to forecast up to a week ahead for the entire northern hemisphere.

Computer-controlled composing systems have broken into the printing trade worldwide. Used by a total of 1,200 companies, they consist of a single computer serving many keyboard inputs.

TRANSPORT, WARFARE AND SPACE EXPLORATION

RUM (Remote Underwater Manipulator), an American tracked vehicle which operates on the seabed under control from the surface, is tested. Equipped with TV cameras and a claw to bring back samples, RUM is operated, to a depth of 10,000 ft, by a coaxial cable from a platform.

Lasers improve bombing accuracy: US bombs, fitted with 'seeker apparatus', react to infrared energy in laser light beamed down by a controller plane and reflected from the target. Bombs guided by this 'echo' are used in Vietnam, with a reported 70% success rate.

A low-power laser beam directed at a tactical missile is seen to make the missile collapse in less than a second. As a result, the US Air Force plans to test a laser with radar direction as a defensive weapon against low-flying aircraft and missiles.

The Apollo 13 mission, dubbed a 'triumphant failure' and launched despite a rash of minor problems, almost costs the lives of its three crewmen when a massive explosion in the craft's oxygen tanks cripples it 200,000 mls (320,000 km) from Earth. After well-judged computation by technicians at Mission Control, the astronauts transfer to the lunar module, in which they return safely to Earth.

ENERGY AND INDUSTRY

Lucas of England make a significant improvement in the design of batteries by introducing polypropylene plastic as the battery's casing, in place of the heavy, traditional bitumastic container.

A furnace powered by the sun is completed at Odeillo-Font Romeu in the French Pyrenees. A parabolic reflector like a huge concave mirror, 130 ft (39.6 m) high by 175 ft (53.3 m) wide, concentrates the sun's energy on to an area 2 ft (0.6 m) in diameter. Sixty-three mirrors, called heliostats, track the sun and direct its rays into the parabolic reflector.

'Sialon', the strongest known ceramic material, which will be used in a high-speed cutting tool for machining metals, is developed by scientists working at the University of Newcastle in England. It is composed of the earth's most abundant elements—silicon, aluminium, oxygen and nitrogen.

MEDICINE AND FOOD PRODUCTION

In Boston, Arthur Herbst and colleagues report that daughters of women treated during pregnancy with diethyl-stilboestrol (to prevent spontaneous abortion), suffer a higher than average incidence of cancer of the vagina 15 years later.

G.W. Horn of Turin University develops an artificial leg which 'walks' up and down stairs. The knee locks and unlocks automatically, activated by electronic signals produced by the contraction of the amputee's remaining thigh muscles. The user wears a rechargeable 6 V battery power pack.

Har Gobind Khorana produces the first man-made gene—the basic unit of heredity—at the University of Wisconsin.

FRINGE BENEFITS

BEA join other major airlines in using computers to trace lost luggage.

The recently developed 'floppy-disc' recorder provides three times more storage space and much faster access than any other computer memory device on the market. Now integrated into IBM's 3740 system, it kills competition almost overnight and establishes an industry-wide standard.

Europe's first fully automatic system for measuring runway visibility is tested at Gatwick Airport, Sussex, England. Three stations along the runway measure the degree of illumination which is then passed over telephone wires—in digital form—to a computer in the control tower.

Marine radar acquires a memory. An auto-plotter, developed in Japan and incorporating a videotape, records the current position of any ship and its position a few minutes previously.

Flash photography is simplified by the Magicube, whose bulbs are fired mechanically, not electrically. A trigger on the camera releases a percussion device on each of the four bulbs in turn, so eliminating the need for a battery.

More accurate US weather-forecasting is promised with the launching of the ITOS 1 (Improved Tiros Operational Satellite 1) weather satellite, the first to relay data by day or night.

TV lasers are installed to monitor air pollution in the West German city of Duisberg. When a major source of smoke is picked up by the TV system, a laser-radar, or lidar (light detection and ranging), unit comes into play to measure the concentration of solid material over a range of 6¼ mls (10 km).

Japan and China become the fourth and fifth nations (after the USSR, USA and France) to launch satellites. The Chinese satellite weighs 382.5 lb (173 kg) and broadcasts the music of the song, 'The East is Red'.

The world's largest railway wagon is built for the Federal German Railways. Capable of carrying 530 tons on its 32 axles, the massive waggon can also move its load hydraulically nearly 2 ft (60 cm) to either side or 1½ ft (45 cm) vertically, to negotiate corners.

The highly successful moon robot, Lunokhod ('moon rover') 1, is landed by the Soviet spacecraft Luna 17. Lunokhod 1 consists of an instrument compartment mounted on an eight-wheel chassis. Each of the four pairs of wheels is powered by an electric motor, and sensors control automatic braking as the vehicle arrives at a dangerously steep slope.

'Nemo', the US Navy's acrylic 'bubble'—a submersible with an acrylic sphere large enough to accommodate two people—is tested. The crew winch it down a cable anchored to the seabed.

Soyuz 9, with a two-man crew aboard, sets a new record for the longest manned space flight as it spends nearly 18 days in space.

British Rail demonstrate the APT (advanced passenger train). Safe speeds of up to 155 mph (250 km/h) are planned on existing track, using a mechanism which tilts the body of the train inward as it hurtles round bends. But on its first real run in 1982, passengers report slight sensations of motion sickness as the train takes the bends; and failure to iron out the technical problems causes the project to be postponed.

Liquid explosives are used for fracturing underground oil- and gas-bearing rock formations. Developed by the Explosives Corp of America, the explosives are successfully tested in Texas and Louisiana. On detonation, shock waves crack the rocks, improving the permeability, and therefore the productivity, of a well. The hope is that they will break up the stubborn shales from such fields as the Peceance Basin in Colorado, which could yield as many as 160,000 million barrels of oil.

Carbon dioxide lasers become a new tool for cutting and welding, and are the only type so far capable of giving the necessary continuous power to cut metals, wood, plastics, paper and cloth. In 1973 John Collier, the English clothing manufacturer and retailer, will use the first computer-controlled laser to cut layers of cloth to make suits and other garments.

A large reinforced concrete solar still is built at the Shafrikan collective farm, Bukhere Oblast, in Russia. It distils and purifies local water, which is high in minerals and sulphur, by evaporation at a rate of about 540 gallons (2,455 l) a day.

Harmful effects of the contraceptive pill, such as raised blood pressure and thrombosis, are becoming more evident. A year after British doctors become more wary of prescribing it, the US Food and Drug Administration warns that the pill can cause blood-clots.

L-dopa therapy, pioneered by Greek-American neurologist George Cotzias, brings dramatic relief to patients with Parkinson's disease. L-dopa counters the lack of dopamine in the brain, which causes the characteristic tremor.

Surgeon Michael Hackett determines the extent of damage in burn victims. By using an infrared scanning camera, he gets a complete picture in 10 minutes. Since destroyed tissue is 3° cooler than living tissue, he can tell which burns are only partial, and will heal by themselves, and which will require skin grafts.

London sees the launch of the first fully automatic navigational buoy, powered by a diesel generator.

Mediator, a computer-assisted system, helps air traffic controllers monitor the crowded skies.

Boeing 747s—soon nicknamed 'Jumbo Jets'—go into service on the North Atlantic route. The wide-bodied jet, developed in reponse to a huge increase in air passenger traffic during the sixties, has a fuselage big enough to have contained the Wright Brothers' first flight, and its engines burn one gallon (4.5 l) of fuel in less than 2 secs. The spacious 747 interior, *left*, can accommodate nearly 500 passengers, with room for a 16-seat 'penthouse' suite above the main cabin and behind the flight deck. In 1974, a Jumbo will airlift a record 674 people to safety, following a hurricane in Darwin, Northern Australia.

COMMUNICATION, INFORMATION AND SPACE APPLICATIONS

A portable hologram camera is developed by the Hughes Aircraft Co in the USA. The camera, to be used initially to test the performance of aircraft wings, uses a form of lensless photography. The object is illuminated by laser lights and a 3–D image captured on a highly sensitive photographic plate.

Eighty per cent of the 2½ million electronic calculators sold around the world are made in Japan. US interest is slow to develop, but the British market picks up, following the decimalization of the currency.

London's Heathrow airport becomes the first airport in the world to computerize the control of incoming cargo.

'Big Bird', a new type of US military reconnaissance satellite, is launched by Titan IIID rocket. This 50-ft (15.2-m) craft contains a camera able to define 1-ft (30-cm) objects from a height of 100 mls (161 km).

TRANSPORT, WARFARE AND SPACE EXPLORATION

The USA mounts a pair of successful manned Apollo moon missions. In Apollo 14, Alan Shepard—America's first man in space—leads his crew through a host of minor technical problems. Using a small handcart they collect 20 lb (9 kg) of soil and rocks. Apollo 15 astronauts benefit greatly from the Lunar Rover, the first lunar car, in which they travel a total of 45 mls (28 km) and collect 35 lb (16 kg) of rock samples.

The crew of Soyuz 11 set a new duration record as they spend nearly 24 days in space, but perish on re-entry to the Earth's atmosphere when an air valve on their spacecraft fails, causing fatal decompression.

Electric cars driven by Frankfurt automobile magnate Dr George von Opel, set six new world records for electrically-propelled vehicles. Dr von Opel proves that electric power does not necessarily result in low-speed, low-performance cars when he reaches 118 mph (188.6 km/h) over 1,100 yds (1 km) from a flying start.

ENERGY AND INDUSTRY

US scientists demonstrate the first motor to be powered by the electric field in the atmosphere. The motor produces less than a millionth of a horse power, but with suitable technology for tapping the Earth's electric field, it could become a supplementary source of power. On a clear day the atmosphere above 1 sq ml (2.59 sq km) of the Earth's surface has enough energy to light a 100 W bulb for 30 secs—electric storms would run 500 such bulbs for over a year.

The first nuclear power station in the world to be cooled by ordinary water begins to generate electricity. Fuelled with natural uranium, the Gantilly power station on the St Lawrence River in Canada promises cheaper nuclear reactors by getting away from the dependence on costly heavy water as a coolant.

The world's first solid state meter for measuring bulk supplies of electricity is introduced by Landis & Gyr. A digital electronic instrument, it is more accurate and reliable than earlier electromagnetic meters.

MEDICINE AND FOOD PRODUCTION

Britain's Royal College of Physicians claims that cigarette smoking causes as many deaths as the great 19th-century epidemic diseases such as typhoid and cholera.

The treatment of pituitary dwarfism in children becomes simpler and cheaper when Choh Hao Li, a Chinese chemist working at the University of California, synthesizes the all-important growth hormone, somatotrophin.

The challenge of microsurgery requires the cooperation of eye surgeons, diamond-cutters, metallurgists and optical instrument makers. The first product of the British Microsurgical Instrumentation Research Association is the diamond-bladed scalpel. Developed for eye surgeons, it is expected to play a role, too, in neurosurgery.

FRINGE BENEFITS

The Wylfa nuclear power station on Anglesey, North Wales, becomes operational. Wylfa is the first nuclear power plant to generate electricity under the control of a central computer. The eighth, and last, first-generation Magnox station to be built, Wylfa is also unique in its fuel storage system, in which irradiated fuel is stacked in air-cooled tubes filled with dry carbon dioxide.

Residents of parts of New York and London can now dial each other direct. The telephone signals travel by wire to exchanges in New Jersey and Cornwall in Britain, from where they are beamed over the Atlantic by satellite.

Kodak XL movie cameras, equipped with such refinements as aperture lenses and faster films, make indoor home movies possible with domestic lighting.

Illiac IV, a machine consisting of a battery of 64 'slave' computers and developed at the University of Illinois, can handle 200 million instructions a second.

The microprocessor, the world's first 'computer on a chip' is introduced by Intel of California. A miniature integrated circuit, contained on a single silicon chip a few millimeters square, can perform calculations previously worked out slowly and expensively by massive machines. Its potential in telecommunications, medical diagnosis, analysis and instrument control is enormous and the microchip will completely change the face of world industry.

Prospero, a British-built research satellite, is launched by the Black Arrow rocket from the Australian site at Woomera.

Mariner 9 is the first spacecraft to orbit another planet. After a 167-day flight, the US craft begins a thorough programme of mapping the Martian surface. The most ferocious dust storm to occur on Mars since 1924 is observed by the craft before it transmits 7,329 TV pictures to Earth.

French SSBS (*Sol-Sol Balistique-Stratégique*) S–2 missiles become operational. The medium-range nuclear missiles are launched from two groups of underground silos in the Haute Provence region.

The US Air Pollution Control Office (APCO) favours the gas turbine engine for the 'clean car' of the future. APCO has found, after studying proposals submitted by a number of US firms, that gas turbine engines—despite having a high fuel consumption—are the cheapest alternative to the internal combustion engine. APCO's enthusiasm is dampened by scientists, who point out that a gas turbine engine emits unacceptably large quantities of nitrous oxide gas.

Glass makes its début in a submersible when it is used to form the viewing hemisphere in the bow of the US Navy's research vessel *Deep View*. Powered by electric motors, the craft can operate to a depth of 1,500 ft (457 m).

The world's first large-scale plant for generating electricity by magnetohydrodynamics (MHD) is completed in Russia. The process converts thermal energy directly into electricity without using turbines. The plant, called the U25, is the successful culmination of the Soviet MHD programme, which was first started in 1960 (the process was first achieved in England in 1964).

Water is commercially applied as a quality cutting tool for the first time in a factory which produces contoured furniture. Pioneered by the McCartney Manufacturing Co, USA, water-jet cutting will spread to shoe manufacture, sweet-making, car production and even the cutting up of fish fingers.

A new 'wonder material', glass-reinforced cement, is invented by the Building Research Establishment in England as a lightweight alternative to concrete, and also as a fireproof, asbestos-free alternative to plastic. It will be used to make boats, garden furniture and hi-fi turntables; until it is known whether it can stand the test of time, the material will also be used to clad buildings, such as the Crédit Lyonnais headquarters in London, but not to construct them.

Research at the University of Pennsylvania Medical School shows that the healing of fractures can be speeded up by passing a low-voltage electric current through the affected bone.

At London's Middlesex Hospital, a new sterile unit is introduced to protect patients especially at risk from infection. First of its kind in the world, the unit comprises a suite of sterile rooms rapidly built from prefabricated plywood panels. Cheaply installed, it offers a sterile environment in which the patient can easily be nursed.

Researchers at the Anderson Tumor Institute in Texas isolate the herpes (cold sore) virus from the lymph-cell cancer known as Burkitt's lymphoma; it is already associated with the early stages of cervical cancer.

A full honours degree course, broadcast on the BBC, is offered by the Open University.

The Victoria line opens, extending London's Underground service. It is the first fully automatic passenger railway in Britain. Train speeds and scheduled stops are controlled electronically, and the driver's tasks are limited to monitoring the train's functioning, opening and closing the doors, and pressing a button to set the train in motion—as well as being on hand to deal with emergencies.

191

COMMUNICATION, INFORMATION AND SPACE APPLICATIONS

Landsat 1, the first of a series of Earth resources technology satellites for the seventies, is launched by NASA. It photographs the Earth's surface, providing data that will aid agriculture and the search for natural resources.

Using electron scan technology, developed by IBM, 100,000 transistors will soon be squeezed on to a single silicon chip only a few millimetres square. As a direct result of this dramatic reduction in the size of integrated circuits, cheaper, more efficient electronic gadgets will be available by the middle of the decade.

Digital TV, which transmits the sound signal within the picture signal, not separately, is introduced by the BBC. The technique cuts the cost and complexity of transmission and maintains high-quality sound over long distances.

TRANSPORT, WARFARE AND SPACE EXPLORATION

The ambitious Pioneer 10 spacecraft is launched from Cape Kennedy on a journey which will take it past Mars, through the Asteroid Belt, and beyond Jupiter. Travelling at 32,375 mph (51,800 km/h)—faster than any previous man-made craft—it reaches the moon in just over 11 hrs. Pioneer 10 will reach Jupiter late in 1973 and send back an immense amount of data. In 1976 it will cross Saturn's orbit and is expected to leave our solar system in 1987.

Apollo 16, the fifth US manned moon mission, brings back almost 43 lb 9 oz (20 kg) of rock samples and establishes the first lunar astronomical observatory.

HMS 'Wilton', the world's first 'plastic' warship, is launched at Woolston, Southampton. The ship's hull is constructed from glass-reinforced plastic to test the potential of the material for warships, such as mine countermeasure vessels, in which non-magnetic qualities are vital.

The heaviest and most complex unmanned non-military spacecraft to date is launched by the USA. Copernicus, the third in a series of Orbiting Astronomical Observatories, returns data on stellar phenomena.

ENERGY AND INDUSTRY

For the first time, central heating systems can be adjusted immediately, according to the size of the house and the needs of the moment, when Matsushita Electric and the Osaka Industrial Research Institute of Japan introduce the ultrasonic kerosene burner. Inaudible to the human ear, ultrasonics are used to atomize kerosene at the burner nozzle, while air is forced into the burner for better combustion.

An experimental coal-fired power station is opened at Lunen, Germany, in an attempt to increase the efficiency of generating electricity by gasifying coal. The present output will be vastly increased by new turbine blades, which are being developed to withstand temperatures of 1,832°F (1,000°C). Once installed, they will enable this gas and steam turbine power station to compete with oil- and nuclear-powered stations.

MEDICINE AND FOOD PRODUCTION

US surgeon Irving Cooper offers epileptics the chance of a normal life. Platinum electrodes implanted in the cerebellum—the centre of voluntary muscle control—receive radio signals which relieve spasticity, paralysis or seizures. The 'brain pacemaker' is powered by a low-voltage battery worn around the waist.

For some time there have been indications that multiple sclerosis is caused by a virus, but no firm evidence of this has come to light. Now, at Sydney University, John Prineas finds that nerve cells examined in the early stages of the disease are packed with what seem to be virus particles, similar to those implicated in measles.

FRINGE BENEFITS

Anti-glare goggles to protect metal workers' eyes from over-bright light are developed by Sandia Laboratories, New Mexico.

CEEFAX, the BBC's 'electronic book' information service, is announced. Subscribers, whose TV sets have to be fitted with decoders, will have instant access to up-to-the-minute data by punching the appropriate 'page' numbers on a keypad. News, weather and stock market prices will figure prominently in the early days of the service, with other data pages being added quickly according to demand. The service will be fully operational in two years.

Computers turn to the problem of job finding. In both the USA and Britain, computer job banks are being used to update print-outs of vacancies. The initial publicity leads to an increase in jobs offered, and speeds the listing and filling of posts.

Kodak pocket Instamatic cameras bring cartridge loading to subminiature photography. Small, easily pocketable cameras are loaded with drop-in cartridges containing high-definition colour film. The popularity of the cameras is boosted by the availability of high-quality processing and printing services for the small negatives.

Philips, the Dutch electrical giant, develop VLP—a video LP disc and recorder—to compete with the video cassette. There are two types of 12-in (30-cm) disc both of which have a grooveless mirror-like surface and, using a laser light source, can be played back on a Philips recorder through a normal TV set. One disc can record a 30-min broadcast on each side and freeze any frame. The other runs for an hour each side but has no freeze-frame facility. However, the system, called LaserVision, will not be marketed for several years.

Assembly line workers producing complex items of communications equipment can work more efficiently now they are supplied with audio instructions, generated by computer and relayed via earphones.

Apollo 17, the last of the US exploratory manned moon missions, is a resounding success. The crew includes a trained geologist who is one of two astronauts who spend a record 7 hrs 37 mins outside the lunar module in one of three long working sessions on the moon's surface. Carrying 50 lb 14 oz (23 kg) of moon rocks, the crew safely concludes the longest ever manned space flight of 1,494,365 mls (2,390,984 km).

Lance, a surface-to-surface battlefield support missile, goes into service with the US Army, to replace the Honest John and Sergeant missile systems. Lance is the first US Army missile to use ready-packaged and stored liquid propellant. Later models will use DME (Distance Measuring Equipment) for increased accuracy over the missile's 75-ml (120-km) range. Eventually a laser-homing system will be fitted to the Lance warhead.

The astounding growth in tanker size reaches a new high with the launch of the *Globtik Tokyo*, a 483,644-ton tanker nearly ¾ ml (1,207 m) long—a far cry from the *Glaukauf* of 1886, a 2,307-ton prototype of the modern tanker. A steam turbine, geared to a single propeller shaft, gives a speed of 14 knots. Machinery control is fully automated and only two watch engineers are required to be on duty in the control room.

The new sodium sulphur battery—invented by the Ford Motor Co in 1967—is used to power an 18-cwt (914-kg) Bedford delivery truck. Developed by the Electricity Research Council Centre in Britain, the truck has a range of 62 mls (100 km) and promises to be the prototype of short-distance electric vehicles.

The world's first manned submersible oil rig to be made mainly from glass-reinforced plastics is built by Slingsby Engineering in Britain.

Experiments based on the life of plants lead scientists in the USA and the USSR to claim that they can produce electricity from sunlight by photosynthesis. By putting the green pigment, chlorophyll, into a solar cell, M. Calvin and H. Tributsch in the USA obtain minute amounts of electricity from solar energy. They optimistically forecast a time—20–30 years in the future—when these devices could become commercially viable.

The British-designed EMI brainscanner is introduced to give cross-sectional X-rays compiled from views taken all around the brain. The technique, called computerized axial tomography (CAT), reveals structural abnormalities—tumours, haemorrhages and swellings—within the brain.

The use of DDT is restricted in the USA while other countries have already banned it. Although DDT does no proven damage to humans, birds and fish, they can suffer behavioural damage—salmon, for example, lose the ability to migrate. DDT will still be used in the developing world because the World Health Organization consider its benefits outweigh its drawbacks.

An electronic lock and key system based on plastic ID cards is used in high-security buildings.

Turn on, tune in, fade out with a sound meter which cuts musical instruments' power when the noise is too loud.

Intelsat IV-F5 is launched, carried by an Atlas-Centaur rocket. To be stationed at a height of about 22,300 mls (35,600 km) over the Indian Ocean, this new communications satellite will provide between 3,000 and 9,000 telephone circuits or 12 TV channels for the 83 nations who are members of the Intelsat organization.

The first single lens instant camera comes on to the market. The fold-up Polaroid SX-70 uses a new kind of film that develops outside the camera and leaves no residue. Instant cameras will shortly become almost as versatile and as fully automated as their more conventional rivals.

The eye in the sky

In May 1963, American astronaut Gordon Cooper announced from his Mercury spacecraft more than 100 miles (161 km) above the Earth that he could distinguish roads, buildings and even chimney smoke from the planet below. Incredulous ground staff accused him of hallucinating. However, excellent pictures taken during subsequent US space missions verified Cooper's claim, and the immense interest they aroused prompted NASA to build a series of Landsat satellites to observe the surface of the Earth.

The first of these satellites, Landsat 1, was launched by NASA in July 1972. Since then, a vast amount of beneficial knowledge has been relayed to Earth by this craft and its two successors. Remote mountain ranges have been accurately mapped and surveyed for the first time. Fishermen have been immeasurably helped by the pinpointing of ocean areas likely to yield good catches. The lives of sailors have been saved by advance warning of impending hurricanes and typhoons.

Earth's surface has also been photographed and studied, with valuable results, by the crews

Off the Florida coast, a huge storm brews. Pictures taken from space, such as this one snapped by the crew of Apollo 8, have increased our understanding of the world's weather. Since the sixties, meteorological satellites have, for example, monitored cloud and snow cover, and air temperatures.

of Soviet and US orbiting space stations; but the Landsat surveys have been particularly useful because their coverage has been both comprehensive and repetitive. Each satellite—about 953 kg (2,100 lb) in weight, and 10 ft (3.05 m) in height—has relayed a continuous stream of information to receiving stations on Earth from a height of 570 miles (917 km), in the course of 14 orbits a day.

Landsats have sent back two sorts of images: television-like pictures, and infrared images which have revealed much information impossible to glean with the naked eye. Everything on Earth, whether living or not, absorbs and reflects infrared heat energy from the sun, and global features such as soil, rocks and vegetation can thus be distinguished by the infrared signals they emit. Scanners on the Landsat spacecraft print these variations in different colours to produce infrared images.

Since infrared paints clear pictures distinguishing between healthy crops, which show up pink or red, and blighted ones of a blackish grey shade, infrared images provide a wealth of agricultural data. And because a plant's infrared signal changes with disease long before that disease is outwardly visible, such images can give advance warning of disaster. The satellite pictures have also made it possible to differentiate crops, and so assess potential yields. In the space of 49 hours, 25 crops were, for example, identified in 8,865 Californian fields. Such monitoring could

eventually lead to a realistic global food policy to avert both famine and over-production.

As NASA builds its fourth Landsat, due for launch before the end of 1983 and designed to provide more detailed pictures than ever before, the recruiting of satellites to monitor man's use—and abuse—of the planet becomes ever more feasible. In Brazil, for example, where forest is being cleared for agricultural development, Landsat images have already

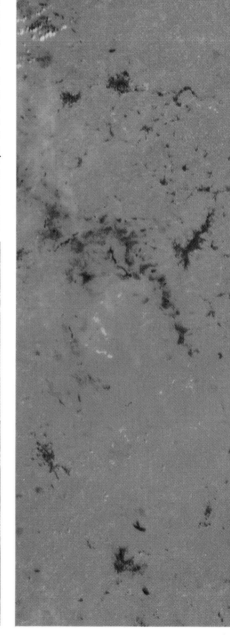

proved to be the only effective way of deterring infringements in the law limiting the amount of forest that can be felled.

In the future, satellites could also be used to police the sea. Captains whose oil tankers spill slicks in coastal waters may soon be swiftly apprehended. Techniques for distinguishing the type and amount of oil spilt are improving so fast that tankers will soon be identifiable by their oily trails.

Three-quarters of the Earth's total reserves of fresh water are stored as snow and ice. Aided by satellite images the water supplies for many areas can be predicted by assessing the winter snow cover. The Sierra Nevada mountains of North America, *below*, were conspicuously bare in the late winter of 1977—a drought year. Satellite photography has also helped map-making enormously. Only about half the world's landmass has been adequately mapped: now, new maps can be prepared twice as fast as by traditional modes.

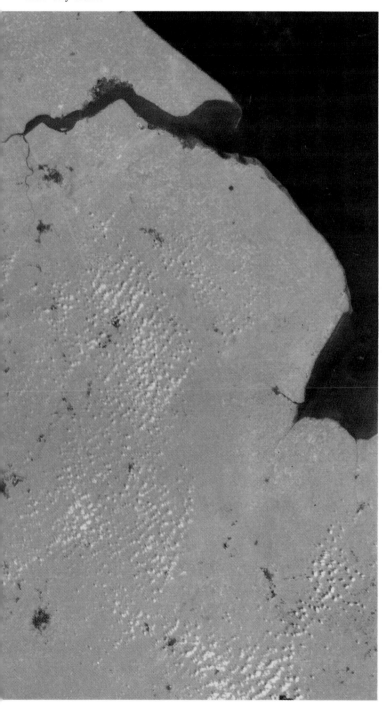

The area of England shown in the Landsat picture is indicated by the shaded rectangle, *left*. Individual photographic frames cover about 115 sq mls (185 sq km). A Landsat can map the whole Earth in 18 days.

Healthy, green vegetation shown in red, predominates in this infrared picture of North East England taken by Landsat 1 in 1973. Blue-black areas mark towns and cities such as Hull on the north bank of the River Humber. Using computers, satellite images can be analyzed within a few days to provide assessments of crop distribution with a 90 per cent accuracy.

COMMUNICATION, INFORMATION AND SPACE APPLICATIONS

In direct competition with the BBC's CEEFAX system, ITV in Britain demonstrates its ORACLE service of news, weather, sports, traffic and financial information. Next year, the BBC and ITV will agree a standard so that, using the same decoder, both CEEFAX and ORACLE can be seen on the same TV set.

The image intensifier, a TV camera tube which produces good outdoor pictures when illuminated only by the stars and moon, is developed in West Germany. The device will prove useful in industry, medicine, traffic control and in scientific research—especially in the study of nocturnal animals.

Duplicating in colour is possible with the new generation of photocopiers. The machines can produce colour reproductions on either plain paper or transparencies for projection.

TRANSPORT, WARFARE AND SPACE EXPLORATION

A British prototype high-speed train travels at 143 mph (230 km/h), setting a world speed record for diesel-electric railway traction. The key to such speed is the engine arrangement: there are two of them, one at each end of the train.

The heat pipe—a British invention—offers one solution to the problem of cleaning up car exhaust fumes, whose noxiousness is largely due to imperfect fuel combustion. A pipe in the engine, heated by the car's exhaust system, ensures that the fuel is fully vapourized; this allows the engine to run on a ratio of fuel to air which produces less carbon monoxide and other gaseous pollutants. The system also decreases fuel consumption, but at the expense of a 30% loss in power.

America's public transport system, badly neglected in the post-war years, shoots into the future with the opening of BART—San Francisco's Bay Area Rapid Transit System. The electric trains and fare collection are both fully automated. An automatic gate records the start of a journey on a passenger's magnetic ticket, which is marked with the amount paid. At journey's end, a second gate subtracts the correct fare, printing the credit sum on the ticket. However, the system suffers from teething problems—in the next two years, one third of the 30 trains will be returned to the repair yards each day.

ENERGY AND INDUSTRY

A new building material, which is five times stronger than concrete and twice as effective as an insulator, is announced by England's Cranfield Institute of Technology. Made from the pulverized fuel ash from power stations, this cheap type of ceramic is impermeable and its attractive surface can be glazed in a number of colours.

Shoes, furnishings and floor coverings are just some of the items which will now be made from 'Cambrelle', the first of a new range of melded fabrics to be made commercially. Developed by ICI, melding involves bonding together different fibres without knitting or weaving them. A heavy-duty fabric known as 'Terram' will also be produced by ICI for such civil engineering uses as the stabilizing of soil.

The world's first truly self-sufficient house is built near Cambridge, England. It receives electricity generated by windmills, makes gas from sewage and refuse, obtains water from a rain tank, and is heated by solar power.

MEDICINE AND FOOD PRODUCTION

Doctors in Helsinki use radio immuno-assay to test for spina bifida in the unborn foetus. Using the technique of amniocentesis to tap off a sample of amniotic fluid from the pregnant womb, they test for the tell-tale protein which indicates the presence of this serious congenital disorder.

Widespread outbreaks of a serious pig disease, swine vesicular fever, show how viruses can change and mutate. British and US scientists trace SVF back to a fairly mild virus, Coxsackie B5, occurring in the human gut. In its new guise, the virus is responsible for a serious, highly contagious disease which can still infect human beings.

FRINGE BENEFITS

The easy-to-use hexagonal screwdriver works from any angle.

A tiny, diver's device calculates how much time must be spent in resurfacing to avoid the bends.

The Hydragas suspension of the Austin Allegro, British Leyland's new car, gives smoother driving. At each wheel, instead of solid rubber springs there are flexible rubber units containing pressurized nitrogen. Front and rear systems are also connected so that if one goes over a bump this also compresses the other—avoiding uncomfortable bumping.

Computer-coded labels are introduced into supermarkets to speed the changeover to electronic cash registers. The cashier simply passes a scanner over the label on each product and the price is extracted from a computer memory.

A miniature microphone, which plugs directly into the ear and makes for inconspicuous communications, is developed by Naval Electronics of California. TEAM (tube earphone and microphone) makes TV interviews easier and allows a privacy of conversation welcomed by police forces.

A do-it-yourself calculator is marketed in Britain by Sinclair, Europe's largest pocket calculator manufacturer. The 'Cambridge' runs on four cheap batteries and takes only $2\frac{1}{2}$ hrs to assemble.

The USSR aims to monitor its complete economy by computer. Emphasizing improved efficiency rather than greater productivity, the Soviet Government plans to introduce 930 computerized management systems into business, and install new equipment in 2,000 computer centres.

Britain's Independent Commission on Transport estimates that, in terms of energy consumed, the bicycle is by far the most efficient means of transport. Using a unit of 'passenger-mile per gallon of petrol equivalent', the Commission finds that whereas a bicycle will travel 1,650 mls (2,640 km) on one such gallon, and a person on foot 370 mls (592 km); someone sharing an average British car with three others will manage only 27 mls (43 km).

London's ambitious motorway programme is scrapped. The newly elected Labour Greater London Council want the £2 billion earmarked for the scheme to be used to fund better public transport in the city.

Trucks carrying supplies to oil workers in Alaska are supported by large inflated rubber bags instead of conventional wheels and tyres. The Rolligon lorry averages 10.6 mph (17 km/h) over a gruelling $687\frac{1}{2}$-ml (1,100-km) Alaskan journey, and is equally at home on powder snow and frozen rivers. It also performs well when exported to the shifting sands of Saudi Arabia.

France's first automatic Personal Rapid Transit System is developed for the city of Lille. Rubber-tyred unmanned railway cars carrying up to 33 seated and 16 standing passengers will run at up to 50 mph (80 km/h) over a 5-ml (8-km) track.

Skylab, the massive 77-ton orbiting US space station, is launched.

France enters the modern nuclear age as her first fast reactor, the Phénix, begins to generate power and breed its own plutonium fuel.

Superheated steam from volcanic rock drives the turbines of a new power station in eastern Russia. Its output of electrical energy is small, but it is seen as a forerunner of other such stations, which would not only be powered by this inexhaustible supply but would also reduce the menace of the 30 volcanoes in Kamchatka.

The steel firm Dorman Long design a revolutionary drilling rig for use in the North Sea oil fields. Constructed from both steel and concrete, it is quick to assemble, considerably cheaper than any other design and can operate to depths of 600 ft (183 m).

Electricity generated by ocean waves looks a stronger possibility when Stephen Salter of Edinburgh University invents a wave power machine. Known as the 'nodding boom' machine, it consists of a number of floats, called Salter Ducks, which nod up and down when a wave passes. It is the most efficient machine for extracting wave power yet devised: 1,000 Ducks stretching for 19 mls (30 km) would supply a twelfth of Britain's power needs.

Scientists at Aberdeen University, led by Professor John Malland, usher in a whole new generation of diagnostic equipment. The nuclear magnetic resonator (NMR) subjects living tissue to a magnetic field, measures the changes in radio wave absorption—which differ between healthy and diseased tissue—and analyzes the results by computer.

Researchers at the University College of Wales demonstrate that communications through the corpus callosum—the bundle of nervous tissue linking the two hemispheres of the brain—are defective in schizophrenics.

Push-through tabs on cans save litter and resources.

Forensic scientists may now catch crooks by using a computer that matches slivers of glass.

IBM introduce a new range of Selectric self-correcting typewriters. These machines are much quieter than their predecessors and have an expanded 96-character keyboard which is ergonomically designed to make typing more efficient. The larger keys have also been textured so as to reduce glare—a common problem in brightly lit offices.

Construction begins on a massive barrier across the River Thames at Woolwich intended to protect London from the increasing threat of floods. Contracted to the Davy Cleveland Barrier Consortium, the revolutionary design incorporates 10 gates installed between nine concrete piers and abutments on each bank. Six 10,000-ton sills (concrete slabs to give support and prevent erosion) will be lowered to the river bed between the seven central piers. Due to be completed by 1982, difficulties arising from the installation of the pivoting gates—lying far enough below the water line, when lowered, to allow a normal flow of shipping—will prevent the flood barrier from being operative until 1983 at the earliest.

Engineering life

In his wildest dreams, man has yearned to breed new and wonderful organisms to solve his food and energy problems, or to change his own and other species for the better. Now those dreams of playing God may have come true. If they have, it is largely because of the way in which genetics—the science of heredity—has evolved from a descriptive into a technological discipline. Using theoretical knowledge of genetics, coupled with agricultural and industrial expertise, man can now not only change the living world through selective breeding programmes, but has also begun to master the skills of genetic engineering.

From the earliest days of agriculture, man has used the fact that 'like begets like' to breed food plants and domestic animals selectively. Even 9,000 years ago, a farmer probably collected seed for next year's crops from the most productive seed heads of the current year, while the healthiest, fattest animals were saved from the cooking pot and used to be parents of the next generation. If any of the desirable traits were inherited, that is, programmed into the organisms by genes, then such selective breeding led to genetic improvement.

Modern agricultural techniques of breeding are based on exactly the same principles. The great difference is that today's plant and animal breeders, because they have a deep insight into genetic mechanisms, can work with greater accuracy. Given this, and the access to vast stocks of organisms, each with a different genetic make-up, plant and animal breeders can in time produce organisms with almost any mix of characteristics.

This availability of the widest possible range of parent stocks has been a major factor in the green revolution, which has dramatically increased the yields of staples such as wheat, potatoes and rice. In a potato breeding programme it might be, for example, that a small Andean strain with a nasty taste had a genetically endowed resistance to a viral or fungal infection crucial to the success of a new strain. A properly designed series of crosses could insert the Andean resistance gene into a new, tasty, high-yield type.

In their eagerness to produce disease-free stock, or new combinations of characters, geneticists have begun to devise short cuts to bypass the time-consuming business of sexual reproduction. In meristematic tissue culture, for example, small clumps of cells are taken from the growing tips of selected plants and grown in a nutrient mixture until they produce whole new plants. These plants are generally free of virus disease and are identical in genetic composition to the plants from which they came. In cell fusion technology, two cells are literally made into one, then grown to make hybrids which combine the characters of the two different parents.

Generations of trial and error may be needed by these Nepalese farmers to obtain a better strain of rice. But using scientific methods, breeders in the Philippines produced a 'miracle' rice with double the normal yield in just three years.

French Charolais cattle grow quickly and produce lean, tender meat. After artificial insemination of Charolais semen began in Britain in 1962, these qualities have been passed on to improve the world's beef and dairy herds.

It is the desire to change the genetic make-up of an animal, plant or micro-organism without using conventional breeding methods which explains much of the current boom in genetic engineering. The main commercial thrust in this field involves attempts to convert single-celled bacteria or yeasts into production units for medically useful proteins which normally have to be laboriously extracted from natural sources—and with minute yields. Two good examples are the anti-virus protein interferon, which may also help fight cancer, and the hormone insulin whose lack leads to diabetes. The genes that direct the manufacture of these molecules in man can now be identified and extracted from human cells then inserted into the genes of a chosen micro-organism. All the offspring of this organism will then have a new synthetic capacity.

Similar techniques will eventually be used to adjust the genetics of man's food-producing animals and plants. The scientific step to tampering with human genes will then be, technically at least, a small one.

Human cells invaded by viruses produce minute amounts of interferon, a protein that is not only effective in fighting viruses but may also be one key to curing cancer. Genetic engineers have devised means of making interferon by factory methods. The gene for interferon production is removed from a human chromosome then inserted into a bacterium which acquires the ability to make interferon. The diagrams *below* describe in a simplified way the steps by which a genetic engineer carries out these changes. The DNA (deoxyribonucleic acid) from which human genes are constructed is extracted from human cells and chopped into pieces with a 'restriction endonuclease' enzyme which cuts the DNA at specific points. The resulting fragments have 'sticky' ends, here coloured red and green, which are eager to join up with each other. One of these DNA fragments contains the interferon gene and is ready for the next step in the process.

The portion of bacterial DNA into which the interferon gene will be inserted is known as a plasmid. It contains genes which confer immunity to two antibiotics: ampicillin (hatched) and tetracycline (stippled). The same enzyme used to cut up human DNA now splits the plasmid in the centre of the tetracycline-resistance gene. Bacteria with recombined plasmids can later be identified since they are resistant to ampicillin but are killed by tetracycline.

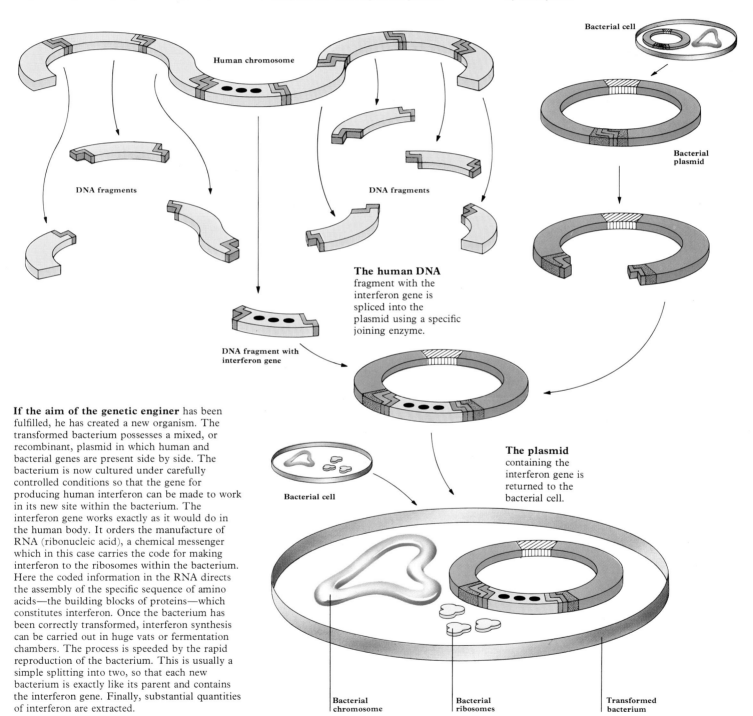

Human chromosome

DNA fragments

DNA fragments

Bacterial cell

Bacterial plasmid

The human DNA fragment with the interferon gene is spliced into the plasmid using a specific joining enzyme.

DNA fragment with interferon gene

If the aim of the genetic enginer has been fulfilled, he has created a new organism. The transformed bacterium possesses a mixed, or recombinant, plasmid in which human and bacterial genes are present side by side. The bacterium is now cultured under carefully controlled conditions so that the gene for producing human interferon can be made to work in its new site within the bacterium. The interferon gene works exactly as it would do in the human body. It orders the manufacture of RNA (ribonucleic acid), a chemical messenger which in this case carries the code for making interferon to the ribosomes within the bacterium. Here the coded information in the RNA directs the assembly of the specific sequence of amino acids—the building blocks of proteins—which constitutes interferon. Once the bacterium has been correctly transformed, interferon synthesis can be carried out in huge vats or fermentation chambers. The process is speeded by the rapid reproduction of the bacterium. This is usually a simple splitting into two, so that each new bacterium is exactly like its parent and contains the interferon gene. Finally, substantial quantities of interferon are extracted.

Bacterial cell

The plasmid containing the interferon gene is returned to the bacterial cell.

Bacterial chromosome

Bacterial ribosomes

Transformed bacterium

COMMUNICATION, INFORMATION AND SPACE APPLICATIONS

A mini tape-recorder, designed by the CIA and small enough to fit into a cigarette pack, is marketed to British detectives. Equipped with a self-contained speaker and microphone, it can pick up conversations from across a room, even if hidden inside a pocket.

The visual synthesizer, the colour TV equivalent of synthesized electronic music, is produced by Electronic Music Studios in the USA and creates continually moving video graphics which can change in size and colour.

The push-button telephone makes its British début. Although initially no faster than the conventional dial model, the keyphone is designed to suit the high-speed electronic telephone exchanges that are soon to be introduced.

NASA launches ATS–6, a direct broadcast TV satellite carrying a powerful TV relay. The first satellite to link remote communities in the USA, this experimental model is later moved to a position over Lake Victoria on the borders of Kenya and Tanzania. From here, it broadcasts educational material on hygiene and agriculture to village communities in India where there are no other means of receiving TV or other telecommunications services.

TRANSPORT, WARFARE AND SPACE EXPLORATION

A bicycle tyre that gives a ride as comfortable as a pneumatic tyre, without the drawback of punctures, is introduced in Britain by Raleigh. The Cairfree is made from 80% natural rubber.

Russia plans to build a new trans-Siberian railway, north of the existing one, to aid development of Eastern Siberia's rich natural resources. Aiming for completion in 1983, the railway will have to be laid across mountain peaks, volcanically active zones and thousands of miles of permafrost.

A research vehicle, run on the US Department of Transportation's test tracks, breaks the world rail speed record as it reaches 255 mph (410 km/h).

ENERGY AND INDUSTRY

The tallest building in the world opens in downtown Toronto. The restaurant at the top of the Toronto communications tower is more than a third of a mile (over 0.5 km) from the ground and on a clear day affords views of distances up to 75 mls (120 km).

A better technique of making optical glass fibres for the telecommunications industry is patented by John MacChesney and Paul O'Connor of the Bell Laboratories, USA. They considerably reduce the amount of impurities in the glass, and this means that telephone calls, relayed along the fibres, do not need to be amplified every few miles.

MEDICINE AND FOOD PRODUCTION

Genetic engineering involves inserting the genes from one cell into the nucleus of another. This fusion of the two, possibly unrelated, organisms could have many applications in medicine. But it could also invite wholesale disaster, such as accidental creation of resistant bacteria, which might cause diseases with no known cure. The National Academy of Sciences in the USA calls a halt to research in genetic engineering until safer techniques are developed.

Some transplant surgeons foresee an end to rejection problems by way of 'anti-antibodies'. These are chemical substances which 'police' the antibodies present in the body, so controlling the response to any foreign elements. Now, doctors at Britain's McIndoe Memorial Research Unit find that specific anti-antibodies can be purified to prevent reactions against skin grafts.

FRINGE BENEFITS

The Glasgow Fire Brigade uses a computer to store information about its area.

Fison's Gro-Bags, compost-filled sacks which are planted with fruit and vegetables, are marketed in England.

The pitted nature of Mercury's surface is at last revealed by photographs transmitted from the US Mariner 10 space probe. A mosaic of pictures, taken at intervals, shows a world heavily cratered and criss-crossed by cliffs running for hundreds of miles across its crust. Other studies conducted by the probe detect a faint trace atmosphere—one trillionth that of the Earth's—and surface temperatures ranging from $-346°F$ ($-210°C$) to $950°F$ ($510°C$).

Minute particles once too small for human scrutiny, can now be revealed with the holographic electron microscope developed at the University of Texas. Magnifying millions of times, the microscope produces an image of the clouds of electrons surrounding an atom. Now the original aim of holography has been realized, this 3–D microscope promises to lead the way to many discoveries about the nature of the atom.

The first of a new generation of submarine cables—it can carry 1,840 two-way channels—is laid between Britain and Canada. It provides double the capacity of the six existing transatlantic cables put together.

The first programmable pocket calculator is introduced by the British company Hewlett Packard. No larger than a man's hand, the HP65 can be programmed to solve scientific, engineering and statistical problems.

Skynet IIb, launched from the USA, is a communciations satellite made in, and controlled from, Britain. It is the first European geostationary communications satellite in orbit.

In the USA, deaths resulting from road accidents fall from 54,000 in 1973, to 45,000. The introduction of a nationwide 55 mph (88 km/h) speed limit may well have contributed to the decrease.

The European Airbus A300B airliner is launched. Four million man-hours have been spent on perfecting a supercritical wing, designed to delay the formation of sonic shock waves at high speeds, while its two turbofan engines give it the lowest fuel consumption per passenger mile of any jet in history.

The French Army uses Pluton, the only known tactical surface-to-surface nuclear missile to be developed outside the USSR and USA. Pluton is mounted on, and fired from, a tank chassis.

Half of Iceland's population of 110,000 enjoys the warmth brought to their homes and offices by water piped directly from hot springs.

A school in Atlanta, Georgia, is the first large building in the world to be equipped with air conditioning which is powered by the sun. Developed by engineers as a result of the 1973 energy crisis, the refrigerating equipment uses solar power to evaporate the water needed to cool the air.

In response to the call for energy conservation, recycling industries step up production. In Britain, the output of steel made exclusively from scrap is doubled; plastic garbage is recycled into building materials and broken bottles into glass fibre; and old tyres are made into shoe soles.

Insidious lead poisoning causes serious brain and nerve damage in humans. According to Professor Derek Bryce Smith of Reading University, England, even minute traces of lead may result in behaviour disturbances leading to outbreaks of irrational violence. Henry Warren of British Columbia links sub-clinical lead poisoning to a higher than normal rate of still births and diseases of the central nervous system, including multiple sclerosis.

Ringworm of the scalp is still being treated with X-rays to the affected area. A study from Israel, however, shows that irradiation of children leads to the development of tumours—some of them cancerous—in the skull and neck. The incidence of brain tumours and thyroid and salivary gland cancers, is three times as common in a group of 11,000 young patients, than in children who have not been treated.

To overcome a shortage of wild yams used to make contraceptive pills, a Japanese firm develops a new process using microbes to synthesize the vital hormones.

A German cigarette lighter uses four solar cells to recharge its battery.

TV subtitles for the deaf are demonstrated in the USA.

Clean, silent and efficient—the electric bicycle is the answer to an ecologist's prayer. Made of steel and alloy and running on either pedal power or from a battery-pack which can be recharged up to 2,000 times, this prototype has an estimated running cost of only 1p (2 cents) for each 10 miles.

The Tornado swing-wing, multi-role, combat aircraft, a joint venture by a British, German and Italian consortium, makes its first test flight. Due to enter service in the eighties, Europe's most important military aircraft will be armed with bombs in its IDS (interdiction and strike) role, and with missiles as a fighter.

201

Speeding up the trains

In the 1820s, when public railways were in their infancy, the fastest any ordinary member of the public could travel by train was about 30 mph (48 km/h). By the 1960s, train travel at 100 mph (161 km/h) had become available to all fare-paying passengers. Then, within less than 20 years, maximum speeds on scheduled services leapt by another 60 per cent as, in 1981, France introduced her TGV (*Train Grande Vitesse*). The TGV was the offspring of a young generation of high speed trains built specifically to provide rapid inter-city travel.

First of these high speed trains of the sixties were the Japanese Shinkansen (New Trunk Line) trains, which began a full service in 1966. Prompted by severe congestion on the meandering line running south from Tokyo, Japanese National Railways had built an entirely new line which passed directly through, or over all natural obstacles and eliminated the curves that have proved to be the major barrier to increased speed and passenger safety. Hikari ('Lightning') trains, each carrying 1,400

Roller-coasting over the hills between Paris and Lyon, the French TGV is powered by electric current drawn by pantograph from overhead wires. Eight passenger cars, designed with the gaps between them virtually eliminated for aerodynamic efficiency, are enclosed at each end by a power car. Offering comfortable travel to ordinary passengers (275 of the train's 386 seats are second class), the TGV is the fastest scheduled train in the world. On a test run in 1981 it easily topped 236 mph (390 km/h).

The bullet-nosed Hikari trains, *right*, serving Japan's Shinkansen line, race along track which bypasses gradients and curves. The electrically powered trains reach their cruising speed of 130 mph (209 km/h) only four minutes after leaving each station. Speeds of 161 mph (260 km/h) are planned on a new line south of Osaka, where tracks are spaced farther apart to cut air turbulence as trains pass each other.

A race of high speed trains built since the twenties, *below*, would reveal amazing progress in average speeds. One hour after the start, the steam-powered 'Flying Scotsman' would have travelled some 60 miles (96 km), the streamlined, diesel-powered 'Flying Hamburger' 78 miles (125 km). Next would come Britain's High Speed and Advanced Passenger trains at 103 and 125 miles (166 and 200 km) respectively. The Shinkansen train would have reached 130 miles (210 km), but the TGV would be the clear winner at 161 miles (260 km).

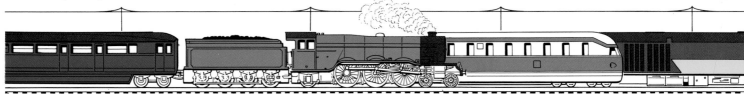

Flying Scotsman 1935   Flying Hamburger 1933   British HST 1976

passengers, sped along this track at an average speed of 130 mph (209 km/h).

Encouraged by this triumph, other nations vigorously pursued the idea of advanced, high speed trains. Like its Japanese counterpart the French TGV runs on an entirely new railway line. Planners elegantly solved the problem of hills by incorporating 3.5 per cent gradients into the line. Aided by a roller-coaster effect, the TGV trains surmount these in their stride without speed loss. The track's broad, sweeping curves are never less than $2\frac{1}{2}$ miles (4 km) in radius, which helps keep speeds high. Since the trains began daily scheduled services between Paris and Lyon in 1981, they have kept up cruising speeds of 161 mph (260 km/h).

Of all the railway planners involved with high speed trains, those in Britain faced particularly thorny problems. Over half the country's existing train lines consisted of curved track over which a conventional 130-mph (209-km/h) train could not pass without causing discomfort, and possibly danger, for passengers. Construction of an entirely new straight line was impossible, since Britain was already criss-crossed with lines passing through or near heavily populated urban areas. So British engineers decided to construct a train uniquely suited to existing track. A train was devised with a lightweight body, low centre of gravity and a mechanism which monitored curves in the track and safely tilted the train's body up to 9° inward in response.

In an effort to win back passengers from road and air, other nations, including West Germany, Italy and the USSR, are also developing high speed trains. But if economics allow, the trains of the future will be totally different from those of today. Engineers in Japan, West Germany and Britain are involved in the development of 'maglev' trains with no wheels and no mechanical connection with the track. They are supported and propelled by the interaction between magnets on the train body and the track. A Japanese test train has already achieved 321 mph (517 km/h).

Speeds on urban railways are rising in tune with those of inter-city services. The ambitious Californian BART (Bay Area Rapid Transit) railway system boasts fully automatic trains which reach 80 mph (129 km/h) and average 42 mph (68 km/h), with stops. A computer controls all functions of the railway, right down to the opening and shutting of the doors.

Britain's Advanced Passenger Train (APT), *above*, able to speed along existing track at 125 mph (201 km/h), is built of lightweight aluminium alloy which makes it 40% lighter than a normal train. Attempts to put this bold design into service have been frustrated by economic strictures and by faults in the tilt mechanism.

The APT's air suspension is supported by swinging bolsters to try to ensure a smooth ride.

— Air suspension
— Tilt jack

— Swinging bolster

As the APT approaches a curve at high speed, automatic spirit-level sensors measure the degree of inward tilt needed. They then activate hydraulic jacks to give the tilt required. When the train returns to straight track, the cars revert to their normal, upright positions.

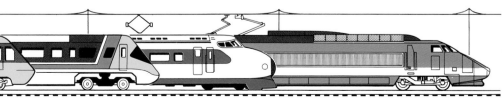

British APT 1982   Japanese Shinkansen 1966   French TGV 1981

COMMUNICATION, INFORMATION AND SPACE APPLICATIONS

Liquid crystal displays for pocket calculators and digital clocks and watches are marketed for the first time by BDH in Britain. Before the end of the decade, the company will have established a monopoly in these crystals. Similar displays have been developed in the USA and Japan, but are not sufficiently stable or long-lasting to compete commercially.

A low-light TV camera—it can detect a person 7 mls (11 km) away on a clear night—is developed in the USA and used by the Iranian militia. The most sensitive system of its kind, it allows faces to be recognized at 5 mls (8 km), and can be used continuously in both light and dark. On the minus side, it is seriously hampered by rain, fog and cloud, so the US Army opt for infrared cameras.

Kodak instant print cameras and film are launched. The film develops outside the camera while you wait.

TRANSPORT, WARFARE AND SPACE EXPLORATION

The European Space Agency (ESA) comes into being, taking over the responsibility for scientific satellites from ESRO and starting work on a programme of applications satellites for communications and observation of the Earth. The Agency also takes on the development of the French Ariane heavy launch vehicle.

COS–B, a scientific satellite developed by ESRO, is launched from the USA to study cosmic rays at up to 62,500 mls (100,000 km) from the Earth.

In a historic link-up, the American Apollo 18 and Soviet Soyuz 19 dock in space. Three hours after docking, the two commanders shake hands; then the crews celebrate with a well-earned dinner of borscht, turkey and lamb. For almost two days the crews visit each others' ships and carry out joint experiments. The Apollo-Soyuz Test Project (ASTP) proves the feasibility of space rescue and shows that successful international cooperation in space research is possible.

ENERGY AND INDUSTRY

A thermonuclear power station, Tokamak 10, begins operation at the Kurchatov Institute in the USSR. It is an experimental attempt to see if the generation of power from nuclear fusion could become commercially viable.

The first oil to flow regularly from the North Sea is pumped to Britain from the Argyll field.

The fastest ever speed for weaving cloth is achieved by a new loom, which lifts the fibres with jets of air rather than with the mechanically operated bars of other machines.

MEDICINE AND FOOD PRODUCTION

Three-quarters of the atmosphere is composed of nitrogen; but, unless it can be 'fixed' into a compound, it cannot be used to increase the protein content of crops. Now Australian and Canadian scientists have adapted *Rhizobium*—a bacteria which lives on pea roots and 'fixes' nitrogen naturally—to 'fix' nitrogen in the laboratory.

During research into drug addiction, scientists at Aberdeen University, Scotland, isolate 'the brain's own opiate'—encephalin—whose action is similar to that of morphine. This raises hopes of producing a powerful natural analgesic without addictive properties: the perfect painkiller.

FRINGE BENEFITS

Swingline, the staple makers, patent their 'multiple shot fastening gun'.

The armless windmill, designed as a cheap power source and irrigation pump for developing countries, finds applications in the developed landscape of Buschland, Texas. Funded by the US Department of Energy, the pump has a 55 hp output and can pump 400 gallons of water a minute. Armless windmills represent a major advance on conventional windmills as they can pick up and use wind from any direction at any time without having to be reoriented. Their low running costs and relatively high energy efficiency make them just as suitable for remote locations in technologically advanced countries, as for the low-technology environments their designers originally had in mind.

Altair, a home computer which can be built from a kit, comes on the US market. Easy to use, and with a choice of programmes, Altair sets a trend quickly followed by many other manufacturers.

The pocket calculator boom peaks with world production hitting 50 million. The £25 ($50) electronic watch also becomes a reality as stern competition forces down the price of electronic gadgets. The US company, Commodore, market an electronic watch accurate to within 5 secs a month.

Less than 50 years after Baird's first TV transmission, the 130 million TV sets in the USA exceeds the number of bath tubs.

The video games craze catches on as Atari/Sears of Japan produce their Hockey Pong for the Christmas market, using the first low-price integrated circuits specifically designed for TV games.

The Toronto communications tower—the world's tallest self-supporting structure—will accommodate all the radio and TV channels for the Toronto area and eliminate interference caused by the city's high-rise buildings.

The Honda Civic is the only car in the world to meet all the anti-pollution requirements of the USA's Clean Air Act without special devices.

The Boeing Jetfoil 929–100, a waterjet-propelled hydrofoil, which can accommodate up to 400 passengers, enters service in Hong Kong. The powerplant consists of port and starboard gas turbines, each connected to a pump through a gearbox. The pumps discharge water at high pressure through nozzles in the base of the hull.

A car that is unplugged before being driven away is marketed in Britain. The Enfield 800 two-seater saloon is powered by lead-acid batteries, recharged while the vehicle is not in use. The car is said to handle and perform well, although the top speed is only about 45 mph (72 km/h). The car is cheaper to run and service than a conventional car and does not emit noxious exhaust fumes, but its high purchase price and the inconvenience of constant battery recharging deter high sales.

The Lucas electric taxi, revealed at the London Motor Show, has more space for passengers than the familiar black cab, despite being 39 in (1 m) shorter. Its bodywork is made of glass-reinforced plastic, with replaceable corners in case of damage. Despite its excellent design and performance, the taxi is not acceptable to London's cab drivers who are deterred by its short range of only 100 mls (160 km) before the battery pack needs recharging.

Fuel tanks in vehicles can now be protected from fire and explosion as manufacturers begin to line them with a new form of expanded aluminium foil. The foil occupies only 0.5% of the tank's volume, and prevents the fuel from igniting after an accident.

A large farm in Phoenix, Arizona, is irrigated with water distributed by one of the first intermediate-temperature solar-powered pumps. When the sun's heat reaches its peak in June, 10.6 million gallons (48 million l) of water are pumped every day. In 18 months' time the solar collectors will be operating at a temperature of 302°F (150°C).

Getting rid of the stink from sewage is the idea behind ICI's 'deep shaft' treatment of effluence. Whole sewage plants will now be economically housed underground in vertical shafts, instead of in the usual overground series of circular tanks.

The first successful cloning of a mammal occurs at Oxford, England, where zoologist Derek Bromhall succeeds in producing a rabbit, identical in all respects to its 'mother', in the laboratory. He replaces the nucleus of a female's egg with the nucleus of a cell taken from elsewhere in the same rabbit's body.

In trials at St Bartholomew's Hospital, London, 15 previously infertile women who have been treated with the fertility drug Bromocriptine, succeed in bearing children.

Cesar Milstein, working in Cambridge, England, announces, in a modest letter to *Nature* magazine, one of the greatest scientific discoveries of the century: the use of genetic engineering to create identical micro-organisms, or monoclonal antibodies (MABs), which will play a vital part in the fight against disease.

The Japanese patent a TV that freezes and displays one frame at the top of the screen while the rest of the programme continues.

BiC introduce their disposable razor to the UK market.

Yielding up to 100 times more information than conventional radiography, EMI's new whole-body scanner, *left*, takes clear cross-sectional pictures through any part of the human body. The scan on the right, for example, shows a 'slice' through the chest, showing bone, fat and muscle, with the heart in the centre. The technique of computerized axial tomography—the process upon which the scanner depends—was originated by EMI researchers in 1967 and made available to the medical profession in the form of a brainscanner in 1972. The Series 2 general purpose system shown here is much quicker than orthodox X-ray examination as well as providing far more information, and is already in regular use around the world for diagnosis and for the planning and monitoring of treatment.

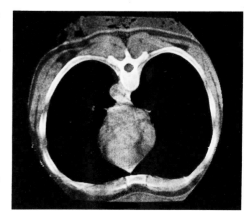

The momentum of the microchip

Chips with everything—that is the menu on which modern man is now fed. And this new diet promises revolutionary changes to the vital statistics of human society, making industry fat in output and lean in manpower, putting muscle into machinery and taking the drudgery out of the office routine. There is seemingly no sphere of human endeavour from which the chip can be excluded.

The secret of the spectacular success of the chip, a slice of silicon only 0.1 in (0.5 mm thick), but with remarkable electrical properties, lies in both its structure and its minute size. A single chip only 0.25 ins (5 mm) square can, for example, form the heart of a computer which, even in the mid-sixties, would have occupied a room 16.25 ft (5 m) square. As for structure, it is the element silicon that holds the key to the way in which the chip is manufactured and behaves.

Silicon is a perfect material for making chips because it is a semiconductor. When absolutely pure, it is a poor conductor of electricity, but when it contains impurities it allows a weak electric current to pass through it. Scientifically, it was the investigation of this property of silicon at the Bell Telephone Laboratories in the USA during the forties that led a team of workers to discover that, if layers of silicon are treated differently, they could be endowed with different electrical properties.

This was how the transistor was born. Silicon layers were selectively and carefully 'doped' with impurities, then combined to provide the ideal slimline replacement for the thermionic valve. Also in the forties came another advance crucial to the eventual success of the chip: the printed circuit which, instead of wires, has its electrical connections printed on to a copper baseplate.

Within another decade, miniaturization really began to get under way with the invention of integrated circuits. These are tiny printed circuits joining separate areas on a single slice of silicon, each area treated to operate in a different way: for example, as transistor, resistor, capacitor and so on. By the end of the sixties, thousands of components could be crammed on to a single slice of silicon. It was this that became christened the chip.

Changing the chip into a tiny computer, or microprocessor, was achieved in 1969, the year in which a chip was first designed as the central processing unit of a computer; that is, the part that carries out all the arithmetical calculations and controls the other, separate parts such as the memory and the programme, which may themselves be in chip form.

As chips continue their inexorable march into all spheres of life, so capacities and capabilities increase—in 1979, the first million-bit memory chip was made. The prospects for the future are indeed momentous.

Working in harness, four of these T3 robots employed by General Motors in the USA can together spot weld car bodies at the rate of 200 welds per car and 48 cars per hour. Unlike the human machines they have replaced, the robots can tolerate deafening noise for indefinite periods and work two or three shifts every 24 hours. But although reliable and resilient, and becoming more sophisticated almost by the day, the bodies of such robots come a poor second to their human counterparts in skills such as precision manipulation. Robots may not suffer from fatigue or take days off for illness, but as yet they cannot see well, nor can they perform simple tasks on command as well as the average three-year-old. The key to improving the skills of robots lies not just in body design but also in changes to the chips of which their 'brains' are made.

Meticulous quality control is an essential part of chip production: even tiny scratches on the silicon can impair performance. Because the chips are so small, microscopic techniques are used to magnify them and the images then projected on a TV monitor. Paradoxically, the checking of the chips is performed with the help of computers which themselves function with the help of chips.

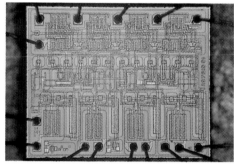

The microprocessor made on a single silicon chip is formed by a series of processes which alter the electrical properties of the silicon crystals so that they will perform correctly. Each area of the chip is treated in a different way, according to the final function it will have. Connections between parts of the chip are on printed circuits.

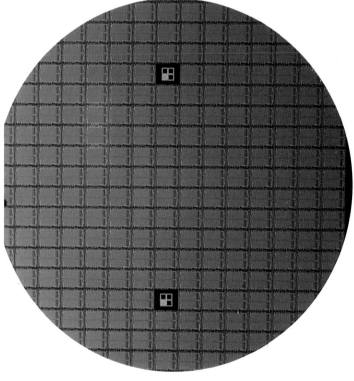

A single silicon wafer, reproduced here to its actual size, yields 200 individual chips, each capable of dealing with some 8 million bits of information every second. To make a robot capable of welding car parts, it may take only a few such chips—what is important is not their size but the way in which each is constructed and programmed to carry out a specific set of instructions devised by its human masters.

COMMUNICATION, INFORMATION AND SPACE APPLICATIONS

The smallest ever TV is produced by Ferranti as a navigational aid for helicopter pilots in the US Air Force. The tiny screen—a bare ¾ in (2 cm) across—forms part of the pilot's visor, while the actual TV tube is built into his helmet.

A watch which measures the heartbeat is developed in Newcastle, England, but the major manufacturers are the Americans and Japanese. Quick to recognize the possible applications in medicine and sport, they add the heartbeat to the existing displays of hours, minutes and seconds. A detector in the watch monitors the pulse in the wrist and translates it into a digital display.

Palapa 1, the first of a pair of geostationary satellites, provides the inhabitants of Indonesia's widely scattered islands with TV, radio and telegraph communications.

The Canon AE–1 camera made by Canon Inc in Japan is the first to incorporate a microprocessor to control exposure. In the years that follow, sophisticated electronic devices will replace the mechanical parts of more and more traditional cameras.

TRANSPORT, WARFARE AND SPACE EXPLORATION

The US Navy tests Tomahawk, a Seá-Launched Cruise Missile (SLCM) designed for use by submarines. Two versions are planned: a tactical model with a conventional high-explosive warhead, and a long-range strategic model carrying a nuclear warhead. Both are fired from a standard torpedo tube and cruise at low levels, the better to penetrate enemy ground defences.

One of the most technically advanced underground railways in Europe opens in Glasgow, Scotland. The 'clockwork orange' system, with its orange cars, runs through cannily updated tunnels and stations built in 1896.

The flexibility and launch-speed of the US Pershing 1A ground-to-ground guided weapon system owes much to its gyrocompasses, which enable the missiles to be fired from an unsurveyed site, and to its SLA (Sequential Launch Adaptor), which can put up to three missiles in flight from a single control station.

ENERGY AND INDUSTRY

Professor W. Spear of Dundee University, Scotland, announces a cheaper way of making silicon solar cells by depositing silicon vapour directly on to glass or aluminium. On a clear day 75 kW of electricity could be generated by 0.4 sq mls (1 sq km), of these cells, with 25 kW generated on an overcast day.

The first two nuclear power stations to generate electricity with Britain's advanced gas-cooled reactors are brought into operation at Hinkley Point in Somerset and Hunterston in Scotland. Fuelled by enriched uranium and cooled by carbon dioxide, they are smaller than Magnox reactors but have a much higher electrical output.

MEDICINE AND FOOD PRODUCTION

Chronic ulceration of the legs is treated by Swedish scientists, who pack ulcer craters with water-absorbent beads to soak up four times their weight of fluid, so reducing the risk of infection.

The Abingdon Hospital Pain Relief Unit in Britain pioneers a technique for freezing nerves which carry the sensation of pain to the brain. This treatment, which can bring relief for several months, is effective for short-term conditions, such as post-operative discomfort, as well as for long-term intractable pain due to neurological disorder, arthritis and some forms of cancer.

While investigating schizophrenia, researchers at the University College of Wales accidentally discover that the drug Nootropyl enhances memory and learning performance. It has the effect of improving 'nervous traffic' between the two hemispheres of the brain. The drug was originally developed in Belgium to combat motion sickness.

FRINGE BENEFITS

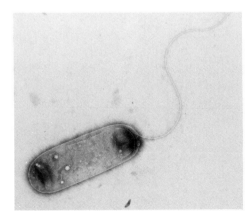

A strain of bacterium unknown to science kills 34 people. At a convention of the American Legion held in Philadelphia, 221 guests at one hotel fall ill with pneumonia-like symptoms. 'Legionnaires Disease' is traced to *Legionella pneumophila*, a hitherto unknown species of a hitherto unknown genus.

IBM develop ink-jet, non-impact printing for addressing labels. A jet of ink, controlled by a magnetic field, is sprayed into a character form of any style and on to any surface. The details of the names and addresses to be printed are stored on the magnetic tape of the computer that controls the operation.

APPLE, one of the most versatile microcomputers, is created in a garage in California by a pair of amateur electronics enthusiasts. The APPLE starts a revolution in home and school learning.

A cassette tape, carrying stills of 1,000 colour pictures and an audiotape, is introduced by Matsushita in Japan. A separate playback machine is needed to display the stills on a TV monitor.

Audio reproduction enters the computer age with the introduction of the ADC Accutrac 4000 by BSR (Birmingham Sound Reproducers) in Britain. The machine's turntable has a computerized memory bank and an infrared scanner for selecting up to 13 tracks on a disc, according to programmed instructions. It also has ultrasonic remote control for armchair listening at a distance of 33 ft (10 m).

A microcomputer for cars has been developed in the USA by General Motors. The Alpha V measures speed, fuel level and consumption, battery voltage and oil pressure, calculates journey times and keeps the engine running.

Hilly San Francisco replaces its ailing bus fleet with the first new electric trolley buses put into service in the USA for more than 20 years.

The Air-Launched Cruise Missile (ALCM) system, under development in the USA, further confuses distinctions between tactical/strategic and conventional/nuclear weapons: the missile's TERCOM (Terrain Contour Matching) guidance system can drop it within 30 ft (9 m) of a target after a 1,500-ml (2,413-km) subsonic flight; and the small, inexpensive missiles can be altered so fast that enemy classification of types and numbers is nearly impossible.

Train journey times across England to South Wales are drastically cut by British Rail's High Speed Train. Averaging 103.3 mph (166 km/h), the trip from London to Cardiff takes just over an hour.

Viking 1, the first spacecraft to make a successful soft landing on Mars, sends back to the USA clear photographs of the Martian landscape—a rusty-brown, rock-strewn desert beneath a pinkish sky.

A plastic aluminium which can be moulded into any shape or stretched to several times its own length is developed for the electronics, automobile and construction industries.

Kidney dialysis, whereby toxins are removed from patients' kidneys, becomes more effective when polythene is used as the material for making a crucial component, known as a Paraflo plate, in dialysing machines. This polythene-based plate spreads out the kidney fluid and facilitates its dialysis.

Work is started on the construction of Europe's largest man-made lake, the Kielder Dam and Reservoir in Northumberland, England. The dam, scheduled to reach its top level in 1982, will contain 42,000 million gallons (190 million l) of water, providing a supply for industry and 85% of the population of north-east England.

The prostaglandins are a group of intriguing substances, found in most parts of the body, whose functions are not yet fully known. But now, in Britain, scientists at the Wellcome Foundation laboratories discover a prostaglandin which prevents blood-clotting. This substance, labelled PGE, could possibly be used as an anti-coagulant and as a prophylactic for coronary heart disease.

A new kind of drug comes on to the market for the treatment of peptic ulcers. Cimetidine (Tagamet) aids healing by blocking the action of histamine on the stomach and so preventing the secretion of excessive acid. This may be the first of many drugs tailored specifically to blocking the action of local hormones.

Doctors at London's Hammersmith Hospital introduce the practice of blood-exchange to rid the blood of excess cholesterol. The conscious patient's blood is painlessly removed and separated into cells and plasma. The cells, recombined with fresh blood, are returned to the patient. This blood-swap principle could equally be applied to the removal from the blood of the huge molecules—called immune complexes—which cause severe pain and inflammation in rheumatic disease.

Press a button on Singer's new electronic sewing-machine, *left*, to select any one of 25 stitches pre-set for all ordinary purposes—a microprocessor does the rest. The machine has no levers or cams, has a needle that slants towards the operator for a better view of the work and is unique in being equipped with a self-winding bobbin.

Concorde becomes the world's first supersonic airliner to operate a regular passenger service. Although it is hailed as a feat of engineering, Concorde has been slow to win permission to fly commercial routes in the face of public anxiety about sonic booms. Only after an exhaustive series of trial flights has the go-ahead been given.

Exploring the solar system

Bound for Uranus and Neptune, unmanned US Voyager space probes have already travelled farther than any other spacecraft. These missions, which carry with them a record of life on Earth—in the hope that by fantastic coincidence they might be found by some intelligent beings far out in the galaxy—are but a small milestone in man's attempts to explore both the solar system and the larger Universe of which he is part.

Despite the immense progress made since Sputnik became, in 1957, the first man-made object ever to escape the pull of the Earth's atmosphere, we have as yet no means of probing any of the ten million million stars the Universe embraces. In our solar system, nine planets revolve around the sun: Mercury, Venus, Earth, Mars, Jupiter, Saturn, Uranus, Neptune and Pluto. By the end of the eighties, only far-off Pluto will remain totally uncharted.

The planets so far explored differ vastly. Mercury, photographed by the US Mariner probes, is a heavily cratered world whose surface temperature reaches a fiery 950°F (510°C) in an atmosphere with a pressure only a trillionth that of Earth's. Venus, in contrast, has an atmospheric pressure 100 times greater than that of Earth, which proved powerful enough to crush Soviet landing craft sent there in the sixties. Two-thirds of the Venusian landmass consists of rolling plains scoured by electrical storms, where temperatures soar to 527°F (275°C)—hot enough to melt lead.

Mars, once thought to host intelligent life forms which had carved 'canals' on its surface, is now known to be a dusty desert from pole to pole. Both Russia and the USA have landed probes on Mars, and both have considered sending manned missions there. Moderate Martian temperatures, and an atmospheric pressure a hundredth that of Earth, would pose no significant threat to human astronauts.

To land a mission on Jupiter would be impossible, since the giant planet is composed

mainly of gas, with a molten centre whose temperature is probably five times that of the Sun's surface. The Jovian atmosphere, formidable radiation belt and four large moons were, however, explored by the Voyager probes—robot ships weighing less than a tonne but each carrying 254 lb (115 kg) of scientific instruments. The spacecraft then flew on to Saturn and, in 1980 and 1981, investigated the planet's spectacular ring system and moons before swinging away towards Uranus, Neptune and beyond.

After a journey of a quarter of a million miles, the US Apollo 11 mission landed Neil Armstrong and Edwin Aldrin, *left*, on the moon. Only nine years earlier, in 1960, no one had travelled more than 25 miles (40 km) above the Earth's surface. Such phenomenal technological progress enabled man to visit an alien world for the first time. Between 1969 and 1972, in the course of six Apollo missions, 12 astronauts explored the lunar surface. They collected 847 lb (384 kg) of soil and rocks, travelled many miles across its surface in the specially built Lunar Rover, and conducted numerous scientific experiments. They concluded that the moon supports no life forms.

Volcanic, red-brown rocks coated in fine dust are revealed by this picture of the Martian surface taken by a US landing craft. The robot probe, whose computerized biology unit was contained in only 1 cu ft (0.028 cu m), conducted experiments to incubate living soil organisms.

An enormous rift valley, 4 mls (7 km) deep in places, stretches one fifth of the way around Mars, *left*. In 1971 the planet's peaceful surface was obscured by a ferocious dust storm which raged around its entirety for two months, destroying two Soviet landing probes. Several dormant volcanoes are dotted on the Martian crust, one of which may be the destination of the first manned planetary mission.

In 1980, when the two Voyager space probes began their investigation of Saturn, *right*, they upset several preconceived notions. The rings, presumed to be several broad bands of icy rubble, were revealed as a complex system of thousands of ringlets. Titan, Saturn's largest satellite, was found to be swathed in nitrogen—not methane. Six new moons were also discovered.

Jupiter, *below, top right*, has a 'mini solar system' of four large and nine small moons. Voyager revealed that one of these, orange-coloured Io, boasts at least eight active volcanoes—first proof of geological activity in the solar system outside Earth. Europa, in contrast, was found to be superficially smooth, while Callisto is scarred by more craters than any other object observed by man. Ganymede has a mysteriously patchy, dark and light crust.

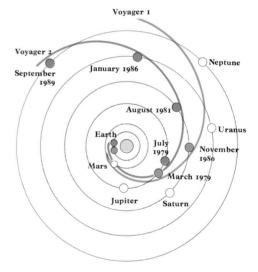

The flightpaths of the US space probes Voyager 1 and 2, and the dates of their planetary encounters, are shown in blue and red, *above*. They were launched in August and September 1977 (clear circles indicate the positions of the planets at that time). They followed an elliptical path which took them roughly halfway around the sun before they reached Jupiter, their first destination. Both probes were launched in the same direction as the Earth's solar orbit, taking advantage of its velocity; this meant that only a small increase of speed—and of fuel expenditure—was needed to put them on course. A planetary mission can only be launched during a 'launch window'—the period of time during which both Earth and the target planet are in suitable positions around the sun.

COMMUNICATION, INFORMATION AND SPACE APPLICATIONS

The Bell Telephone Co is the first to use optical fibres to transmit TV signals. Their $1\frac{1}{2}$-ml (2.4-km) cable forges a link which will make broadcasting more efficient and economical.

A controversial bugging device, the size of a match head and claimed to be the world's smallest, is sold in Britain. The mini-mike can pick up a whisper 6 mls (10 km) away—but only against a backdrop of complete silence.

TRANSPORT, WARFARE AND SPACE EXPLORATION

A Vosper Thornycroft VT 2 military hovercraft is used for troop landing exercises. Developed from the VT 1 passenger hovercraft, the 99-ft VT 2 carries 130 soldiers and their vehicles. The lift and propulsion system is powered by two Rolls-Royce Proteus marine gas turbines, giving a speed of more than 60 knots.

The crew of the Soviet spacecraft Soyuz 26 set a new space endurance record as they spend 96 days 10 hours in orbit around the Earth, most of it in the Salyut 6 space station.

A man-powered aircraft, Gossamer Condor, wins the Kramer prize for flying a figure-of-eight course of over 1 ml (1.6 km). Designed by Paul Macready, who uses advanced plastics and carbon fibre materials, a later model will cross the English Channel.

The US Space Shuttle makes its first gliding test flight, after being carried aloft on the back of a Boeing 747. The Space Shuttle, whose development was approved by President Richard Nixon in 1972, is planned as the first reusable spacecraft for manned flight. One of the early operational missions, following its launch in 1981, will be to carry Spacelab, a workshop and laboratory developed by the European Space Agency, in which valuable scientific and technological research can be carried out in conditions of zero gravity.

ENERGY AND INDUSTRY

Twice as heavy as the Eiffel Tower and standing 12 storeys high, the largest hydraulic press in the western world is finally assembled at Issoire in France. Manufactured in the USSR, the machine will be used for pressing, shaping and cutting the metals needed to make parts for aircraft, railway and defence industries around the world.

'High tech' architecture for a technological age finds expression in the Georges Pompidou Centre in Paris. This museum, research centre and library complex is reviled by critics as appearing to be inside out—the working parts of the building, such as pipes and shafts, are exposed on the exterior and painted bright colours. Antagonistic at first, the people of the old Beaubourg district where it stands, soon grow to enjoy its accessible atmosphere.

MEDICINE AND FOOD PRODUCTION

Since the discovery of the naturally occurring 'opiate' encephalin, two years ago, researchers have found more endorphins (as this whole group of substances is now known). At Johns Hopkins, Solomon Snyder succeeds in mapping specific pathways in the brain where endorphins act, including one in the limbic system which is associated with emotions and mood. This has implications for pain relief and for the possible role of endorphins in mental disturbance.

Post-mortem studies of the brains of known schizophrenics reveal chemical differences between them and normal brain tissue. Cambridge University biochemists track down a disorder in a substance called dopamine, a neuro-transmitter involved in communications between brain cells.

FRINGE BENEFITS

'Super call', an electronic line judge, helps to resolve disputes among tennis players.

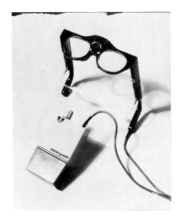

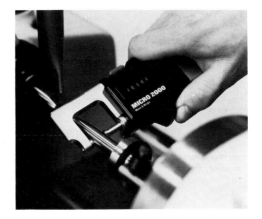

Sonicguide, an environmental sensor built into a spectacle frame, helps overcome the problems of the visually handicapped. Its purpose is to substitute sound for sight. The device bounces high-frequency sound waves off nearby objects and converts the returning 'echo' into audible sounds that are directed by small tubes to each ear. Sonicguide has been developed in New Zealand by Wormald International Sensory Aids and is effective at distances up to 16 ft (5 m). Users learn to integrate the auditory 'picture' they receive of their immediate environment with ordinary ambient sounds, and can then move around with a new freedom and confidence.

Philips of the Netherlands launch their 1700 video cassette recorder which halves the cost of tapes and doubles playing time, simply by halving tape playing speed. For the first time, a whole video tape of a feature film can be seen on a home TV set without breaks.

The BBC makes its first quadrophonic radio broadcasts, but technical adjustments are needed since the stereo reception is slightly fuzzy. The new system seems to stand a good chance of being adopted in Europe, but manufacturers must wait for standards to be agreed on before marketing new equipment.

The Japanese car industry now employs 7,000 robots which are used for welding, painting, controlling sheet metal pressing and assembly. Robots keep costs low, so boosting foreign sales.

Hydrogen gas is used to fuel motor vehicles in two Californian experiments. A 1975 Pontiac, claimed to be 'the world's first wind-powered car' is demonstrated, and the city of Riverside experiments with hydrogen-powered buses. A wind turbine converts the gas into usable form.

Three satellites, developed for ESRO, are launched from the USA and put into operation as part of ESA's established programme. They are the GEOS for geomagnetic studies, METEOSTAT for meteorology and ISEE-B (International Sun-Earth Explorer).

The French Naviplane N500 hoverferry begins trials in the English Channel. The N500 can accommodate 400 passengers and 45 cars. Power is supplied by five gas turbines, two for lift and three for propulsion. The maximum speed is 75 knots.

Since 1974, the numbers of Americans travelling by public transport has been increasing steadily, after declining for the previous 30 years. Massive federal support, including money to buy 3,808 new buses, has produced this change.

Satirically dubbed the 'capitalist bomb' because it kills people but leaves property intact, the neutron bomb is developed by the US military. A small fission (or atomic) bomb triggers a fusion reaction which releases about 80% of the bomb's energy as neutron radiation.

Forty million gas appliances—domestic cookers, heaters and industrial machines—have been converted to use natural gas from the North Sea, as the British Gas Corp completes its unique 10-year programme.

Engineers at IBM's Yorktown Heights Laboratory in New York use gallium arsenide for making solar cells, and increase the efficiency of converting sunlight into electricity to 22%. The cells are more expensive than the less efficient silicon solar cells, but they function better at high temperatures.

United Technology start to use lasers to glaze materials. The lasers rapidly fire a liquid on metallic surfaces, producing a finish which is hard, strong, abrasion-resistant and corrosion-free.

Scientists at Britain's University of Cambridge develop a laser which is capable of concentrating power equal to that generated by all the power stations in England. For a fraction of a second, they focus this power on hydrogen atoms to discover if the conditions necessary for nuclear fusion can be achieved. The success of the research may lead to nuclear fusion becoming a commercial energy source in the future.

A mysterious disease which has killed hundreds of people in northern Zaïre and the southern Sudan is now identified as a virus infection called Lassa fever. Related to the green monkey disease which erupted in Marburg, Germany, nine years earlier, it is highly contagious. There is no known cure.

West German scientists develop a new drug, praziquantal, to conquer the debilitating parasitic disease, bilharzia.

The New Jersey-based pharmaceutical company, Merck, Sharp and Dohme announce an entirely new anti-inflammatory drug which has been developed only after synthesizing more than 500 compounds. Said to be safe and non-narcotic, it will be marketed under the trade-name Dolobid.

Car wheel alignment may now be more easily checked by an electronic device.

The world's first hand-held electronic micrometer, *left*, gives its readings instantly on a digital display. Made by Moore and Wright of Sheffield, England, it is not only easier to use than existing mechanical micrometers, but is even more accurate, giving precise measurements in laboratories and on shop-floors.

The Dounreay Fast Reactor goes out of commission. After generating 500 million units of electricity, the station, at Caithness, Scotland, is shut down by the United Kingdom Atomic Energy Authority. Dounreay started operating in 1959, built up to its full output of 15 MW by 1963 and has provided vital information about the engineering aspects of fast breeder reactors. It is superseded by the PFR (Prototype Fast Reactor), which was built on a nearby site in 1974 and is now reaching its designed output of 250 MW—enough to supply a city of 300,000 people.

Power from the sun

Every day the Earth is bathed in an abundant source of natural power: sunlight. It has been calculated that three days' worth of sunshine provides as much potential energy as all the world's coal, oil and natural gas put together. The only problem is to find a way of harnessing it; for the amount of available sunshine varies enormously from day to day, from season to season, from latitude to latitude. If it could only be concentrated or conserved, energy from the sun could be made to drive motors, or power the turbines that generate electricity. Only in the twentieth century has there been a large-scale attempt to do just that—an attempt that grows more determined as our fossil fuel reserves dwindle.

Smaller-scale operations for trapping solar energy have been around at least as long as the greenhouse. For over a century, solar cookers have found favour in tropical countries—small aluminium reflectors focus the sun's rays on to a pot or pan. Solar stills can evaporate sea water to provide valuable salt and fresh water supplies. A still in Patmos in the Aegean sea, for example, gives the islanders well over 8,000 gallons of water a day. The application of solar power is far more practicable for tropical and subtropical peoples than for the heavily populated areas of the industrial northern hemisphere. At noon on a clear day, all the solar energy falling on an area in the tropics eight kilometres square, is equivalent to Britain's total output of energy. Nevertheless, it is still unrealistic to think of solar energy as a source of regular electricity supply. Its uses must remain small-scale or local—for heating buildings, providing hot water, driving air conditioning systems or pumps. A wide range of solar collectors, usually in the form of panels fitted to rooftops, will transfer the sun's heat to air or water. For instance, 200,000 such panels, each about two meters square, successfully supply hot water to homes in Israel.

The power of solar energy has been obvious since at least 212 BC, when Archimedes is said to have set the Roman fleet on fire by focusing the sun's rays on the ships. The same principle is employed at the solar furnace built in the French Pyrenees during the thirties: hundreds of adjustable mirrors concentrate the sun's rays on to a concave mirror, which then transfers the accumulated heat to a furnace. 'Solar One', in New Mexico, is typical of the experimental solar power stations which have begun to flourish in flat desert regions. Its many concentric rings of mirrors direct the sunlight on to a 'power tower' where the heat is gathered to drive an electricity generator.

Perhaps the most important innovation in solar energy technology this century, was the advent of the solar cell in the fifties. Originally a spin-off from the transistor revolution, solar—or photovoltaic—cells use the proper-

ties of a mineral such as silicon to transform the photons in sunlight into electricity. Once the small electric currents generated in each cell are linked together, enough power can be accumulated to run, say, the instruments of a communications satellite. Telstar, launched in 1962, carried 5,600 silicon solar cells instead of conventional batteries, whose limited life-span make them unsuitable for space.

Solar cells at present generate electricity at roughly ten times the cost of a fossil fuel-fired generating plant; but there are claims that solar power will shortly be cheaper than any other energy source. Already there are ambitious—some would say lunatic—schemes to put a solar power station into orbit. Huge arrays of solar collectors, several kilometres square, would transmit energy to a receiving station on Earth in the form of microwaves (highly dangerous if the microwave beams were misdirected). At a more mundane level, it seems probable that solar cells will continue to be improved and solar furnaces developed. So, if power from the sun cannot exactly promise the world free energy, it can at least cut its cost and help to keep the planet clean. Nor is there any fear of it running in short supply.

Rays of sunlight, converted into electricity by 16,000 solar cells, power *Solar Challenger* on its 200-ml (322-km) maiden flight from Kent, England to France in the summer of 1981. Every cell is 14.5% efficient in its conversion of solar to electrical energy. Only the fifth aircraft to be powered by the sun, *Solar Challenger* was built by US engineer Paul MacCready to promote interest in the development of solar cells. Robust, and weighing 209.4 lb (95 kg), it is constructed from the most advanced materials to emerge from Du Pont, who sponsored the whole project.

Temperatures as high as 4,000°C are reached at this solar furnace at Odeillo-Font Romeu in the French Pyrenees. Rows of adjustable mirrors, carefully arranged on a hillside, reflect the sun's rays on to a large concave mirror which focuses them on to a central furnace. Here, instead of making electricity, the perfectly clean heat is used in metallurgical research programmes—it can melt up to 132.3 lb (60 kg) of iron every hour.

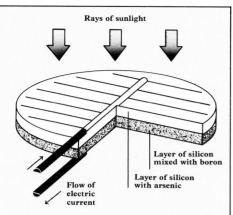

Rays of sunlight

Layer of silicon mixed with boron

Layer of silicon with arsenic

Flow of electric current

The solar, or photovoltaic, cell can be made from minerals such as silicon, gallium arsenide or cadmium sulphide. Sunlight striking the cell causes electrons to flow from one layer to the other, producing a tiny electric current. Individual cells, connected in series in a panel, are able to generate usable, though expensive, electrical power.

The light of the sun powers this radio telephone installed beside a highway in the barren reaches of the Saudi Arabian desert. An array of solar cells, joined together in the square panels at the top of the post, trap the solar energy and convert it into the electric power the Arab needs to establish radio contact with civilization.

COMMUNICATION, INFORMATION AND SPACE APPLICATIONS

NASA's Seasat 1 satellite explores the vast oceans of the world. Its instruments measure sea surface temperatures, wind and wave movement, icebergs and ocean currents. Although its working life is less than four months, Seasat provides a wealth of data on over 95% of the Earth's oceans—70% of the total surface—every 36 hours.

An ear plug, which not only receives sound but also transmits it, is patented in Tokyo, and allows walkie-talkie communication even against loud background noise. Whenever the wearer speaks, the ear plug transmits the vibrations as electrical signals. When listening, it translates these signals into vibrations which can be sensed by the human ear.

A chess-playing programme on a high-speed computer steals a game from San Fransisco Grand Master Peter Biyasis. On the mass market, sales of a talking Chess Challenger, electronic dice, microvision and other TV games are booming.

TRANSPORT, WARFARE AND SPACE EXPLORATION

Three spacecraft are docked together for the first time when Soyuz 27 docks at the forward airlock of the space station Salyut 6, to which Soyuz 26 is already linked.

West German drivers may soon benefit from radar warning systems, following tests aimed at reducing car collisions, particularly on roads carrying high-speed traffic. A microprocessor in a car converts radar signals into information about the speed and acceleration of vehicles in front of the driver, who can then assess any potential danger and be warned if he is too close to other cars.

A Greyhound 'Americruiser'—it is claimed to be the world's only turbine-powered bus—is exhibited at the International Gas Turbine Conference in London. Powered by an engine 1,000 lb (450 kg) lighter than an equivalent diesel unit, the bus uses low-grade fuel, which causes little pollution, and gives a comfortable ride.

ENERGY AND INDUSTRY

Washing machines reach the point where they are programmed to follow different instructions, leading to different washing and spinning cycles. Microchip technology and improved mechanics have brought more accurate control over a wide range of different fabrics, with better cleaning and faster spinning.

The number of nuclear power stations operating in the world now stands at 204. Of the total amount of electricity generated, the USA produces 46%.

Tibet puts its first geothermal power station into operation near the capital, Lhasa, where there are many hot springs and lakes.

MEDICINE AND FOOD PRODUCTION

The undesirable side-effects of oxytocin, which is used to induce labour in pregnant women, prompts US authorities to ban elective induced labour except in emergencies.

In Britain, the search for more effective anti-rejection drugs for organ transplants yields Cyclosporin A. This new immunosuppressive compound is non-steroidal and can sometimes be used to fight rejection without the need for the long-term steroid treatment which causes such unpleasant side-effects in transplant patients.

Researchers at University College and the National Hospital for Nervous Diseases in London identify myasthenia gravis as an auto-immune disease. This mysterious illness affects voluntary muscles, causes crippling weakness and can be fatal. Now it is recognized that the myasthenia gravis victim produces antibodies which attack receptor centres in the muscles. This may explain why complete blood transfusions—temporarily 'flushing out' the rogue antibodies—effectively reduce symptoms.

FRINGE BENEFITS

The pocket maths teacher, the Mathemagician calculator, is introduced by Videomaster.

The British Post Office continues trials of Prestel, its public TV information, or viewdata, service. Anyone with a telephone and a TV set can gain access to computerized data and services by means of a module which links both instruments to the terminal. The system will eventually be launched in 1980 and go international in 1981.

Louise Brown, the world's first test-tube baby, is born in July at Oldham, England, after doctors implanted a fertilized egg into her mother's womb. Patrick Steptoe and Dr. Robert Edwardes—pioneers of this particular technique—fertilized the egg in their laboratory using sperm from the husband, and kept it in a test-tube for $2\frac{1}{2}$ days before implanting it.

The Pentax 110 single lens reflex camera is the first 'system' camera in the subminiature format with a range of interchangeable lenses and accessories.

The Global Atmospheric Research Programme (GARP) of 1978–9 aims to discover how accurately the world's weather can be forecast. It uses five geostationary satellites provided by ESA and by the USA, USSR and Japan, to aid observation of air, cloud, snow and moisture movement over the entire Earth.

The Orbital Test Satellite (OTS), constructed for ESA with Britain as the prime contractor, is launched to form the basis of a European regional satellite system for telecommunications and experiments in TV distribution.

The arm of the law grows longer as lasers enter the field of forensics. Canadian scientists discover that a laser beam can reveal fingerprints, up to 10 years old, which fail to show up with ordinary methods.

Konica of Japan launch the world's first automatically focusing camera—the user has only to position the subject within a small square in the viewfinder, and the focus is set at the press of a button.

The Panapic, a miniature gramophone which plays discs embedded in the pages of a book, is successfully marketed as an educational toy by Matsushita of Japan.

Kenneth Warby achieves the official world water speed record of 319.627 mph (514.2 km/h) in the hydroplane *Spirit of Australia* on Blowering Dam Lake, New South Wales.

A road tanker, which promises safer transportation of dangerous and flammable chemicals, is tested in Britain by Shell. The tanker is the first in the world to carry its load within a double casing of glass-reinforced polyester. Polyurethane foam, treated with a fire retardant, is sandwiched between the two layers to give added protection in case of accidents. A low centre of gravity makes the tanker safe and easy to drive.

One train will test all Britain's railways every year. Ultrasonic equipment, backed up by 14 microprocessors and a minicomputer, can instantly process data, which currently has to be recorded on film and sent back to the laboratory. Any cracks detected in the line are marked with a splash of paint, while an alarm alerts the train's crew.

Engineers in Britain develop a thermoplastic form of natural rubber—the first that can be moulded, shaped and recycled. Invented by the Malaysian Rubber Producers' Research Association, it will offer new uses for natural rubber, such as lightweight body panels for cars.

One of a second generation of industrial robots is demonstrated at the Third Industrial Robot Conference and Exposition in Chicago. Made commercially available by Unimation and called PUMA, it is the first robot to be designed exclusively to assemble the hardware components of computers and motors.

The world's largest terminal for holding refrigerated containers from ships is built at Tilbury on the Thames estuary in England.

Specialists can only 'view' unborn children indirectly, using techniques such as ultrasound. Now, the laparoscope is developed at King's College Hospital in London. This flexible telescope-like instrument can be introduced through the mother's abdominal wall to give doctors their first direct glimpse of the living foetus in the womb.

Following the discovery of the cause of 'Legionnaire's disease', US health authorities investigate other outbreaks similar to the one which struck the American Legion convention in Philadelphia two years ago. They find the same bacterium, *Legionella pneumophila*, implicated in epidemics of this acute form of pneumonia in several other cities. The bacterium thrives in a variety of moist conditions from muddy streams to water-pipes.

British scientists succeed in transplanting a live egg cell from a freshly-killed female animal to one recently inseminated. This makes it possible to breed from pedigree females after their death, for the eggs can be deep-frozen, then implanted and fertilized in a host animal months or years later.

A panel of solar cells power a new calculator on the US market.

A plastic strip containing electric contacts activated by pressure is tacked to skirting (base) boards to provide an alarm system for the elderly.

The world's largest hovercraft, the SRN 4 'Super 4' enters service between England and France on the Dover/Boulogne/Calais route in July. The *Princess Anne* weighs in at 300 tons and has a cruising speed of 55 knots. The first SRN 4 carried 254 passengers and 30 cars; the 'Super 4' takes a 70% larger load—424 people and 55 cars—but costs only 15% more to operate.

COMMUNICATION, INFORMATION AND SPACE APPLICATIONS

Philips launch LaserVision, a digital video disc system smaller than many cassette decks. The disc is read by a helium neon laser and the system is free from the two problems that have dogged other video discs—dust and scratching.

Faster and more compact integrated circuits are now possible, using graphoepitaxy, MIT's new technique for growing silicon crystals by which artificial grooves are made in the crystals to control their natural growth. This breakthrough allows etched circuits to operate more quickly at reduced power and will, it is hoped, lead to 3–D circuits to provide larger programmes.

Micropad, the world's first computer terminal to accept direct handwritten data is introduced by Quest Automation in the USA.

Work begins on the development of robots able to 'see'. They will be programmed with a 'visual' coded memory and could revolutionize such industrial processes as quality control.

Bell Telephone Laboratories unveil their electronic blackboard. Identical in appearance to the traditional model, it transmits each image on to a visual display unit and automatically records the information.

TRANSPORT, WARFARE AND SPACE EXPLORATION

Skylab, the orbiting US space station, falls back to Earth on 11 July, after travelling 87 million mls (139 million km) around the planet since its launch in 1973. Once the largest, most sophisticated craft in space, Skylab breaks into thousands of pieces, two-thirds of which are burnt up in the Earth's atmosphere. Most fragments fall into the oceans, but some land in Western Australia—fortunately without causing damage to persons or property.

The moons of Jupiter are explored in fascinating detail by the US space probes Voyagers 1 and 2. The two nuclear-powered spaceships are heavier and better equipped than their predecessors, Pioneers 11 and 12, and reveal that Io, the innermost of the larger Jovian moons, is the most volcanically active body yet found in the solar system.

ENERGY AND INDUSTRY

An English inventor, R. Hawes proposes his Gemini wave energy power station. Its turbines would be driven by air compressed by floats, as they are moved by the waves.

The Tele-Mole, based on a British invention, is marketed by Iseki Poly-Tech of Japan. Since the tunnel-boring machine is laser-guided and remotely controlled by a computer at the surface, no human work-force is needed underground. The Tele-Mole works fast: fully-lined tunnels, up to 3.3 ft (1 m) in diameter, can be bored at the rate of 295 ft (90 m) per week.

The biggest dry dock in the world, designed to accommodate the largest ships afloat—some oil tankers weigh nearly a million tons—opens at Dubai in the United Arab Emirates. Built by British firms Costain International and Taylor Woodrow International, it has three docks, which can be emptied of water within three hours, and huge gates, which can be opened within 15 mins.

MEDICINE AND FOOD PRODUCTION

Interferon, a protein made by human body cells under attack from a virus, prevents viruses from reproducing and so controls the spread of infection. Burroughs Wellcome, the drug company, pioneers the large-scale production of interferon (cultured in human cells), making it available for experimental use against virus diseases and cancer.

The World Health Organization reports that *Mycobacterium leprae*, the causative agent of leprosy, is becoming resistant to antibiotics, so an effective vaccine is needed. Dr Dick Rees at the National Institute for Medical Research in London uses the nine-banded armadillo to grow sufficient quantities of *M. leprae* to make the first vaccine.

FRINGE BENEFITS

Wealthy US executives benefit from the 'Tera' pocket calculator, linked to a company's computer by two-way radio.

The US company Mattel receive their millionth chip for use in electronic games.

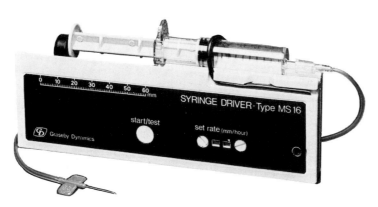

This microelectronic 'syringe driver' offers a unique way of infusing small volumes of liquid into the body over a period of time. Used by patients who need gradual doses of hormones, antibiotics or analgesics, for example, it can release measured amounts into the bloodstream over a period varying from $\frac{1}{2}$ hr to 50 hrs, according to need. Any standard small disposable syringe can be fitted to it, and when the syringe driver, which is battery powered, is fitted in its shoulder holster the patient experiences a minimum of inconvenience. A later model will be developed specifically for the continuous infusion of insulin to help in the control of diabetes.

JVC (Japan Victor Co) introduce a new video and digital sound disc. The disc is 'read' by a sapphire stylus with a playing life of 2,000 hrs. Picture quality is good and, unlike LaserVision, the system can be used to play both audio and video discs.

BASF of W. Germany demostrate their LVR (longitudinal video recording system) which offers 3 hrs of colour video from the world's smallest cassette.

Following rumours that pollution and the use of aerosol sprays may be changing the delicate balance of the Earth's atmosphere, a NASA Explorer–B satellite carries the Stratospheric Aerosol and Gas Experiment (SAGE) into orbit to assess any changes in the ozone level of the stratosphere.

A computerized laser printing method is developed by the Monotype Corp in Britain for publishing houses in Shanghai and Peking. The new method will change the lives of Chinese printers: previously they had to rollerskate between rows of type to select from the 60,000 characters in the Chinese language.

Canada becomes the first country to operate a satellite TV broadcasting service. The Anik B, which relays directly to home TV sets, requires only a small rooftop dish as an antenna.

Pioneer 11 becomes the first spacecraft to reach Saturn. Launched in 1973, primarily to study Jupiter, the probe reveals that the famous rings of Saturn are composed of ice-covered rocks. The spacecraft also photographs the planet from a distance of 12,500 mls (20,000 km); it is blue, with an area of bright bands near its North Pole.

In an effort to comply with proposed legislation limiting the amount of dangerous chemicals in a vehicle's exhaust fumes, US scientists develop the DISC (Direct-Injected Stratified Charge) engine. The new engine combines the fuel economy of a diesel engine with the better pollution control of a gasoline one.

Ariel 6, a British scientific satellite, is launched from the USA to study X-ray and cosmic ray astronomy.

The cost of producing silicon is reduced by one sixth. The Silane process, invented by Union Carbide Corp in the USA, means that solar cells can be made cheaply enough to put the production of electricity from sunlight on a cost-effective footing.

The most effective filter yet devised to keep the air clear of noxious airborne substances is announced by the Chemical Defence Centre at Porton Down in England. Made of 100% pure activated charcoal in cloth form, the filter will have many applications in the military, medical and industrial fields, since it prevents the inhalation of chemicals and germs.

West German researchers develop solar collectors which can capture diffuse, as opposed to direct, sunlight. Fitted to the roofs of houses, these collectors will provide enough solar power to heat domestic water and central heating systems, for they can generate temperatures of 212°F (100°C).

The infectious hepatitis virus is cultured in the laboratory for the first time. At the Merck Institute in Pennsylvania, Philip Provost and Maurice Hilleman round off 25 years of effort by successfully growing the virus in live kidney cells from a rhesus monkey foetus. This is the vital first step towards development of a vaccine.

At the McIndoe Unit of the Victoria Hospital in England, surgeons cover skin grafts with amniotic membrane—the sac surrounding a foetus in the womb. Professor Page Faulk suggests that the same substance in amniotic tissue which prevents the mother rejecting the 'foreign' foetus, may help the body accept a graft.

Throwaway toothbrushes are moulded from one piece of plastic by a firm in Milan.

Philips' new video computer toy uses plug-in cartridges that offer a variety of TV games selected by a touch-sensitive keyboard.

Private telephone exchanges are planned by Britain's GPO for small businesses.

One hundred new-style payphones controlled by microprocessors are installed at mainline railway stations in London and at some British airports. Dials are replaced by buttons and payment in advance—with an automatic money-back system for unused time—relieves local exchanges of the task of monitoring the cost of calls.

The speed of change in office equipment is emphasized by the Rank Xerox 9400 copier. Fully automated, it will print both sides of the paper, collate, produce 7,200 copies an hour and, as a bonus, it can diagnose many of its own faults and tell the operator what action to take to rectify them.

COMMUNICATION, INFORMATION AND SPACE APPLICATIONS

Designing a microchip which can pass through the eye of a needle is made easier with Stereoscan, an improved scanning electron microscope installed at Britain's Science Research Council laboratories.

Self-repairing microchip circuits, in which the functions of a damaged circuit are taken over by a neighbouring circuit, are designed by Dr John Barker of Warwick University, England. Multi-purpose chips are another electronic novelty. They are arranged so that they can perform a variety of functions, depending on the way they are connected up.

A 'listening' computer has been installed in the state of Illinois to give clearance for long-distance calls. The caller dials up the computer and reads in his credit card number which the computer then checks. If the caller's credit is acceptable, the computer switches the caller to an available long-distance line.

Third World countries can benefit hugely from electronic rain and river-flow gauges designed by Britain's Department of Agriculture to forecast floods and droughts.

TRANSPORT, WARFARE AND SPACE EXPLORATION

The US spacecraft Voyager 1 flies past the planet Saturn and makes the first close study of Titan (Saturn's largest moon), passing within 2,500 mls (4,030 km) of its surface. Excellent pictures of the planet's rings, and the discovery of six new moons, are among the fruitful results of the probe.

Commercially viable electric vehicles become more of a practical proposition with the announcement of a link-up between the British Chloride Company and GEC in America. By pooling resources, the two firms hope to achieve swifter production of a sodium-sulphur battery weighing 75% less than an equivalent lead-acid battery. The proposed battery would make an electric vehicle's power unit light enough to be an attractive alternative to the conventional engine.

ENERGY AND INDUSTRY

A large underground deposit of hot water, discovered near Southampton, England, is earmarked as a source of geothermal energy which could heat 1,000 houses for several decades. Meanwhile, the British Department of Energy and the European Economic Community together donate £7 million ($14 million) to tap the energy found in the hot granite rocks deep beneath the surface of Cornwall.

Biotechnology enters the energy-saving arena as micro-organisms are developed to ferment organic waste to produce alcohol. The eventual aim is to substitute alcohol for oil as a major source of fuel.

Two of Britain's largest glass-makers, Rockware Glass and United Glass, open big industrial plants for recycling cullet, or waste glass—remelting old glass is far cheaper than making new glass, which burns up more reserves of costly fuel. The companies aim to recycle 250,000 tons of glass each year until the end of 1983.

MEDICINE AND FOOD PRODUCTION

A US company, Dista Products, introduce a new anti-inflamatory drug: Opren works by preventing the attraction of white blood cells to arthritic joints.

Genetic engineering gets its first trial in humans when Martin Cline of the University of California attempts to treat thalassaemia, an hereditary blood disease. Cline tries to insert a corrected version of a defective gene into two patients' bone-marrow, but the procedure fails to cure the disease.

Investigators at Stanford University, USA, put monoclonal antibodies (MABs) to work in the early detection of disease. Various MABs, known to react to specific disease agents in the body, can be used to detect the presence of infectious illnesses and cancer at an early stage.

FRINGE BENEFITS

Streamlined roller skates made largely of lightweight plastics and alloys are in vogue.

Carrying the hopes of the British motor industry, the Austin Mini Metro is launched with enormous publicity. Designed to provide economical motoring in the Mini tradition, the Metro is much roomier inside than its small overall dimensions would suggest. The layout is the now-classic, transversely mounted engine, driving the front wheels, and body features include the 'hatchback' tailgate access facility that has proved so popular with buyers of small cars. British Leyland, the makers, look to large and continuing sales of the Metro to put the ailing company back on its feet.

The first of the Intelsat–V series of satellites is launched. The largest communications satellite put into Earth's orbit to date, Intelsat–V can relay 12,000 telephone calls and two colour TV channels.

The Xerox 5700 electronic printing system combines word-processor printing, electronic masking, remote control computer printing and direct copying in a single unit. Worldwide, the word processor market is booming. Sales are increasing by 25% a year: in the USA alone the market is worth well over $100 million a year.

AUGMENT, the automated office which offers a wide range of electronic facilities including note taking, editing, typesetting and spelling corrections, dialogue recording, calculations and computer graphics, is made available to the US public by the Stanford Research Institute. A similar system, SCRAPBOOK, developed by the National Physical Laboratory, is available in Britain.

A document can now be sent from London to Toronto in minutes with Intelpost, the first public international electronic facsimile service.

Discs are becoming as compact as cassettes. Philips in the Netherlands and Sony in Japan produce digital discs $4\frac{1}{2}$ in (11.25 cm) wide, which can play for several hours on each side. The discs are played back on a record player the size of an A4 sheet of paper, with a laser stylus which never touches—and so never wears out—the disc.

Although seat belts have been standard in US cars since the mid-sixties, it is estimated that only 20% of US drivers wear them. In contrast, 10 European countries have some form of law compelling car drivers and their passengers to wear seat belts.

Two Soviet cosmonauts return to Earth from the Salyut 6 space station after spending a record 184 days (about 6 months) in orbit. The mission commander, Valery Ryumin, took part in the 175-day Soyuz 32 mission in 1979, and so breaks the space dwellers' world record.

A female voice alerts the driver of the Datsun 810 luxury car, if the vehicle's lights have been left on. A miniature recording system in the dashboard reminds forgetful motorists: 'Please turn off your lights.'

Reduced pollution and the ability to burn a wide range of coals are the main advantages of the pilot power plant—the biggest of its type in the world—completed at Grimethorpe in Yorkshire, England. The plant, which represents the most important advance in coal combustion technology this century, will try out the technique of fluidized-bed coal combustion to determine whether the process is commercially viable on a large scale.

Bacteria continue to amaze the technological world when it is discovered that they can make fibres. Edward Atkins identifies many different fibres which, like cellulose at the turn of the century, could be exploited commercially. Malcolm Brown shows some bacteria actually making already-twisted fibres which could be stronger than cotton.

The fully automatic factory comes closer to actuality as computer-aided manufacture is developed in Japan, the USA and Britain. Computers will soon be used to design the components of machines and to control their manufacture in an automatic production system, which includes the use of robots and computer-controlled machining and assembly.

Scientists have determined the change in radio waves caused by selective absorption when a normal healthy organ is placed in a magnetic field. Now, at the Radcliffe Infirmary in Oxford, England, the topical magnetic resonator (TMR) is used to check the suitability of donor kidneys for grafting.

Page Faulk of the McIndoe centre for transplant biology in Sussex, England, discovers the protein ferritin which surrounds the foetus and protects it from its mother's immune system. Faulk shows that cancer cells have a ferritin layer and suggests that its removal would open the way to attack by antibodies.

Bone-marrow is particularly vulnerable to irradiation. Now, in Britain, West Germany and the USA, doctors adopt the practice of removing bone-marrow from cancer patients requiring heavy doses of X-ray treatment. Kept in a deep-freeze, the bone-marrow can later be reimplanted, unharmed.

The mapping of Venus nears its end. Ultraviolet pictures taken by the Pioneer Venus Orbiter spacecraft show swirling cloud formations over the planet, but for two years now the craft has been methodically mapping the planet's surface under the cloud by radar. Pioneer records continents and mountain ranges, but, on the whole, the surface of Venus is found to be flat. The survey also shows that Venus is rounder than the Earth, without either Earth's bulging equator or its flattened poles.

Sony's Walkman 1 is the runaway audio success of the year. It is a tiny tape player, not much larger than a tape cassette and so light that it is worn rather than carried. Sound comes through headphones only; and the sight of joggers, rollerskaters and cyclists wearing both headphones and happy expressions quickly becomes commonplace.

COMMUNICATION, INFORMATION AND SPACE APPLICATIONS

The space-saving Sony Typecorder aims to change the face of the average office. The typewriter-cum-tape-recorder uses plain paper, but stores up to 120 A4 pages of type on a single tape and prints out like a large desk calculator. Sony also launch a matching word processor with miniature disc stores and a full-page display monitor.

Fibre optics may soon be used to replace neon lights. Although costly, IMTECH, a new design based on thousands of short optical fibres, saves energy, lasts twice as long as its neon equivalent and is also weatherproof.

Safer landing at busy airports—and the early detection of toxic wastes—are the twin promises of SODAR (sonic detection and ranging). The giant device is installed at Frankfurt and other major West German airports to measure wind movement and strong air currents created by other aircraft in busy flightpaths. SODAR is also installed at a West German nuclear power station to predict the direction and speed of radioactive dust clouds in case of emergency.

TRANSPORT, WARFARE AND SPACE EXPLORATION

World railway routes now total 780,000 mls (1,248,000 km), of which 100,000 mls (160,000 km) are electrified.

The latest BMW car informs its driver when it needs a service or a change of oil. Electronic sensors monitor and analyse the engine's condition, taking into account not only speed and mileage, but also the way in which the driver handles the car and whether it is subjected to the rigours of city driving. A light on the dashboard warns when a service is due.

France chooses gas turbine engines to power her experimental high-speed train, which shatters the world rail speed record with a 235 mph (380 km/h) run. The Train Grande Vitesse, using specially constructed straight track, is expected to slash two hours off the journey time between Paris and Lyons.

ENERGY AND INDUSTRY

Britain celebrates 100 years of public electricity supply. Since the power was switched on from a generator connected to a waterwheel on the River Wey in Godalming, Surrey, Britain has developed the largest electricity supply organization in the world: the number of generating stations, fuelled by coal, gas, oil, water or nuclear fission, has grown to 127. They supply electricity to over 20 million customers in all parts of the country via the grid system.

British Aerospace develop a new method of shaping and moulding superplastic metal alloys to reduce the weight and cost of future aircraft. The wings of the Airbus A310 will be made from a titanium alloy which can be stretched and blown into shape, yet still retain its heat-resistant property during flight.

The world's longest single-span suspension bridge opens over England's Humber estuary. At 4,626 ft (1,410 m), its span is 367 ft (112 m) longer than the previous record-holder, the Verrazano Narrows Bridge, New York.

MEDICINE AND FOOD PRODUCTION

Essential blood proteins, such as those needed by haemophiliacs, can be genetically engineered in the laboratory. Instead of extracting these substances from whole blood, Speywood Laboratories of Nottinghamshire, England, engineer yeast cells to combine with the proteins, and then encourage them to multiply.

Sleeping sickness is still endemic in Africa and South America. Daunorubicin, an antibiotic, is excreted from the patient too quickly to kill the parasite. Dr James Williamson overcomes the problem by attaching daunorubicin to albumin or ferritin, two human proteins, which readily absorb it and increase its potency in the body.

FRINGE BENEFITS

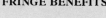

The first pocket-sized TV goes into production. Sinclair Radionics, of Cambridge, England, present Microvision, the result of five years of research and development (Sinclair also pioneered the pocket calculator). Microvision will receive black-and-white pictures on its 3-in (7.5-cm) screen almost anywhere in the world, and doubles as an FM radio receiver. It will cost £50 ($100).

A 19th-century dream is realized in the print industry. Gravure, a printing method that gives high quality results, has always been restricted by the problems of preparation of material for the process. Now, Crosfield Electronics' digital modular scanner, linked with a laser gravure cylinder engraving machine, makes gravure readily accessible.

Personal microcomputers are still dropping in price. Sinclair's latest model, the ZX81 sells for £70 ($140), which is just over two-thirds of last year's price. New features include animated graphics, and complex mathematical programmes.

Gallium arsenide may replace silicon as the linchpin of microelectronics. Each molecule emits light, conducts electricity and causes high-speed reactions.

A mini computer with the capacity of a mainframe model is introduced by Intel. The iAPX 432 uses three silicon chips, equivalent to 225,000 transistors, to perform functions at a speed that would make a mainframe overheat and consume too much power. Much of the programme, or software, is built directly into the hardware, or chips.

Holograms add an extra dimension to video games. Players of Cosmos, the latest game from Atari of California, see two-dimensional characters against a 3–D background, generated by holograms.

A videodisc which allows viewer participation is released in the USA by First National. The 'Kididisk', designed as a home teaching device, has fast forward, playback and freeze-frame facilities.

The Americans step up spending on laser weapon development—$200 million (£117 million) a year at the latest count. Initial hopes of producing a 'satellite-killing' beam are dashed by its prohibitive cost and susceptibility to jamming. But lasers fired from the ground or mounted in aircraft look promising for more conventional warfare—to say nothing of commercial laser power for generating electricity and launching satellites.

Suspended over the rails by magnetic levitation, and driven by linear induction motors, two 'maglev' trains each carry 32 passengers between Britain's Birmingham Airport and the National Exhibition Centre in Birmingham. Due to open officially in 1984, this will be the world's first commercial maglev service.

The first Soviet nuclear-powered surface warship, the battlecruiser *Kirov*, is commissioned. Capable of a speed of 35 knots, its nuclear reactors are supplemented by oil-fired boilers to drive the steam turbines.

The USSR's oil output reaches 12.2 million barrels a day. This makes Russia the largest oil producer in the world, a position it reached in 1974 and has kept ever since. Its target for 1985 is between 12.4 and 12.9 million barrels a day. It is the second largest exporter of oil at 3.2 million barrels a day, and is the largest exporter of natural gas at 1.6 million million cu ft (45,307 million cu m) per year.

Thorn Lighting in Britain announce their new, very thin domestic lamp which produces as much light as a 100 W bulb but consumes a fifth of the power. Called 2D—its fluorescent tube is folded into the shape of two Ds—it is designed to last for 5,000 hrs, five times longer than normal light bulbs.

ICI announce that a bacterium may soon be helping them to manufacture plastic goods for the home. This bacterium—*Alcaligenes eutrophum*—can store over two-thirds of its body-weight as PHB (polyhydroxybutyrate) when food is in short supply. ICI have harnessed this ability and use PHB as an ingredient in the making of certain plastics. This latest example of biotechnology may be expanded in the future by genetically engineering the bacterium to produce different substances for use in a wider range of plastics.

Premature babies are often overwhelmed by breathing difficulties due to a thin liquid film covering the surface of the lungs. Now Alec Bangham of the Institute of Animal Physiology at Cambridge, England, develops a substance to overcome the surface tension. It can be inhaled by babies in powder form to give a life-saving coating to the lungs.

The US Food and Drug Administration approves a vaccine against serum hepatitis. Developed by Merck, Sharpe and Dolme, it is in its final testing stages. With an estimated 200 million people throughout the world chronically infected, this long-awaited vaccine is likely to be in wide demand.

Rubik's cube, a mind-bending toy, is introduced to Britain.

The BAe 146 begins test flights. The makers, British Aerospace, have designed their 80-seat 'Feederliner' to collect passengers from smaller airports and 'feed' them to larger ones. The aircraft shows many innovative features in an effort to compete with US planemakers, and it is exceptionally quiet; but there are doubts about its likely fuel economy.

COMMUNICATION, INFORMATION AND SPACE APPLICATIONS

Since the first electronic computer appeared in 1951, the speed of large-scale scientific models has doubled approximately every two years. The latest US supercomputers, Cray I, built by Cray Research Inc, and CYBER 205 from the Control Data Corp, can perform 100 million arithmetical operations in a second. Aerodynamics, meteorology, seismology and atomic research all demand these speeds to unscramble complex problems.

Kodak introduces a film format that is truly revolutionary—it is a 15-exposure disc which uses a new high definition emulsion and carries coded information to facilitate processing and printing. Kodak's new range of cameras have microprocessor control.

The American Broadcasting Company and Britain's Channel 4 have bought the first video picture library to conform to national TV standards.

Satellite TV is to be introduced commercially into Britain by the Marconi Co before the end of 1986. The BBC plans to run two channels— one with edited highlights of old broadcasts and a second running feature films.

TRANSPORT, WARFARE AND SPACE EXPLORATION

The Dutch sloop *Flyer*, skippered by Cornelis van Reitschoten completes the Whitbread Round-the-World yacht race in 120 days, breaking the previous record for the 27,000-ml (43,200-km) journey by a remarkable 14 days.

The first Boeing 757 takes off in February at the start of a year's worth of final tests. Its advanced wings, built on to a 727-style fuselage, carry two Rolls-Royce RB 211-535C turbofans—Boeing's first venture into non-American engines for a new aircraft. Competing for the short/medium range airliner market, the 757 will have to contend with Airbus Industrie's new offering, the A310.

During the conflict between Britain and Argentina over the Falkland Islands, the *HMS Sheffield* is sunk by an Exocet missile, bought from Aérospatiale of France. Known as the 'Fire and Forget' missile, the Exocet uses its own radar to home in on, and strike, a target out of the blue from up to 25 mls away, skimming the surface of the sea to avoid being picked up by any defensive radar.

ENERGY AND INDUSTRY

Engineers in France devise a cheap and simple way of laying deep-water pipelines for future use by the offshore oil industry. A barge, fitted with a machine which employs electron beams to align and weld joints, can automatically lay steel pipes up to six times quicker than conventional, less secure methods.

The US Whirlpool Corp announce that over 10 years they have cut the energy consumption of refrigerators by 47%, washing machines by 42%.

Engineers at Inverness, Scotland, complete the tallest—and probably the last—giant oil platform for use in the North Sea. At a height of 611 ft (210 m), made of steel and weighing 41,000 tons, it will support equipment which will, in 1983, pump oil ashore from British Petroleum's Magnus field—the most northerly North Sea field yet to be developed.

MEDICINE AND FOOD PRODUCTION

British doctor Michael Epstein identifies the first virus implicated in human cancer: the Epstein Barr, present in Burkitt's lymphoma—a highly malignant cancer common in African children.

A 49-year-old man, whose diseased heart is said to have stopped 70 times, is the first Briton to be fitted with a computerized heart pacemaker. A tiny microprocessor warns the artificial pacemaker if his heart's rhythm becomes erratic.

Israeli doctors report success with interferon (an anti-virus protein compound) in treating severe infectious hepatitis. They recommend large-scale trials with the drug, which could be especially useful in stimulating the natural immune system.

FRINGE BENEFITS

A robot machine that is able to crawl over sheer surfaces may relieve sailors of cleaning ships' hulls.

An electronic pass enables security systems to monitor workers' movements in high-risk jobs.

A lie detector for home use is now available.

Sony preview a prototype all-electronic camera, the Mavica, which uses a magnetic disc to store up to 50 pictures in digital form. The discs can be viewed on a TV monitor, transmitted over a telephone line and developed in conventional printed form. The discs may also be reused by erasing the pictures.

National Panasonic launch the NV-7900, Britain's first domestic video recorder with a stereo sound facility. It can be used in conjunction with stereo TV sets, or conventional hi-fi systems in tandem with ordinary TV sets. The accompanying hand-set allows 25 of the NV-7900's functions to be remotely controlled.

Toward 2000
the question of
the future

Part of the appeal of science fiction lies in the glimpses of future machines and future life-styles. Human beings are fascinated by the future as much as the past and like to try and foresee events, to look beyond the boundary between the world as it is and the world as it will be.

This book has made an inventory of 20th century technology and the accompanying scientific expertise; the machines and processes featured have shaped the world we live in today. Now the book has reached the boundary between present and future. To what extent can future technology be predicted, particularly the technical advances between now and the end of the century?

Futurology, a science of sorts, is the nearest thing to a systematic way of predicting the shape of the future. The work of futurologists, though, is shackled by powerful constraints that complicate even straightforward predictions about the technology to come. Why is prediction so difficult a task? There is one profound philosophical answer to this question, and a host of practical reasons best summarized as the interaction between trends and serendipity.

First, the philosophic reason: the commonsense answer to the question 'Does every event have a cause?' is yes. Trees fall down because lightning strikes them; oaks grow because acorns germinate. But, at the level of the atomic fabric of nature, commonsense is not always a good guide. As demonstrated by the disintegration of atoms in radioactive substances, each atom will eventually break down. Every disintegration is a distinct event, but there is absolutely no way of predicting when

any specific atom will explode. Atomic detonations are events without causes and this central uncertainty seems to extend to almost all aspects of atomic behaviour. It is intrinsically impossible to pin down the motions of individual atomic particles in space and time.

The shadowy imprecision of cause and effect underlying this most fundamental structure of the world is a clue that larger events might have equally imprecise causes.

The practical reasons for the difficulty of prediction are more obvious. Predictions based on trends are usually made by examining the past pattern of change and extrapolating this previous trend on to the future. With sufficient information and in unchanging conditions, this approach can give good results in the short-term. In practice, however, vital information is often lacking, the environment itself is constantly changing and chance events can drastically alter circumstances.

Such chance events are the serendipity factor. An Arab-Israeli war here, a seven-year drought there and a million other uncontrollable factors, up to and including World War III, can all make utter nonsense of any predictions based on trend analysis. For example, the experience gained in the 1982 South Atlantic war will undoubtedly affect developments in weapon technology.

This said, given a reasonably stable world in the next 20 years, there are technological developments that are reasonably certain to occur. Well-founded predictions can give a good insight into the world of technology up to—and even beyond—the end of the 20th century.

The future / 2

Following the launch by Novo in 1982 of a pig-derived human insulin, an entirely microbiological human insulin is now being marketed by Eli Lilley.

Large-scale trials in Pakistan of the first plant bred specifically for biomass energy conversion have been successful. The small trees grow rapidly, with an astounding cellulose production rate, and can be cropped when three years old. They flourish in semi-arid conditions because of their extensive, deep root system and can be grown in areas unsuitable for food crops. The trees provide a cash crop for subsistence farms, are a domestic heating source and can be used as fuel in a range of specially designed electrical generators.

Fear of dentists becomes a thing of the past as a new chemical, GK–101, replaces the dreaded drill in removing the decayed portions of teeth. GK–101 is simply and painlessly squirted into cavities where, within minutes, tooth decay breaks up, leaving the healthy part of the tooth ready for filling.

Thinking out the thinking machine

Computers and other micro-electronic devices have utterly transformed communications. Traditional communication is the transfer of information from one person or place to another and this information is always thought of as part of whoever or whatever carries it. Now that machines can ingest, store, manipulate and transfer information, it can be conceived as an entity with its own existence.

Information is still collected, processed, stored and transmitted in the form of sorting, typing and printing in words and pictures on paper, even in highly industrialized societies. By the end of this century, there seems to be no doubt that this position will have changed dramatically and more and more information will be handled electronically.

Before the information revolution can take hold among ordinary people, certain thresholds of convenience and cost must be passed. In industrialized countries these thresholds have already been passed for some functions such as everyday arithmetic computation, typing/word processing and data storage. Over the next two decades, real unit costs for the integrated circuits at the heart of the new information technology will continue to fall. This will make the machines available to more people and overcome the cost barrier.

Once the machines are cheap they must also be convenient. At present it is impossible to imagine newspapers being completely replaced by an electronic information transmission system. The news can be gathered and transmitted quickly and efficiently by electronic means, but one cannot fold up a television receiver and watch it on the way to work. But, with the trend towards smaller and more portable receivers, the 'foldable' TV becomes a possibility. Smaller, flatter cathode-ray tubes which use less power but have increasing signal sensitivity will be one important trend in TV development.

Computers have become a far more familiar part of everyday life in the last ten years. Wage slips are computerized, many households own an electronic calculator, or even a small home computer; children play with electronic toys.

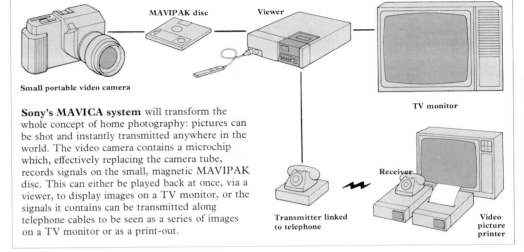

Small portable video camera — **MAVIPAK disc** — **Viewer** — **TV monitor** — **Receiver** — **Transmitter linked to telephone** — **Video picture printer**

Sony's MAVICA system will transform the whole concept of home photography: pictures can be shot and instantly transmitted anywhere in the world. The video camera contains a microchip which, effectively replacing the camera tube, records signals on the small, magnetic MAVIPAK disc. This can either be played back at once, via a viewer, to display images on a TV monitor, or the signals it contains can be transmitted along telephone cables to be seen as a series of images on a TV monitor or as a print-out.

The huge surge of development in computer technology over the last two decades will certainly continue over the next two.

The crucial central technology in computers is the silicon integrated circuit (SIC). SIC is the Model T Ford of the micro-electronics industry. A SIC is at present produced by cutting an extremely thin slice of silicon from a single huge crystal. On this semi-conducting substrate, circuitry is produced on a microscopic scale. Researchers in the USA, Europe and Japan are currently working to improve the basic processing power of SICs or even to supplant them with different types of logic circuitry. This research should spawn a few competing systems in the next 20 years.

One feature almost certain to enter commercial computer production is the obvious one of packing more and more components into each square millimetre of silicon surface—'ultra-high-level' integrations. Photoreduction has been developed to the point where circuitry patterns less than 3 microns ($\frac{3}{1000}$mm) across are the commercial norm, and packings of submicron dimensions can already be produced in the laboratory. But wavelength considerations mean that this is the theoretical limit to lithography using light. In the near future, electron beams or X-ray sources, both with shorter wavelength characteristics than visible light, will almost certainly be used to achieve circuit printing of even greater density. When such developments are commercially available, the single memory chip, which now contains about 64,000 memory elements, may contain more than a million elements.

Also under consideration are more revolutionary options that might take off commercially before the end of the century. IBM for instance is extremely interested in 'Josephson junction' technology. Such junctions in micro-circuits depend for their operation on the fact that some materials become super-conducting at temperatures close to absolute zero ($-273°C$). In 1979, IBM demonstrated that, in laboratory conditions with massive cooling equipment to generate the necessary low temperatures, Josephson circuits could be made to operate ten times faster than SIC systems.

Other computer companies, such as Fujitsu in Japan, are investigating whether semiconductors other than single crystal silicon—gallium arsenide, for instance—might produce advantages in operating speed.

Information transfer over long distances can take place between computers via telephone networks. An alternative system for transmitting digital information uses electronically

Heart disease, one of the century's most insidious killers, is rendered less likely by the introduction in the USA of a synthetic vegetable oil which eliminates harmful cholesterol. This sucrose polyester has no calories, spreads like margarine and can be eaten in quantity without the dangerous accumulation of cholesterol. Its one disadvantage—interference with Vitamin A and E absorption—can be overcome by including vitamin pills in the diet.

The NASA space telescope, with computer control and memory facilities, is now in orbit. Sited above the Earth's atmosphere, and with a reflecting mirror unaffected by gravitational distortion, the optical telescope is able to respond to much fainter signals than those detectable by even the largest ground-based telescopes.

A safe, short-acting contraceptive for use by men has been produced by organic chemists. It works by inhibiting the enzymes that enable migrating sperm to penetrate mucus and fuse with a female egg. The inhibitor is taken in pill form before intercourse and rapidly achieves effective levels in the seminal fluid. Once the ejaculated sperms are inside the sexual partner, the inhibitor prevents them from moving and from fertilizing the egg. The drug has no effect on sperm production, hormone levels or libido, and 24 hours later the sperm is effective again.

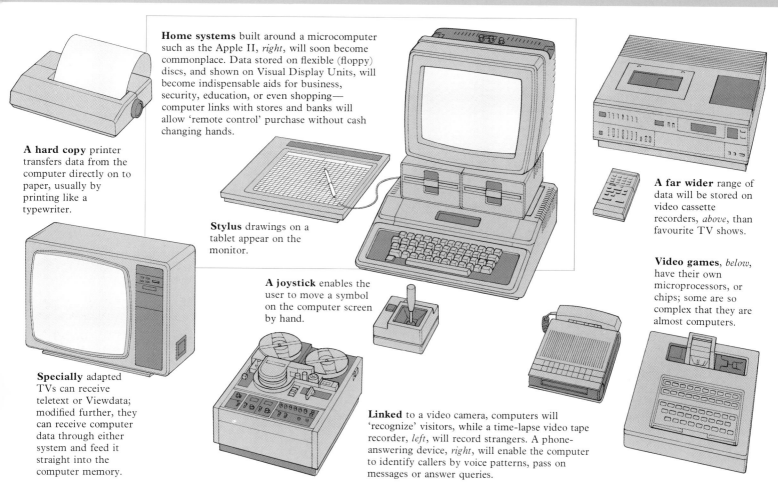

Home systems built around a microcomputer such as the Apple II, *right*, will soon become commonplace. Data stored on flexible (floppy) discs, and shown on Visual Display Units, will become indispensable aids for business, security, education, or even shopping— computer links with stores and banks will allow 'remote control' purchase without cash changing hands.

A hard copy printer transfers data from the computer directly on to paper, usually by printing like a typewriter.

Stylus drawings on a tablet appear on the monitor.

A far wider range of data will be stored on video cassette recorders, *above*, than favourite TV shows.

Video games, *below*, have their own microprocessors, or chips; some are so complex that they are almost computers.

A joystick enables the user to move a symbol on the computer screen by hand.

Specially adapted TVs can receive teletext or Viewdata; modified further, they can receive computer data through either system and feed it straight into the computer memory.

Linked to a video camera, computers will 'recognize' visitors, while a time-lapse video tape recorder, *left*, will record strangers. A phone-answering device, *right*, will enable the computer to identify callers by voice patterns, pass on messages or answer queries.

modulated light signals sent along glass or silica fibres of hairlike fineness. Digital information from the first computer is converted into visual form by modulating a semi-conductor laser or light-emitting diode. The optical signals are then transmitted along the inside of the fibre and reconverted into digital form in the second computer. The advantages of these fibre optic signals over other systems include: increased security, low basic material costs, light, flexible cables and low signal loss per unit of cable length. Such advantages make it extremely likely that gossamer-fine optic cab-

leways, laid next to roads or railway tracks, or slotted inside power transmission cables, will be as common as copper cables by 2000.

The great breakthrough to AI, artificial intelligence, the final barrier that hovers before all computer scientists, might just come in the next two decades. In Japan there is already a gigantic, subsidized effort toward the so-called 'fifth generation' level of computing power. The aim of this work is to produce computers that properly duplicate the human powers of hearing and vision, thus opening up the possibility of direct communication between man

and the machines he has created.

Even more breathtaking is the fact that these 'fifth generation' machines will have the ability of 'creative thought'. Concepts in programming will have to be revolutionized and software in such computers will use human 'fuzzy' or open-ended logic.

If such systems can be made to work, they can be set the problems of improving their own programmes. By 2000, computers may have left us behind. They might be busy making improvements to themselves, the nature of which we do not understand.

The future /3

Electric cars become practical with the development of powerful batteries only $\frac{1}{10}$ the weight of conventional batteries. The new batteries, which contain porous polyacetylene films used as electrodes, will, by 2000, put 8 million electric cars on US roads.

A joint working group from NASA, the World Bank and UNESCO have announced plans for an ambitious scheme to provide the potential for domestic satellite communication between every town on Earth. A large number of geostationary satellites with huge 'open access' data transmission ability will be launched by Space Shuttles. The satellites can be used for speech or TV transmission between any point on the globe with the relevant transmitter system, to any other point equipped with high-sensitivity dish aerials for reception.

'Smart' rooms now figure in 10% of US houses and offices. Designed as energy-savers, their scanning electronic 'people sensors' switch on lights—and heating—when a person enters a room and switch them off when the last person leaves.

Weapons that hide and seek

Computer logic, squeezed into smaller and smaller spaces and using less and less power, will have a huge impact on all types of weapon systems over the next 20 years. Every gun might have its own integral computer; thus the infantry rifle of 1999 would provide a magnified day or night view of the target zone, ask for a target to be identified on its viewing screen, decide which type of projectile to fire, aim itself, make allowance for wind speed and direction, then fire on command.

Equipment for warfare has become the work goal of increasing numbers of the world's most gifted minds. There are probably more qualified scientists and technologists working in the world today than have ever existed through all of man's history, but at the same time, more money is spent on the research and development of military technology than on any other sector of human activity. This trend is almost certain to continue, and all conventional weaponry existing at present can be refined with the new technology.

The most deadly and potent technology is reserved for the massive killing machines—strategic nuclear weapons. In the USA and USSR the development of strategic weaponry over the next 20 years will be constrained in three ways: by technological possibilities, by funding levels, and by the self-imposed, reciprocal nuclear arms agreements. Whatever patterns these constraints take, the basic organization of strategic weaponry will remain the same—a mixture of fusion weapons (H-bombs), housed in a trio of delivery systems. The delivery systems are land-based ICBMs (inter-continental ballistic missiles), nuclear-powered submarines carrying ICBMs, and strategic bombers. How will these delivery systems and warheads change in the future?

There will be a greater range of warheads. Some will simply get bigger in order to counteract increasingly well-protected targets, or to neutralize many targets at once. Others will be multiple, with perhaps 10 to 20 independently targetable warheads, capable of separating in complex patterns to confuse defensive radar, and of releasing bogus war-heads against which anti-missile missiles will be pointlessly expended. Current trends suggest that the guidance systems of all missiles will become even more accurate using ultra-detailed satellite mapping of enemy areas.

New delivery systems take a long time to plan and produce. The next 20 years in the USA should see the deployment of the next generation of ICBMs—the MX system. A variety of deployment methods has been considered, but the latest scheme, which might well be adopted, is the 'dense pack' strategy. Missiles, each carrying 10 warheads, are placed in some of a densely packed array of dummy and functional silos—dense packing means placing missiles only one or two kilometres apart. If an enemy attempts to destroy this array with a shower of warheads, the dense pack defends itself because the first incoming warhead will detonate so close to its trailing companions that it will cause them to detonate prematurely. In military jargon this mutual destruction between warheads is termed 'fratricide'. The first 'fratricide-inducing' dense packs could be in position by 1987.

The efficiency of submarine missile delivery systems depends on their position being unknown up to the instant when they launch their missiles. Over the next few years, technology will be working towards two opposing ends. First, methods of locating well-hidden submerged submarines will be improved, perhaps by the computer analysis of sound patterns detected by fixed and temporary networks of underwater microphones. Second, submarines will become even larger, deeper diving and quieter in order to maintain their effectiveness.

Paradoxically, the most dramatic developments of the next years could occur in what was previously the least sophisticated and most

Commercial cargoes of the future may be carried in aerial freighters, *below*, in which a flatbed between nose and tail is fitted with containers that are simply slotted in to form the fuselage. The giant, six-engined McDonnell Douglas Spanloader, *bottom*, may carry over 260 tons of cargo non-stop across the USA by stowing containers in its thick 300 ft long (91 m) wings.

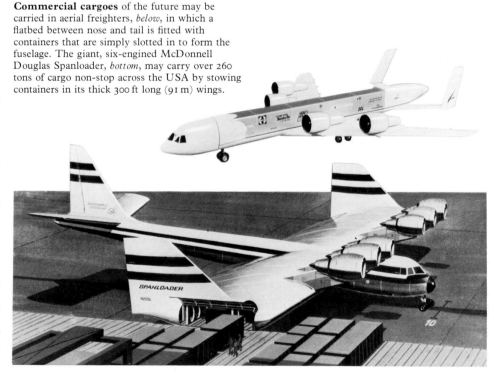

easily countered delivery system—the manned strategic bomber. Bombers, typified by the aging B–52s, are vulnerable to surface-to-air missiles and supersonic interceptors. The bomber's relatively slow speed is only part of the problem; even a supersonic bomber is still an easy target because its position can be quickly assessed by radar.

Since its development in World War II, radar technology has transformed air warfare. Defending forces can accurately locate and identify attacking planes by using increasingly subtle radar-based methods. Bombers and fighter planes can only survive if they can baffle the radar 'eyes' of the defending forces. If aircraft can be made that do not significantly reflect the microwave radiation utilized by radar systems, they would effectively be invisible to them.

Weapons systems technologists in the USA

are trying to produce just such an aircraft—the advanced technology bomber or 'Stealth'. The plane is still highly secret, but some of the components of its design can be deduced. It will have a smooth, uncluttered outline and the surface might be coated with a layer of a material that reduces the reflected radar signal energy. The body of the aircraft is likely to include a large proportion of non-metallic materials, for instance carbon fibre-containing composites. Stealth should have a radar image so feeble that it will be extremely difficult to locate by any known radar.

As well as the direct developments of existing weapon technology, there is an outside chance that, before the end of the nineties, completely new weapons systems might appear. At the moment these might seem straight out of 'Star Wars', but there are serious suggestions that laser or particle beam weapons are

practical possibilities. Such weapons might be located in earth orbit and used to destroy enemy satellites or ICBMs in mid-course trajectories. Gigantically powerful energy sources would be needed to produce beams of sufficient intensity to destroy such targets over long distances, but this is probably the least of the problems. Any lasers would have great difficulty inflicting damage on a target with a reflective, mirror-like surface. The charged particle streams that would be produced by the weapon could be reduced by interaction with the atmosphere and bent by magnetic fields.

While it is difficult to predict the exact course of developments, one thing is certain: the turn of the century will see us with a clutch of even more terrifying armaments—unless the weapons we have now are used to their full effect before we reach that date, or good sense intervenes in the political arena.

Lockheed's supersonic transport, *right*, for the nineties may revitalize aluminium which, mixed with lithium, say, can withstand temperatures of 300°F (130°C), yet remain 10% lighter than conventional alloys.

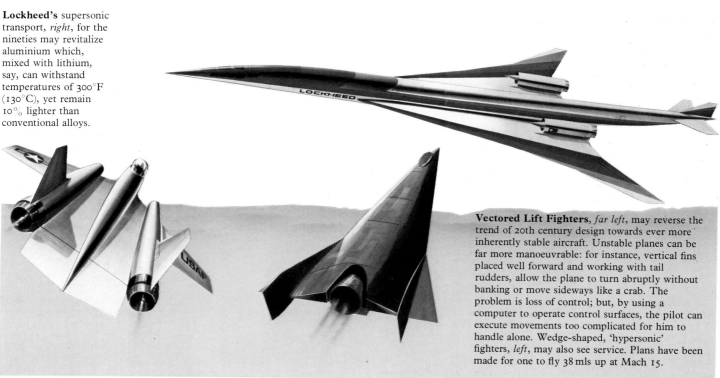

Vectored Lift Fighters, *far left*, may reverse the trend of 20th century design towards ever more inherently stable aircraft. Unstable planes can be far more manoeuvrable: for instance, vertical fins placed well forward and working with tail rudders, allow the plane to turn abruptly without banking or move sideways like a crab. The problem is loss of control; but, by using a computer to operate control surfaces, the pilot can execute movements too complicated for him to handle alone. Wedge-shaped, 'hypersonic' fighters, *left*, may also see service. Plans have been made for one to fly 38 mls up at Mach 15.

The future /4

The successful use of computers as aids to medical diagnosis has led to their adoption by psychiatrists. Flashing questions up on a video screen—the patient types in answers—the computer is able to make a preliminary diagnosis of the patient's condition, freeing the doctor from much of the donkey-work and allowing him to devote more time to people who need personal attention. Patients report that they often relate more openly to the sympathetic, objective machine than to its human counterpart.

The French Government converts all exchange-to-exchange mainland telephone routes from copper cable to optical fibre systems. Soon, exchange-to-subscriber links will also be converted to this system.

An executive speech processor is launched commercially. This minicomputer can unerringly transcribe normal speech into text, while storing the material with a running keyword indexing system. It comes with a basic vocabulary of 75,000 words and sophisticated grammatical knowledge, but must be 'trained' to understand the speech idiosyncrasies of the person dictating to it.

More power to energy

The sun is the supreme energy source. Without it, the Earth's temperature would never rise above $-450°F$ ($-280°C$). So, the ultimate, high-technology answer to the world's insatiable appetite for energy is to create a miniature, controlled sun on earth, and multi-million dollar experiments in fusion power, imitating the nuclear processes which fuel the sun, are already in progress. Although the technological difficulties are immense, the dream may well become reality early in the twenty-first century.

The energy industry is expanding fast, both by developing existing techniques and sources, and by exploring new possibilities. But just what you will fill your car with in 2001 is hard to foresee because of the unpredictable effects of social attitudes and political change. In the last 20 years, for example, fears about the safety of nuclear fission power plants have effectively curtailed nuclear energy developments in some countries. Arab-Israeli conflicts and Islamic politics have dramatically changed the financial structure of the world's oil markets—in ten years, prices rose from two dollars a barrel to over 40 dollars. World upheavals as much as scientific research will determine which energy sources will be in use at the end of the century.

Today, fossil fuels reign supreme. In developed countries with their gargantuan energy consumption, oil, coal and gas provide the bulk of energy for domestic and industrial purposes. But, since the fifties, commercial, uranium-fuelled fission power plants have produced an ever-increasing, if minor, proportion of the total energy demands of these countries. Other sources of usable energy still represent only a tiny proportion of the global sum.

Ultimately, the relative proportions of the energy sources used must change because, at present, the world is committed to profligate use of non-renewable, natural resources. Coal, gas, oil, even peat, represent the accumulation of hundreds of millions of years of carbon fixation by long-dead plants. However imprecise our estimates of the world's fossil hydrocarbon reserves are, one fact is sure: those reserves are finite. Twentieth century people alone will have used the bulk of that great inheritance.

The oil shocks of recent years—embargoes, price rises—have given the industrialized world strong warning of its energy vulnerability. The resulting anxiety has stimulated a remarkable number of attempts to prove the viability of energy forms using renewable resources. All of these techniques—wind power, wave and tidal power, geothermal sources, solar energy, biomass conversion, fast breeder reactors, nuclear fusion—existed in embryo before, but have been the subject of much closer scrutiny since the eventful years of the seventies.

The eighties and nineties will see three main strategies of development in energy technology. The first will be the increasing diversity and sophistication of fossil fuel recovery techniques. After the success of the North Sea and Gulf of Mexico fields, more and more remote, hazardous, continental shelf sites will be probed for hydrocarbon reserves. Large-scale reserves are likely to be discovered in the Antarctica area, and between mainland China and Australasia. To extract those reserves, increasingly adventurous marine platforms will be needed.

The oil industry will also expand its efforts to extract oil from sources hitherto considered uneconomical. Shale-oil reserves—oil locked in rock formations—are gigantic, particularly in the USA, and, as oil prices rise, the complex and expensive extraction techniques seem more worthwhile. Another, perhaps more rapid, change in secondary extraction methods will be achieved through biotechnology. Bacteria will be isolated, or genetically engineered, that can be injected underground to loosen presently unextractable oil so that it can be removed economically.

The second strategy in the energy technology of the near future will be to upgrade one or more of the possible renewable energy sources to the level of importance that nuclear fission has today. Different methods will suit different parts of the world. Biomass conversion and solar energy techniques are good possibilities for the tropical, developing nations. In Europe and the USA the next 20 years might just see the culmination of the scientists' energy dream: fusion power.

Fusion power fuels the sun and every star in the universe. Within the sun, gravitational forces are so immense that sufficiently high temperatures are achieved to make hydrogen atomic nuclei fuse together. In the chain of linked nuclear reactions at this temperature, matter itself is turned into energy. Hydrogen

bombs are uncontrolled examples of the power of nuclear fusion, but, if the process could be achieved under controlled conditions on earth, it could provide virtually limitless energy.

Two large-scale prototype installations exist that might achieve controlled nuclear fusion before the century is out: the Joint European Torus project (JET), near Oxford in Britain, and the Tokamak Fusion Test Reactor at Princeton, New Jersey, USA. Both use the Tokamak, a device that employs electromag-netic coils to create the extreme conditions necessary for nuclear fusion.

Fusion is still a dream, but fission, the third major strategy of energy development, exists now. In the USA it already provides one-tenth of the electricity supply and its use is bound to expand over the next 20 years. The accident at the Three Mile Island nuclear plant in Pennsylvania showed the dangers of this power technology, but demonstrated that, even in the face of catastrophic human errors, the safety margins built into a normal commercial reactor avoid serious leakage and loss of life.

Between now and the end of the century, a combination of new reserves, new technology and fuel economies will offset the declining potential of known energy sources. But economic growth and wealth are utterly dependent on energy and the race is on to find new ways of coping with ever-increasing demands. The world will soon have to choose the energy source of the future.

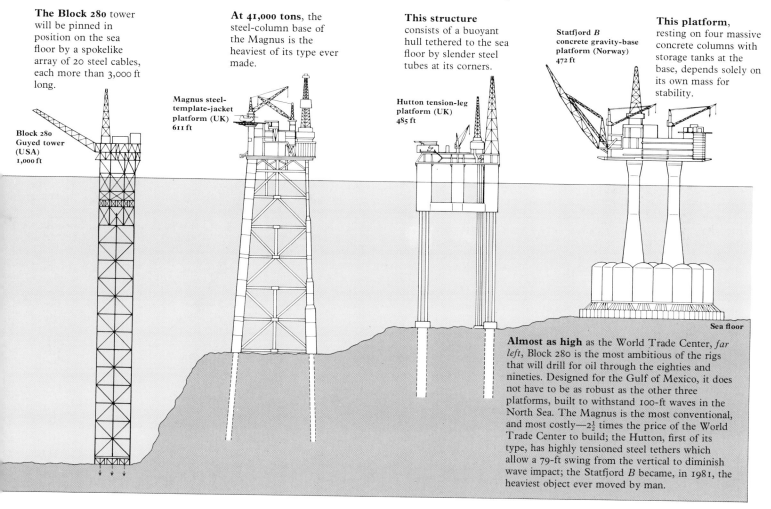

The Block 280 tower will be pinned in position on the sea floor by a spokelike array of 20 steel cables, each more than 3,000 ft long.

Block 280 Guyed tower (USA) 1,000 ft

At 41,000 tons, the steel-column base of the Magnus is the heaviest of its type ever made.

Magnus steel-template-jacket platform (UK) 611 ft

This structure consists of a buoyant hull tethered to the sea floor by slender steel tubes at its corners.

Hutton tension-leg platform (UK) 485 ft

Statfjord *B* concrete gravity-base platform (Norway) 472 ft

This platform, resting on four massive concrete columns with storage tanks at the base, depends solely on its own mass for stability.

Sea floor

Almost as high as the World Trade Center, *far left*, Block 280 is the most ambitious of the rigs that will drill for oil through the eighties and nineties. Designed for the Gulf of Mexico, it does not have to be as robust as the other three platforms, built to withstand 100-ft waves in the North Sea. The Magnus is the most conventional, and most costly—$2\frac{1}{2}$ times the price of the World Trade Center to build; the Hutton, first of its type, has highly tensioned steel tethers which allow a 79-ft swing from the vertical to diminish wave impact; the Statfjord *B* became, in 1981, the heaviest object ever moved by man.

The future / 5

The first wave-power production platform, tethered off the Japanese coast in 1991, is now supplying power to the Japanese electricity grid.

The prototype of the 797 'Century Airplane' is revealed. A wide-bodied, fuel-efficient aircraft, it weighs over twice as much as the legendary 747 'Jumbo' and will seat 1500 passengers. Thanks to economies of scale and new, high-efficiency jet engines, the real unit passenger cost will be significantly lower than that of the 747. Direct computer control of all wing surfaces during take-off and landing will mean that the 797 needs only 10% more runway length than its predecessor.

Nuclear power plant technology takes a step forward with the development of an efficient vitrifying process for the stabilization of dangerous radioactive waste.

The Princeton-based nuclear fusion research team succeed in producing sustained fusion energy. The project director predicts that a power-generating fusion plant will be operating commercially within 20 years.

Changing the facts of life

Genetic engineering, long predicted by science fiction writers, is now a reality, and could conceivably help us toward a cure for cancer. It is part of an ever-expanding biotechnology explosion that could change the face of medicine in the next two decades.

After years of being considered a soft, unrigorous science, biology has sprung into the limelight and is becoming an increasing force in the chemical and pharmaceutical industries. The subject areas of cell biology, cellular genetics and biochemistry have now fused to provide the world with the framework of techniques known as genetic engineering. Scientific journals even contain advertisements for customized DNA-making machines; individual human genes can be extracted from our cells, and those same genes can be inserted into the genetic blueprints of other organisms. Each of these facts of life of the early eighties would have been thought whimsical fantasy only 20 years ago; where will these techniques take us in the next 20 years?

Progressively, scientists will acquire the extraordinary ability to make proteins of our own choosing. Proteins are the key, and the most complex, molecules from which living matter is constructed. Every practical task that living things carry out is mediated by structural and enzymic proteins. They are the ultimate, all-purpose molecules, big enough and variable enough to be structurally tuned to perform any molecular task. More than three billion years of organic evolution on Earth have been built on the very nearly infinite variety of these substances. And now we can manipulate them.

Basic genetic engineering technology allows us to choose any of the presently existing multitude of proteins (from any of the millions of species on Earth) that we wish to use, and then mass produce that protein. The power to isolate particular genes also makes it possible subtly to change their structure and hence adapt the structure of the proteins for which they are blueprints.

The manipulatable genes can be inserted into workhorse micro-organisms, such as yeast or bacteria, to produce proteins, but they could also be inserted into the gene banks of domesticated animals and plants. New breeds of cattle or new strains of rice with desirable traits could be produced, short-cutting lengthy selective breeding programmes.

New genes could even be inserted into man himself. Many serious congenital diseases are the result of the lack of a particular enzyme, or the presence of a protein that itself produces disease symptoms. Phenylketonuria of the newborn, which can severely damage the brain, is an example of the first group; sickle-cell anaemia and thallasaemia instances of the second. Within the next 15 to 20 years it might be possible to diagnose these genetic defects in the womb, remove a group of the foetus's cells, insert corrective genes and then replace the cells into the growing child.

There are proteins worth producing commercially in large quantities. Two of the many that would be sufficiently valuable to warrant

One of the least likely candidates for keeping the torch of technological progress burning is the tiny rare, nine-banded armadillo. Frustrated scientists spent years trying either to culture the leprosy organism in laboratories, or to encourage it in animals used for vaccine production. Then it was found that the organism flourishes in this delightful creature. A leprosy vaccine was at last developed in London from armadillos housed at Porton Down's Microbiological Research Establishment. Already successfully used to treat advanced cases in Venezuela, the vaccine will soon contain the tide of leprosy—owing to increased resistance to existing drugs, the estimated 15 million victims are growing in number—and eventually eradicate the disease.

the expense of the genetic engineering techniques are neuropeptides and interferons.

Neuropeptides are a group of small protein molecules that have powerful effects all over the body, but are particularly important in the brain. Some, such as endorphins and encephalins, seem to be involved in the ways in which we perceive and regulate pain. The most potent artificial pain-killers, such as opiate drugs, work because they crudely mimic the pain-regulating functions of the endorphins

that our own brain and other organs can produce. It is highly likely that, using the gene for pancreatic endorphin (which passes easily from bloodstream to brain), a bacterium will be engineered to produce pounds of this completely natural analgesic. It, and substances like it, could give powerful and controllable pain relief almost certainly without the risk of addiction that accompanies the opiates.

Interferons are protective proteins, which are only synthesized by cells under attack by

viruses or foreign nucleic acids. Although produced in miniscule quantities, they provide multi-faceted protection against the spread of virus disease through body tissue. And there is an increasing suspicion that they may act in a defensive way against the development of cancers. Over the next 20 years, genetic engineering methods will produce natural interferons, which will then be clinically tested against many types of infective disease.

Besides genetic engineering there are other clear areas of advance in high-technology medicine. Spin-offs from biotechnological advances will be new synthetic antibiotics, tailored to avoid the enzyme defences of harmful bacteria. Transplant surgery will become increasingly successful as more aspects of the rejection phenomenon are overcome, either by drugs or by the elimination of donor antigens (foreign proteins) and recipient antibodies.

Antibodies themselves will be at the centre of another medical breakthrough. Using complex new medical techniques, scientists will produce monoclonal antibodies: antibodies directed at a single specified protein. Such monoclonals represent the ultimate 'magic bullet' of chemotherapy. They can be designed to attack specific cells, such as cancerous cells, or bacteria and virus organisms.

By 2000, monoclonals might be used to carry powerful drugs to specific areas of a patient's body. Thus drugs that might harm some parts of the body could be targeted straight to diseased cells. Monoclonal antibodies could become the pharmaceutical, and benevolent, equivalents of guided missiles.

While industrialized countries are developing these highly sophisticated techniques, the Third World countries still face the enormous problems of infectious disease, parasite disease, malnutrition and bad living standards. The technology already exists to combat most of these problems, but implementation is costly and difficult. The present plans of the World Health Organization for the next 20 years include the simple yet powerful strategies of health education, the provision of clean, piped water, vaccination programmes and parasite control.

Bibliography

General

Asimov, I. (Ed.) *Biographical Encyclopedia of Science and Technology*; Pan 1975 (UK), Doubleday 1975 (USA)

Baker, R. *New and Improved : Inventors and Inventions that have Changed the Modern World*; British Museum 1976 (UK)

Bronwell, A. B. *Science and Technology in the World of the Future*; Wiley 1970 (USA)

Cardwell, D. S. L. *Technology, Science and History*; Heinemann Educational 1972 (UK); *Turning Points in Western Technology*; Neale Watson Academic 1972 (USA)

Carter, E. F. *Dictionary of Inventions and Discoveries*; Muller 1966 (UK), Crane, Russack 1966 (USA)

Crowther, J. G. *Discoveries and Inventions of the 20th Century*; Routledge and Kegan Paul 1966 (UK)

de Bono, E. (Ed.) *Eureka : An Illustrated History of Inventions from the Wheel to the Computer*; Holt, Rinehart and Winston 1974 (USA)

Dictionary of Scientific Biography; Scribner 1970 (USA)

Feldman, A. & Ford, P. *Scientists and Inventors*; Aldus 1979 (UK)

The Inventions That Changed the World; The Reader's Digest 1982 (UK)

Jewkes, J. & others *Sources of Invention*; Macmillan 1969 (UK), W. W. Norton 1969 (USA)

Kivenson, G. *The Art and Science of Inventing*; Von Nostrand Reinhold 1977 (USA)

Williams, T. I. & Withers, S. (Eds.) *A Biographical Dictionary of Scientists*; Black 1969 (UK)

Williams, T. I. (Ed.) *A History of Technology Vols VI and VII*; Oxford University Press 1978 (UK and USA)

Communication & Information

Baker, W. J. *A History of the Marconi Company*; Methuen 1970 (UK), St Martins Press 1973 (USA)

Braun, E. & MacDonald, S. *Revolution in Miniature : History and Impact of Semiconductor Electronics*; Cambridge University Press 1978 (UK and USA)

Burkitt, A. & Williams, E. *The Silicon Civilization*; W. H. Allen 1980 (UK)

Chappell, W. *A Short History of the Printed Word*; André Deutsch 1972 (UK)

Clair, C. *A History of Printing in Britain*; Cassell 1965 (UK)

Clarke, A. C. *Voice Across the Sea*; Muller 1958 (UK), Rocket 1958 (USA)

Coe, B. *Colour Photography : The First Hundred Years 1840–1940*; Ash & Grant 1978 (UK)

Dummer, G. W. A. *Electronic Inventions and Discoveries*; Pergamon 1978 (USA)

Eames, C. & R. *A Computer Perspective*; Harvard University Press 1973 (USA)

Evans, C. F. *Making of the Micro : A History of the Computer*; Gollancz 1981 (UK), Van Nostrand Reinhold 1981 (USA)

Fox, L. (Ed.) *Broadcasting and Communications*; Marshall Cavendish 1978 (UK)

Gernsheim, A. & H. *The History of Photography*; Thames & Hudson 1969 (UK), Grosset & Dunlap 1968 (USA)

Hill, J. *The Cat's Whisker : 50 Years of Wireless Design*; Oresko/Jupiter Books 1978 (UK)

Metropolis, N. (Ed.) *A History of Computing in the Twentieth Century*; Academic Press 1981 (USA)

Moran, J. (Ed.) *Printing in the Twentieth Century ; A Penrose Anthology*; Northwood 1974 (UK)

Porter, R. W. *The Versatile Satellite*; Oxford University Press 1977 (UK and USA)

Renmore, C. D. *Silicon Chips and You*; Sheldon 1979 (UK), Beaufort 1980 (USA)

Robertson, A. (Ed.) *From Television to Home Computer*; Blandford 1979 (UK)

Thomas, D. B. *The First Colour Motion Pictures*; HMSO 1969 (UK)

Wheeler, L. J. *Principles of Cinematography : A Handbook of Motion Picture Technology*; Fountain Press 1963 (UK)

Transport & Warfare

Batchelor, J. & Hogg, I. *Artillery*; Jane's Publishing Company 1972 (UK), Ballantine Books 1972 (USA)

Bird, A. *Early Motor Cars*; Allen & Unwin 1967 (UK)

Boddy, W. *The History of Motor Racing*; Orbis 1977 (UK), Putnam 1977 (USA)

Canby, T. Y. 'Skylab, Outpost on the Frontier of Space', *National Geographic*; October 1974

Chant, C. (Ed.) *How Weapons Work*; Marshall Cavendish 1976 (UK)

Cornwall, E. L. (Ed.) *History of Ships Vols 1–4*; New English Library 1973–4 (UK)

Davies, W. J. K. *Diesel Rail Traction*; Almark 1973 (UK)

Davis, P. *Veteran and Vintage Cars*; David & Charles 1981 (UK)

The Flier's Handbook; Pan 1978 (UK), Crown 1978 (USA)

Gatland, K. *Space Technology*; Salamander 1981 (UK), Crown 1980 (USA)

Georgano, G. N. (Ed.) *The Complete Encyclopedia of Motorcars, 1885 to the Present*; Ebury 1973 (UK), Dutton 1982 (USA)

Gibbs-Smith, C. H. *Aviation : An Historical Survey from its Origins to the End of World War II*; HMSO 1970 (UK)

Gore, R. 'What Voyager Saw: Jupiter's Dazzling Realm', *National Geographic*; January 1980

Gunston, W. *The Illustrated Encyclopedia of the World's Rockets and Missiles*; Salamander 1979 (UK), Crown 1978 (USA)

Hartcup, G. *The Achievement of the Airship*; David and Charles 1974 (UK), Wren 1974 (USA)

Hough, R. & Frostick, M. *A History of the World's High Performance Cars*; Allen & Unwin 1967 (UK)

Hough, R. & Setright, L. J. K. *A History of the World's Motorcycles*; Allen & Unwin 1973 (UK), Harper & Row 1966 (USA)

Kenyon, L. *Discovering the Undersea World*; University of London Press 1966 (UK)

Koenig, W. J. *Weapons of World War 3*; Hamlyn 1981 (UK)

Macintyre, D. & Bathe, B. W. *The Man-of-War*; Methuen 1968 (UK), McGraw-Hill 1968 (USA)

Nock, O. S. *World Atlas of Railways*; Mitchell Beazley 1978 (UK), Rand McNally 1978 (USA)

Quick, J. *Dictionary of Weapons and Military Terms*; McGraw-Hill 1973 (USA)

Reder, G. *World of Steam Locomotives*; Blandford 1974 (UK), Putnams 1974 (USA)

Spratt, H. P. *Merchant Steamers and Motorships*; HMSO 1949 (UK)

Taylor, J. W. R. *A History of Aerial Warfare*; Hamlyn 1974 (UK)

Taylor, J. W. R. & Munson, K. *History of Aviation*; New English Library 1972 (UK)

Taylor, J. W. R. & Munson, K. *Jane's Pocket Book of RPVs : Robot Aircraft Today*; Macdonald and Jane's 1977 (UK), Macmillan 1978 (USA)

Taylor, M. J. H. (Comp. & Ed.) *Jane's Encyclopedia of Aviation Vols 1–5*; Jane's Publishing Company 1980 (UK)

Turnill, R. *The Observer's Book of Manned Spaceflight*; Warne 1978 (UK)

Turnill, R. *The Observer's Spaceflight Directory*; Warne, 1978 (UK)

Worker, C. F. *The World's Passenger Ships*; Ian Allan 1967 (UK)

Energy & Industry

Alexander, W. & Street, A. *Metals in the Service of Man*; Penguin 1969 (UK)

Byers, A. *Centenary of Service : A History of Electricity in the Home*; Electricity Council 1981 (UK)

de Haan, D. *Antique Household Gadgets and Appliances*; Blandford 1977 (UK), Barrons Educational Series 1978 (USA)

Douglas, R. W. *The History of Glassmaking*; Foulis 1972 (UK)

Dunsheath, P. *The History of Electrical Engineering*; Faber 1969 (UK)

Fishlock, D. *The New Materials*; John Murray 1967 (UK)

Hardingham, M. (Ed.) *Illustrated Dictionary of Fabrics*; Studio Vista 1978 (UK)

Hayden, M. *The Book of Bridges*; Marshall Cavendish 1976 (UK)

Holt, L. T. C. *Tools for the Job*; Batsford 1965 (UK)

Katz, S. *Plastics : Designs and Materials*; Studio Vista 1978 (UK)

Landes, K. *Petroleum Geology*; Wiley 1959 (USA)

Larsen, E. *New Sources of Energy and Power*; Muller 1976 (UK)

Longstaff, M. *Unlocking the Atom : A Hundred Years of Nuclear Energy*; Muller 1980 (UK)

McNeil, I. *Hydraulic Power*; Longman 1972 (UK)

Metalworking : Yesterday and Tomorrow; McGraw-Hill 1978 (USA)

Patterson, W. C. *Nuclear Power*; Penguin 1976 (UK)

Thévenot, R. *The History of Refrigeration Throughout the World*; International Institute of Refrigeration 1979

Williams, J. R. *Solar Energy : Technology and Applications*; Ann Arbor 1977 (USA)

Wright, J. P. *The Vital Spark*; Heinemann Educational 1974 (UK)

Medicine & Food Production

Asimov, I. *The New Intelligent Man's Guide to Science*; Nelson 1967 (UK), Basic Books 1965 (USA)

Asimov, I. *Words of Science*; Harrap 1974 (UK)

Bankoff, G. *The Story of Plastic Surgery*; Faber 1952 (UK)

Cartwright, F. F. *A Social History of Medicine*; Longman 1977 (UK), Longman Inc 1977 (USA)

Cole, H. H. & Ronning, M. (Eds.) *Animal Agriculture*; Freeman 1974 (UK)

Inglis, B. *A History of Medicine*; Weidenfeld & Nicholson 1965 (UK), World Publishing 1965 (USA)

Janick, J. & others *Plant Science*; Freeman 1974 (UK)

Keen, H. & Jarrett, J. (Eds.) *Triumphs of Medicine*; Elek 1976 (UK)

Longmore, D. *Machines in Medicine*; Aldus 1969 (UK)

Lyons, A. S. & Petrucelli, R. J. *Medicine : An Illustrated History*; Abrams 1978 (USA)

Margotta, R. *An Illustrated History of Medicine*; Hamlyn 1968 (UK)

Novotny, A. & Smith, C. (Eds.) *Images of Healing*; Macmillan 1980 (UK)

Parish, H. J. *Victory with Vaccines : The Story of Immunization*; Livingstone, 1968 (UK)

Pyke, M. *Food Science and Technology*; John Murray 1970 (UK)

Robinson, D. *The Miracle Finders : Stories Behind the Most Important Breakthroughs of Modern Medicine*; Robson 1978 (UK), David McKay 1976 (US)

Sourkes, T. L. *Nobel Prizewinners in Medicine and Physiology 1901–1965*; Abelard-Schumann 1966 (UK)

Trotter, W. R. *Man the Healer*; Wayland 1975 (UK)

Venzmer, G. *Five Thousand Years of Medicine*; Macdonald 1972 (UK), Taplinger 1972 (USA)

Wangensteen, O. H. & S. D. *The Rise of Surgery : from Empiric Craft to Scientific Discipline*; Dawson 1978 (UK), University of Minnesota Press 1979 (USA).

Weitz, M. *Health Shock*; Hamlyn 1982 (UK)

Index

Index

238

Acknowledgements

Photographic credits
r = right, l = left, t = top, c = centre, b = bottom

Page 10l Crown Copyright Science Museum, London: 10r Institute of Agricultural History & Museum of English Rural Life; 11 Bildarchiv Preussischer Kulturbesitz; 12 Marconi Co Ltd; 13l Crown Copyright Science Museum, London; 13r Peter Roberts Collection; 14l Mary Evans Picture Library; 14r Crown Copyright Science Museum, London; 15 Crown Copyright Science Museum, London; 16l Mary Evans Picture Library; 16r BBC Hulton Picture Library; 17 Gillette UK Ltd; 18l Ann Ronan Picture Library; 18r Crown Copyright Science Museum, London; 19 H. Roger Viollet; 20l Mary Evans Picture Library; 20r BBC Hulton Picture Library; 21 Crown Copyright Science Museum, London; 22/3 Esso Petroleum Co; 23r Hughes Tool Co; 24 Hamlyn Picture Library; 25 Crown Copyright Science Museum, London; 26l H. Roger Viollet; 26r Osram-GEC; 27 BBC Hulton Picture Library; 28 Imperial War Museum; 29l H. Armstrong Roberts/Zefa; 29r National Film Archive/Stills Library; 30l Crown Copyright Science Museum, London; 30r Crown Copyright Science Museum, London; 31 Mary Evans Picture Library; 32t BBC Hulton Picture Library; 32c BBC Hulton Picture Library; 32b H. Armstrong Roberts/Zefa; 32/3 BBC Hulton Picture Library; 33tl BBC Hulton Picture Library; 33tr Mary Evans Picture Library; 33c H. Armstrong Roberts/Zefa; 33b Sony; 34 The Bettmann Archive; 35 Crown Copyright Science Museum, London: 36l Kobal Collection; 36r Crown Copyright Science Museum, London; 37 John Topham Picture Library; 38 H. Roger Viollet; 39l BBC Hulton Picture Library; 39r H. Roger Viollet; 40 Sikorsky Aircraft, Connecticut/MARS; 41 Crown Copyright Science Museum, London; 42 Imperial War Museum/MARS; 43l Crown Copyright Science Museum, London; 43r Hamlyn Picture Library; 44/5 Yves Bresson/Frank Spooner Pictures; 45l Ann Ronan Picture Library; 45r David Scharf/Oxford Scientific Films; 46l Crown Copyright Science Museum, London; 46r Imperial War Museum; 47 Imperial War Museum; 48 The Mansell Collection; 49 Lent to Science Museum, London by Nat. Physical Laboratory, Teddington; 50t Mary Evans Picture Library; 50bl Ferranti; 50br Philips; 51t Ann Ronan Picture Library; 51bl Paul Brierley; 51br Photri/Zefa; 52 John Topham Picture Library; 53 Imperial War Museum; 54 Peter Roberts Collection; 54/5 G. Kalt/Zefa; 55t Peter Roberts Collection; 55b Nigel Snowdon; 56/7 Imperial War Museum; 58 Kodak Museum; 59tl Polaroid (UK) Ltd; 59bl Barry Moscrop; 59br Chris Thomson/The Image Bank; 60 Mary Evans Picture Library; 61l Photri/Zefa; 61r Peter Roberts Collection; 62 J.M. Jarvis/Zefa; 62/3 J.M. Jarvis/Zefa; 63t J.M. Jarvis/Zefa; 63b Terence Spencer/Colorific!; 64 The Bettmann Archive; 65l Western Electric Co Ltd; 65r Camera Press; 66/7 Tony Latham/Courtesy of the Science Museum; 68 Imperial War Museum; 69 Crown Copyright Science Museum, London; 70/1 Paul Brierley; 72 Crown Copyright Science Museum, London; 73 Hamlyn Picture Library; 74l Crown Copyright Science Museum, London; 74r National Film Archive/Stills Library; 75 BBC Hulton Picture Library; 76l Imperial War Museum; 76r BBC Hulton Picture Library; 77 BBC Hulton Picture Library; 78l BBC Hulton Picture Library; 78r Science Museum, London; 79 Crown Copyright Science Museum, London; 80 Crown Copyright Science Museum, London; 81l British Cellophane Ltd; 81r National Motor Museum; 82 H. Armstrong Roberts/Zefa; 83 Crown Copyright Science Museum, London; 84 Popperfoto; 85l BBC Hulton Picture Library; 85r Kellogg's; 86 Lufthansa Archiv Photo/MARS; 87 Dunlop; 88 IBA Broadcasting Gallery; 89 Novosti Press Agency; 90l BBC Hulton Picture Library; 90r Kodak Museum; 91 BBC Hulton Picture Library; 92l BBC Hulton Picture Library; 92r Crown Copyright Science Museum, London; 93 The Mansell Collection; 94 The Boeing Commercial Airplane Co, Seattle/MARS; 95 John Topham Picture Library; 96 BBC Hulton Picture Library; 97 Popperfoto; 98 Hank Morgan/Colorific!; 99 Patrick Ward/Daily Telegraph Colour Library; 100 Popperfoto; 101 BBC Hulton Picture Library; 102/3 Electricity Council; 103l John Prizeman/LEB; 103tr Electricity Council; 103br Electricity Council; 104l H. Armstrong Roberts/Zefa; 104r Penguin Books Ltd; 105 Eastern Airlines, Florida/MARS; 106l Grundig International Ltd; 106r Peter Smith; 106/7 Sony (UK) Ltd; 107l Ben Rose/The Image Bank; 107tr Michael Holford; 107br Paul Brierley; 108 Fritz Curzon/Sylvia Katz; 109l H, Armstrong Roberts/Zefa; 109r The Bettmann Archive; 110/1 Michael Freeman/Daily Telegraph Colour Library; 111 Shaun Skelly/Daily Telegraph Colour Library; 112l Biro Bic Ltd; 112r Crown Copyright Science Museum, London; 113 BBC Hulton Picture Library; 114tl Ann Ronan Picture Library; 114bl Mike Hooks; 114br Mike Hooks; 114/5 Spectrum Colour Library; 115tl Mike Hooks; 115bl Mike Hooks; 115r Austin J. Brown/Zefa; Background photo: Simon Blacker; 116l Fox Photos; 116r L.L.T. Rhodes/Daily Telegraph Colour Library; 117 The Bettmann Archive; 118/9 Frank Spooner Pictures; 120l John Topham Picture Library; 120r Walt Disney Productions/The Tither Collection; 121 Sikorsky Aircraft, Connecticut/MARS; 122l BBC Hulton Picture Library; 122r Crown Copyright Science Museum, London; 123 British Aerosol Manufacturers Assoc.; 124l Popperfoto; 124r H.J. Heinz Co Ltd; 125 Imperial War Museum; 126l Novosti Press Agency; 126r Popperfoto; 127 National Coal Board; 128 Cruft Laboratory, Harvard University; 129 Michael Taylor; 130 BBC Hulton Picture Library; 131l John Frost Historical Newspaper Service; 131r BBC Hulton Picture Library; 132l H. Armstrong Roberts/Zefa; 132r Popperfoto; 133 BBC Hulton Picture Library; 134l Popperfoto; 134r American Petroleum Institute Photographic & Film Services and Kerr-McGee Corporation; 135 D.J. Jackson; 136 John Topham Picture Library; 137 National Motor Museum; 138 BBC Hulton Picture Library; 139 British Railways Board; 140l Kobal Collection; 140r BBC Hulton Picture Library; 141 Popperfoto; 142 John Topham Picture Library; 143 Kobal Collection; 144l Dave Falconer/Camera Press; 144r BBC Hulton Picture Library; 145 Boeing Commercial Airplane Co/MARS; 146 Photri/Zefa; 146/7 Douglas Kirkland/Colorific!; 147t Dana Duke/Colorific!; 147b Computer Aided Design Centre/Clark Shoes Ltd; 148l Sony; 148r Popperfoto; 149 Peter Roberts Collection; 151 Jean Gaumy/John Hilleson Agency; 152/3 Popperfoto; 154 Photri/Zefa; 154/5 Daily Telegraph Colour Library; 156l Popperfoto; 156r Peter Roberts Collection; 157 Popperfoto; 158tl NASA/David Baker; 158tr NASA/David Baker; 158bl NASA/David Baker; 158br Spectrum Colour Library; 159t Spectrum Colour Library; 159b NASA/David Baker; 160l Popperfoto; 160r NASA/David Baker; 161 Popperfoto; 162/3 Colin Caket/Zefa; 163t Robert Estall; 163b Spectrum Colour Library; 164l Popperfoto; 164r John Topham Picture Library; 165 Popperfoto; 166 Anthony Howarth/Daily Telegraph Colour Library; 166/7 Bergström & Boyle Books Ltd; 167 Bergström & Boyle Books Ltd; 168l John Topham Picture Library; 168r Novosti Press Agency; 169 John Topham Picture Library; 170l Novosti Press Agency; 170r John Topham Picture Library; 171 The Family Planning Assoc.; 172 Novosti Press Agency; 173l The Royal National Institute for the Blind; 173r Digital Equipment Co Ltd; 174 Novosti Press Agency; 175 Camera Press; 176 US Navy Official Photo, Washington DC/MARS; 177 Camera Press; 178 Kodak Museum; 179l John Topham Picture Library; 179r NASA/MARS; 180l The British Tourist Authority; 180r Kodak Museum; 181 Chris Smith/Camera Press; 182l Popperfoto; 182r UKAEA/Camera Press; 182 Illustrated London News/Camera Press; 184 British Petroleum; 185 Lockheed Missile & Space Co USA/MARS; 186l NASA/David Baker; 186r Popperfoto; 187 Patrick Thurston/Daily Telegraph Colour Library; 188l IBM; 188r Photri/Zefa; 189 Boeing Airplane Co, USA/MARS; 190 UKAEA; 191 Fox Photos; 192l BBC; 192r NASA/Science Photo Library; 193 Polaroid (UK) Ltd; 194 NASA/David Baker; 194/5 NASA/David Baker; 195 NASA/Aspect Picture Library; 196l Peter Roberts Collection; 196r IBM; 197 Andy Beard/Camera Press; 198t Terry Fincher/Colorific!; 198b Robert Harding Picture Library; 200l Jet Propulsion Laboratory/David Baker; 200r The Design Council; 201 British Aircraft Corp/Mike Hooks; 202 Rapho; 202/3 Orion Press/Zefa; 203t Pictor International; 203b British Railways Board; 204 Grant Heilman/Lititz/Zefa; 205l Thorn/EMI; 205r Science Photo Library; 206/7 Milacron; 207t Paul Brierley; 207c Don Thomson/Science Photo Library; 207b Georg Fischer/Visum; 208l E.H. Cook/Science Photo Library; 208r The Singer Co (UK) Ltd; 209 British Aerospace, Bristol/MARS; 210t NASA/David Baker; 210c NASA/David Baker; 210b Spectrum Colour Library; 211t NASA/David Baker; 211b NASA/David Baker; 212l Wormald International Sensory Aids Ltd; 212r Neill Tools Ltd; 213 Popperfoto; 214 Jean Guichard-Sygma/John Hilleson Agency; 214/5 Pierre Vauthey-Sygma/John Hilleson Agency; 215 Robert Azzi/Susan Griggs Agency; 216l Courtesy of the Post Office; 216r Associated Newspaper Group Ltd; 217 The Times/Camera Press; 218 Graseby Dynamics; 219l British Telecom; 219r Rank Xerox; 220 National Motor Museum; 221l NASA/David Baker; 221r Sony; 222l John Topham Picture Library; 222r Crosfield Electronics; 223 British Aerospace/Mike Hooks; 224l Sony; 224r Panasonic; 228 McDonnell Douglas Corp/Mike Hooks; 229t Lockheed; 229bl McDonnell Douglas Corp/Mike Hooks; 229br McDonnell Douglas Corp/Mike Hooks; 230 Spectrum Colour Library; 230/1 © Scientific American April 1982; 232/3 Joe Van Wormer/Bruce Coleman
Special thanks to Steve Mansfield, Stan Nelson (Biro Bic Ltd), Dr C.A. Redfarn.

Artwork
Arka Graphics: 114–5/154–5/162
Hayward and Martin: 106/226–7
Tom McArthur: 150–1/199
Scientific American (c): 231

Line Artwork/Retouching
Roy Flooks

Typesetting
Servis Filmsetting Ltd, Manchester

Origination
Gilchrist Bros. Ltd, Leeds